Psychotherapeutic Treatment of Cancer Patients

Psychotherapeutic Treatment of Cancer Patients

JAN 27 1983

Edited by
Jane G. Goldberg, Ph.D.

The Free Press
A Division of Macmillan Publishing Co., Inc.
NEW YORK

Collier Macmillan Publishers
LONDON

The Free Press
A Division of Macmillan Publishing Co., Inc.
866 Third Avenue, New York, N. Y. 10022

Collier Macmillan Canada, Ltd.

Library of Congress Catalog Card Number: 81-66326

Printed in the United States of America

printing number
1 2 3 4 5 6 7 8 9 10

Library of Congress Cataloging in Publication Data
Main entry under title:

Psychotherapeutic treatment of cancer patients.

   1. Cancer—Treatment. 2. Psychotherapy. 3. Cancer—
Psychological aspects. I. Goldberg, Jane
[DNLM: 1. Neoplasms—Therapy. 2. Psychotherapy.
QZ 266 P974]
RC271.P79P78   616.99'406   81-66326
ISBN 0-02-911960-X   AACR2

To my mother, whose commitment to life continues to inspire me
and to my father, who taught me the meaning of earth
and to the rest of my family, Lee, David, Sanford, Lenny, Kim, and Lisa.

Contents

Acknowledgments

A book, like a child, grows and develops from the converging influences of many individuals. It is with deep gratitude that I acknowledge those people whose thoughts and feelings I have been able to assimilate and integrate into my own.

Ruth Sackman, Director of the Foundation for Alternative Cancer Therapies, has generously given to me her time and her immense knowledge of cancer. Her tireless efforts toward maintaining the integrity of humankind deserve enormous recognition.

Phyllis Meadow has given me the belief in myself that enabled me to accomplish the task of editing and writing part of a book. And most importantly, she has taught me that love emerges from the feeling of being understood.

Lou Ormont has modeled for me an openness of heart and mind, and paid me the high compliment of allowing the influence to be mutual.

Hyman Spotnitz has provided me with a framework within which to organize the immense amount of data one gathers from observing the phenomenon of cancer.

Jack Kirman and Stanley Hayden both shared with me an enthusiasm for the project, and gave me the emotional communication necessary for me to tolerate the inevitable frustrations of putting together a book.

Lancelot Fletcher, June Bernstein, Florence Deitz, and Richard Soghoian read parts of the manuscript and helped with editing and offering suggestions to improve the material.

Kitty Moore, my editor at The Free Press, gave me invaluable advice in determining the final manuscript.

My friends, Eleonore Ament, Judith Chusid, Cynthia Harter, Lynn Bultman Jahncke, Jody Kraft, Nancy Minchenberg, and Caroline Paine Sontheimer have stayed with me through the time of this work, and all other times, as well.

And finally, with profound appreciation, I acknowledge my patients, both with and without cancer, who privilege me with the gift of their words, and continue to help me to learn and love and learn to love.

J.G.G.

Contributors

STEPHEN A. APPELBAUM, Ph.D., was on the staff of Menninger Foundation for over two decades. He is currently in private practice and on the faculty of the Topeka Institute for Psychoanalysis. He is the author of more than seventy journal articles and several books, including his most recent *Out in Inner Space—A Psychoanalyst Explores the New Therapies.*

HERBERT BILICK, Ph.D., is a clinical psychologist in private practice in New York City and Director of Training at Poulin and Lunger Associates. His prior positions include Director of Oncology Psychiatry Services at Roosevelt Hospital in New York City, and Co-Director of Cancer Counselling and Training Center of Westchester, New York.

ROBERT DEW, M.D., is an internist and in private practice in medical orgonomy in Wayne, Pa. He has written several articles on somatic biopathies, published in the *Journal of Orgonomy* and lectures at New York University in a course on Wilhelm Reich.

LENA BLANCO FURGERI, Ed.D., is the Director of Group Therapy at the Long Island Consultation Center and a faculty member of the Fordham University and New York University Schools of Social Work. She is also in private practice.

JANE G. GOLDBERG, Ph.D., is currently in private practice of psychoanalysis and psychotherapy in New York City. Dr. Goldberg serves as Managing Editor of the journal *Modern Psychoanalysis.* She has published in the areas of experimental psychology, psychoanalytic theory and technique, and psychological aspects of cancer.

MICHAEL E. KERR, M.D., is Clinical Assistant Professor of Psychiatry and Director of Training of the Georgetown Family Center. He was trained in family therapy and therapy by Dr. Murray Bowen. In addition, Dr. Kerr has been on the faculty of the Family Institute of Chicago, a consultant in family therapy at the National Institute of Mental Health, and is presently on the editorial advisory board of the journal *The Family.* He has authored journal articles and book chapters, and along with Dr. Bowen, has made over fifteen teaching videotapes on family therapy.

ANITA LANSNER, M.S.W., is on the staff of Long Island Jewish–Hillside Medical Center.

RUSSELL LOCKHART, Ph.D., is Associate Research Psychologist in the Department of Psychiatry at UCLA Medical School, Director of the Psychophysiology Research Laboratory at the Camarillo–NPI Research Program, and Director of Research at the C. G. Jung Institute in Los Angeles. He has written on the application of Jungian concepts and is a practicing Jungian analyst.

BONNIE MASLIN, Ph.D., is Director of Research and Training at the Employee Counseling Service, Department of Health in New York City. She also serves as a consultant to the American Health Foundation. She has authored many journal articles and books, and has made numerous presentations at professional conferences.

STEVEN G. McCLOY, M.D., practices internal medicine in Barrington, Rhode Island, and serves as the Assistant Director at the Rhode Island Group Health Association. He was formerly the Medical Coordinator in the Departments of Community Medicine and Medicine at Long Island Jewish–Hillside Hospital. In his practice, he emphasizes psychosomatic interactions in health and disease.

YEHUDA NIR, M.D., is the Director of Pediatric Psychiatry and Associate Attending Pediatric Psychiatrist at Memorial Sloan-Kettering Cancer Center in New York City. He has held faculty positions at Mt. Sinai School of Medicine, New York University, and Cornell Medical College. He has authored many journal articles and has co-authored with Dr. Maslin a book entitled *Attachments*.

WILLIAM NULAND, M.D., is an internist and Medical Director of the Cancer Counseling and Training Center of Westchester. He is a past President of the Society for Clinical and Experimental Hypnosis and past Associate Director of the Morton Prince Center. He has authored numerous articles on psychosomatic medicine and hypnotherapy.

STEPHEN OHAYON, Ph.D., is a psychotherapist a the Long Island Consultation Center and in private practice in Manhattan and Brooklyn.

LOUIS ORMONT, Ph.D., is a practicing psychoanalyst in New York City, specializing in group treatment. He is a Training Analyst at NPAP, and on the faculties of the Center for Modern Psychoanalytic Studies, Adelphi University, the Washington School of Psychiatry, and numerous other analytic institutes and medical schools. He has authored numerous articles on group analysis, and recently co-authored *The Practice of Conjoint Treatment*.

KATHLEEN PHILBIN, R.N., M.A., practices in the Boston, Mass. area. She was formerly a faculty member of the State University of New York at Buffalo, Molloy College.

RICHARD RENNEKER, M.D., is a practicing psychoanalyst in Los Angeles. He did seminal research on the psychosomatics of cancer thirty years ago. Dr. Renneker is currently associated with Cedar Sinai Medical Center.

PAUL ROSCH, M.D., has worked with Dr. Hans Selye, the founder of the stress concept and Dr. Flanders Dunbar, who introduced the term "psychosomatic" into American medicine. He has served as Chairman of the International Foundation for Biosocial Development and Human Health, and is currently Adjunct Clinical Professor of Medicine at the New York Medical College, President-elect of the New York State Society of Internal Medicine and President of the American Institute of Stress. He is widely published in journals and books, and is listed in *Who's Who in the World, Who's Who in the United States,* and *The Dictionary of International Biography.*

WENDY SCHAIN, Ed.D., is a certified psychologist in private practice in the Washington, D.C. area. She serves as Medical Care Consultant to the National Institute of Health Clinical Center.

HAROLD SEARLES, M.D., is currently in private practice of psychoanalysis and psychotherapy in the Washington, D.C. area. He is a Supervising and Training Analyst in the Washington Psychoanalytic Institute and has served as its President. Dr. Searles is the author of four books, including his collected works, numerous journal articles, and is widely known for his work on schizophrenia.

HYMAN SPOTNITZ, M.D., is a psychoanalyst in private practice in New York City. He is the founder of the school of thought called Modern Psychoanalysis. He has authored several books and numerous published articles on psychoanalytic psychiatry, group therapy, and neurology.

Foreword

Important insights about the therapeutic import of the emotional state of the cancer patient while undergoing orthodox medical treatment are conveyed in this book. It focuses, however, on the adjunctive and still experimental field of psychological treatment. Observations, speculations, and findings drawn from individual, group, and family therapy are reported.

Over the centuries, medical advances and growing understanding have transformed many life-threatening diseases into curable and ultimately preventable conditions. Cancer researchers have long been working toward those ends, and the prognosis attached to some forms of the disease has gradually brightened with the introduction of more powerful therapeutic agents. As the pursuit of the "miracle drug" continues, some of these approaches may become obsolete; but until its advent we will perforce adhere to our present policy of applying in each case the most effective of the methods currently available, singly or in combination. It may be helpful to view the psychotherapy of cancer in that long-range perspective.

The general principles delineated in this book leave little doubt in the reader that there is an important psychological component in cancer. This is explored in various contexts by the contributing authors and valuable guides to influencing it therapeutically are discussed.

Cancer has destroyed people I loved. It is a heart-rending experience, one that implants a determination to do everything possible to eliminate this merciless killer. That is one reason why I agreed to write this foreword. Another reason is that, although I have devoted myself for many years to clinical research in schizophrenia, cancer has been a related research interest of mine since I began to study medicine. And recently, in the process of actively renewing the clinical study of cancer, I have been impressed with the similarity of the emotional attitudes of people suffering from cancer and those of schizophrenic patients. This and other common characteristics have often been noted by research-oriented psychotherapists.

The frequent equating of cancer with schizophrenia is, in great measure, a reflection of the dreaded prognosis that has traditionally been attached to each condition. Groddeck's statement, in the *Book of the It*

(1923), that "what is not fatal is not cancer," is reminiscent of the impression once conveyed in the psychiatric literature that what is curable is *not* schizophrenia.

Objective evidence to the contrary—recoveries and remissions—has weakened these attitudes. Subjectively, however, a fatalistic view of cancer persists in the minds of many patients. Characteristically, they experience feelings of hopelessness; their emotions convince them that they are incurable.

Practitioners may have the same pessimistic attitude for reasons of their own, such as their indoctrination or previous experience with similar cases. Nevertheless, it is important that they consider the possibility of their feeling that the patient is doomed is being induced by the patient. Even though one does not sense that the patient is the source of the feeling, intellectual knowledge that this is the situation puts the practitioner in a far better position to help the patient.

In other words, the presence of the feeling that a patient is incurable does not mean that the patient is actually incurable. Moreover, it militates, consciously or unconsciously, against the successful handling of the case if the therapist is unaware that he is operating in terms of that feeling. If, on the other hand, one is aware that such a feeling may be a product of the relationship with the patient, this factor may be nullified, and the patient may be helped to recover.

By and large, a spirit of realistic optimism pervades this book. It emphasizes and demonstrates that in specific situations and with certain methods—even autosuggestion—cancer becomes curable, thus pointing the way to the conquest and eventual elimination of cancer as an illness of mankind.

HYMAN SPOTNITZ, M.D.

Preface

Theories of science, like clothes, follow the fashions. The changes in our concepts of disease have been no exception. In recent years, the theory that cancer is a disease susceptible to psychological intervention is one that has not been fashionable. Professionals and the lay public alike have shared the notion that cancer represents a strictly somatic disease. Most of the monies appropriated for research on cancer have been in pursuit of identifying those physical causative agents responsible for the disease. To date, there have been no governmental or large industrial support for research into psychological determinants of cancer. It was not until 1979 that the NCI arm of the NIH called for proposals for investigation into the psychotherapeutic treatment of cancer.

Despite the lack of popularity of the notion that cancer has important psychological components, a small cadre of independent researchers and clinicians has been interested in the problem and applied the disciplines of their arts in attempts to isolate pertinent variables by studying cause and effect relationships. There is now an extant body of literature that describes the pre-cancer psychological state, the defenses and coping mechanisms that are mobilized once the disease has been contracted, and the final psychic processes that take place when the cancer has proven stronger than the person.

Our understanding of the physiological determinants of cancer has advanced rapidly in the last several years. Researchers have tracked down agents with the capability of producing carcinogenic mutation on the cellular level. Our environment has been found to be virtually replete with cancer-causing substances; they are found in the food we eat, the air we breathe, and the things we play with, work with, and wear. Viruses, as well, have been found to play a catalytic role in the development of cancer, and have been isolated in experimental animals and in human breast tissue.

The value of accurate understanding of causative factors in disease is the optimalization of treatment techniques. Progress in the development of innovative treatment techniques has lagged behind the research on physiological causation. The view of cancer as a strictly somatic disease has yielded treatment techniques designed to correct physiological dysfunction.

A view of cancer as a disease with psychological cause or effect, however, demands a treatment designed for efficacy on the psychological level. It is here, then, that the psychotherapy of cancer becomes relevant.

Psychotherapeutic treatment of cancer is still an experimental science. Of all the currently available treatment techniques for cancer, it is the one about which the least is known and is the least frequently applied. Understanding cancer as a psychological, as well as physiological, disease makes the treatment issues certainly as complex as those involving physical causative factors. Yet, most of these issues have not yet been addressed scientifically. We do not know, for instance, how the feelings of the patient toward the therapeutic agent (physician or psychotherapist) influence the course of malignancy. Similarly, we do not yet know how the feelings of the physician (or psychotherapist) toward the patient influence the course of the disease. We do not know when to tell the patient the truth about his illness and when to conceal the truth. We do not know whether some communications to the patient will aid in his recovery and others will make him sick.

Medical treatment of cancer is the deliberate application of toxic stimuli to the patient. There is no proof that psychotherapy cannot be similarly toxic to the individual. Research has validated that psychological intervention is, at best, beneficial to the patient, and, at worse, has no effect at all. Experimentalists have not yet looked into the notion that psychotherapy can make the patient worse instead of better.

It is perhaps a question that we clinicians would rather have left alone. Since Freud's unveiling of the impact of childhood trauma on adult life, we have had a notion of parenting that can be insensitive to the maturational needs of the child. Freud did not carry the analogy over to the psychotherapeutic relationship, and preferred to see failure of the patient to mature as the fault of the patient rather than the fault of treatment. The recent interest in the narcissistic and pre-oedipal conditions have led clinicians, however, to conclude that it is largely the communications, both conscious and unconscious, to the patient that determine the patient's response. Even the consciously well-intentioned therapists, like the well-meaning mother, can make interventions to the patient that are experienced as toxic and damaging. Psychotherapists, like mothers, are not perfect.

With such a notion, the issue of identifying those psychotherapeutic communications to patients which will aid in recovery becomes critical. It was with the intent of exploring this question that this volume on the psychotherapeutic treatment of cancer was compiled.

JANE G. GOLDBERG

Introduction:
The Fight Against Cancer
Yesterday and Today

Jane G. Goldberg

Cancer was not always considered to be the strictly physiological dysfunction that it is today. Physicians in the eighteenth and nineteenth centuries gave wide acceptance to the idea that cancer patients had particular personality characteristics that influenced the contraction and progression of the disease. Cancer was variously attributed to melancholy,[1] fright, grief,[2,3,4] gloominess,[5] depression,[6] and rage.[7,8]

The art of the clinician in eighteenth and nineteenth century Europe, however, proceeded along quite different lines from the new science of the laboratory experimentor. It is the findings of the early laboratory researchers, not the clinicians, that have determined the thrust of most contemporary thinking about the nature of cancer.

Modern-day cancer research has its origins in the nineteenth century laboratory of Louis Pasteur. Pasteur's isolation of the microbe gave modern medicine its most influential theory of disease—the theory of the germ. The idea here is that the virus or bacteria intrudes into the innocent bystander, whose only mistake was to appear unwittingly in the wrong place at the wrong time.

When Pasteur announced his discovery of the germ and its importance in disease, he was sharply criticized. His contemporary, Claude Bernard, debated with him frequently, and insisted that the microbe itself (the virus) was not what was most important; rather, what should be studied is the *terrain,* or the soil in which the disease develops.

The question becomes more comprehensible when we apply it to the human organism. Germs, in the form of viruses and bacteria, surround us constantly. Yet, only some of us "catch" them, and only some of the time. Bernard's point was that the entry of the germ into the system is not in itself disease-producing. The state of the system will determine whether or not the germ damages us, we damage the germ, or we and the germ live in peaceful co-existence.

To pay proper tribute to Pasteur, it is in all likelihood that he himself came to understand the germ to have not quite the unilateral potency that modern-day medicine has come to attribute to it. Although his major life research was on isolating, identifying, and studying the virus, Pasteur was also interested in the concept of immunity induced by serums and vaccines. It was not until on his deathbed, though, that Pasteur recognized with shocking inconsistency that his life-long preoccupation with the virus had been nearly inconsequential, and he uttered:

> Bernard avait raison. Le Germ n'est rien, c'est le terrain qui est tout. (Bernard was right. The microbe is nothing; the soil is everything.)[9]

Simultaneous to Pasteur's isolation of the virus, a small group of Viennese scientists were attempting a parallel task—the isolation of the human psyche. Scientific methodology was well entrenched by that time, and while the material Freud studied was revolutionary, his method was not. Proper scientific discipline demanded the phenomenon in question to be studied in its most elemental form, and apart from the influence of extraneous variables. The consulting room became Freud's laboratory, where his patients dutifully lay on the examining table and described their dreams, hopes, fears, fantasies—the data from which he derived the theory we call psychoanalysis.

The isolation of the contaminant seeking to destroy the organism became as important to Freud as it was to Pasteur, and equally difficult. Hour after hour of listening to his patients convinced him that psychic injury was the result of an actual trauma suffered at an early age. Many women patients described sexual seductions which confirmed Freud's belief in the significance of the traumatic event in the etiology of the neuroses.

The problem in treatment was in getting the patient to remember the trauma. Memory was, at times, too vague to permit sufficient isolation of the trauma. At an early stage of psychoanalysis, the hypnotic method appealed to Freud as an ideal method to separate out the memory of the trauma from all other mental confabulations impeding recollection.

Freud, like Pasteur, met with something unexpected, requiring reformulation of his whole theoretical construct. The unexpected finding was the discovery that his patients were lying. The traumatic events described were often imaginary. The stories his female patients told of sexual assaults by male relatives and friends existed only in the minds of the patients.

Freud was, however, more fortunate than Pasteur; he discovered his error with more than half his life still remaining. Material reported by patients as memory reflected their hopes and fears and could not be separated out from the whole of their mental life. Freud dropped the technique of hypnosis, where isolated memories were sought. He resorted instead to free association, whereby the patient was instructed to report everything. In his pursuit to understand the totality of the mental life of his patients, rather than isolated traumatic events, Freud gave the first attention to the *terrain* of the human psyche.

The implications of a discovery, however, are not always left to the discoverer. Cancer research began in earnest some sixty years after Pasteur's isolation of the bacteria and Freud's pursuit of the human psyche. The concept of the isolated, external, noxious stimulus invading the system (the microbe for Pasteur; the traumatic event for Freud) has provided the point of departure for almost all the cancer research that has been funded, published, and publicized.

The germ theory, however, leaves one vital question unanswered. It is the same question that obsessed Pasteur on his deathbed, and that Freud, similarly, needed to answer in order to make his psychological theory of neurosis comprehensible. If, as both Pasteur and Freud realized, the *terrain* was all-important, what was it about the *terrain* that led some organisms into health and others into disease?

For Pasteur, on the physiological level, organisms were exposed to the same germs, yet some organisms succumbed to the destructive properties of the germs and some did not. For Freud, on the psychological level, the fantasies and fears of his patients were remarkably similar; yet, again, some patients were profoundly sick and others reasonably appropriately functioning. What could the differences be attributed to?

Fortunately for the advancement of science, different laboratories generate different hypotheses to test different theories. While it is true that the mainstream of cancer research has been directed toward the isolation of the virus, a few researchers have made simultaneous investigation into the make-up of the *terrain* of the human organism that would permit a noxious agent to render its destruction.

Pasteur's preliminary research into an immunological agent which would serve to protect the body from disease agents foreshadowed later developments. The year 1891 marked a dramatic turning point in the history of this new line of research. A German physician, E. A. von Behring, treated a young girl dying from diphtheria with serum made from a sheep. Research a year earlier had shown that the serum appeared in the bloodstream of animals after infections, and that the serum was capable of neutralizing poisons. The girl revived, and von Behring won a Nobel Prize for the first medical cure of an infectious disease.[10]

In the same year, an American surgeon, William Coley, observed that certain infections seemed to have a beneficial effect on cancer patients. He, too, injected, patients with bacterial toxins in order to induce responses that could change the course of the malignancy.

In spite of the fact that these findings had profound therapeutic implications, immunology, as a science, was neglected by most medical laboratories. It was only in the mid-1950's that a renaissance occurred in the investigation of the relationship between the immunological defenses and cancer. At that time Dr. Lewis Thomas, the new president of Sloan-Kettering, postulated that the immune system has the function of policing the body from internal threat as well as protecting it from outside invaders.[11] The nature of this threat from the inside, he argued, was the daily production of thousands of cells which are abnormal, genetically different, and potentially cancerous. Others speculate even further, and feel that cellular immunity may have evolved phylogenetically as a specific surveillance mechanism against the cancer cell.[12] In point of fact, all research designed to study the immunological system suggests that the organism normally has the capacity to successfully fight cancer.

Immunology is now referred to as the "brain-child" of the century. It is the area of research that inspires most optimism about the possibility of break-throughs in the treatment of cancer. Though still in its relative infancy, the ideas generated by knowledge of the laws governing the body's immune apparatus, have been put to practical use, and are now responsible for the treatment of a great many cancer patients.

Advances in research applicable to cancer have not been, however, limited to the medical and physiological laboratories. While the physical scientists were making advances toward an understanding of the body's immunological capacity, the social scientists were making parallel discoveries in the laboratories of the psychoanalytic consulting rooms.

Freud, whose training was in the physiological and neurological sciences, conceptualized the psyche as a biological system. Just as the body wards off destructive agents to insure its survival, so too does the psyche. But, what were the psychic counterparts to the germ and the immune system? Freud's answer changed as his clinical experience broadened.

When Freud entered the University of Vienna at the age of seventeen, he was already under the spell of Darwin, whose writings attempted a unification between the realms of rational human behavior and animal impulses. Freud's early work reflects Darwin's influence. Instincts were the deepest drives, those permanent, somatic demands which lie at the bottom of all human activity. Loyal to the Darwinian distinction between the individual and the species, the young Freud emphasized the demands of the self-preservative, ego instincts, and the pleasure-seeking, sexual instincts. It was these internal drives which were the dangers that threatened psychic equilibrium.

The discovery of the repetition compulsion in 1920 forced Freud to revise his theory on the ego and sexual instincts. Freud noticed that his patients seemed compelled to repeat the past, and he identified this compulsion as yet another instinct. Instincts, though, are biological, and a return to the past for any living thing means a return to the inanimate state—the death instinct. Every living thing dies for internal reasons, and in death becomes inorganic once again.

Paradoxically, at this same time, Freud began to understand that external threats could be as potentially destructive as those operating from within the organism. In *Beyond the Pleasure Principle,* Freud conceptualized the living organism as a tiny vesicle "suspended in the middle of an external world" against which this vesicle needs a protective barrier. This protective shield has the function of insulating the personality against stimulation that would work towards the destruction of the self.

The analogy to the germ and the immune system is complete then. Just as only some organisms succumb to the destructive power of germs through physiological deterioration, so too do only some organisms succumb to the destructive power of the id and other agents threatening the survival of the ego through psychological deterioration.

What mechanisms, then, protect our psyches from the ravages of forces threatening destruction? For Freud, the answer was the defense—the psychological representation of the physical immune system. The defense mechanisms offer opposition to both the emergence of dangerous impulses, and the danger of externally threatening forces. It is necessary for the survival of every self that it mobilize its defenses against the threats of these forces. Anna Freud's systemization and codification of the defenses identified each of these mechanisms: regression, repression, reaction-formation, isolation, undoing, projection, introjection, turning against the self, denial, and identification with the aggressor. Defenses are seen, then, as devices used for the maintenance of psychic and systemic equilibrium.

By the 1950s, the mechanisms of resistance to disease had been formulated on both the psychological and physiological levels: the defense mechanisms protect us against intruding agents on the psychic level and the immune system protects us from intruding agents on the physical level.

What would cause these defense systems to be sufficiently inoperative that the organism would get sick? The answer is the same for both the physiologic and the psychologic. If the defenses are weakened, for any reason, they are unable to adequately perform their task of protection.

Researchers have identified many of the factors with the capability of weakening these defense systems. The human organism consists of the summation of a multitude of components, all of which can be broadly classified under genetic, prenatal and postnatal factors. In each of these determinants, proper nutrition, adequate physical and mental stimulation, emotional and physical care, and avoidance of damaging, noxious stimuli are necessary.

Most of the research that has identified these pertinent variables has been done in laboratories investigating either strictly physiological or strictly psychological phenomenon. Since Freud's time, research in both the physiological and psychological areas has been essentially conducted in different laboratories with different methods. This situation has resulted in a Cartesian dualism, whereby the physiologic and psychologic are seen as dichotomous. This situation is made more complicated by the fact that even within those primarily interested in the psychological aspects of cancer, this dualism is evident, and has resulted in the break-down of theory and technique into two camps. Since scientists are eternally interested in the notion of causation, clinicians and researchers have engaged in a sort of reductionism, whereby the psychological is seen as a pre-determinant of the physiological, or, the physiological as a predictor of the psychological. Those who represent the former theoretical view have come to be known as the psychosomaticists; those who represent the latter view have no cohesive identification, and for the sake of such, can be referred to as the cancer managers.

Psychotherapeutic Treatment of Cancer Patients

The history of ideas of how to cure the mind of disease is not unlike the evolution of ideas of how to cure the body. Mental illness has in the past been regarded as the intrusion of an alien outside force—like the germ—and variously understood to be an evil spirit or the devil. Freud's formulation, however, placed the enemy squarely within the psyche of man himself.

The shift in emphasis of the agent responsible for the affliction has meant a concomitant shift in treatment approaches. In one, the sick patient is the passive recipient of the expert's ministrations and the cure is performed without his necessary participation. In the other, the cure consists of helping the patient to use healthy resources within himself, and in this way, he becomes an active participant in the therapeutic process.

Since Freud's emphasis on the instincts, psychoanalysis and psycho-therapy have become interested in finding treatment techniques that strengthen the defensive structure of the ego. The elaboration of this idea into treatment techniques parallels the advances made in physiological laboratories, where the immunological defenses of the body are strengthened. In both, structures inherent to the organism are enabled to ward off both internal and external noxious stimulation, and the goal is to build an immunity to future contamination and deterioration of the organism.

Research on the psychosomatic aspects of cancer poses the idea that malevolent psychological change promotes disease. Correlary to that idea is the notion that beneficial psychological change promotes physiological cure. It was an idea that was recognized as useful in the same historical period that physicians were first noticing particular personality attributes of cancer patients. In 1885, Parker recommended that breast tumor patients develop a positive attitude and be cheerful.[13] Cutter, in 1887, advised that the depressive attitude needed to be reversed through restoring the patient's faith and will to live.[14] Walsh, in 1846, suggested counseling and encouraged his patients to not give way to despair.[15]

Early clinicians, however, had only rudimentary knowledge of how to go about effecting such changes. As the notion of cancer being a disease with psychological components has become experimentally validated, treatment techniques have, accordingly, been refined. We now understand the mind to have an extraordinary capacity to influence the body's physiological processes. Control of the autonomic nervous system has been demonstrated within the laboratory.[16] It seems not so far from conscious controlling of the basal temperature of the right index finger to the control of the T-cells that build a healthy immune system.[17]

The effect of pushing the responsibility for the contraction and cure of disease to the *terrain* of the individual is not, however, without its disadvantages. Information on how the individual needs to act and feel and think in order to reverse the disease process include specifics on how to breathe, eat, work, and play. Techniques such as meditation, visualization, biofeedback, dietary regimes, and exercise programs are all given as aids to help the cancer patient. There is ample evidence to conclude that these techniques, when performed properly, are indeed helpful and may be, at times, curative. Involvement in these techniques requires, however, a cooperative patient who is willing to exercise sufficient self-discipline to both implement and maintain the program. Securing the cooperation of the patient in his own treatment is not always possible, though, as is evidenced by the growing interest of physicians in an area called patient compliance.[18] Contemporary physicians have found that patients have great resistance to following medical regimens, even where the regimen is as simple as swallowing a pill. Freud, years earlier, had discovered the same thing and found that his patients would rather be sick than remember and verbalize those thoughts and feelings that would aid in their cure.

Emphasizing the role of the individual in the development and treatment of disease has yet another disadvantage. Illness is seen as the end-product of some characterlogical deficiency. This notion, carried to an extreme, is a more sophisticated version of the Calvinistic notion that any form of physical disease is indicative of personal misdeed and a fall from grace. The patient, then, suffers not only from the affliction of the disease, but from the affliction of the responsibility of the disease, as well.

Susan Sontag, herself a cancer victim, has written what may well become known as the *locus classicus* of the patient's rebuttal against this idea.[19] She likens the history of the public image of cancer to the parallel history of tuberculosis, which was, like cancer, thought to be a disease with psychosomatic components. Isolation of the tuberculosis bacillus, however, made those psychological theories of the disease obsolete. The so-called "romantic" tuberculosis personality was never experimentally identified, and because of the rareness of the disease now, makes research of such a theory largely irrelevant.

So, too, it may be with cancer. Increasing sophistication in the use of physical agents that enable the body to rid itself of destructive cancer cells may render the field of psychosomatics of cancer irrelevant. Freud himself predicted that the whole field of psychology and psychotherapy would go by the wayside when more precise understanding of the physical processes of the body were acquired. Unfortunately, we are not yet at that point. In the meantime, we can proceed toward the development of a science of psychotherapy. Perhaps the day is not so far off when we will have learned to immunize our patients through psychological, as well as physiological, interventions against the ravages of cancer.

Notes

1. Wiseman, R., *Severall Chirurgicall Inestises,* London, 1676
2. Gendon, D., *Enquiries into the Nature, Knowledge, and Cure of Cancer,* London, 1701
3. Amussat, J. Z., *Quelques Reflexions sur la Curabilité du Cancer,* Paris, 1854
4. Burrows, J., *A New Practical Essay on Cancer,* London, 1783
5. Walshe, W. H., *Nature and Treatment of Cancer,* London, 1846
6. Paget, Sir James, *Surgical Pathology,* Third Edition, London, 1870
7. Snow, H., *Cancer and the Cancer Process,* London, Churchill, 1893, p. 34
8. Von Schmitt, G., *On the Curability of Cancer,* Paris, 1871
9. Selye, H., *The Stress of Life,* McGraw-Hill, N.Y., 1956, p. 205
10. Issels, J., *Cancer: A Second Opinion,* Hodder and Stoughton, London, 1975, p. 93
11. Thomas, L., "Cellular and Humoral Aspects of the Hypersensitive States," in *Symposia of the Section on Microbiology,* edited by H. S. Lawrence. New York Academy of Medicine, Cassel, London, 1959
12. Solomon, G. F., "Emotions, Stress, the Central Nervous System, and Immunity," *Ann. N.Y. Acad. Sci.,* 164, no. 2, 1969, pp. 335–343
13. Parker, W., *Cancer: A Study of Three Hundred and Ninety-Seven Cases of Cancer of the Female Breast,* N.Y., 1885
14. Cuttoo, E., "Diet on Cancer," *Albany Medical Annals,* 1887
15. Walshe, W. H., 1846
16. Miller, N., "Visual Learning," Colloquium given at Rutgers University, Nov. 1970
17. Green, E., "Biofeedback and Voluntary Control of Internal States," in *The Frontiers of Science and Medicine,* edited by Carlson, Henry Regnery. Chicago, 1975
18. Gentry, W. D., "Noncompliance to Medical Regimen," in *Behavioral Approaches to Medical Treatment,* edited by R. Williams and W. D. Gentry. Ballingor, Cambridge, Mass., 1977
19. Sontag, S., *Illness as Metaphor,* Vintage, 1979

PART I
Theoretical Considerations

It has not yet been possible to formulate a theory of cancer that includes its every aspect. Despite research that enables us to more successfully identify personality patterns of the cancer-prone person, patients defy the statistics, and all kinds of personalities are found to develop the disease. Despite massive epidemiological studies that help us to predict expected survival time for all types of cancers, patients still defy the statistics. Some live longer than their bodies seem to have the strength for, while others die without physiological reason.

To put some theoretical construct around a disease that is as varied and unpredictable as cancer is surely an attempt to impose order on apparent chaos. While the study of cancer has generated no new theoretical ideas, it has yielded creative and useful application of old ideas in new ways.

Virtually every theory from the fields of psychology, psychiatry, and medicine have been applied to cancer. It has been seen alternatively as a virus, a lowering of immunological defenses, a biochemical imbalance caused by nutritional deficiencies, a breakdown of cellular communication, a characterological defense against aggression, a resistance to a positive transference to a psychoanalyst, a somatization of pre-oedipal

1

impulses, a freezing of energy, and much more. Research can be found to support any of the above hypotheses.

Both clinical practice and research share a problem inherent to the process of investigation; they cannot see everything at once. Isolating a single factor as contributory to the cancer has been a successful method of investigation. The state of the art is such that we now have many separate, single factors that have been pinpointed as relevant. We know little, however, about the cumulative or synergic effects of these variables. Most practitioners and researchers now agree that cancer is surely a multi-determined phenomenon.

Treatment is often designed to address only one of the variables considered to be catalytic or causative. Nutritional therapies, for example, aim to restore the bodily biochemical balance, but a body wracked with psychological stress will not be able to digest and utilize the proper nutrition. Similarly, psychological therapy may relieve psychic discomfort, but an organism that has cellular malnutrition needs nutritional support from food, as well as from words. Ideal treatment, then, may consist of approaches that address more than one of the determinants of the disease.

The amazing recuperative powers of the body often permit patients to get well even without ideal treatment. Psychological factors are only beginning to receive attention, and until very recently, most cancer patients who have gotten well did so without the benefit of psychological treatment. Nutritional and immunological supports are also now thought to provide considerable help in aiding the body to restoration of health. These too have only recently received sufficient attention that cancer patients have begun to profit from the scientific advances in these areas.

Psychological approaches to an understanding of cancer are themselves varied. In spite of equally convincing alternative theories about what treatment technique works, patients claim to be helped by individual analysis, family treatment, groups with leaders, groups without leaders, by the release of aggression, by the release of love, and so on. We can only conclude that, although our knowledge and our ability to apply our knowledge remain partial, we are still able to offer considerable help to the cancer patient.

Part I outlines prominent theoretical approaches to the psychology of cancer. Chapter 1, by Jane Goldberg, provides the reader with some of the theoretical background and pertinent research to view cancer as a disease with psychosomatic components. Chapter 2 gives a historical perspective to the concept of psycho-physiological interaction in disease. Carl Jung was one of the first analysts to see that illness manifested on a somatic level may have psychological meaning. Russell Lockhart, in chapter 2, applies Jungian thought to an understanding of the symbolic meaning of cancer. Chapter 3 regards stress as a determining factor in the development of cancer. Stress is usually thought of as a psychological mechanism, but it effects physiological change. Hans Selye's discoveries about stress show that deterioration of an organism occurs with either too much or too little stress. Paul Rosch applies Selye's ideas to cancer, and documents the fact that cancer is a disease which is highly responsive to stress. Chapter 4, by Herb Bilick and William Nuland, represents a new concern in the treatment of cancer. A model is presented whereby the cancer patient actively participates in his or her own treatment plan.

1 Experimental Validation of Psychosomatic Aspects of Cancer

Jane G. Goldberg

The popular notion that cancer can strike any one at any time, in democratic fashion, is largely a myth. Most of the literature—both research and clinical—points to the fact that certain pre-existing conditions must obtain before the disease is contracted. Because of the long latency period during which the symptoms of the disease are not yet overtly manifest (some cancers can take up to twenty years from the time of exposure to the triggering substance), the determination of cause and effect is particularly difficult.

Research to determine the various psychological and social-psychological precursors of cancer have included the personality of the individual and various life events, such as death of a loved one or divorce. It is postulated that these psychological and psychosocial phenomena find representation on the physiological level through the mediating mechanisms of the limbic system, the endocrine system, hormone levels, and/or the central nervous system.

The idea that somatically manifest disease can be traced to psychological phenomena has its roots in the early observations of Breur. In 1895, he observed that psychopathological symptoms come into being as a result of pent-up emotion. Freud thought this was correct, and mentioned "strangulated affects" (eingeklemnte affekte).

Freud, himself, however, was not particularly interested in the concept of the conversion of psychological conflict to physiological effect. His initial interest in conversion hysteria may have foreshadowed the mantel taken up by his followers—most notably Franz Alexander. Here, though, despite the fact that symptoms mimicked those of physical diseases (paralysis, anesthesia, blindness, convulsions, or headaches), there was no actual physiological involvement. These diseases were, then, strictly diseases of the mind.

Freud's disinterest in psychosomatic disease is actually explained by his

5

own theory. Psychoanalytic theory of disease is a psychosexual developmental schema, where disturbance can occur at any point along the ascending developmental ladder. Inadequate mastery of any stage inhibits further progress onto the next stage. Freud was primarily interested in the neurotic conflict of the oedipal period, which reaches culmination in the child at the age of seven. Here, separation from the primary love object has become sufficiently strong that the child is permitted the *choice* between the old love object (mother) and yet another love object (father). It is in the possibility of choice that the conflict arises.

The psychosomatic diseases are thought to differ from the psychoneurotic symptomotologies in the date of origin of the repression. In cases where the trauma becomes manifest in somatic symptomotology, the fixation point is before such separation-individuation has occurred, and, importantly, before acquisition of language (usually the first two years of life). Thus, the conflict arises out of and centers around the primary love relationship (mother and infant). And since language is not accessible as a means of discharge or resolution of the conflict, the body itself becomes the vehicle through which the conflict gains physical representation.

Psychological research on cancer patients has validated many of these psychoanalytic concepts. Two broad ideas have generated most of the work done in this area: (1) the "personality" hypothesis, which specifies that there are particular personality characteristics found more frequently in the cancer patients than in normal controls, and (2) the "loss-depression" hypothesis, which suggests that an emotional trauma of separation or loss precedes the development of cancer, with ensuing feelings of helplessness and hopelessness. The personality hypothesis offers the construction of a type C personality, analogous to the type A personality found to be prone to heart disease.

The idea that certain types of emotional conflicts predispose a person to developing cancer (the personality hypothesis) has a history as old as medicine itself; it was a prevalent view of physicians for large segments of time. Galen, as far back as the second century, observed that women who manifest depression seem more inclined to develop breast cancer than those with less melancholic dispositions.[1] The idea finds its next recurrence in seventeenth and eighteenth century England, where physicians alternatively ascribed cancer to black bile and melancholy (Wiseman),[2] to fright or violent grief (Gendron),[3] to "uneasy passions of the mind" (Burrows).[4] These ideas continued in England into the nineteenth century: Walshe mentioned the "habitual gloominess of temper;"[5] Sir James Paget was convinced of the vital role of depression;[6] Snow, who performed the first statistical analysis of the relationship between cancer and personality, stated neurotic tendency to be the most powerful causative factor.[7] Similarly, in nineteenth century France, ideas were promulgated: Amussat considered cancer to be caused by grief;[8] and von Schmitt suggested ambition, frequent rage, and violent grief as primary causes.[9]

Despite the historical popularity of these notions among physicians, twentieth-century medicine was not initially interested in pursuing these ideas. Cancer treatment was developing rapidly from art to science, and the physical treatments of surgery and radiation seemed to be adequate and powerful tools. Further, Freud's broad influence had not yet taken hold, and the ability of physicians to cope with emotional problems was still quite limited.

While early medicine may have contented itself with clinical observations, modern science has become more demanding. The twentieth-century development of sophisticated assessment and statistical procedures has dramatically altered the method of investigation. Complex studies with analysis of multiple variables can now be performed on large numbers of people. This research method is a far cry from the mere observations made by a single physician who was limited by the number of patients in his practice.

Research has been successful in validating a number of observations on the cancer personality made by the early clinicians. A "personality profile" for the cancer patient has now been experimentally established. A comprehensive analysis of these studies yields three dimensions of emotional qualities that seem to characterize the cancer patient. Segmentation of these dimensions does not imply independence from one another; rather, there is much overlapping both within the personality profile dimensions and with the alternative loss-depression hypothesis, as well. Many studies have looked at and confirmed a number of variables to be coincidental to both theories. The three main character traits found to describe the typical cancer patient are: repression of feeling, inhibition of aggression, and, finally, an inordinately pleasant personality.

The idea that cancer can be caused by a repression of emotions follows the earlier thinking of Breuer and Freud. Experimental validation is found in the research of Thomas, Bahnson, and Kissen. Caroline Thomas' study of medical students at Johns Hopkins in 1946 spurred the interest of researchers to identify and quantify more exactly the psychological dimensions of the cancer personality.[10] At that time, she began a longitudinal epidemiological study to discover the precursors of coronary heart disease, hypertension, mental disorders, malignant tumors, and suicide. She initially conceived of cancer as being a condition without psychological factors, and was startled to find striking similarities between those who developed cancer and those who committed suicide. These were people who reported a history of cold and remote parental relations, and who were little given to the expression of emotion.

Studies done subsequent to the Thomas study have used many of her seminal findings as hypotheses. Bahnson tested experimentally the idea that cancer patients are more likely than others to repress feelings.[11] He administered a test to cancer patients and controls where each gave verbal associations to a neutral sound (a kind of auditory Rorschach). The finding that cancer patients gave more positive and benign associations was interpreted as an indication of greater repression of negative thoughts and feelings.

Kissen compared heavy smokers who had lung cancer with those who did not.[12] Test scores were interpreted as indicative that cancer patients suffered from denial and repression of emotions, with "poorly developed outlets for emotional discharge." Kissen concluded that the more repressed the individual, the fewer cigarettes it took to induce cancer.

Other experiments have attempted to identify what particular emotions are repressed. One which has been repeatedly identified is aggression. In order to understand how inhibition of aggression can lead to the somatic state of cancer, one must understand the notion of discharge. For Freud, the normal functioning of the mind is governed by a "control apparatus that organizes, leads, and inhibits deeper archaic and more instinctual forces."[13] The ability to discharge is one of the mechanisms the psyche utilizes to maintain a state of economic stability. Neurotic phenomena are understood, then, to be based on insufficiencies of the normal control apparatus. The insufficiency can be attributed to alternative disturbances. Excitation that is more stimulating than the ego can master can enter the mental apparatus; such experiences are traumatic. Or, alternatively, there can be a blocking of discharge, whereby tensions dam up, and normal excitations are experienced as traumatic.

Motoric discharge is the first form of tension release available to the infant. When he acquires the use of language, his words supplant his actions in providing adequate release from the instinctual demands. The person who somatizes remains fixated in the pattern of motor discharge, even after the acquisition of language.

Research on cancer and aggression confirms this psychodynamic relation. Bacon studied breast cancer patients and found an inordinant amount of unconscious repressed hostility, which he related to an early, pathological relationship with the mother. Many of these patients said that they had never been angry, and there was evidence that relations with others were excessively pleasant.[14] Similarly, Greer and Morris found suppression of anger was correlated with breast malignancy.[15] Epidemiological studies have also been made. One researcher did a state-by-state analysis on manifest aggression, as measured by rates of homicide (aggression turned outward) and suicide (aggression turned inward). He found leukemia and lymphatic neoplasms to be highly correlated with the aggression-in dimension.[16]

A correlate to the idea that inhibition of aggression is implicated in the occurrence of cancer is the idea that expression of aggression has a beneficial effect on malignancy. Derogatis and Abeloff noted that in women with breast cancer, those who expressed anger toward the treating physician or toward the disease itself lived longer than those who were compliant and cooperative.[17] Isreal cites a study where strains of rats bred for susceptibility to a high incidence of spontaneous leukemia are placed together. These animals fight constantly, bite each other, wound each other, and are constantly vigilant for any sign of aggression from the other. The frequency of cancer drops abruptly in rats placed together as opposed to rats who live alone.[18] Blumberg compared patients with fast-growing and slow-growing tumors and found substantial differences. Patients with slow-growing tumors exhibited greater flexibility in responding to emotional trauma, and greater ability in reducing tension through motor discharge.[19] Both Blumberg, in this study, and Klopfer, in another study,[20] found slow-growing tumor groups to be lower in ego defensiveness. Fast-growing tumor patients expended considerable energy in their attempts to maintain an image of themselves as good.

Data on the "loss-depression" hypothesis has given an even more precise picture of the cancer personality. LeShan is the leading spokesman for this theory and has amassed data on more than four hundred cancer patients over a twelve-year period. He found that 72 percent of these patients suffered a loss of a central relationship anywhere from eight years to a few months before the onset of the disease. This figure is in contrast to the controls, where only 10 percent showed a similar pattern.[21] Correlation between separation and cancer was further confirmed in psychosocial data collected by Stephenson and Grace. Cervix cancer patients had a high incidence of divorce, desertion, and separation.[22] Renneker et al. found cancer development to be preceded by object-loss or some other intensely charged emotional experience resulting in depression.[23] A study conducted by the New York City Cancer Institute revealed the consistent pattern of a dominant mother and psychologically or physically absent father in cancer patients. Differences were noted between breast and cervix cancer patients: those with breast cancer married relatively late in life and remained married; those with cervix cancer married earlier, and their marriages were typically broken.[24] Schmale and Iker identified hoplessness as the primary emotional tone of the cancer patient, and found the existence of a conflict with no apparent resolution six months prior to diagnosis.[25]

The loss of a loved object does not, however, inevitably lead to cancer. Rather, adequate coping mechanisms will enable the person to pass through a natural mourning process without resorting to prolonged regression and melancholia. Where cancer is the end result in melancholia, the indication is of inadequate resolution of early conflicts.

The most fundamental anxiety the infant experiences is associated with his state of biological helplessness; he is physiologically unable to satisfy his drives himself. The first fear, then, is the fear of experiencing a state of unpleasure (drive) which the infant is impotent to change. The development of an ego that is adequate to master and satisfy the impulses will discourage the idea that one's own instinctual demands might be dangerous. If the ego does not acquire this ability, however, the infant remains exclusively dependent on external means of satisfaction. He begins to fear that these supplies might fail to arrive. The fear of inadequate protection and nurturance becomes synonymous with the fear of loss of love.

When this fear remains intense, the ego structure is harmed. The development of self-esteem is rooted in and regulated by the infant's experience of gratification of instinctual demands through external means. The infant who knows that his needs will receive satisfaction will develop a strong ego; an ego that feels unloved and unprotected will fear desertion and not have adequate resources to cope with abandonment should it happen.

Elida Evans describes just this psychodynamic situation in cancer patients as extroverts, who invest their psychic energy in an external object. (e.g. a person, activity, or actual object). A chronic imbalance in the direction of the psyche's energy occurs. A traumatic loss, then, results in the energy suddenly becoming free-floating. The person must reinvest the energy back into the self, but he is left without the ability to do so, and the energy recedes into the realm of the unconscious.[26]

The infant whose instinctual demands are inadequately met through external means has, however, another recourse. He can develop a rich fantasy life, and thus substitute for the unpleasant reality (frustration at lack of gratification) a fantasized wish that is more pleasant and more gratifying to his needs.

It has been observed that psychosomatic patients have psychological histories which reveal that fantasy was not a mechanism accessible to them.[27] These patients are poor in producing fantasies when they are in psychoanalytic treatment. Clinicians have described cancer patients in much the same way. Indeed, it may be hypothesized that the somatic symptom of cancer is a biological acting out of the fantasy, and thus replaces the fantasy.

The idea that the psychological history of a person may be a determinant in the creation of organic disease is a thesis which opens up a Pandora's box of unanswered questions. Freud's original patients who displayed hysterical paralysis, deafness, and the like, were, in some ways, more comprehensible. Because no physiological involvement could be discerned, the method of investigation remained exclusively psychological, and the theory divined was a primarily psychological one.

Our current understanding of cancer, though, is that it is a disease with both psychological and physiological involvement. If, as the psychosomatic theorists claim, the progression of systemic disturbance is from the mental to the physical, what, then, is the apparatus for this transformation?

Recent research has shown the neuro-hormonal system to be implicated as a mediating mechanism. It is, in fact, the endocrine (hormonal) system which renders the human oganism capable of translating emotions into chemicals. This process is extremely complex, but, in short, the grand master of the whole neuro-hormonal system is now thought to be the hypothalamus, through which neural impulses pass, are decoded, and finally sent on through either the nervous system or the endocrine gladular system. Psychological distress (or stress), then, is translated directly into physiology.

Adrenal-cortical hormones are known to interfere with the immune system's ability to make antibodies. Recognition of this fact led researchers to use these hormones in organ transplants, where the attempt is made to "fool" the body so that it does not recognize the new organ as foreign. The exceedingly high incidence of cancer in transplant patients is a direct effect of the suppression of the immune system. The danger of rapid spread of bacterial and viral infections from the adrenal-cortical hormone called cortisone is further evidence of the relationship between the immune system and the hormonal system.

Stress and the Hormonal System

The role of stress on the production of hormones and disease was formulated by Hans Selye.[28] Selye had been following up Walter Cannon's idea that the hyperactivity of our own organs and hormones could cause disease. Cannon termed this hyperactivity the emergency fight/flight response. Selye was looking for *the* hormone which would activate the reactivity of the body. He found that when he injected hormones into the body, he would get a stress reaction. This stress reaction consisted of a stress ulcer. He thought he had discovered *the* hormone. Subsequent research, however, revealed that the application of a host of stimuli would cause this same stress ulcer—noise, x-rays, excess activity. Indeed, any stimulus which provoked the organism into its emergency fight/flight response was discovered to be a stressor.

Research subsequent to Selye's has verified that the neuro-hormonal system is extremely vulnerable to stress. The term has been broadened to include psychological agents of stress, as well as physical. If it is true, as has been postulated, that the mind-body dualism is more a product of investigative method than a reflection of the way in which the human organism operates, (see Introduction), then, we would expect psychological trauma, identified as precursors to cancer, to have physiological representation, as well.

Physiological research linking neuro-hormonal and immune dysfunction with psychological data has this aim in mind. While a relationship between the hormone system and the immune system has already been observed, research has not always verified that the two work in concert. Studies have looked at the specific role of the immune system and the hormone system on cancer, independent of each other, as well as their interaction.

Evidence of the direct effect of hormone activity on cancer is provided by P. M. West, who found that performing a lobotomy on a cancer patient had the effect of completely eliminating the cancer.[29] Lobotomy is a surgical procedure invading the hypothalamus, and was used in the mid-part of this century to treat mental illness and, in cases such as the ones reported here, physical pain. The suggestion is that some forms of cancer cells thrive on hormones stimulated by the hypothalamus and that when the hormone supply is cut off, the cancer dies. The hypothalamus is the gland most initimately tied to the affective, emotional system.

Other studies on the hormone system have measured psychological determinants as well as hormone activity in cancer. In these studies, where the person's psychological make-up is correlated with abnormal hormone production, the stressor is defined as "character," or the chronically habituated coping mechanism of the individual, rather than the introduction of some noxious stimulus. Katz et al. found psychological covariants of hydrocortisone production in women with breast cancer.[30] Kissen and Rao have studied steroid excretion patterns and personality attributes of patients with lung cancer.[31]

Research implicating the immune system has continued and has successfully identified stress as a determining factor (Solomon;[32] Weiss;[33] Rasmussen[34]). Bathrop has looked at the physiological response to the stress of the loss of a spouse, and found depressed lymphocyte function, though without any corollary change in hormonal activity.[35] Pettingale et al. found an inverse relationship between inhibition of expression of anger and serum IgA levels (a component of the immune system), and have demonstrated the use of IgA level as a prognostic indicator in the metastatic spread of breast cancer.[36]

Studies investigating the three-way link between emotions, specific hormonal states, and immune functions are scarce and contribute only a fragmentary picture. Mason found the level of a particular adrenocortical hormone (17-hydroxy-corticosteroid) was raised in mothers of leukemic children. He also found raised levels in the urine of Army recruits who had lost their mothers, although the level was lowered in cases where the father was the one who died.[37] While the interaction between the parental loss, psychological defenses, and hormone level is confirmed, the evidence that different losses are associated with different hormonal reactions suggests that the matter is a complex one.

Riley injected animals with a corticosteroid antagonist, and found that previously impaired immune systems were restored to adequate functioning. He also injected mice with a mammary tumor virus, and found that mice who were exposed to a stressful atmosphere developed tumors much more quickly than those who were in a protected environment.[38]

In summary, the idea that cancer is a disease with psychosomatic implications, and possibly origins, is quite old. The work of psychoanalysts has been the major theoretical contribution in this area. Modern experimental research in the psychology and psychophysiology laboratories has validated much of these theoretical concepts. The mediating mechanisms of the limbic, endocrine, and central nervous system have been implicated.

Notes

1. Galen, *De Tumoribus.*
2. Wiseman, R., *Severall Chirurgicall Treatises,* London, 1676.
3. Gendron, D., *Enquiries into Nature, Knowledge, and Cure of Cancers,* London, 1701.
4. Burrows, J., *A Practical Essay on Cancer,* London, 1783.
5. Walshe, W. A., *Nature and Treatment of Cancer,* Taylor and Walton, London, 1846.
6. Paget, J., *Surgical Pathology* (2nd ed.) Longman's Green, London, 1870.
7. Snow, H., *The Reappearance of Cancer after Apparent Extirpation,* J. and A. Churchill, London, 1870.
8. Amussat, J. Z., *Quelques Reflexions sur la Curabilité du Cancer,* Paris, 1854.
9. Von Schmitt, G., *On the Curability of Cancer,* Paris, 1871.
10. Thomas, C. B., and Duszynski, D. R., "Closeness to Parents and the Family Constellation in a Prospective Study of Five Disease States: Suicide, Mental Illness, Malignant Tumor, Hypertension, and Coronary Heart Disease," *The Johns Hopkins Medical Journal,* 134 (1974):251-270.
11. Bahnson, C. B. and Bahnson, M. B., "Denial and Repression of Primitive Impulses and of Disturbing Emotions in Patients with Malignant Neoplasmas." In D. M. Kissen and L. LeShan (eds.), *Psychosomatic Aspects of Neoplastic Disease,* Lippincott, Philadelphia, 1964, 42-62.
12. Kissen, D. M., "Lung Cancer, Inhalation, and Personality," In D. M. Kissen and L. Leshan (eds.), ibid.
13. Fenichel, Otto, *The Psychoanalytic Theory of Neurosis,* W. W. Norton, New York, 1945.
14. Bacon, C. L., Renneker, R. and Cutler, M., "A Psychosomatic Survey of Cancer of the Breast," *Psychosomatic Medicine,* 14 (1952):453-460.

15. Greer, S. and Morris, T., "Psychological Attributes of Women who Develop Breast Cancer. A Controlled Study," *Journal of Psychosomatic Research,* 19 (1975):147-153.

16. Field, P. B., "Mortality Rates and Aggression Management Indices," *Journal of Health and Human Behavior,* 4(2), 1963

17. Derogatis, L. and Abeloff, M., cited in "Cancer and the Mind: How Are They Connected," by Constance Holden, *Science,* 200 (June 23, 1978):1363-1368.

18. Israel, L. *Conquering Cancer,* Vintage Books, New York, 1979.

19. Blumberg, E. M., "Results of Psychological Testing of Cancer Patients," In J. A. Gengerelli and F. J. Kirkner (eds.), *Psychological Variables in Human Cancer,* U. of Calif. Press, Berkeley and L.A., Calif., 1954, 30-61.

20. Klopfer, B., "Psychological Variables in Human Cancer," *Journal of Projective Techniques,* 21 (1957):331-340.

21. LeShan, L., *You Can Fight for Your Life,* Lippincott, Philadelphia, 1977.

22. Stephenson, I. H. and Grace, W., "Life Stress and Cancer of the Cervix," *Psychosomatic Medicine,* 16 (1954):287.

23. Renneker, R. et al., "Psychoanalytic Explorations of Emotional Corrolates of Cancer of the Breast," *Psychosomatic Medicine,* 25 (1963):106.

24. New York City Cancer Institute, unpublished monograph.

25. Schmale, A. H. and Iker, H., "The Psychological Setting of Uterine Cervical Cancer," *Annals of the New York Academy of Sciences,* 125 (1966):807-813.

26. Evans, E., *A Psychological Study of Cancer,* Dodd, Mead, New York, 1926.

27. Meadow, P., private communication.

28. Selye, H., *The Stress of Life,* McGraw-Hill, New York, 1956.

29. West, P. M., In *The Psychological Variables in Human Cancer,* In Gengerelli, J. A. and Kirkner, F. J. (eds), University of Calif Press, 1954, 92-93.

30. Katz, J., Gallagher, T., Hellman, L., Sachar, E., and Weiner, H., "Psychoendocrine Considerations in Cancer of the Breast," *Annals of the New York Academy of Sciences,* 164 (1969):509-516.

31. Kissen, D. M. and Rao, L. G. S., "Steroid Excretion Patterns and Personality in Lung Cancer," *Annals of the New York Academy of Sciences,* 164 (1969):476-482.

32. Solomon, G. F., "Emotions, Stress, the Central Nervous System, and Immunity," *Annals of the New York Academy of Sciences,* 164 (1969):335-343.

33. Weiss, D. W., "Immunological Parameters of the Host-Parasite Relationship in Neoplasma," *Annals of the New York Academy of Sciences,* 164 (1969):431-448.

34. Rasmussen, A. F., Jr., "Emotions and Immunity," *Annals of the New York Academy of Sciences,* 164 (1969):458-462.

35. Bathrop, R., "Depressed Lymphocyte Function after Bereavement," *Lancet,* April 16, 1977, 834-836.

36. Pettingale, K. W., Gree, S. and Tu, D. E. H., "Serum IgA and Emotional Expression in Breast Cancer Patients," *Journal of Psychosomatic Research,* 21 (1977):395-399.

37. Mason, J. W., "Psychological Stress and Endocrine Function," In E. J. Sachar (ed.), *Topics in Psychoendocrinology,* Grune and Stratton, New York, 1975.
38. Riley, V., "Mouse Mammary Tumors; Alteration of Incidence as Apparent Function of Stress," *Science,* 189 (August 1975):465-467.

2 Cancer in Myth and Dream

An Exploration into the Archetypal Relation Between Dreams and Disease

Russell A. Lockhart

Cancer is a family of diseases often characterized by rapid and relatively unrestrained proliferation of undifferentiated cells that invade bodily organs and tissues and spread from original growth sites to distant areas in the body. It is an invasive, powerful growth that consumes and destroys vital life processes. Cancer is modern man's most dread disease, an insidious process seemingly victimizing without warning, without reason, without meaning. Even the word *cancer*[1] strikes horror, bringing to mind images of the physical body eaten away by the ravenous advance of a consuming malignancy. It becomes a genuine *mortificatio*[2]—a true dark night of the soul. Perhaps in no other way does an individual experience the deepest possible meaning of "autonomous" than in cancer attacking, seizing, and consuming his life. In it, he is confronted by a truly other, a powerful *numen*[3] threatening his very existence.

Cancer is experienced by nearly one of every four individuals in modern industrialized societies and the cancer death rate is increasing, despite attempts to diagnose and treat the disease at ever earlier stages. One frequently hears the view that cancer is a "disease of civilization". Its relative absence and slower growth in primitive cultures, psychotic individuals, the mentally retarded, and wild animals supports this notion. Cancer may be an inevitable price modern man pays for separating himself too far from the life of nature.

Cancer grows in many different bodily fields producing a whole flora of types and species. The language of cancer is one of earth and plants. Even the patron saint for cancer, St. Peregrine,[4] has a name which means "to cross the fields."[5] Fantasy connects cancer to the earth. I consider cancer in

This chapter originally appeared in *Spring,* 1977, pp. 1-26.

certain forms to be related with something of the substance of one's self denied, undernourished, or cut down; something of one's psychic and bodily earth not allowed to live, not allowed to grow. Cancer lives something of life unlived. Carl Jung put it this way:

> I have in fact seen cases where the carcinoma broke out . . . when a person comes to a halt at some essential point in this individuation or cannot get over an obstacle. Unhappily nobody can do it for him, and it cannot be forced. An inner process of growth must begin, and if this spontaneous creative activity is not performed by nature herself, the outcome can only be fatal. . . . Ultimately we all get stuck somewhere, for we are all mortal and remain but a part of what we are as a whole. The wholeness we can reach is very relative.[6]

We know that no matter how conscious one is, impulses to life may be blocked by ego, encapsulated by repression, surrounded by a hard shell of inhibition, and hidden away crab-like in unconsciousness. The connection between cancer and the crab is not accidental and carries symbolic significance. The crab is an animal hidden from view, shrinking back, yet holding tenaciously to what it seizes. Its hard shell protects its vital life process. This is an introverted image. Yet, one of the most outstanding features seen in the majority of cancer victims is an extraordinary degree of libidinal investment in an outer object, coupled with a severe denial of something inner. That is an extraverted image.

It has been repeatedly observed that cancer often emerges within six to eighteen months following some major emotional loss, particularly when the suffering individual falls into a "hopeless-helpless" psychology. Such an individual's reason for living frequently is carried by an outer object— be it person, work, possession, goal, or idea. When that is lost, a common reaction is loss of will to live. This is fertile soil for the growth of cancer. Libido turns inward and, unable to find there a compensating value, begins to feed upon the body as outer object to the psyche. It is for this reason that Elida Evans, in one of the few works on the psychology of cancer,[7] concluded her analysis of cancer patients with the observation that cancer is primarily a disease of the extravert, in Jung's special sense of extravert. It is often difficult for the extravert, whose libido has been overly invested in an outer object, to reinvest his energy when the object is lost. This idea of extraversion as an etiological factor in cancer has not been tested directly. However, there are studies which show cancer patients scoring in the extraverted direction on both objective and projective personality tests.

Along these lines, I have been impressed by the extent to which causes and cures for cancer—in fact and fantasy—have been uniformly sought in external factors. A recent United States governmental report suggests that 80 to 90 percent of cancer is environmentally "caused." And the treatment of cancer is based almost entirely on the use of external chemicals, radiation, and surgery. Cancer is considered the most somatic of diseases both in origin and treatment. A common medical view is that there is no psychosomatic aspect in cancer. It is not an underestimation to say that the psyche is left out of treatment, nor is it considered a factor in the genesis of the disease. In a recent issue of *Harper's*,[8] there is a special section reviewing the causes and treatment of cancer. There is no mention of psychological factors. This reflects a persistant attitude, in spite of accumulating evidence attesting to the importance of psychological factors in the background of cancer patients, which would support the hypothesis that environmental factors work to create cancer primarily in those individuals whose psychology has prepared the way for susceptibility. Along these lines, the so-called surveillance theory of disease pictures cancer as a natural life process, growing or induced in us all the time. But there exists a natural suppressive mechanism—primarily the immune system—which operates to inhibit the growth of these undifferentiated cells.[9] It is very likely that the immune system is extraordinarily sensitive to psychic influences. When this system is disturbed, the resistance to environmental agents, the suppression of the natural tendency toward undifferentiated proliferation, is diminished, and the possibility of cancerous growth increases. This is one of the basic principles underlying the work of investigators who are developing techniques for "recruiting" the psyche in the treatment of cancer.[10]

It is proposed that mental processes are able to interact with the immune system in such a way that, for example, by visualizing the immune system actively attacking the cancerous growth, the immune system is mobilized, strengthened, and its natural antagonism toward cancerous growth reawakened. In this way, the patient participates in his own treatment, a kind of psychic biofeedback which not only affects the body but often increases the person's will to live. Of course, in accepting this proposition one must accept the corollary proposition that one's psyche has also played a role in the development of the disease. The mechanism works both ways—an idea not many are willing to accept.

In studying the relation of psyche and cancer, I have found the psyche responds with some of the same characteristics of the disease itself. It becomes very consuming; it proliferates; it goes from its starting place to very distant sites. It consumes time as well as energy. I have experienced this proliferation in the form of ideas and fantasies as well as synchronistic occurrences. It is important to provide ground for this by writing and telling some experiences. For thoughts, like feelings and emotions, do not disappear. They fall into unconsciousness where if ignored, they will continue to feed and breed. Because of the power of the cancerous process, working with cancer is not without dangers.

One can feel almost victimized in this work. For this reason, it is of interest to me that the phrase *cancer victim* is such a prominent one in the language of cancer. Cancer victimizes. A modern dictionary illustrates the meaning of victim as one that is injured or destroyed under any of various conditions with the phrase: "a victim of cancer."[11] The phrases we use carry unconscious images within their meanings. Herman Paul more than a hundred years ago wrote: "The old word meanings have an after-effect, chiefly imperceptible, within the dark chamber of the unconscious of the soul."[12] This can be coupled with Jung's statement: "What an archetypal content is always expressing is, first and foremost, a figure of speech. . . ."[13]

If the modern meaning of "victim" is epitomized by the cancer victim, we may learn something by inquring into this word's hidden images. The oldest meaning in English of victim is *a living creature killed and offered as a sacrifice to some diety or supernatural power.*[14] In Latin, the word is *victima* and refers to the sacrificial beast. Paradoxically, this word comes from older roots (*veg-* and *vic-*) meaning "increase" and "growth." It is remarkable how frequently the word growth is used in relation to cancer and tumerous enlargement. In Greek, victim derives from the root *auxo,*[15] meaning "increase," and is the name of one of the Charities. More remotely, the term refers to a fertility Goddess whose name was Auxesia.[16] At Epidaurus, her cult involved human sacrifice.

Victim and growth are integral aspects of the fertility Goddess, for in almost all ancient cultures, the fertility of the earth required human sacrifices. The Goddess devours the sacrificial offering as an essential precondition to her participation in new growth. "Victim" and "growth" are also part of the imagery of cancer's patron saint, St. Peregrine, who is feasted on the first day of May. Since antiquity, May Day has been celebrated as a spring-time fertility festival symbolic of the return of life, and defeat of winter, the hope of an abundant harvest. The ritual celebration centered around the sacred tree which in time became the maypole.

In these various connections there is a hint that a potentially important part of the psychic and mythic background of cancer lies in the realm of the earth mother as fertility Goddess. We might ask whether there is a connection between man's destruction, ravaging, and polluting of the earth in modern times and the increasing emergence of cancer? It is an important fact that cancer was essentially absent in the American Indian culture prior to the white man's invasion. A moment's reflection reveals that the white man's behavior was not unlike cancer itself. More recently, when John Dean told Richard Nixon, "There is a cancer on the presidency," he captured in this image something of our modern values. Cancer is not just an illness of our time but is a symptom of our spirit. We know that such problems have an inner and outer aspect. So we may ask ourselves: to what extent do we destroy, ravage, and pollute our earth, that is, our material body and its counterpart in psychic earth, the ground of our being?

"Victim" implies an image of sacrifice. Sacrifice comes from the Latin term *sacrum facere,* meaning "to perform a sacred ceremony," that is, an offering to the Gods. What does modern man offer the earth Goddess?

Where are the sacred ceremonies in her honor? And what is her retribution for this neglect and violence to her precincts? What is not sacrificed willingly finds itself sacrificed unwillingly. Is the cancer victim one who is sacrificed unwillingly?

The phenomenology of cancer is full of images of guilt and retribution ("What have I done to deserve this?") and promises to one's self and others that, should there be a recovery, sacrifices will be made, there will be a change of ways, life will be lived properly. The psychology of such unwilling sacrifice is quite different from that of the willing sacrifice. There are moments and seasons in one's life when genuine sacrifice of the most valued thing is essential for further growth. If this sacrifice is not made willingly, that is, consciously and with full conscious suffering of the loss, the sacrifice will occur unconsciously. One then will not sacrifice to growth, but be sacrificed to growth gone wrong.

Some time ago, an old man came to see me because of my interest in dreams and cancer. His wife had just died of cancer, and he wanted to tell me something he thought might be important. Prior to his wife's diagnosis, she began to have terrible nightmares filled with conflagrations and vicious, pursuing animals. She woke in the night screaming in response to dream images of dogs tearing at her stomach, fires burning her flesh, and other horrors. These nightmarish experiences lasted about two weeks. Several months later she was diagnosed with terminal stomach cancer, and within three months she was dead. The old man told me: "You know, those dreams were the beginning of it. The cancer was announcing itself. I feel the truth of this in my bones. But people won't listen to an old man." He was echoing the tradition growing out of man's experienced connection between his dreams and his bodily afflictions. In ancient times, dreams were believed to be diagnostic of somatic conditions, revealing the presence of disease and disorder and, moreover, often announcing the required treatment. Even the famous rationalist physician Galen took his dreams seriously. It is written that he was:

> . . . twice admonished in his sleep, to cut the artery that lies between the forefinger and the thumb, and doing it accordingly, he was freed from a continual daily pain with which he was afflicted in that part, where the liver is joined to the midriff; he was testified to this at the end of his book of Venesection. It is certainly a very great example, when a man so great as he was in the medical art, put so much confidence in a dream as to try experiments upon himself; where he was to run the risque of his life, in his very own art. I cannot help admire his probity in the next place, that where he might have arrogated the merit of the invention to himself, and place it wholly to the account of the subtlety and penetration of his own genius, he attributed it to God, to whom it was due.[17]

It was to the Gods that the ancients attributed the diagnostic dream, the treatment dream, as well as those healing dreams through which the divinity worked directly. Aristotle, in his essay on prophetic dreams, wrote:

> . . . since the beginnings of all events are small, so it is clear, are those of the diseases and other affections about to occur in our bodies . . . it is manifest that these beginnings be more evident in sleeping than in waking moments.[18]

Thus, to dreams were attributed the power of signaling bodily disturbance. Aristotle went further:

> . . . it is not improbable that some of the presentations which come before the mind in sleep may even be causes of the actions cognate to each of them . . . it is quite conceivable that some dreams may be tokens and causes of future events.[19]

This is a remarkable idea. Together with the ancient idea of divine action, we might say that Gods work their will in and through dreams—not only in healing, but in creating sickness as well. Dreams bring healing and sickness. Ancient theurgic medicine was centered in the proposition that sickness and healing issued from the hands of Gods. Disease and affliction were a consequence of improper relationship to the divine. The purpose of sickness, the meaning of affliction, was to force the individual to confront his disconnection from the Gods, to sacrifice his hubristic acquisitions, and to replace himself in the proper spirit of relationship by binding himself (religio)[20] through suffering in service to the Gods.[21]

Modern man and his medicine have lost touch with this special sense of the importance and value of sickness, and the central role that dreams play in connecting his soul to the powers beyond himself. We are indebted to Jung because he rediscovered this religious attitude not only toward the dream but toward man's ills as well. "Man needs his difficulties," he said, "they are necessary for health."[22] Unfortunately, this attitude has not permeated medical practice, and the dream is rarely mentioned in the current medical shrines. The dream is no longer consulted for diagnosis, no longer recruited in treatment, no longer sought for in healing or cure. We may ask the question: Is there a place in modern culture for a revival of the ancient theurgic attitude toward sickness, suffering, healing, and the central role of the dream?

In Deuteronomy, the Hebrew God proclaims: "I wound and I heal; there is no rescue from my grasp."[23] This drama of necessary suffering, of inevitable wounding and healing at the hand of the God, is pictured in dreams. Dreams are the voice and vision of the soul, and it is the soul that is man's organ of perception and connection to the gods that work in his depths. It is soul that first feels and sees the smiting and curing hand of the God at the root of one's sickness. Soul reveals these fateful events to the conscious mind through dreams. Pindar put it beautifully: "The soul slumbers while the body is active; but when the body slumbers, she shows forth in many a vision, the approaching issues of woe and weal."[24]

Is it possible to learn from the dream life of an individual whether the "woe and weal" there pictured will express itself in a somatic cancer? Are there dream themes or images premonitory of a developing cancerous condition? Do different cancers symbolize themselves differently? Are dreams prognostic? How is cancer treatment pictured in dreams? How might dreams be utilized in the treatment of a cancer patient? Is there a healing dream process in relation to cancer? Do dreams prepare the way to death?

In spite of the many hints by Jung, the study of these issues relating to the dream-disease relationship has not been a prominent part of analytical psychology and certainly not a visible part of psychosomatic medicine. Analysts and patients feel on much safer ground interpreting a dream psychology than in regarding a dream from its organic aspect, even though, as Jung pointed out, a dream with an organic implication often has a peculiar effect not only on the dreamer's body but on the body of the analyst as well.

A dream may speak organically both before and after the emergence of bodily disturbance. That is, dreams may not only anticipate the development of somatic involvement, but may also reflect bodily disturbance in process. Working out the means for identifying the organic dream is a formidable task. However, the possibility that dreams distinguish different bodily disturbances, and picture them differently, is a proposition that finds considerable support in Jung's comments on the dream-disease relation, and serves as a basis for the beginnings of systematic research in this area. An example might be helpful.

In 1933, Dr. T. M. Davie submitted a patient's dream to Jung for interpretation. No other information about the patient was provided. The dream was as follows:

> Someone beside me kept asking me something about oiling some machinery. Milk was suggested as the best lubricant. Apparently I thought that oozy slime was preferable. Then, a pond was drained and amid the slime there were two extinct animals. One was a minute mastadon. I forgot what the other one was.[25]

Jung told Dr. Davie the dream indicated an organic condition and that the drainage of the pond referred to the damming up of cerebrospinal fluid. Dr. Davie was very impressed with Jung's diagnosis and concluded his own published report of the case with these words:

> Dreams . . . do not merely provide information on the psychological situation, but may disclose the presence of organic disorder and even denote its precise location.[26]

When later asked how he arrived at such a diagnosis, Jung told his medical audience at Tavistock:

. . . why I must take the dream as an organic symptom would start such an argument that you would accuse me of the most terrible obscurantism. . . . When I speak of archetypal patterns those of you who are aware of these things understand, but if you are not you think, "This fellow is absolutely crazy because he talks of mastadons and their difference from snakes and horses." I should have to give you a course of about four semesters about symbology first so that you could appreciate what I said.[27]

The dream Jung interpreted has an obvious "mechanical" aura, being concerned as it was with lubricating machinery and draining a pond. Such a mechanical focus often has implications for the "machinery" of the body. But there is much more in this dream. Jung knew Latin and it could not have escaped his attention that the Latin word for slime is *pituita*. From this word comes pituitary. The slimy colloidal secretions of the pituitary gland are essential to certain bodily processes. These secretions flow into the third ventricle, one of those hollow subterranean womb-like caverns through which the cerebrospinal fluid has the function of lubricating these cavities and provides a mechanical barrier against shock to the brain. It is as if the brain floats in this fluid. There are many aqueducts—even named so—through which this fluid pours on its course. If cut off or blocked, the effect, as in a real aqueduct, is a drainage of the cerebrospinal pool downstream.

Milk is suggested as a lubricant. This detail of the dream is understandable in connection with the image of the mastodon—an origin Jung was certain to have known. The element *odon* refers to "teeth" and comes from the Latin *odontia*. The *mast* element comes from the Greek words *mastos,* meaning breast. So, a mastodon is an animal that has "breast teeth," and in fact was given this name because of the nipple-like projections on its rounded teeth—the distinguishing feature of this animal among the mammoths. And, now, those of you who know brain anatomy will immediately think of the *mamillary bodies,* those breast-shaped structures of the hypothalamus lying at the base of the third ventricle with nipple-like projections protruding at the base of the brain.

There is much more to this dream, but already we see a drainage of fluid Jung felt to be the cerebrospinal fluid, an oozy slime that could refer to the secretions of the pituitary, and a mastodon whose etymology is related to breast, and therefore, to milk symbolism—all elements physically related to the third ventricle. Jung might argue that extinct animals still live in the diencephalon, that ancient part of the brain that is essentially unaltered in creatures that have brains at all. Perhaps in this dream the two extinct animals are images of the hypothalamus and the pituitary that lie beneath the cerebrospinal pond. The case was medically diagnosed as a neurological disturbance in the third ventricle.

To put this material in the form of an hypothesis, we would say that *bodily organs and processes have the capacity to stimulate the production*

*of psychic images, meaningfully related to the type of physical disturbance
and its location.* It follows that we must look for correspondences between
type of cancer and the images in dreams that may symbolize the disease and
its location. This hypothesis has enormous implications, not only for
psychosomatic medicine, but for an emerging image of health and health
care in which the individual consciously carries ever more responsibility for
his own illness, not only in its origin, but in its treatment as well. As Ivan
Illich makes clear in his book, *Medical Nemesis,* this is not yet a medical
reality. He writes:

> The medical enterprise saps the will of people to suffer their own reality. It
> destroys our ability to cope with our own bodies and heal ourselves. . . . Our
> hygienic hubris is rooted in our attempt to engineer an escape from suffering.
> We medicalize the entirety of life.[28]

Whereas traditional cultures equipped every person with the art and
meaning of suffering, healing, and dying, we have become separated from
the physician of the psyche. We have lost contact with the medicine of the
soul. The dream provides a way back, a connection to the voices and images of the psyche, a relationship to the inner physician who also diagnoses, prescribes, and treats. Paracelsus said:

> Even while still in the womb, unborn, man is burdened with the potentialities of
> every disease, and is subject to them. And because all diseases are inherent in his
> nature, he could not be born alive and healthy if an inner physician were not
> hidden in him.[29]

A young man with leukemia reported the following dream:

> I hear voices . . . eventually I shut myself in a room . . . I'm very scared. Three
> "beings" burst into the room. It turns out they are humanlike. A doctor is asked
> to help out. The beings are just as confused and frightened. The doctor brings
> up jokingly that he's part of a crazy group of physicians. He explains that he's a
> holistic doctor. They announce: "so are we."

The patient was encouraged to contact these inner figures, in dialogue and
fantasy, as a means of connecting consciousness with this inner source of
healing. The patient, near death and told he would die shortly, began this
relationship. He discovered the inner physician would answer his direct
questions and, in so doing, tell him exactly what to do. His therapist told
me that when the patient called her, he told her what the doctors were saying and what they were telling him to do. She thought he meant his outer
doctors, but he corrected her at once. His *inner* physicians had ordered a
change in diet, in exercise, in relating to others and the patient was col-
laborating enthusiastically with these inner prescriptions. This is an example of the role a dream can play in relating even a dying patient to something of his inner substance and the distinct reality of the psyche within.
The essential question must not be that of prolonging life only to be lived in

the old ways and on the same paths. Cancer as an image in dreams or as a reality in the body signifies something wrong in one's relation to life, and so cancer is both a warning and an opportunity to seek out the paths of unlived life—in whatever period of time one has remaining. Dreams can play a momentous part in discovering a new relation to life, as well as a new relation to death. As both life and death are journeys that must be taken, shrinking back from either is fuel for the tragedy of meaninglessness.

In approaching the issue of the relationship between dreams and disease, we are confronted immediately with one of our deepest sources of fantasy and paradox: the relationship between body and soul, soma and psyche. Our approach to this problem in the study of cancer assumes that dreams are capable not only of picturing disease process and organic conditions, but may do so prior to any appearance of somatic symtoms, and may in fact be the birthplace, the seeding ground of disease. Our image is one which J. Kirsch pictured more than thirty years ago in an article entitled "The Role of Instinct in Psychosomatic Medicine," when he wrote that the psyche is "quite frequently the matrix of many diseases."[30] It is useful to remember that matrix means *womb* in Latin.

C. A. Meier has taken the psyche-soma mystery as an expression of synchronicity. He proposes a tertium,[31] an unknown "third" factor beyond body and psyche, which synchronistically produces symptoms in both realms. Symptom comes from the Greek roots *syn-,* meaning "together," and *pitein,* meaning "to fall." A symptom then refers to two or more things which fall together. For Meier, it is body and psyche that "fall together" in symptoms. In Latin this image of falling together is preserved in the word *concido,* which has the additional meaning of "to fall dead." Cuvosier said that every sickness carries the germ of death.[32] We see it in the language of sickness. The word *concido* is the root of our English words "coincidence" and "accident." We meet here the underlying idea that chance plays the crucial role in our symptoms. We are unlucky. As G. Bennette says of the man who holds this view,

> . . . he is victimized by sickness and illness, afflicted more or less unpredictably and at random by external or accidental influences of which he is quite independent and for which he can hardly be held responsible.[33]

This idea is nowhere more deeply expressed than in the reaction of most cancer patients upon learning their diagnosis. Symptom and chance come from the same root, and mirror in language an age-old attempt of ego-consciousness to picture its afflictions as the result of accident, rather than to itself.

Symbol is related to symptom. From the Jungian perspective, we tend to view symptoms symbolically. What image is hidden in this word "symbol"? It comes from the roots *syn-,* meaning "together," and *ballein,* meaning "to throw." Thus a symbol refers to two or more things "thrown together." A cancer patient, just before she died, painted a spontaneous and unexpected image of a crocodile holding a clock. The images of clock and crocodile were "thrown" together, becoming a symbol[34] that meant more to her than "your time has come," because it gave her a distinct, unique, and personal symbol of her situation as she approached the reality of death. The symbol came to her very forcefully. The idea of "force" is in the word itself. In contrast to symptom, where things *fall* together, in symbol we have the feeling of things actively coming together, *thrown* together. *Ballein* originally had the meaning to throw as to hit, from which comes our English word ballistics. Thus, symbols are as if something thrown, aimed, intentionally to hit.

Taking Meier's statement one step further, we could say that the body and psyche fall together producing symptoms, but are thrown together producing symbols. There is a feeling of passivity in the image of falling together, while there is a feeling of action in the image of throwing together. Following this along, I am impressed by how active patients and doctors are in relation to symptoms, and how inactive most patients and doctors are in relation to the meaning, or symbolic significance, of the illness. This seems backwards. Perhaps there is something important in being patient with one's symptoms, while actively exposing and opening oneself to the symbol thrown at consciousness by the tertium that lies beyond body and psyche. It is there where psyche and soma meet in psychoid[35] interaction, where body is psyche and psyche is body, and where both are subject to the play of archetypal forces. It is the meeting ground of man and the gods.

If the gods wound, and if the gods become diseases, as Jung used to say, then it is necessary to understand sickness—even cancer—as a *wounding* and to go in search of the God at work in it. Gods are angered and strike when they are denied, defiled, or devalued. What is needed is to go into the symptom, into the sickness, and connect again with the God hidden there.

A cancer patient reported the following dream that had been recurrent since childhood:

> I open the door of a darkened bedroom and with the light shining from my back across the room to a window, I see a glowing face outside the window looking at me. I immediately become paralyzed, lift up off the ground so that I am floating and begin floating slowly toward the face. The dream never resolves beyond this point.

This dream illustrates an important distinction that E. F. Edinger has recently amplified.[36] The ego must come to *know* the unconscious—here pictured as the dreamer "seeing the face." But equally important, although often forgotten, is that the ego is also *known by* the unconscious. The face sees the dreamer too.

But something is wrong. The dreamer loses his ground and is in danger of being assimilated by the powerful face. The dream never resolves, coming again and again. The dreamer is here going into the God, perhaps into what ultimately became the devouring cancer, but he does not do so consciously. It is not the *knowing with* that Edinger describes as the essential condition to bring consciousness to the God.

Recurrent dream and recurrent cancer may be related. Recurrent dreams are a significant feature in the dream life of cancer patients. One of the mythical themes that can be gleaned from reports of cancer patients is the myth of Sisyphis,[37] the king who was sentenced to Hades with the punishment of pushing a huge boulder up a mountain, only to have the boulder roll again to the bottom every time he reached the peak. It is a theme of recurrence without resolution, like the recurrent dream. It was only when the above dreamer completed the dream by consciously exposing himself to the awesome emotional power of the face that he experienced a release from this Sisyphean fate. The dream has not returned, nor has his cancer.

Dreams play a critical part in our search for contact with the God hidden in our sickness. The God is not easily found, because, like Eros, he is often hidden in darkness. It is Psyche who brings the light to see the God. The inevitable task of Psyche is to bring the God into view. That is her mission. For this, she is afflicted and tormented and put through impossible tasks. Through her willing suffering and ever-close awareness and risk of death, she earns her marriage to the immortal realm. The Eros and Psyche myth is as well a story of the mystery of soma and soul, and may hold the hidden meaning of the union of body and psyche.[38]

Perhaps cancer is an experiment, an experiment in the creation of greater personality, urging it on to the frontier of its existence in order to constellate there the meaning and purpose of one's destiny previously denied. Jung said, "it was only after my illness that I understood how important it is to affirm one's own destiny."[39] And it was after his illness that his most creative work was done, by his own admission.

The hurting body forces us to remember that the body is the temple.[40] Sickness—even cancer—is an invitation to re-enter the temple in search of our connection to what is beyond constricted consciousness. Sickness can be a road to individuation, holding within it the *massa confusa,* the confused mass, not yet transformed.[41] Sickness—and particularly cancer— pulls consciousness to ever deeper recesses of the self.

Cancer has been described as a type of suicide, a way out, a mode of death, as one of the ways we *choose* to die. Cancer has even been pictured as an alternative to psychosis.[42] Bodily destruction and images of bodily consumption are frequent in psychosis, and the dreams of cancer patients too are filled with images of bodily rending and consumption. Recently, a patient told me he experienced his cancer as consuming him. Then, he added: "It's more than that. It's like I'm consuming myself." What God is at work here?

It was in reflecting on this question that I recalled the myth of Erysichthon. As Ovid tells it, Erysichthon takes a company of axemen to the sacred grove of Demeter to obtain sufficient timber for an elaborate banquet hall.[43] He is warned by the female spirits of the trees to desist from his plan. Intent, despite all warnings, he cuts down the sacred oak of Demeter. In so doing, he angers this gentle Goddess to a fury nearly unparalleled in Greek mythology. She inflicts upon him an insatiable hunger. After exhausting all possible food, he devours himself. This is a particularly graphic image of a victimization in relation to the Goddess of growth and increase.

In pursuing this myth I was startled to come across a fairytale which may be a living rendition of the Erysichthon tale. It comes from an old woman on the Greek island of Cos, around the turn of the century, and illustrates dramatically what I have been saying. It is called, "The Fairy's Revenge."[44]

This tale begins as a tragic love story. Dimitroula, a young woman, loves a ploughman. The king, however, greedily wants her for her beauty, and so devises a plot to kill the ploughman. On a high plain, amidst lovely and sacred trees, the king gives a sign to his men to attack the approaching ploughman. The men fail to see his sign. This so enrages the king, he jumps angrily in the air, gives the sign more forcefully, and then falls backward onto his throne. The king's men see his sign and attack the ploughman with waves of arrows. The ploughman falls. A great female voice from the trees shouts out: "His blood shall open a pit to smother you." The men, in fear, turn to their king, but he is nowhere to be seen. In his anger, he had fallen onto his throne, and, tipping it backwards, fell into an old broken well—smothering himself in the mire. As the men looked down upon their fallen king, the ploughman in one last gasp of strength, fell upon them knocking everyone into the well, drowning them all. The king's son, upon hearing the news, swears to cut down the woods to the roots, because of his spite against the spirits who had punished his father so harshly.

This is the background of the tale. I would emphasize the psychological importance of the transition between the old king and the new king. The old king reflects aging and exhausted values. Transition to a new king constellates the *possibilities* of a new ruling principle of the realm. In this story, however, the new king begins his kingship caught in a psychology of power, vengeance, and retribution against the feminine spirits who brought his father to a bitter but just end. The son carries on in the psychological tradition of the father. An improper relation to the feminine spirit runs through this family, a kind of "psychological genetics" that may not be unrelated to the fact that cancer too seems to be carried through the family tree. And now to the ghastly story of the prince's fate.

Filled with the powers of revenge, the prince, now king, set off with his axe-men to lay low the sacred trees and offending spirits. All went speedily at first as they fell flat the tall trees one after another. Their youthful vigor was slackened, however, by a huge oak in the center of the grove that seemed to resist each blow. Using their sharp axes with all their strength, they had cut nearly half through the mighty tree when they heard a plaintive cry from the heart of the oak. The axemen were ready to drop their axes and flee when the king shouted to them, "Smite it again, you dogs, pay no heed to spirits!" And because their fear of him was greater, they took their axes to the tree and dealt still more telling blows. Then, upon reaching the very center, a mighty gush of blood jetted forth, and a voice cried: "Oh, ye who fear not God!" As the tree trembled, and swayed, and finally crashed to the ground, the voice was heard again: "Even as God has punished your father, even so and three times worse will he punish you." From the direction of the voice there appeared a young woman's head, her hair disheveled and drenched with the blood of the tree, which now filled the ground on which they stood. The youths were seized with terror and ran, but the king turned on the female spirit like a madman and raised his sword and brought it down on her with all his strength. But when he tried to withdraw his sword, he could not; for in his blind anger, he had missed her and wedged it deep within the tree stump. Without his weapon, he too was gripped with fear and fled to his palace and took to his bed. That night, as he slept, he saw a dream. A fairy came to him and took him forcefully by the hand and led him to the place where the trees had been cut down. "Stay and behold what you have done," she said. As he looked, he saw each felled tree become a flame, and in an instant there were fires all around him burning furiously, singeing his hair and licking at his feet. He was powerless to flee, as the fires united into a single holocaust that seemed bent on destroying him completely. As the tongues of flame leaped to mid-heaven, he saw there the fairy pointing at him and saying, "This and much worse is the lot of those who destroy my beautiful trees." As she faded, a terrible cold wind blew through the fire-ravaged place as if all the north winds of the earth had united against him. The king began to shiver and his ulcerous fire wounds broke into dry cracks to the very bone, and with each shake of his body they stretched and slackened, bringing him wracking pain and terrible anguish.

As he stood helpless and afraid, an old woman approached him. She was hunch-backed, horrid, filthy and scabby—a terrible figure. She came right up to the king and with her bony and decrepit hand reached out for his sword, still lodged in the tree trunk. Without strain or difficulty, she snatched it free from its bond and raised it to her ghastly face. Like a priest performing a ritual, she breathed upon it three times, each time filling the blade with virulent seeds from her poisonous breath. "I am the Ravening Hunger," she intoned in a voice filled with hate and prophecy. As the king opened his mouth in fright, she raised herself high and plunged the sword into his gaping mouth and down into his belly, and as she drew it out, all the seeds of the ravening hunger planted themselves in his entrails. So immediate was the effect that he strained to lick the blood from the sword as it was withdrawn from his mouth. An overpowering and insatiable hunger and thirst came over him. Cisterns and wells he drank, full rivers and lakes, but nothing could quench his thirst. All the victuals of the world were placed before him, but nothing could sate his awful hunger. So great was his distress and overpowering his need, that he awoke from his dream.

"I am hungry," were his first words. The palace servants made ready all the foods of the realm, but the king's ravenous hunger knew no bounds. In short time, he had consumed all the food of the land and waters of the realm. Still he hungered and thirsted for more. There was nothing left to sell for food, nothing but a son and daughter. When he could find no buyer for his daughter, he tried to eat her. But the king's desperate plan was thwarted by her brother, and the two children fled for their lives. Now totally alone, without family, without friends, without servants, and only an empty kingdom, the king began to tear at his own flesh, gnawing it greedily with his teeth until he had devoured himself to death.

The prince's fate is revealed to him in a dream, and his hunger is begun therein, a clear expression of the idea that dreams may be the psychological matrix of disease and divine retribution.

The prince, like Erysichthon, is intent upon felling the sacred trees. Jung has described the tree as the symbolic seat of transformation and renewal, and thus, of the self.[45] The tree has its roots in the earth, and its branches reach toward the heavens. The tree carries the image of connection both downward into maternal earth and upward into paternal sky. To fell the sacred tree is to sever one's connection to the Gods below and above. It is an attack on the self. Ultimately, the prince's attack on the self is visited back upon himself. Behind this, is the retribution of the fertility Goddess whose trees are felled. Demeter is the highest expression of the fertility Goddess and her tree is not the tree of knowledge, but the tree of life. To attack it, to try to make it one's own, as does the prince, is to destory oneself, to literally consume one's own life.

The prince is warned but does not listen.[46] His ego cannot submit to the will of the autonomous spirits. The self sends warnings when the ego oversteps its bounds by invading the sacred precincts with hubristic intention. These warnings are carried in dreams. If the warnings go unheeded, the God's punishment may likewise be carried in dreams, as was true for the prince, and for the wife of the old man who told me of her dreams of fires and attacking dogs.

A contemporary version of this story was told to me recently by a young woman who has experienced cancer. Her dream went something like this:

> I am in a field . . . watching . . . and I see some men . . . they are wearing grotesque masks whch make them look very tall . . . they shoot some trees with fire and the leaves immediately burn up and then the fire goes out . . . but the trees look burnt . . . they take off their masks . . . they have business suits on and they are satisfied with what they have done and they want to continue . . . I

can see helicopters in the distance shooting something that I know will kill the fruit on the trees. . . .

I have seen in the background of many cancer patients something corresponding to a powerful psychological growth cut down or cut off. It is as if something very alive in themselves was killed. The person severed some living connection to the self, in service of an ego that would assimilate the self. Instead, the wounded self begins an inevitable course of assimilating the ego, and when it comes out in psychosis, or in cancer, we see man reduced to eating himself, feeding on his own flesh, rather than on the fruits of the earth whose spirits he has violated in himself.

Perhaps we could learn something of Demeter's perspective from the American earth. It is heard in the voice of an old holy woman of the Wintu tribe, when she says:

> The White People never cared for land or deer or bear. When we Indians kill meat, we eat it all up. When we dig roots, we make little holes. When we build houses, we make little holes. When we burn grass for grasshoppers, we don't ruin things. We shake down acorns and pinenuts. We don't chop down the trees. We only use dead wood. But the White People plow up the ground, pull down the trees, kill everything. The tree says, "Don't. I am sore. Don't hurt me." But they chop it down and cut it up. The spirit of the land hates them. They blast out trees and stir it up to its depths. They saw up the trees. That hurts them. The Indians never hurt anything, but the White People destroy all. They blast rocks and scatter them on the ground. The rock says, "Don't. You are hurting me." But the White People pay no attention. When the Indians use rocks, they take little round ones for their cooking . . . How can the spirit of the earth like the White Man? . . . Everywhere the White Man has touched it, it is sore.[47]

I met a patient recently who epitomizes the prince in his psychology of power against the earth spirit in himself. He had widespread cancer and should not have been alive at all. But he had an unexpected encounter with his psyche in the form of several dreams which had such a profound effect on him that the term transformation is hardly suitable. It was like a conversion experience to the reality of the psyche. After this, the cancer began to regress. But what struck me was not the regression of the cancer and the prolonged life. (That type of quick and temporary healing without transformation of the individual and the quality of his life is seen too frequently—a lull before an even more virulent cancer returns. It is as if the ego has healed its wounds in order to maintain the same relation to life. Such power is effective for a time.)

But with this man, there was more than healing. This was a patient cured in the truest sense of the hidden meaning contained in this word cure. Cure comes from the Latin *cura* meaning care, concern, trouble, anxiety, as well as sorrow. The Indo-European root is *kois* meaning to sorrow for something. Thus, cure is related to an active process of bringing to illness one's anxiety, one's care, one's sorrow, one's concern. These are images that do not avoid the deep emotions of sickness, and even suggest that it is the care and concern that is essential to cure. For the patient to get well, the patient—not just the physician or therapist—must show care, concern, sorrow. The patient must become emotionally involved in his own sickness. That is, he must suffer it as the first ingredient on the way to cure.

The root *cura* also gives rise to *curiosus,* which in our language becomes *curiosity.* What is this relationship between curiosity and cure? Since curiosity is a desire for knowledge, there is the archiac implication that curiosity was the basic sin that led woman to seek out and eat the fruit of the tree of knowledge of good and evil. On the same model, we find in all cultures that some institution functions as the keeper of the secret knowledge—whether it be priest, shaman, medicine man, or doctor. Historically, curiosity has been linked with man's impulse to find out the secrets, not just of nature, but the sacred secrets as well. There is no harm in learning the secrets in hubristic aspiration rather than in service of relationship to one's self, to others, and to the divine spirits at the root of nature.

There is something more. From the point of view of "normalcy," anything that deviates becomes a "curiosity." On the one hand, our interest flows out to such curiosities. When we encounter someone quite mad, someone quite misshapen or horrible, do we not yearn to see, to look, to take in? Yet, at the same time, do we not try to hide our glance, or flee, or experience great relief when the situation has returned to normal? We treat our own pathologies, whether psychic or physical, in the same way. They fascinate and invite our libido to participate; yet, we fight, become fearful, and rid ourselves of them as quickly as possible. The relation between cure and curiosity, however, suggests that these are not to be kept apart. Perhaps the cure comes when one is motivated by curiosity to go into the pathology rather than away from it. Jung used to say the only real disease was normality, that man's illnesses and his neuroses were his riches and that by going into them, one would find the completeness that is so missing in what we consider normalcy. Perhaps curiosity is what leads the healer, be he physician, analyst, or anyone else, into contact with sickness and disorder. Of course, we must wonder about the extent to which we become genuinely curious about our own sickness. Knowing why we are sick leads to knowledge about the part we play in developing our own sickness, a painful knowledge not many are willing to seek.

In Greek, cure is rendered by the work *aki.*[48] It means silence, calm, lull. It reflects the quietness in the image of suffering one's pains in silence as an essential step in the process of healing. It is a *meditatio* in the original sense: to take the measure of one's self by reflection. If our pains are driven or taken away without suffering, we avoid this *aki,* this *meditatio.* That is why quick healing often is so temporary. One may be healed of the sickness, but not transformed by it. But from the genuine journey into one's sickness—even the horrors of cancer—one could learn what Paracelsus revealed:

> . . . it is God who has given us disease. He could, when the time were proper and the limit of our purgatory had come, take it away from us, even without the physician. If he fails to do so, it is only because he does not want this to be accomplished without the help of man.[49]

NOTES:

1. *Cancer* and related words (e.g., *canker; cancre, chancre*) derive from the Latin word *cancer* meaning "crab." The ancient association between crab and the disease of cancer developed from the physical resemblance between the legs of a crab and the radiating engorged veins surrounding a cancerous tumor. The word itself derives from two roots: *can* meaning "to surround" and *cer* meaning "hard." It is this image of a hard surrounding that is distilled in the animal's name. The use of the term cancer goes much beyond its specific medical referent, most importantly in its metaphoric use as "an often malignant source of spreading and corroding destructive evil." (Definition 3, *Webster's Third New International Dictionary,* Springfield: Merriam, 1971).

2. *Mortificatio* literally means "death-bringing." It sums up the dark experiences accompanying the gradual loss of life's energies, the pain and suffering of hard punishment and cruel affliction. Symbolically, it refers to the "extraction" of soul and spirit from the body. It is in this sense that *mortificatio* is a major operation in the alchemical process and refers also to the idea that a new birth requires a death of the old. Re-birth and resurrection imagery are always associated with prior mortification (e.g., Christ's crucifixion). I use the term here for the purpose of bringing together the imagery of alchemy and the imagery of sickness. As Jung has shown (e.g., *Psychology and Alchemy,* CW 12), alchemy may be considered a model of the individuation process. The "alchemy of sickness" and its relation to individuation will be the subject of another paper.

3. *Numen* is a Latin word meaning generally "command," "will," and "authority," especially in a religious sense in which it comes to mean "divine will," "power of the gods," "divine sway," "supreme authority." By metonymy it refers specifically to "a divinity," "diety," "god," "goddess." (See Charlton T. Lewis, *A Latin Dictionary for Schools,* Oxford: O.U.P., 1889/1964). The word literally means "nod as if to beckon," and carries the image of a God beckoning man to approach the divine. Rudolph Otto (*The Idea of the Holy,* Oxford: O.U.P., 1923/1950) used this word to coin the term numinous to describe the "awful," "overpowering," "urgent," "wholly other" and "fascinating," quality of the *mysterium tremendum*—the direct phenomenological experience of the divine. I characterize cancer as a numen and its experience as numinous because it shares these qualities with religious experience,

particularly in those experiences of a God's wrath, fury, and punishment (or the "demonic dread," which is the fear of such experience).

4. St. Peregrinus Laziosi was born in 1260, in Forli, Italy. During the course of a political demonstration, he slapped St. Benizi on the cheek. St. Benizi offered Peregrinus the other cheek in return. Peregrinus was so affected by this that he was instantly converted. He joined the Servite order at Sienna and later founded a Servite chapter at Forli. He was tireless in his service and devotion, and it is said he never sat down. He developed a cancer on his foot, and as it worsened, it became necessary to amputate. The night before surgery, Peregrinus had a dream in which his cancer was healed by God. In the morning, the cancer was gone. His devotions and service continued for many years without recurrence of the cancer. He died in 1345. Documented evidence of his cure played an important part in his canonization in 1780. Since that time he has been the patron saint of the cancer victim.

5. The Latin word *peregrinus* is formed from two roots: *per* meaning "through," "across," "through the midst of," "traverse," and *ager* meaning "land," "field," "pasture." Hence, the image "to cross the fields." In its development, the word came to mean "from foreign parts," "stranger," "alien," "foreigner." In its sense as "one who journeys in foreign lands," the word is the source of our English word *pilgrim*.

6. From a letter of C. G. Jung to his cousin, Rudolf Jung, May 11, 1956. In C. G. Jung: *Letters* (Princeton: Princeton University Press, 1975), II, p. 297.

7. Elida Evans, *A Psychological Study of Cancer* (New York: Dodd Mead and Co., 1926). The title page suggests the introduction was written by C. G. Jung but apparently this is not correct. The editors of *The Collected Works of C. G. Jung* have made the decision not to include this introduction in the final volume of miscellaneous works (CW 18.)

8. "The Antisocial Cell," *Harper's,* June 1976, pp. 43–64.

9. L. Stein, "Introducing Not-Self," *Journal of Analytical Psychology,* vol. 12, 2 (1967), has introduced the notion of the self as manifesting in "the lymphoid stem cells and/or the undifferentiated mesenchyme cells of the reticulo-endothelial system," in a sense connecting the concept of self with the body's immune system. The breakdown of the immune system as an important factor in the emergence of cancer would mean that in some crucial way the self loses its immunity against "not-self." From this point of view, cancer would reflect a breakdown in the self's defenses, and more generally, that psychosomatic disease represents an attack upon, and/or a breakdown of, the self. Some implications of this extraordinary view are discussed by M. Fordham, "Jungian Views of the Body-Mind Relationship," *Spring* 1974.

10. For examples of this work see the following and references contained therein: O. Carl Simonton and Stephanie Simonton, "Belief Systems and Management of the Emotional Aspects of Malignancy," *J. Transpersonal Psychol.,* 1975, 7, pp. 29–47; "Second Conference on Psychophysiological Aspects of Cancer," *Annals N.Y. Acad. Sci.,* 1969, 164, pp. 307–634; D. M. Kissen and L. L. Leshan (eds.), *Psychosomatic Aspects of Neoplastic Disease,* Philadelphia; Lippincott, 1964.

11. Definition 2a(1), in *Webster's New Collegiate Dictionary,* p. 1304.

12. The quotation is from Herman Paul, *Prinzipien der Sprachwissenschaft* (Halle: Niemeyer, 1880), as cited by Theodore Thass-Theinemann, *The Interpretation of Language,* (N. Y.: Aronson, 1968/1973), I, pp. 81–82.

13. From Jung's essay, "The Psychology of the Child Archetype," in C. G. Jung and C. Kerenyi, *Essays on a Science of Mythology* (N. Y.: Pantheon, 1949), p. 105. In R. F. C. Hull's later translation (CW 9, 1, p. 157), the sentence became: "An archetypal content expresses itself, first and foremost, in metaphors."

14. The earliest printed use of the term is found in 1497: "Obedyence excellith al vyctyms (printed *vyayms*) and holocaustis in the whiche was sacrefyced ye flesshe of other creatures." Definition 1, in *The Compact Edition of the Oxford English Dictionary,* p. 3623.

15. In Greek this term means "increase" and later "increase in power" as "to strengthen," later still in the sense of "to bring up to manhood." It is a combining form with many words, giving them the meaning of "increase" or "growth."

16. Reference to Auxesia may be found in *The Oxford Classical Dictionary,* p. 155. Her worship at Epidaurus is described by Herodotus in his *History,* 83: ". . . they fixed a worship for the images [of Auxesia and Damia], which consisted in part of sacrifices, in part of female satiric choruses. . . . These choruses did not abuse men, but only women of the country. Holy orgies of similar kind were in use among the Epidaurians, and likewise another set of holy orgies, whereof it is not lawful to speak."

17. From "A Medial Dream," by an anonymous author, in Ralph L. Woods and Herbert B. Greenhouse (eds.), *The New World of Dreams* (N. Y.: Macmillan, 1974), p. 46.

18. From *De Divinatione per Somnum* ("On Prophesying by Dreams"), (Chicago: Encyclopedia Britannica, Inc., 1952, VIII, *Great Books of the Western World*), p. 707.

19. Ibid, p. 706.

20. *Religio* is said to derive from two roots: *re* meaning "again," "anew," and *ligio* meaning "tie," "bind," "fixed to." Religio thus would mean "to bind oneself anew."

21. A particularly useful analysis of this idea and its practical implications has been provided by R. M. Stein in his paper "Body and Psyche: An Archetypal View of Psychosomatic Phenomena," *Spring,* 1976.

22. C. G. Jung, "The Transcendent Function," CW 8, p. 73.

23. *The New English Bible,* Deuteronomy 32:39.

24. This passage is from Pindar's funeral poetry preserved as a fragment (Number 131) of a larger but lost work.

25. From T. M. Davie, "Comments upon a Case of 'Periventricular Epilepsy,' *Brit. Med. Journ.,* 1935, p. 296.

26. Ibid, p. 297.

27. From C. G. Jung, *Analytical Psychology: Its Theory and Practice* (N. Y.: Pantheon, 1968), pp. 73–74.

28. Ivan Illich, *Medical Nemesis* (N. Y.: Random House, 1976).

29. From Paracelsus: Selected Writings (N. Y.: Pantheon, 1951), p. 150.

30. From J. Kirsch, "The Role of Instinct in Psychosomatic Medicine," *Am. J. Psychotherapy,* 1949, 3, pp. 253-260.

31. *Tertium* here takes on the meaning of "the third thing." Meier elaborates this idea and particularly its relation to synchronicity (". . . it presupposes a ter- tium, higher than soma or psyche, and responsible for symptom formation in both . . .") and the theory of the "subtle body" in his paper, "Psychosomatic Medicine from the Jungian Point of View," *J. Analyt. Psychol.,* 1963, 8, pp. 103-121.

32. As cited by Paul Tournier in an important but little-known book, *A Doctor's Casebook in the Light of the Bible* (N. Y.: Harper and Row, 1960), p. 170.

33. From Graham Bennette, "Some Ideas Toward an Interpretation of Cancer in Psychophysiological Terms," *Harvest,* 1966, 12, pp. 35-70.

34. A genuine symbol stimulates the *imagination.* This is the critical difference be- tween *sign* and *symbol.* A "sign" enables one to translate an "unknown" into "known" categories. But a symbol, because it moves the imaginal realm to ac- tivity, always produces or leads to something not yet known. Jung writes: "The place or the medium of realization is neither mind nor matter, but that in- termediate realm of subtle reality which can be adequately only expressed by the symbol. The symbol is neither abstract nor concrete, neither rational nor irra- tional, neither real nor unreal. It is always both. . . ." (CW 12, p. 283). The "place" or "medium" referred to by Jung is precisely the imagination, or the *imaginatio* of the alchemists, that "psychic realm of subtle bodies whose characteristic it is to manifest themselves in a mental as well as a material form" (ibid., pp. 278-279). Sickness as *a symbol* also will stimulate the imagination. This imaginative activity must not be avoided—although that is one's usual response to the fantasies that our or others' illness brings. The *imaginatio* was the most important alchemical operation and it may prove to be an essential operation in the psychological treatment of sickness.

35. Jung uses the term *psychoid* to mean the "irrepresentable" nature of the collec- tive unconscious, that is, the archetypal psyche which in itself is not subject to experience by the conscious psyche. To use Plato's allegory of the cave, the shadows would be "representable" and thus effects of the fire of the collective unconscious that can be made conscious. But the fire itself is not subject to ex- perience, although nonetheless "real." In this sense, the fire would be the *psychoid* determinant of the experience of the shadows.

36. From Edward Edinger, "The Meaning of Consciousness," *Quadrant,* 1975, 8, 33-48.

37. Although all antique sources agree on the nature of Sisyphus' fate in Hades (to roll the rock up the hill only to have it endlessly fall back before reaching the crest), the reasons for this punishment are quite varied. In one account it is a nameless impiety (Mary Grant, ed., *The Myths of Hyginus,* Lawrence: Univ. Kansas Publ., 1960, p. 62). In another tale, Sisyphus subdues Thanatos (Death) so that no one dies until Ares unbinds Thanatos. Sisyphus is sent to Hades, but because Sisyphus did not have proper funeral rites, Hades gave him permission

to return briefly to earth. He did not return and in fact lived to old age. But Hades put him to the rock in order to keep him from escaping once again (see *The Oxford Classical Dictionary,* p. 1050). This is a psychology of attempted escape from the fate of death.

38. The myth tells us that Voluptas (Pleasure) is the offspring of the union of Eros and Psyche. Reflection on this myth as one of relationship between body and psyche would be guided by the idea that genuine pleasure requires a union of soma and soul in relatedness, rather than in opposition, or in hierarchical notions of superiority, of one over the other.

39. From *C. G. Jung, Memories, Dreams, Reflections* (N. Y.: Vintage 1961), p. 297.

40. This point is made most clearly by St. Paul (1 Co 6:19): "Or know ye not that your body is a temple of the Holy Spirit in you, which ye have from God; and ye are not your own?" (The Englishman's Greek New Testament, Grand Rapids: Zondervan, 1970, p. 445). In *The New English Bible* (ibid., p. 286), this verse is translated: "Do you not know that your body is a shrine of the indwelling Holy Spirit, and the Spirit is God's gift to you?" The word temple is a translation of a Greek word which has the more specific meaning of "the inmost cell of the temple in which the image of God was placed." The body as temple means that the image of God dwells hidden there. This idea perhaps bears upon the current fascination with the body.

41. In alchemy, *massa confusa* refers to the "chaos" of elements in active conflict and hostility with one another. All bonds are broken, all connections dissolved. It is a state of complete disorder and undifferentiated chaos. The cancer cell likewise is undifferentiated and chaotic in its organization and spreading growth. The psychological approach to the treatment of cancer is likely to be most effective when the cancer itself is regarded as the *massa confusa* which must be differentiated and transformed. The alchemist reduced the disorder of the alchemical chaos by his devotion to his operations and putting himself in a condition in which the "miracle" of transformation was possible. As Jung points out, ". . . transformation was a miracle that could take place only with God's help" (CW 14, p. 283).

42. See, for example, C. B. Bahnson and M. B. Bahnson, "Cancer as an Alternative to Psychosis: A Theoretical Model of Somatic and Psychologic Regression," in D. M. Kissen and L. L. Leshan (eds.), *op. cit. sup.,* pp. 184–202.

43. The story of Erysichthon is to be found in the Eighth Book of Ovid's *Metamorphoses* (Lines 738–878). A beautiful verse rendition is the Sir Samuel Garth translation (*Ovid's Metamorphoses,* N. Y.: Heritage Press, 1961).

44. The story in its full rendition may be found in R. M. Dawkins, *Forty-Five Stories from the Dodekanese* (Cambridge: Cambridge University Press, 1950), pp. 334–349. The main events of the first part of the story are told here in broad outline. The second part is presented in a much reduced "retelling." I am grateful to my assistant, Caroline West, for her help in reworking this story.

45. C. G. Jung, "The Philosophical Tree," CW 13.

46. The warnings come not only from the tree spirits but from the instinctive responses of the Prince's men, e.g., shrinking back from, and fear of, the tree

spirits. The Prince pays no heed. Even when the Prince through manipulation forces his men to continue the attack on the sacred trees, there remains *one alone who hesitates.* This is important psychologically as a kind of muted voice of conscience warning the hubristic ego. These warnings urge redirection. When unheeded, the fateful play continues to its tragic end.

47. From T. C. McLuhan (ed.), *Touch the Earth: A Self-Portrait of Indian Existence* (N. Y.: Pocketbooks, 1972), p. 15.

48. This word refers to "silence" as well as to "cure" and "point." The point reference is to the barbs of hooks and points of arrows and the resulting sharp pains upon puncture. It would seem to refer to the quiet suffering of sharp and acute pains.

49. From Paracelsus, ibid., p. 155.

3 Stress

Cause or Cure of Cancer?

Paul J. Rosch

Speculation concerning the possible relationship between stress and the onset or course of cancer has been receiving increasing attention in the past few years. I first became interested in the subject when invited to contribute a chapter to the current Sloan Kettering Series, *Cancer, Stress and Death,* which was the result of a joint symposium held under the auspices of the International Institute of Stress and the Sloan Kettering Foundation at Montreal in 1977. When the subject was first proposed, my attitude was skeptical, partly because of the recognition that after having been involved in stress research and a familiarity with the literature for thirty years, the subject did not ring any resonant chords. Furthermore, it became immediately apparent that any attempt to authenticate such a relationship, from a clinical point of view, might be a nightmare for a variety of reasons.

What Is Stress?

The first and most obvious problem is, "What is stress?" Decades of work in this subject have failed to produce a definition which is accepted by all investigators. The term obviously means different things to different people. Most commonly, it is used interchangeably to reflect some outside adverse agency such as extremes of temperature, noise, or altered emotional states due to pain, anxiety, or grief. More properly, however, the term "stressor" should be reserved for such factors and, as originally defined by Selye, it was viewed as the "non-specific response of the body to any demand." His early classic experiments demonstrated that the organism's response to noxious stimuli was manifested first by an "Alarm Reaction," which was a call to arms of the body's resources, followed by a "Stage of Resistance," during which increased defenses to the stressor occurred, and finally a "Stage of Exhaustion" resulting in disease or death.

Selye termed this tripartite response, the "General Adaptation Syndrome," and the disorders that resulted (peptic ulcer, hypertension, arthritis) he called "Diseases of Adaptation."

The tools available in those early days of stress research were crude by comparison with the resources available today. Selye's observations were confined predominantly to alterations in the pituitary-adrenal axis, and consisted of biochemical measurements of these parameters as well as gross microscopic morphologic alterations noted in experimental animals. Subsequent refinement in endocrine measurements and techniques led to an appreciation of a vast repertoire of hormonal participation in the response to a variety of stressors, particularly by Mason and others. It quickly became apparent that, in addition to the stereotype response to nonspecific stress, there was superimposed a whole spectrum of biochemical and hormonal responses with marked individual variation. Some of these can undoubtedly be explained by intrinsic genetic influences, while in other instances "prior conditioning" might play a role.

Aside from the obvious problems imposed by the semantic difficulties, it is immediately apparent that, from a practical or clinical viewpoint, what is stressful for one person may not be so for another. For example, it is generally conceded that the death of a spouse represents the most stressful type of life change event in terms of producing adaptive coping requirements. That may be true for most successful marriages, but on the other hand, a widow of a wife-beating alcoholic may be filled more with relief than with grief. As a practicing physician, the distinction in individual response to the same event is even more impressive and instructive. For some patients recuperating from a coronary thrombosis, the ideal prescription is three or four weeks rest in a tranquil environment removed from the pressures and anxieties of work. For another individual with the same diagnosis, to prescribe a three or four week vacation on a deserted tropical beach would be lethal.

This brings us to another aspect of the subject which is particularly germane to our topic, namely, the concept of eustress. We are increasingly impressed with the fact that not all stress is bad. We should like to characterize harmful stress as "distress" and pleasurable or productive stress as "eustress." Thus getting married is as likely to be as stressful as getting divorced; winning a race or an election may be as stressful as losing; a passionate kiss may be as stressful, but we would hardly place it in the same category as walking on burning coals or being in a traffic jam for three or four hours on the way to the airport.

Finally, we must distinguish between acute stress and chronic stress, and it is also necessary to make a distinction between those situations in which successful adaptive or coping mechanisms have supervened as opposed to those in which such resources were not available.

What Is Cancer?

Aside from the semantic and philosophic problems imposed by attempting to provide a universally acceptable definition of stress, there are equally challenging and inscrutable dilemmas associated with the diagnosis of cancer. To be sure, the diagnosis is simple enough when one is able to examine a piece of tissue under the microscope or observe certain characteristic changes in specific laboratory tests, x-rays, or other sophisticated imaging studies. In terms of dating the onset of malignancy, however, the problem is quite different.

If a lump is detected in the breast and is subsequently found to be malignant, when did the cancer start? One month ago? six months ago? a year ago? at birth? If we are unable to determine this, then how can we logically expect to associate a stressful event with the subsequent development of cancer? Is it possible that cancer cells frequently circulate through our system but are detected and destroyed by an effective surveillance and immunologic mechanism? Are various forms of cancer equatable, so that they can be grouped under the same heading for our purpose? Should an indolent basal cell carcinoma of the skin be considered in the same breath with a rapidly growing anaplastic carcinoma of the lung, a brain tumor, acute leukemia, or cancer of the cervix?

These were some of the seemingly insurmountable problems that occupied my attention as I began this investigation. The results of those studies, however, have more than vindicated the appropriateness of such an inquiry and will provide the basis of this report.

Historical Considerations

The notion that cancer might in some fashion be linked to altered emotional states is probably as old as the history of medicine itself. The ancient Greek physician Galen, in his treatise on tumors, *De Tumoribus,* noted that melancholy women (women supposedly having too much black bile— Greek *melas chole*) were much more susceptible to cancer than other females. At the beginning of the eighteenth century, the English physician Gendron noted the effect of "disasters of life as occasion much trouble and grief" in the development of malignancy. Eighty years later, Burrows attributed the disease to "the uneasy passions of the mind with which the patient is strongly effected for a long time." Early in the nineteenth century, Nunn emphasized that emotional factors appeared to influence the growth of tumors of the breast, and Stern commented on the fact that cancer of the cervix appeared to be more common in sensitive and frustrated married women. Toward the middle of the century, Walshe's treatise, *The Nature and Treatment of Cancer,* drew attention to the "influence of mental misery, sudden reverses of fortune and habitual gloomings of the temper on the disposition of carcinomatous matter. If systematic writers can be credited, these constitute the most powerful cause of the disease." By the end of the century, another English physician, Snow, in reviewing the case histories of 250 patients at the London Cancer Hospital, concluded that "the loss of a near relative was an important factor in the development of cancer of the breast and uterus."

I tend to attach special importance to such observations simply because the practice of medicine in the eighteenth and nineteenth centuries was slightly different than it is today. The physician was apt to have a more personalized relationship with his patient, which included not only a knowledge of his complaint and illness but an awareness of the setting in which they had arisen. More than likely, he was well aware of environmental factors at home and at work, of familial and genetic influences, as well as emotional factors that could play a role in the development of the patient's illness or response to it. A practitioner of those days was more apt to be a true "family" physician and, not having the "advantage" of modern-day technology, he would have to rely more upon his senses, intuition, and clinical acumen in arriving at a diagnosis and prescribing treatment, as contrasted with his modern counterpart who is more apt to use the laboratory, x-ray, or computer in managing the patient. The training of physicians of the eighteenth and nineteenth centuries was also more apt to be heavily grounded in the humanities, in literature and philosophy, than is the current medical curriculum with its necessary emphasis on the sciences, biochemistry, mathematics, etc. The physician of one or two hundred years ago probably had more time to spend with his patient and, more importantly, was apt to have the opportunity to observe him frequently at home in a family setting, both of which factors may have been able to provide him with greater insight into possible emotional factors in the genesis or perpetuation of the patient's illness. Thus by virtue of his own orientation and education and the personalized approach referred to above, physicians of the eighteenth and nineteenth centuries could well be expected to exhibit a greater sensitivity to the relationship I should like to propose. For this reason, I find their observations exceedingly important. The frenetic nature and pace of modern medical practice almost precludes such broad and, at the same time, in-depth knowledge of the patient, or the leisure of speculating on the relationships we wish to consider here.

Cancer and Civilization

One of the most interesting recurring themes in my research appeared to be the observation that an increasing incidence of cancer was directly proportional to the degree of "civilization." This appears to have been first expressed by Tanchou in 1833 in his "Memoir on the Frequency of Cancer" addressed to the French Academy of Sciences. Much of this information derived from Le Conte's "Statistical Researches," which noted:

> M. Tanchou is of the opinion that cancer, like insanity, increases in a direct ratio to the civilization of the country and of the people. And it is certainly a remarkable circumstance, doubtless in no small degree flattering to the vanity of the French savant, that the average mortality rate from cancer at Paris during 11 years is about 0.80 per 1,000 living annually, while it is only 0.20 per 1,000 in London!!! Estimating the intensity of civilization by these data, it clearly follows that Paris is four times more civilized than London!!!

Le Conte noted also that in the Orient, cancer appeared to be more frequent among Christians than Muslims, and also, interestingly enough, he commented on the fact that the incidence of insanity similarly appeared to be directly related to the degree of civilization. Of course, one might correctly attribute such observations as being related to greater diagnostic skills in civilized countries, more accurate registration and reporting of illness, changes in diet, and increasing contact with potential carcinogens as civilization progresses. But none of these factors singly or in combination provide a satisfactory explanation when scrutinized carefully.

Dr. William Bainbridge, a surgeon at the New York Skin and Cancer Hospital, in his book, *The Cancer Problem,* published in 1914, noted that, "Man in his primeval condition . . . has been thought to be very little subject to new growth, particularly to those of a malignant character. With changed environment, it is claimed by some, there came an increase in susceptibility to cancerous disease, this susceptibility becoming more marked as civilization develops. . . ." The following year, Frederick Hoffmann, under the auspices of the Prudential Life Insurance Company, published a treatise entitled, *The Mortality of Cancer throughout the World,* in which he noted:

> The rarity of cancer among native races [primitive races] suggests that the disease is primarily induced by the conditions and methods of living which typify our modern civilization. . . . A large number of medical missionaries and other trained medical observers, living for years among native races throughout the world, would long ago have provided a more substantial basis of fact regarding the frequency of occurrence of malignant disease among the so-called uncivilized races, if cancer were met with among them to anything like the degree common to practically all civilized countries. . . . Quite the contrary, the negative evidence is convincing that, in the opinion of qualified medical observers, cancer is exceptionally rare among the primitive peoples including the North American Indians and the Eskimo population of Labrador and Alaska.

A decade later, Dr. Stanton Hooker in an article entitled, "Eclecticism in Cancer Therapy," urged less emphasis upon cancer research and study of artificially induced cancer in laboratory animals, in the hope of retarding the malignancies they themselves had produced, and more emphasis upon the observation of people.

> There is, as a matter of fact, a growing group of independent thinkers both lay and professional, who are anything but impressed with the story of the discovery and isolation of the "cancer germ." . . . Mr. Ellis Barker has also written reiterating his views, in common with those of Sir Arbuthot Lane, my own and many others, that cancer is *a disease of civilization.* [Italics mine.]

In the same year, Dr. Morley Roberts in *Malignancy and Evolution* noted, "I take the view commonly held that, whatever its origins, cancer is very largely *a disease of civilization."* [Italics mine.] The following year, Dr. William H. Hay in an article entitled, "Cancer: A Disease of Either Election or Ignorance," opined:

> A study of the distribution of cancer among the races of the entire earth shows a cancer ratio in about proportion to which civilized living predominates; so evidently something inherent in the habits of civilization is responsible for the difference of cancer incidence as compared with the uncivilized races and tribes. Climate has nothing to do with this difference, as witness the fact that tribes living naturally will show a complete absence of cancer until mixture with more civilized man corrupts the naturalness of habit; and just as these habits conform to those of civilization, even so does the incidence of cancer begin to show its head. . . .

Roberts referred to a volume by Dr. Charles H. Moore, published in 1865, entitled, *The Antecedents of Cancer,* that "connects the progress of civilization with the increase of cancer which has remained an incontestable theory to the present day." Another author of the same period, Dr. W. Mitchell Banks, is quoted as stating that, "Cancer is on the increase in this country. Is it possible that this is coincident with our full habit of living as a people?" And still another source, Dr. Charles Powell, is quoted as observing in his *The Pathology of Cancer* that, "There can be little doubt that the various influences grouped under the title of civilization play a part in producing a tendency to Cancer."

One of the most exhaustive reviews of this aspect of the subject is to be found in Dr. Alexander Berglas' book, *Cancer: Its Nature, Cause and Cure* (Paris 1957) which has for its dominant theme the theory that cancer is a disease from which the native peoples are relatively or wholly free. "I have come to the conclusion," Berglas noted, "that cancer may perhaps be just another intelligible natural process whose cause is to be found in our environment *and mode of life.* . . . Everyone of us is threatened with death from cancer because of our inability *to adapt to present living conditions."* [Italics mine.]

In the preface to Dr. Berglas' book, the renowned medical missionary Albert Schweitzer commented:

On my arrival in Gabon in 1913, I was astonished to encounter no cases of cancer. . . . I cannot, of course, say positively that there was no cancer at all; but like other frontier doctors, I can only say that if any cases existed, they must have been quite rare. In the course of the years, we have seen cases of cancer in growing numbers in our region. My observations incline me to attribute this to the fact that the natives are *living more and more after the manner of the whites.* . . . [Italics mine.]

These observations were not limited to medical personnel. The great explorer Vilhjalmur Stefansson wrote an extensive study entitled, *Cancer: Disease of Civilization?,* an anthropological and historical study ultimately published in 1960. Stefansson quoted from Sir Robert McCarrison's observations among the Hunza in Kashmir (1904–1911). Dr. McCarrison had surveyed 11,000 natives and concluded that cancer was unknown among them. "In addition to their diet, the Hunzas were 'far removed from the refinements of civilization. Certain of these races were of magnificent physique, preserving until late in life the characters of youth; they are unusually fertile and longlived and *endowed with nervous systems of notable stability.' "* [Italics mine.] Stefansson suggested that in the argument between vegetarians and meat eaters, Hunzas versus Eskimos, that both may be right in praising their respective diets and wrong in condemning the other. "The most general conclusion . . . I have been able to reach appears to be that relative, if not complete, immunity to malignant disease is a by-product of good health. The peoples believed to be free from cancer were believed also to be longlived and to die eventually of old age, in the sense that they did not appear to die of any specific trouble but just from wearing out."

Modern Clinical Research

A few decades ago a Jungian psychoanalyst, Elida Evans, pointed out that many cancer patients appeared to have lost an important emotional relationship before the onset of illness. In contemporary times, the pioneer efforts of David Kissen, a British chest surgeon, called attention to the fact that there were certain personality traits which appeared to characterize patients with cancer of the lung, and these could best be described as an inability to express emotions adequately. Another study done by Schmale and Iker dealt with healthy women who had no symptoms but merely an abnormal Pap smear detected on a routine physical examination. Without any knowledge of the results of the Pap smear, they were able to predict with almost 75 percent accuracy those individuals who had early cancer, simply by utilizing a questionnaire which differentiated between various emotional states. They found that cancer was most apt to occur in those women with a "helplessness prone personality," or some sense of helpless frustration which could not be resolved in the preceding six months. William Greene, a hematologist at the University of Rochester, reporting on a fifteen-year study of patients who developed lymphoma or leukemia noted that it was apt to occur in a setting of emotional loss or separation which in turn brought about feelings of anxiety, sadness, anger, or hopelessness. Excellent reviews of these and other investigations were reviewed, analyzed, and extended in elegant, in-depth surveys by the Bahnsons and more recently, the Simontons. Lawrence LeShan, a psychoanalyst, has written extensively on this subject in the past two decades. He utilized Rorschach techniques, Thematic Apperception Tests, Worthington Personal History and structured personal interviews, and most importantly, interviews with close relatives of the patients. The conclusion was that the strongest clue to the possible development of malignancy was loss of the patient's *raison d'être* (hopelessness and helplessness), inability on the part of the individual to express anger or resentment, a marked amount of self dislike and mistrust, and most significantly, for our purposes, *loss of an important emotional relationship*.

About thirty years ago, Caroline Thomas, Professor of Medicine at The Johns Hopkins Hospital, began a psycho-social study of medical students, initially designed to determine whether or not the development of hypertension could be predicted by certain personality traits. She decided to study medical students since they could be followed very closely during their four years of medical school, and as intelligent physicians, could be relied upon to cooperate in follow-up studies for the remainder of their lives. Over the course of the last three decades, Thomas has accumulated very detailed data consisting of demographic and familial factors, as well as genetic, physiologic, psychologic, and metabolic characteristics. She obtained these by utilizing a variety of psychological stress tests, a Habits of Nervous Tension Questionnaire, as well as projective psychological tests such as the Rorschach and Figure Drawing Tests. As the data evolved and could be analyzed by computer techniques, the results seemed to indicate that it was possible also to predict a population with an increased tendency to develop cancer. Thomas' data suggested that malignancy tended to occur in individuals who were non-aggressive and who could not express their emotions. Many of them tended to be rather lonely persons without any close parental affiliation or who had figuratively "lost their parent."

Emotional loss as well as loss due to political defeat was viewed by various commentators as playing an essential role in the subsequent development of cancer in Napoleon, Ulysses S. Grant, Robert Taft and Hubert H. Humphrey. More recently, the flare up of cancer which had previously been dormant in the Shah of Iran over a period of six years, was viewed as directly related to his loss of homeland and power and enforced exile. Tolstoy's *The Death of Ivan Iliyich* echoes a similar theme, and it was intuitively reiterated by the poet W. H. Auden in "Miss Gee."

Doctor Thomas sat over his dinner
  Though his wife was waiting to ring,
Rolling his bread into pellets,
  Said, 'Cancer's a funny thing.

Nobody knows what the cause is,
  Though some pretend they do;
It's like some hidden assassin
  Waiting to strike at you.

Childless women get it,
  And men when they retire;
It's as if there had to be some outlet
  For their foiled creative fire.'

The Effects of Emotions on the Rate of Cancer Growth

All practicing physicians have observed that the rate of cancer growth may vary widely from patient to patient despite apparent similarities in age, sex and cell type. Numerous studies suggest that the rate of tumor growth can indeed be predicted based upon certain personality traits similar to those we have described above. About twenty-five years ago, Blumberg examined two groups of cancer patients matched for age, intelligence, and the state of their malignancy, all of whom knew their diagnosis. They were studied following their initial treatment when they were, relatively speaking, "feeling well." Patients dying in less than two years were compared with those living for more than six years and were found to have significantly poorer outlets for emotional discharge.

A similar study done about ten years ago on 204 cancer patients again concluded that the group with the most favorable outlook could be characterized as individuals who were able to show strong feelings under severe stress without loss of emotional control. A more recent study at the National Cancer Institute on a group of patients who had been operated on for malignant melanoma, with apparently successful results, revealed that relapse did not tend to occur among those patients who maximized the significance of their illness with an active positive approach. Ikemi noted that faith and belief appeared to be a major factor in spontaneous remission of cancer. Greer's observations that suppression of anger was significantly correlated with the finding of cancer in women coming to biopsy for a lump in the breast prompted an editorial on "Mind and Cancer" in *The Lancet*. The same author also called attention to the fact that serum IG-A levels were significantly higher in women who habitually suppress anger, implicating the immune system in this relationship. Thus emotional loss, feelings of "helplessness and hopelessness," and inability to express emotions appear to be influential factors in determining the course as well as the development of cancer.

Animal Studies

Laboratory workers provide additional support for the theories expressed above. Workers in the school of the great Russian psychologist and physiologist Pavlov found that dogs subjected to severe and chronic stress had a marked increase in "malignancy of the internal organs." Researchers at the Pacific Northwest Research Foundation in Seattle studied a strain of mice that is highly cancer prone and, under usual laboratory conditions, developed tumors within 8–18 months after birth in 60% of the cases. When the mice were raised in a soundproof protected area which insulated them from the stress of laboratory commotion and noise, only 7% of the mice developed cancer during a 14 month period. In another experiment, it was noted that in stressing the animals by simply rotating them gently on a turntable, the incidence of cancer could be significantly increased. Other studies done at the Stanford University School of Medicine on virus induced tumors in mice, revealed that the tumor size could be increased by three days of electric shock stress following the virus inoculation. It was also noted that female mice that appeared to have aggressive or fighting behavior developed much smaller tumors than passive or docile subjects.

Bereavement and Cancer

We have previously referred to the difficulties in defining stress because of its highly personalized and individualized nature. One of the most ambitious and impressive attempts to quantify human stress is to be found in the work of Dr. Thomas Holmes, Professor of Psychiatry at the University of Washington, whose group identified 43 life change events and rated them according to magnitude. The criterion utilized was, how much the individual had to cope with or alter his life style as a result of the event. The following is an abridged version of the scale with the arbitrary values assigned:

Event	Score
Death of a spouse	100
Divorce	73
Marital separation	65
Death of a close family member	63
Jail term	63
Marriage	50

Event	Score
Fired from job	47
Retirement	45
Sex difficulties	39
Death of a close friend	37
Change in number of arguments with spouse	35
Son or daughter leaves home	29
Trouble with in-laws	29
Outstanding personal achievement	28
Change in eating habits	15
Vacation	13
Traffic tickets	11

Using a questionnaire which measures the number and types of life change events in the preceding six months, year, or two-year period, it became possible to predict with some accuracy the likelihood of an individual becoming ill within the next six months, and to some extent, how serious that illness might be. The first five items have been copied directly and, looking at the chart, one notes that death of a spouse is considered to be the most significant stressful life change event. More than one-quarter of the way down the scale is divorce, followed by marital separation and death of a close family member. Thus all the items of greatest magnitude represent loss of a close personal relationship, with death of a spouse easily outdistancing the rest. It would also seem obvious that in terms of serious illness, cancer would have to rank at the top.

This relationship is further borne out by the following two studies. Table 3.1 shows the relationship of marital status of females in the United States to mortality from cancer of the breast, female genital organs, and other sites. Table 3.2 displays age-mated statistics from Great Britain which show similar findings. Both of these studies clearly indicate that mortality rates are higher for widowed and divorced individuals as compared to single and married women regardless of age, and specifically with respect to malignancy of the female genital organs. These findings assume increased significance in terms of a modus operandi when one notes other evidence for a strong correlation between depression and decreased immunologic capacity. This had been thought to be mediated through the endocrine system, but more recently, workers in Sydney, Australia, demonstrated that loss of a spouse was regularly accompanied by a marked reduction in immune function, two to six weeks after the event, and that this impairment could occur apart from any apparent significant change in hormonal activity. Other research indicates that interferon, a non-specific polypeptide, which is one of the basic defenses against virus infections and is now being intensively investigated in the treatment of cancer, is also suppressed under conditions of emotional stress.

TABLE 3.1 Cancer Mortality Rates per 100,000 Living Population of the United States 1929–1931

MARITAL STATUS	BREAST	UTERUS	OVARY-FALLOPIAN TUBES	VULVA AND VAGINA	ALL OTHER SITES	TOTAL
Single	15.0	9.0	3.3	.5	3.4	61.2
Married	24.5	35.0	4.7	.8	11.8	137.7
Divorced	29.3	57.2	6.0	1.5	81.8	175.8
Widowed	74.4	94.4	0.6	4.3	344.4	527.1

TABLE 3.2 Death Rates per 100,000 Living, All Forms of Cancer, England and Wales, 1930–1932

MARITAL STATUS	AGE 25	AGE 35	AGE 45	AGE 55	AGE 65	AGE 70 AND OVER
Spinsters	126 ± 0.6	68 ± 2.0	219 ± 4.1	416 ± 6.7	635 ± 13.1	961 ± 14.5
Married	169 ± 0.5	75.1 ± 2.0	202 ± 1.0	401 ± 3.3	639 ± 8.1	962 ± 11.2
Widowed and Divorced	161 ± 3.6	89 ± 3.9	246 ± 5.1	432 ± 5.1	692 ± 9.3	1084 ± 7.8

Theory of Cancer

It is a curious observation that just as cancer seems to be relatively uncommon in less civilized or developed humans, so it appears to be increasingly rare in lower forms of life. In fact, as one descends the phylogenetic scale, it is apparent that the incidence of cancer progressively decreases. On the other hand, the ability of the organism to regenerate tissue, organs or even parts of the body increases proportionately. Certain lower forms of invertebrates have the ability to sever parts of their anatomy when irritated, and obviously, such a capacity would have evolutionary or survival value only if the animal possessed an equally remarkable capacity to regenerate the cast-off portion from the available cell remnants. The starfish is able to grow a new appendage and the newt can regenerate its tail. Is it not possible that the human cancer chromosome, or whatever else one wishes to call it (genome, virus, DNA molecule), is the modern day replica of this regenerative trait which was once vital to the organism's survival or adaptation, but like many of man's present adaptive responses, has actually become harmful or dangerous. The primitive cellular response to loss, injury, or irritation is apparently purposeful new growth or regeneration. In man this capability is no longer preserved, and new growth or neoplasia, with far more sinister consequences, results in cancer.

There is support for such a hypothesis in recent experiments which disclose that if one injects into the limb of a newt chemicals which are known to result in the development of cancer in humans, malignancy does not occur. Instead, the newt grows an accessory limb. Similarly, if the lens of the eye of this animal is removed surgically and carcinogenic agents are implanted, cancer does not result, but instead a new lens is regenerated. In other words, the identical stimulus apparently induces either regeneration or malignancy, depending upon the organisms's stage of evolution.

There is one exception which almost appears to prove the rule. Much attention was attracted recently to the phenomenon of the "born again spleen." A series of cases of rupture of the spleen were reviewed in which, although this organ had been surgically removed, remnants of functioning splenic tissue could be demonstrated many years later, suggesting for the first time that successful regeneration of an organ could occur spontaneously in humans. It is interesting that splenic tissue should have this capacity in which the regenerative mechanism of the organ does function purposefully, and it is therefore not surprising to note that the spleen is also unique in that it is the only organ in humans that does not give rise to primary cancer. Anatomists also observe that accessory spleens or spleniculi occasionally occur; in rare cases several hundred have been present, representing a reversion to a *more primitive condition* in which splenic tissue was not localized in a definite organ, but was scattered throughout the gastro-intestinal tract. Thus from the standpoint of comparative anatomy, the spleen retains certain vestigial characteristics from which it may derive such potential.

If physical loss and injury can provide the stimulation for new growth (cancer), it is not too difficult to conceive that emotional loss may provide a similar stimulus to the highly developed cerebral cortex of man. Even in lower forms of life, the ability to regenerate tissue must involve something more than a simple local response and include, through some systemic humoral or nervous system pathway, the participation of the organism as a whole. Quite likely, the phenomenon of loss is appreciated by the organism via a chemical or humoral messenger or some aspect of stimulation of the nervous system which allows it to mobilize and integrate its activities for reparative processes.

Man is unique in that he responds not only to actual danger but also to the threats and symbols of danger. Indeed the anticipation of a noxious stimulus may elicit responses of a far greater magnitude than the actual injury itself. One clear example of this is sitting in the dentist's waiting room. Similarly, a protective adaptive response may overshoot the mark and be more damaging than the actual or anticipated offending agent. Secretion of adrenalin with its effects on the heart and blood pressure may be purposeful responses in the animal poised for flight or fight. However, the vexed and apprehensive exeecutive whose blood pressure boils over and who subsequently has a stroke in response to some argument at work is clearly having an inappropriate adaptive response far more dangerous to his life than the original irritant. There is no question that emotional stress in humans may have more profound effects than physical stress, as demonstrated by the hormone secretion studies performed on the Harvard crew team which clearly demonstrated a more profound influence on the coxswain than on the actual rowers. All these observations are consonant with our notation that emotional stress may result in adaptive responses which once might have been useful in our ancestors, but have now become injurious to us.

I concede that it is difficult to think of cancer as ever having been linked to anything that was useful or purposeful. Today's cancer patient is reminiscent of the Biblical leper who was similarly consumed by a process that was decaying or putrifying, one who is not infrequently avoided by family, friends, and even physicians. The diagnosis is considered to be an ill omen and tantamount to a death sentence with its fear of prolonged pain, suffering, loss of attractiveness and social esteem, or the contemplation of disfiguring surgery. Cancer is defined in the *Oxford English Dictionary* as being "offensive to the senses or to taste or refinement; disgusting, repulsive, filthy, foul, abominable, loathsome." The distinguished psychiatrist Karl Menninger noted that "the very word 'cancer' is said to kill some patients who would not have succumbed [as rapidly] to the malignancy from which they suffer." Our abhorrence is reflected by the notation that "moon children" has replaced "Cancer" in astrological charts. Even a federal law, the 1966 Freedom of Information Act, singled out cancer as the only disease exempt from disclosure since it would be "an unwarranted invasion of personal privacy."

Thus because of sociocultural considerations, it is difficult to think of cancer as ever having been related to something that was useful or purposeful. From a teleologic viewpoint, however, and based upon information presented above, such a conclusion seems valid. The most profound effects of stress are to be found in endocrine changes and effects upon the immunologic system. Similarly, immunotherapy and hormones represent two of the most powerful weapons employed in the treatment of cancer. It would therefore seem most unlikely that a strong relationship did not exist between stress and cancer.

Practical Considerations

What is the significance of all this? Do these observations contribute anything to our understanding of the nature or treatment of cancer? I think so. It should be obvious that if the observations of Thomas and others have merit, then it should be possible to predict a high-risk cancer group on the basis of certain personality traits, and to have an extraordinarily high index of suspicion in evaluating such patients. Similarly, if noxious influences or distress can play a role in the causation or aggravation of cancer, then is it not possible that positive emotions such as faith and laughter or eustress can have the reverse effect? Such a phenomenon is suggested in the case of other illnesses, as in Norman Cousins' recent book, *Anatomy of an Illness* and in Adam Smith's *Powers of Mind*. Several years ago, J. I. Rodale, the founder of *Prevention,* wrote a book entitled *Happy People Rarely Get Cancer*. I have never been able to obtain a copy of this, but it is of interest that nuns, Mormons, Christian Scientists, Seventh Day Adventists and other individuals who have found some "inner peace or life style" which apparently insulates them from distress appear to have less cancer. Finally, there is increasing evidence that the patient's emotional participation may play a vital role in the course of his illness. This has been emphasized by LeShan, and more recently by the Simontons who, using visual imagery and other techniques such as biofeedback and hypnosis, report increased survival rates in cancer patients who have embarked on such programs. A recent feature article in the *New York Times* indicated that spiritual healing was gaining ground among Catholics and Episcopalians citing certain cancer patients who "recovered or enjoyed long remissions or whose final days were painless."

There are any number of claims for cancer cures, all with zealous advocates. They include mineral waters, comfrey and other herbs, voodoo, yoga, faith healing, krebiozen, acupuncture, laetrile, various shrines, and the list goes on and on. All of these are supported by fervent anecdotal evidence, and yet it is perfectly obvious that no one agency appears to be successful in all or even a signficant number of cases. On the other hand, it does seem unreasonable to categorically dismiss all of these as not having a scintilla of truth, and it is certainly difficult to deny that documented cases of spontaneous remission of cancer do occur. I believe that there is a common thread which runs through all these experiences.

A hint of this may be found in the interesting case history noted by Klopfer, who described a patient with far advanced lymphosarcoma who begged to be treated with krebiozen after he had learned of a number of fantastic cures with this new chemical from Germany. After the patient's initial series of treatments, his tumor masses "melted like snowballs on a hot stove." Where previously he had required an oxygen mask to merely sustain himself during daily activities, he was now able to fly a plane at 12,000 feet without any effort. He continued to do well, but following some unfavorable publicity suggesting that krebiozen was ineffective, he again became bedridden. In desperation his physician told him that the adverse reports were not accurate and had been based on faulty preparations of the drug. He indicated that he now had available a supply of a fresher, more active potent principle, which the patient eagerly accepted. Actually, he was given distilled water, and again, the disease disappeared rapidly with clinical remission. Subsequently, it was announced that the Food and Drug Administration and the American Medical Association had found krebiozen to be worthless. Following this, the patient succumbed to his disease almost within a matter of days.

Another aspect of this phoenomenon, more scientifically documented, may be found in a discussion of one of the papers presented at the New York Academy of Sciences International Conference on Immunology of Cancer (1976). The comments were directed at some curious results noted in a research project utilizing BCG vaccine in patients with lung cancer at McMaster Unversity in Toronto. The initial program was undertaken by an enthusiastic thoracic surgeon given the pseudonym "Berkley-Smythe" who had a positive, personalized, optimistic approach to patients and who achieved rather remarkable results. Because of this, the study was subsequently greatly expanded, but was now carried out by different staff physicians. Although the identical protocol was followed, no improvement was noted in the new patients. I should like to quote from the discussion:

> We then sat down and said, why is this? Why are we seeing no beneficial effect? Why did the first four patients do so much better? We said, let's try to visualize the patient who is in the cubicle when Berkley-Smythe walks in and says, "Good afternoon, Mr. Featherwick. It's good to see that you've recovered from your operation. You are feeling much better now, aren't you? Mr. Featherwick says, "Oh yes, I'm feeling a hell of a lot better than I did when I

had my chest tube in, and I really feel like I'm on the road to recovery." Berkley-Smythe then agrees that he's doing very well, indeed, but that his outlook might be even better with some additional treatment. "We now have a good way to treat you that we've learned about from experimental animal studies and from other people's work with patients who have a similar problem to yours. We would be glad to do this for you, if you would like to try it; wouldn't you Featherwick? OK, just sign this consent form. You know it's a pretty benign treatment. There are some complications that could occur, but they aren't nearly as bad as the operation that you came through well." All of which is true. So the patient is entered into the study and comes back every visit to see Berkley-Smythe, who is smiling and enthusiastic, and the patient is smiling enthusiastically and doing well.

On the other hand, there are doctors in the immunotherapy clinic who don't have the aura of Berkley-Smythe. Dr. Marvin Milquetoast is one. Marvin goes to see a patient (let's call him Mr. Thanapolensis) whom he has never seen before and introduces himself as Marvin Milquetoast, the immunotherapist. "Your doctor," says Marvin, "has referred you here for our experimental treatment protocol. Now, we really don't have any idea whether this treatment is any good or not, but there isn't much else we can do for you, so we'd like to include you in this experiment. You may get the treatment or you may not, but if you'd like to join anyway and maybe get a chance at it, we'd be happy to have you. Before you sign, though, I have to tell you that you'll get sores on your arms and legs, you may get a fever or throw up, and you may get granulomatous hepatitis, or even anaphylaxis and die. But you'll probably be okay. Now you understand that, don't you? So Mr. Thanapolensis signs up, and away we go. But somehow, Dr. Milquetoast's patients don't do very well.

We've all seen in one way or another this phenomenon, which I have termed the Berkley-Smythe effect, the powerful influence of psychologic suggestion. We have recently learned that it is sometimes possible to convince a patient to lower his own blood pressure. Maybe it is even possible that psychologic forces might help a patient to subdue his own tumor. We also see the Berkley-Smythe effect acting on ourselves and other investigators, and I think we must be very careful that it does not influence our objectivity, particularly as we report our results in meetings like this one.

Both of these anecdotes are strongly reminiscent of a well-recognized phenomenon in clinical medicine variously referred to as "the placebo effect" or the power of faith. While widely acknowledged, the placebo effect is poorly understood, and only recently have we had some hint as to how such a mechanism may operate. The recent discovery of the endorphins, hormones secreted by the brain and capable of supplying the body's own morphine-like substance for pain relief, reinforces the view that the body has its own intrinsic mechanisms for the relief of pain. It has been proposed that release of beta-endorphin may account for the beneficial effects of acupuncture in relief of certain painful conditions and also explain the ability of certain individuals, such as yogi, to withstand the extreme pain of lying on a bed of nails. There are apparently numerous other allied humoral agents secreted by the brain which appear to have a role in determining emotional states or reactivity or in promoting homeostasis in other spheres of physiologic activity. It is therefore significant to note that what is known about the current physiology of endorphin secretion is that it is increased under stress and appears to be governed by the same influences that govern the secretion of ACTH and cortisone, the premier stress hormones.

In any event, it seems clear that the body possesses awesome capabilities to protect itself and to restore itself to a normal state when threatened by outside agencies. Many of the adaptive responses which occur no longer serve a useful purpose, and indeed may be harmful. While cancer may represent an example of the latter, it appears obvious that the body in its wisdom still retains the capacity to right this wrong. We are on the threshold of elucidating those factors. While harmful stress may have an important role in the pathogenesis of cancer, it appears equally plausible that eustress may have a significant opposing effect, as has been suggested in other diseases. Dr. Lawrence Burton, an immunologist working in the Bahamas, has apparently developed a unique immunologic test for the detection of cancer which is now undergoing intensive investigation in the United States. In a private communication to me he noted, "Death in family, family sickness, financial problems, etc. have produced depressed immune mechanisms as expressed 24–48 hours later in blood results as well as in later tumor exacerbations." Of even greater interest is his notation of substantial alterations in the immune mechanism of such patients *before* any participation in his immuno-augmentative therapy program, simply as a result of their hope and enthusiasm on being informed that they will be *accepted* for treatment.

Thus the future of cancer research may well lie in a greater understanding of the nature of stress for man, how these effects are mediated through hormonal or immunologic pathways and how the natural wisdom of the body can be enhanced to promote a healing or reparative effect. Clearer understanding of how placebos, positive emotions such as faith, love, and happiness exert their beneficial effects should be a top priority item of research. Behavioral modification, biofeedback, and other truly holistic measures may ultimately provide more gratifying and sustained results than the current *armanentarium* of chemical and physical poisons which direct their actions at the results rather than the causes of cancer.

References

DUNBAR, F., and ROSCH, P. J. Illness syndromes: High disability. In *Psychiatry in the Medical Specialities*. New York: McGraw-Hill, 1959, pp. 155–317.

Fox, B. H. Premorbid psychological factors as related to cancer incidence. *J. Behav. Med.* 1:45–133, 1978.

HOLMES, T. H., and RAHE, R. H. The social readjustment rating scale. *J. Psychosom. Med.* 11:213–218, 1767

LESHAN, L. *You Can Fight for Your Life.* New York: M. Evans, 1977.

MASON, J. W. Psychologic stress and endocrine function. In Sachar, F. J. (ed.), *Topics in Psychoendocrinology.* New York: Grune & Stratton, 1965.

ROSCH, P. J. Stress and cancer: Disease of adaptation? In Tache, J., Selye, H., and Day, S. B. (eds.), *Cancer, Stress and Death.* New York: Plenum, 1979, pp. 187–212.

———. Mind and cancer. *Lancet,* 1:1302, 1979.

———. Should the patient know? *JAMA,* 242:615, 1979.

———. Stress: Its relationship with illness. In *Traumatic Medicine and Surgery for the Attorney.* London: Butterworths, 1960, pp. 261–364.

———. Growth and development of the stress concept and its significance in clinical medicine. In *Modern Trends in Endocrinology.* New York: Paul B. Hoeber; London: Butterworths, 1958, pp. 278–297.

SELYE, H. *Stress without Distress.* Philadelphia: J. B. Lippincott, 1974.

———. *The Stress of Life.* New York: McGraw-Hill, 1956.

———. *Stress.* Montreal: Acta, 1950.

SELYE, H., and ROSCH, P. J. The renaissance in endocrinology. In *Medicine and Science.* New York: International University Press, 1954, pp. 30–49.

———. Integration of endocrinology. In *Glandular Physiology and Therapy.* Philadelphia: J. B. Lippincott Co., 1954, pp. 1–100.

SIMONTON, B. C., SIMONTON, S. M., and CREIGHTON, J. *Getting Well Again.* Los Angeles: J. P. Tacher, 1978.

STEFANSSON, V. *Cancer: A Disease of Civilization?* New York: Hill and Wang, 1960.

THOMAS, C. B., and GREENSTREET, R. L. Psychological characteristics in youth as predictors of five disease states: Suicide, mental illness, hypertension, coronary heart disease, and tumor. *Johns Hopkins Med. J.,* 132:16–43, 1973.

4 A Psychological Model in the Treatment of Cancer Patients

Herbert Allen Bilick and
William Nuland

This chapter will describe a psychological approach in the treatment of the emotional aspects of cancer. In recent years the fight against cancer has expanded beyond traditional medical treatment. The enormous expenditures of resources in developing more powerful and sophisticated chemotherapy, radiotherapy, and surgical procedures have yielded relatively disappointing results. Cures for a majority of cancer patients continue to elude medical investigation. The incidence of cancer is on the increase. Toxic side effects from medical treatments produce additional suffering for the patients and their families. As a result there has been a growing public dissatisfaction with orthodox medical treatment. New areas of investigation which have stimulated interest and which offer exciting new possibilities include nutrition, elimination of environmental carcinogens, immunotherapy, and psychological components of malignancy. In these new developments cancer as a disease entity is conceptualized in a more holistic framework. Malignancy is not only a disease of the body, but also encompasses the total person as well as the person's environment. It is this growing awareness of the complex nature of cancer that has led to the development of new approaches which, when used in conjunction with medical intervention, promise a more comprehensive and more effective treatment model.

This chapter will describe one of these new approaches—a psychological treatment model which is used as an important adjunct therapy with medical treatment. This approach was first developed and articulated by Dr. Carl Simonton and Stephanie Matthews Simonton.[1] Patient attitudes and beliefs, stress and its relationship to the immune system, early childhood experiences, visual imagery as a bio-feedback system, secondary gains of illness, family support systems, life goals, and possibility of recurrence and death are important components of this treatment model. The addition of clinical hypnosis as a therapeutic tool has greatly enhanced the effectiveness of the psychotherapeutic interventions in this approach.

Before describing these treatment components, it is important to state the underlying assumptions and working hypotheses of this model.

Underlying Assumptions and Working Hypotheses

There has been a great deal of research done on the emotional aspects of cancer, which will be briefly cited in this paper. For a more thorough review of this area, the interested reader should consult LeShan,[2] Bahnson,[3] and Achterberg and Simonton.[4] One of the most critical assumptions in this approach is the underlying unity between mind and body. If a person is suffering from physical disease, particularly a life-threatening disease, he is also suffering from serious emotional problems. Because the dichotomy of mind and body is eliminated in this model, psychological and physiological stresses are continually influencing one another. Holmes' work has demonstrated that the higher the emotional stress, the greater the risk of physical breakdown resulting in many kinds of diseases, including cancer.[5] The development of a life-threatening illness such as cancer reflects serious unresolved emotional conflicts which can adversely affect the course of the disease (Klopfer[6]).

In this approach, the cancer cell is conceptualized as a weak, poorly formed cell that develops because the immune system is suppressed and does not carry out its normal protective functions. According to the surveillance theory of cancer,[7] malignant cells are routinely manufactured by the body throughout a person's life. Normally, the white blood cells of the immune system destroy these cancer cells as they would any alien invader. When cancer develops it is not as a result of the cancer cell's inherent power, but because of a breakdown in the immune system. This hypothesis sharply contrasts with the more common belief which pictures cancer as an overwhelmingly destructive force that cannot be defeated. Even with the best medical technology, the body has little chance of destroying this devouring disease. In the present model, it is the cancer which is assumed to be weak, while the deficit lies in the factors that are interfering with the immune system's normal functioning.

Related to this model is the hypothesis that the immune system is suppressed by emotional and psychological stress (Bathrop et al., 1977[8]). The psychological stresses, which can emanate from many sources (e.g., intrapsychic and family conflicts, work problems, and personal loss) are usually untreated in the cancer patient. Limiting the treatment to medical remedies only is analogous to trying to save a sinking ship using modern, sophisticated pumps to bale out the water while doing nothing about the holes in the bottom of the ship. Without alleviation of his or her psychological stresses, the patient must rely solely on medical treatment, which not only overlooks the importance of psychological stresses on the disease process but often further suppresses the immune system, thereby increasing the probability of additional medical complications.[9]

Another important working hypothesis is that immune system functioning can be influenced by specific psychological techniques. Recent developments in the field of bio-feedback[10] has demonstrated that autonomic functioning, which previously had been assumed to be involuntary, can be brought under conscious control. Autogenic training, relaxation techniques, bio-feedback machines, and hypnosis have proven to be invaluable tools in the treatment of a variety of pathological conditions, such as pain, headaches, gastrointestinal disorders, impotence, and heart problems, among others. In this model, clinical hypnosis is utilized to control pain, to stimulate immune system functioning, to control side effects of medical treatment, to deepen relaxation and visual imagery, and to facilitate personal awareness and growth. A more detailed description will follow later in this chapter.

Finally, it is assumed that patients who take responsibility for participating in their own recovery, by actively involving themselves in their fight against cancer, do better than those patients who experience themselves as helpless victims of their overwhelming disease. This assumption often generates intense controversy because responsibility is equated with blame. Those who do not understand the concept of responsibility feel that the cancer "victim" is burdened enough by the disease. Subjecting them to take responsibility for their illness and recovery is perceived as blaming, cruel, guilt-producing, and punishing for the patient and the family. It is unfortunate that this misconception arises, because it deprives the patient and his or her family of important psychological resources which are based on the assumption of responsibility. This concept has nothing to do with blame. Rather, patients have the option of taking the responsibility to examine and explore the meaning of their illness and the psychological stresses which may be contributing to their cancer. These factors are often outside of the patient's awareness. Without taking the responsibility to look at the emotional problems which are interfering with their recovery process, patients lose the opportunity to initiate health producing changes in their lives. It is emphasized that the exploration of this largely unconscious realm is done without judgment or blame. Of course, many patients and their families respond in a blaming way. When this occurs, it is dealt with as a therapeutic issue, as it usually serves as a resistance to personal or family change.

These assumptions and hypotheses have been operationalized into a powerful clinical approach which will be described below.

Intensive Residential Groups

The cancer patient and a support person, usually a family member, are asked to participate in an intensive five-day residential group with other cancer patients and support people. Because of the life-threatening nature of cancer, the patients and their families experience the burdens, the devastation, and the anguish of this disease in relative isolation. The fear of cancer is prevalent not only among the general population but also among professionals who treat cancer patients. It has, for example, been observed that when a patient is diagnosed as having terminal cancer, the amount of attention and contact with the doctors and nursing staff in hospitals is reduced significantly. An intensive group setting with cancer patients and their family members who are struggling with similar economic, social, psychological, and medical realities alleviates this deep sense of alienation, isolation, and desperation. In addition, since time is a luxury for cancer patients, an intensive group experience facilitiates the examination of personal conflicts, the process of personal and family change, and the acquisition of important self-help tools in a relatively short amount of time. In these groups, psychological and family resources are mobilized in the fight against cancer.

Positive Belief System and Expectations

Cancer patients' underlying beliefs and expectations about their illness and their chances for recovery are often characterized by defeat, despair, hopelessness, and fear. Even when the patient is more optimistic, he is given little to do except to rely on his medical treatment. In this approach, through the use of visual imagery, the patient has the opportunity to examiné his underlying beliefs and attitudes, to develop a positive belief system about his body's immune system and medical treatment, and to learn a self-help tool which fosters the patient's confidence and self-reliance. The patient is taught an active meditative process with a casette tape and individualized instruction. After relaxing himself, the patient develops a weak and confused image representing his cancer. In contrast, the patient visualizes his white blood cells, the body's immune system, and his current medical treatment, either chemotherapy or radiotherapy, using strong and powerful images. The patient then sees in his mind's eye his white blood cells and medical treatment aggressively and totally destroying the cancer while leaving the healthy tissue relatively unharmed. The dead cancer cells are then flushed out of the body and the patient visualizes himself completely healthy. Physiological accuracy is not necessary in this visual imagery process. Rather, the focus is placed on symbolic images which represent positive beliefs in the potency of the patient's immune system, in the medical treatment, and in the goal of recovery. For example, the cancer may be visualized as dough or a spongy material while the white blood cells may be seen as white knights or sharks and the medical treatment as a powerful poison directed at the cancer. The patient uses this meditation three times per day.

In the groups, each patient draws and discusses his visual imagery, which is then reviewed by the staff. By examining what the patient actually sees, his unconscious attitudes toward the cancer are uncovered. Very often the patients believe that the cancer is indeed a very powerful and destructive force, which is reflected in their visual imagery. The image for the cancer may appear to be weak, but is visualized with very strong attributes. For example, one patient drew a very dense, large spongy mass as the cancer, while the white blood cells were comparatively small piranha fish which could only nibble at the outside of the tumor mass. If the piranha penetrated the spongy mass too deeply they risked suffocation. When these negative beliefs come to the surface, corrective feedback is given to the patient, who then incorporates these suggestions into his imagery to promote more positive expectations.

This visual imagery process can be an effective stress management and powerful bio-feedback technique. It is presented as an important self-help tool and not as an automatic and guaranteed cure. In times of discouragement and high stress, the use of this process is particularly effective in mobilizing inner psychological resources by giving the patient a channel in which to vent his feelings.

Finally, we have found that the toxic, debilitating side effects of the chemotherapy, radiotherapy, and even surgery can be alleviated and frequently eliminated through the use of hypnotic suggestion and visual imagery. Patients who experience these toxic side effects usually have negative expectations about their medical treatment. The treatment is seen as "a necessary evil," "a dangerous poison," or "an enemy" which is encountered with trepidation and fear. Patients are encouraged to develop more positive attitudes by visualizing their medical treatment as a friend and an ally which acts as an adversary only to the cancer while doing negligible damage to their healthy tissue and their immune system. Expecting the most positive effects very often results in reduced or minimal side effects.

Stress, Response to Stress, and Secondary Gains

Cancer patients are introduced to the mind-body unity concepts by identifying the current stresses in their lives and the psychological conflicts prior to their diagnosis which may be related to the onset and course of their disease. The patients examine their response to these stresses and begin to examine their response patterns to stress. Through the use of guided fantasies and hypnotic regression, they are able to deepen their awareness of these unconscious conflicts and defense patterns stemming from their childhood which are mirrored in their present lives. By examining their emotional conflicts and maladaptive defense patterns, the patients are able to begin the important process of internal and behavioral change.

During this period of self-exploration, patients are asked to confront the secondary gains they derive from their illness. This challenges them to look at their disease from a different perspective, namely the unconscious benefits from disease. Usually there are two major kinds of gains.

In one situation, the patient finds himself in a very stressful position with unreasonable demands from which there is no perceived escape except illness. The cancer allows these patients to leave untenable life situations from which, because of their rigid psychological structure, there is no other escape. These conflicts can occur, for example, at work or in the family. In the second situation, the patient receives some significant interpersonal gratification, such as love, attention, or nurturance, as a result of the illness which he was not able to request prior to his disease. In both of these situations, it is emphasized to the patient by the therapist that the secondary gains are legitimate and positive. It is his means of obtaining these gains, however, which needs change. In the course of the five-day group, some very serious problems and conflicts arise which require follow-up treatment. The purpose of this aspect of the group is to challenge the patient to become aware of his inner emotional conflicts and to begin the process of internal change.

Life Goals

Cancer patients are so frequently confronted in the course of their disease with the expectations of physical deterioration and death that they give little thought or emotional energy to their life goals, i.e. purposeful, meaningful, fulfilling activities. Their energies and those of their families are engaged in coping with the hardships of malignancy and in surviving day-to-day. As a result, the quality of their lives is severely diminished. Satisfying, goal-oriented behavior is buried under the strain and quiet desperation of the disease. In the group, patients develop a set of meaningful, satisfying, and realistic goals which are life sustaining and enhance the quality of their lives. This is often difficult for patients to do because they have long been preparing for the worst instead of living as fully as they can in the present. The patients are urged to implement these goals immediately. They are cautioned, however, to develop these goals as part of their internal changes rather than as window dressing to prove to their families that they are really trying. Patients will sometimes develop a set of goals which has little personal meaning to them. Optimally, goals should reflect an earnest desire to change on the part of the patient.

Family Support Systems

Cancer puts an enormous stress on any family system. There is a great need in the families of cancer patients for ventilation of unexpressed feelings, mutual support, and validation. In the group, families are given the opportunity to express their pent-up feelings, such as frustrations, fears, pain, anger, and hopelessness. This not only relieves some of the family tensions but tends to foster mutual support within and among the different cancer families as well. The patients and their families are asked to begin to identify and change their maladaptive roles and family conflicts which interfere with mutuality and family support. For example, the patient is frequently relegated to the role of victim. This fosters unhealthy dependency and blocks open communication among the family members. The families are also helped in identifying the long-standing unresolved emotional conflicts which have gone "underground" when the cancer was initially diagnosed. Unexpressed feelings, maladaptive roles, blocks in communication, pathological family responses to stress, and other unresolved problems are examined in the group with each family while the other families observe. The observers then offer constructive feedback to the family members. The feedback and the close identification with different family roles and conflicts promotes trust and openness which facilitates the process of family change. Family therapy may be recommended for follow-up treatment.

Possibility of Recurrence and Death

In line with the underlying philosophy of this treatment approach, recurrence and death are viewed within the context of the events and conflicts which are occuring in the patient's life rather than as mysterious, unpredictable, inevitable outcomes of this disease. Patients and family members experience a guided fantasy which is designed to elicit the unspoken feelings—the anguish, the fears, the dread—about the possibility of recurrence and death. Although there are no easy answers to cope with these issues, the group members experience relief in airing their feelings and are able to face these possibilities with renewed courage and determination. Patients are encouraged to give themselves enough time to explore the psychological and emotional factors which may be related to their physical deterioration. For example, a patient may be avoiding a particularly painful conflict in his marriage which may have an adverse effect on his physical condition. In the event of a recurrence, patients are encouraged to give themselves enough time (at least two weeks) to grapple with the meaning of the recurrence and to make a conscious choice whether they want to continue to fight or whether they feel it is time to die. A patient may feel that his physical deterioration and emotional anguish are too great an obstacle to overcome and that it would be better to say his last goodbyes to his family and friends. For patients who decide to give up in this way, their death, although painful for the family, leaves fewer psychological scars and unresolved issues because all concerned are given the opportunity to express their deepest feelings to one another during this final separation. It is important to remember that the majority of patients continue to fight at these crossroads but that they now fight as a result of choice rather than out of guilt, family obligation, or unexpressed fears.

The Use of Hypnotherapy

Hypnotherapy as a clinical tool has proven to be invaluable with cancer patients, both in groups and in individual sessions.

Patients who wish to attend an intensive five-day, residential program in group therapy, are carefully screened to ensure that they continue with their medical treatment and are not seeking only an emotional approach. At least two weeks elapse before the patient is seen in the group. This not only gives the patient time to decide whether he is willing to proceed with the approach, but also gives him the opportunity to use the basic visualization tape. This tape has been recorded by Dr. Carl Simonton for the purpose of teaching the patient relaxation and the ability to visualize his cancer, his medical treatment, and his body's immune system.

A limitation of the Simonton tape is that it uses only one standard induction technique, and some patients have found difficulty relating this tape to their individual needs. Therefore, it is important for each patient to be seen in individual therapy sessions prior to his attending the intensive five-day group session. In the individual sessions, the patient's responses to the Simonton tape are evaluated and an individual tape is made for him using an induction procedure and deepening technique most suited to his needs. Most of the difficulties in inducing hypnosis arise from the patient's unconscious defenses against hypnosis. A particular defense may be completely refractory to one method of induction, but may be easily circumvented by another method.

Individual Sessions (Prior to Entering Group Therapy)

In the individual sessions, any one of the numerous hypnotic induction techniques can be used, such as eye fixation, progressive relaxation, or arm levitation, that will best enable the patient to achieve a profound alteration of his state of consciousness. This state helps the patient to achieve a more intense and sustained focusing of attention and concentration, which will greatly assist him in intensifying his image in the visualization process. The deeper the relaxation and the more vivid the imagery, the more effective the meditative process becomes for the patient. After reaching a relaxed state, a patient may have difficulty in moving into the mental imagery process. This may involve difficulty in picturing the image of the cancer, or in visualizing the body's immune system mobilizing against the abnormal cancer cell. Because of the individual problems and differences that may exist, these sessions are designed to help each patient develop the most effective mental imagery process (in both the waking and the trance states) that will enable him to alter the course of the malignancy. This imagery is incorporated into an individual tape.

A variety of hypnotherapeutic techniques are employed by the clinician to best fit the particular needs and personality of the patient (Kroger and Fezler).[11] Thse methods include the following:

1. *Ego Strengthening Techniques.* These are positive suggestions which support the patient's ability to cope and master difficulties he may be encountering in his life. In the individual tape, the sequence of simple psychotherapeutic suggestions is designed to remove tension, anxiety, resentment, and resistance to change. These suggestions are quite often applied very effectively to somatic symptoms such as appetite loss, fatigue, insomnia, headaches, and nausea. Furthermore, these ego strengthening techniques are useful in enhancing the patient's self-image, confidence, and control over his feelings, needs, thoughts, and actions. One advantage of this technique is that a deep trance state is not essential.

2. *Hypnotic Suggestions Related to Pain.* Since many of the patients suffer from pain related either to their disease or to their medical treatment, suggestions are given on the individual tape which significantly or totally diminish the amount of pain the patient experiences. This is accomplished in several ways: direct suggestions of pain reduction, altering the experience of pain, or directing attention away from the pain and its source (Hilgard and Hilgard).[12]

3. *Autohypnosis.* The patient is taught by the hypnotherapist to put himself in a trance state. The suggestions which the patient will give himself while in a trance are reviewed with the clinician to insure that they are realistic as well as enhancing of the patient's belief in his body's ability to restore health. Autosuggestion techniques are also effective in helping the patient to cope with pain and other side effects of his medical treatment. Very often these distressing side effects are dramatically reduced or eliminated through the use of self-hypnosis.

An important advantage of the individual tape recordings is the ability to alter the tapes to meet the changing conditions of the cancer patient.

Group Sessions

Following the individual therapy sessions, the duration of which varies with each individual, the patient will enter the group process in a five-day retreat center, accompanied by his spouse or another significant person. Hypnosis in group therapy offers multiple and creative varieties of intervention to the center patient. It is seen as a productive innovation in the group interaction, with clearly beneficial effects on the life of the group. The group interactions, while in the state of altered consciousness, often bring forth altered levels of cognitive activity more spontaneously than in individual hypnotherapy. Group cohesion and the sense of belonging and attachment are enhanced, thereby reducing frustration, stress, and loneliness.

Some of the hypnotherapeutic techniques (Kruger and Fezler, 1976)[13] which are used in the group are as follows:

1. *Positive Revivification and Age Regression*. While in a hypnotic trance, patients are brought back to certain significant events in their childhood, both positive and traumatic—events which helped to shape their psychological defense structure and their ways of coping with stress. Utilizing progressive relaxation and a script or guided imagery in which all five senses are recalled from this earlier scene, the patients are helped to retrieve therapeutic material that has been repressed for many years. Regression, which is quite commonly a first step in therapeutic intervention, is facilitated by these techniques.

2. *Age Progression*. While in a trance state, the patients project themselves into their future. One benefit of this technique is that patients are helped to revise or choose meaningful goals (usually two to six months in the future). The steps taken to activate the goals, the means taken to achieve the goals, and the positive feelings associated with completing the goals are important elements used in this technique to reinforce the patients' reinvestment of their energies in meaningful activities. Age progression is also useful for future conflict resolution. Patients are asked, while under hypnosis, to develop in their imagery constructive ways of confronting particularly stressful situations which are occuring or will occur in their lives. Seeing themselves mastering a conflict in their lives often provides the impetus to relate to these conflicts in a more constructive, meaningful way.

Case Example

The patient (Ms. G.) is a 45 year-old white female, who was diagnosed as having inflammatory carcinoma of the breast with metastasis to the bone. Her cancer was inoperable and she was put on a regimen of chemotherapy. Ms. G. began psychological treatment when her cancer was first detected.

At the time of her diagnosis, Ms. G was in a state of psychological shock, feeling bewildered, scared, helpless, and angry. These are common initial reactions among cancer patients. She was immediately introduced to the tape recorded by Dr. Simonton and began meditating three times each day. This visual imagery process allowed Ms. G the opportunity to mobilize her psychological resources and channel her anger in a positive direction, toward health. In addition, the meditation served as a counter-balance to her helplessness and fear. Frequently, patients who are not given psychological treatment at the time of their diagnosis lapse into states of resignation, passivity, and a quiet despondency.

Ms. G. was a good hypnotic subject. She was taught self-hypnosis and was able to develop clear, strong imagery. Her cancer was pictured as a soft sponge-like substance which was actively and aggressively destroyed by her white blood cells (men with large paddles "beating the cancer to death"), and her chemotherapy, a strong poison. The cancer cells then disintegrated in a garbage disposal and were flushed out of her body through the kidneys.

In the group sessions and in follow-up individual psychotherapy, Ms. G. became aware of her early psychological conflicts which were replayed in her adult life. Growing up in a family of six children, Ms. G. experienced a lot of competition for both her mother's and her father's attention. Her early childhood was marked by strong feelings of isolation, fear, despair, and psychological neglect by both parents. Her father was "explosive, un-predictable and detached" from her. She was afraid of him and avoided him when possible, thus experiencing little contact or warmth from him. Her mother was an overburdened, depressed woman who was at times con-trolling and demanding and at other times unavailable to meet Ms. G.'s emotional needs. The patient thus experienced strong, unfulfilled de-pendency needs in relation to her mother as well as feelings of guilt and rage which were later repressed. Her conflicts around dependency and separation were somaticized as a child. Her frequent headaches and other childhood illnesses elicited her mother's attention and love. This reinforced Ms. G.'s reliance on physical illness as a way of expressing her psycho-logical conflicts. Ms. G., in the course of the group sessions, realized some of her secondary gains in her cancer, such as, "I'm getting love and atten-tion from my brothers, sisters, and children. I'm finally special to my fam-ily. I'm allowing myself to be dependent and helpless."

Ms. G.'s first marriage of twenty years (which ended in divorce five years prior to the onset of her cancer) and her subsequent relationships with men, reflected her earlier conflicts. These relationships were unhappy and unfulfilling, in which Ms. G. "could never get the understanding and approval" she desperately sought. She was experiencing intense feelings of despair, rejection, and hopelessness in one relationship approximately one-and-a-half years prior to her diagnosis. In addition, she was changing her career goals at that time and felt very frightened and helpless with these changes.

Ms. G. has been working hard in her psychotherapy to understand herself and to change her characteristic responses to her life stresses. The use of hypnosis has been very valuable in her visual imagery, in deepening her level of awareness of her unconscious conflicts, and in bolstering her confidence and esteem in changing her life career goals. Five months after the medical and psychological treatment began, there was no sign of metastases to the bone and the size of the mass in her breast was significantly reduced.

Ms. G. is currently continuing with her medical and psychological treatment. In addition to her physical improvement, Ms. G.'s quality of life has been improved. She is changing her behavior in her new relationship with a man by being more assertive and expressing more of her emotional needs. She is also in the process of changing her relationships with her family members in more satisfying ways. Finally, Ms. G. is beginning to confront her career changes in ways which are less frightening and more positive and creative.

Conclusions

The major hypothesis put forth in this chapter is that the cancer patient's chances for survival and quality of life are improved when medical treatment is combined with psychological intervention. The particular model outlined here is a recent development which reflects years of research and psychological investigation into the etiology of cancer. The use of hypnotherapy with other psychotherapeutic techniques creates a powerful intervention model. Life style changes, personal growth, and psychological mobilization toward recovery are important tools for the cancer patient in this approach.

As is true of any new treatment model, definitive answers to such issues as treatment effectiveness and improvement in treatment intervention lie in the future with well-designed, controlled research. There are, however, some preliminary results reported by the Simontons which offer a promising beginning.[14] They report that of 159 Stage IV terminal patients who have been at their center, 63 are still alive (20 have been lost to follow-up). Of these 63 patients, 22 percent are cancer-free, 19 percent are in partial remission, 27 percent are stabilized, and 32 percent report new tumor growth. In addition, 76 percent of these patients are maintaining a 75 percent or better activity level in their daily lives. Dr. Larry LeShan, who has worked extensively with cancer patients using individual psychotherapy, reports that patients can improve both physically as well as in the quality of their lives if they receive psychological help.[15] He maintains the psychological changes in a positive, life-fulfilling direction are one of the best tools cancer patients have in their fight against malignancy.

Expanding the treatment model in a more holistic direction, employing stress management techniques as well as nutritional and dietary changes, offer the cancer patient hope and new possibilities of more effective treatment breakthroughs.

References

1. SIMONTON, O. C., MATTHEWS-SIMONTON, S., CREIGHTON, J. *Getting Well Again,* Los Angeles, California: J. P. Tancher, Inc., 1978.
2. LeSHAN, L. L. "An Emotional Life History Pattern Associated with Neoplastic Disease." *Annals of the New York Academy of Sciences* (1966) 125:780–793.
3. BAHNSON, C. B., BAHNSON, M. B., "Role of the Ego Defenses: Denial and Repression in the Etiology of Malignant Neoplasm." *Annals of the New York Academy of Sciences* (1966) 125:277–286.
4. ACHTENBERG, J.; SIMONTON, O. C.; MATTHEWS-SIMONTON, S. (eds.) *Stress, Psychological Factors, and Cancer.* Fort Worth, Texas: New Medicine Press, 1976.
5. HOLMES, T. H.; MASUDA, M. "Life Change and Illness Susceptibility, Separation and Depression." *American Association for the Advancement of Science* (1973) 161–168.
6. KLOPFER, B. "Psychological Variables in Human Cancer." *Journal of Projective Techniques* (1957) 21:331–340.
7. RILEY, V. "Mouse Mammary Tumors: Alteration of Incidence as Apparent Function of Stress." *Science* (1975) 189:465–467.
8. BATHROP, R. W.; LUCKHURST, E.; LAZARUS, L.; KILOH, L. G.; PENNY, R. "Depressed Lymphocyte Function after Bereavement." *The Lancet* (April 16, 1977) 834–836.
9. MILLER, N. "Learning of Visceral and Glandular Responses." *Science* (1969) 163:434–446.
10. FULLER, G. D. "Current Status of Bio-Feedback in Clinical Practice." *American Psychologist* (January, 1978) 39–48.
11. KROGER, W. S.; FEZLER, W. D. *Hypnosis and Behavior Modification.* Philadelphia: J. B. Lippincott Co., 1976.
12. Hilgard, E. R.; Hilgard, J. R. "Hypnosis in the Relief of Pain." Los Altos, Califnornia: William Kaufmann, Inc., 1975.
13. Op. cit.
14. MATTHEWS-SIMONTON, S. Personal communication, 1978.
15. LeSHAN, L. *You Can Fight for Your Life,* New York: M. Evans and Company, Inc., 1977.

PART II
Treating Cancer as a Psychosomatic Disease

The treatment of cancer has traditionally been strictly based on physiologic correction. There now exists a substantial body of research and clinical literature which proposes the contribution of the psyche to the development of cancerous growth. Methodologies of investigation vary widely, and research ranges from tumor implants in laboratory rats to complex studies of human cancer populations. While the mediating mechanisms remain largely unknown, several have been proposed, with immunological factors and neurohormonal pathways receiving the largest attention.

Within this predominantly psychological approach to cancer, there are two principal hypotheses. Some have posited a "loss-depression" concept, which proposes that the loss of a valued object—a relationship or material asset—is often an antecedent to cancer. Others see that there is a particular personality pattern that can be identified. In general, these "personality profile" researchers postulate the cancer-prone person as having a greater tendency to repress emotions. Anger is the emotion that is most often cited as the one which cancer personalities do not like to feel or show. These two hypotheses—emotional loss and personality profile—interface in studies taking the position that there are childhood and developmental considerations, and that these, in part, affect or determine the coping mechanisms of the adult who is confronted with the emotional truma of loss. These studies showed cancer patients to perceive their parents as being less close and less accessible than did non-cancer patients.

Part II offers chapters which present cancer as a disease having psychosomatic components. Stephan Ohayon emphasizes the role of impulses and regressive fantasies in the development of tumors. Robert Dew presents a detailed understanding of Wilhelm Reich's views on character analysis, and how cancer develops in the human system. Stephen Appelbaum discusses his use of a visual meditation technique, and the resistances that patients exhibit to getting well.

5 The Psychopathology of Self-Mutilation in the Life of the Contemporary Patient

Stephen Ohayon

CREON. Thus saith Phoebus, our Lord and Seer, in clear command.
An unclean thing there is, his in our land, eating the soil thereof.

Sophocles, *Oedipus Tyrannus*

In Freud's "Inhibitions, Symptoms and Anxiety" we find this revealing passage:

> What we have learnt about anxiety in phobias is applicable to obsessional neuroses as well. In this respect it is not difficult for us to put obsessional neuroses on all fours with phobias. In the former, the mainspring of all later symptom-formation is clearly the ego's fear of its super-ego. The danger situation from which the ego must get away is the hostility of the super-ego. There is no trace of projection here; the danger is completely internalized. But if we ask ourselves what it is that the ego fears from the super-ego, we cannot but think that the punishment threatened by the latter must be an extension of the punishment of castration.[1]

To comprehend Freud, in our viewpoint, is to understand the meaning of the dread of and wish for castration in the individual and group, in the transience of one's life, and in the historical process.

Freud, in our perspective, is the psychologist of the Super-ego. As a Jew, a cultural anthropologist, and a psychoanalyst of man and civilization, Freud preoccupied himself with the phylogenetic ancestry of the Super-ego and the power it has accumulated through millenia of repression (*Totem and Taboo, Moses and Monotheism*). On an ontogenetic level, Freud investigated in the microscopic mental space of the individual the ancestral battle of the Ego against the outbreak and flowering of Super-ego impulses. In this inner conflict the body serves, in the case of conversion hysteria, as a battleground. Target organs suffer from the invasion and occupation of Id impulses on the one hand, and the vengeful forces of conscience on the other.

73

Our thesis in this chapter is that the dynamics of somatization are propelled by a retaliatory Super-ego. It is our attempt to illustrate the law of Talion (castration, Super-ego) which governs our inner psychic life. We believe that a great number of cases of organic lesions, benign or malignant cysts are precipitated by the punitive assault of an "archaic" Super-ego on a target organ of symbolic importance to the individual. By "archaic" Super-ego we understand an internalized conscience of great severity, strictly adherent to the vengeful law of retaliation. The organ is selected because of genetic cellular weakness which renders it prone to Super-ego cathexis. A particular organ could be selected as well for its special history in the life of a patient, its vulnerability or accessibility. Thus, in some cases of conversion hysteria, the guilty organ, or symbolic region of the culprit organ, is stricken with paralysis or decreasing functioning (Super-ego cathexis). Where Super-ego strikes there Id shall be, we might say. Thus, according to Ferenczi, "conversion hysteria genitalizes part of the body at which the symptom manifests."[2]

In this project, we are broadening the perspective of conversion hysteria to include any organic lesion, cellular growth, or functional deficiencies attributable to unconscious or semiconscious psychogenic factors. We wish to introduce the term Psychotic Conversion to label such phenomena. By "psychotic" we understand a rather extreme outbreak of unconscious material of a toxic nature, unfiltered and non-metabolized by the agency of the Ego. In fact, the cases of somatization we will present are psychotic episodes acted-in, so to speak, using the territoriality of the body as a stage for its manifestation. It is more than a symptom as in the case of hysteria conversion, but a radical pathological resistance which often leads to organ-severance (surgery) or death. This transmutation deflects the attention from the pusuit of self-exploration, if the patient is in psychoanalytic treatment, to the focussing on organicity. We believe this dynamic detour to be plotted and orchestrated by the Ego defenses of repression and avoidance.

It is a conversion because a metamorphosis has taken place of a regressive nature where the Ego has been refractory, forcing an impulse fallout on a specific or general anatomical region selected for persecution.

Psychotic Conversion illustrates, in our view, the core of the law of Talion, which is in itself the infrastructure of the Super-ego. The somatized dialectics of guilt and subsequent symbolic castration has found in the psychotic conversion its Judaeo-Christian resolution (Judaeo: the partial sacrificial mutilation of circumcision; Christian: the total sacrificial mutilation of Christ)—the payment for an ideational transgression by self-mutilation.

The responsibility of the Ego in the etiology of Psychotic Conversion cannot be denied. It is the defense of repression, coupled with avoidance and denial of guilt, which is mainly accountable for this turn of events. The Ego's refusal to make conscious the taboo wish and the subsequent guilt feelings will lead to the literal "execution of an organ."

Of all the physiological disturbances precipitated by the Super-ego, we will introduce the cases of three contemporary patients undergoing psychoanalysis (individual or group therapy or both): Celia (uteral cyst), Stephen (penal wart), Mr. G. (oral cyst and facial paralysis). In these three patients the theme of castration as penalty for oedipal wishes will be made clear. Individually these patients have incorporated a harsh Super-ego, rigid and exacting.

The Case of Celia

Celia is a forty-year-old woman who was a group patient for two years. During the process, she put an end to a twenty-year marriage to a depressed husband, Michael, and began experiencing a new feeling of emancipation. After the departure of her twenty-one-year-old son from home, an off-spring to whom she was symbiotically attached, she developed a relation-ship with a nurturing man, Bruce. During her treatment, Celia began ex-periencing sexual wishes toward the male therapist. These feelings would cause her an unusual amount of anxiety. The patient, it seems, was process-ing materials of an oedipal nature. She began producing reminiscences of her relationship with her father, in particular a memory of significant im-portance. After returning from her first date at the age of sixteen, her father administered to her bodily punishment. Analysis revealed that her father's reaction was interpreted by the young woman as an act of love.

The sexual transference with the therapist-father blossomed pro-gressively. Celia began to dress in vivid colors, surrendering her bland wardrobe for tasteful and feminine styles. In the twentieth month of treat-ment, Celia informed the group that her gynecologist had discovered a uteral fibroid tumor at an advanced stage. Celia compared it to a "three month fetus." Celia did not exhibit any sign of anxiety as she described her condition; on the contrary, she exhibited a calm in her voice and a serenity in her demeanor which perplexed the group. Analytic exploration revealed a substantial amount of fantasies of pregnancy. During the previous few months Celia had felt lonely and wished she could have a child. At the next session, Celia informed the group that her gynecologist suggested surgical intervention—a hysterectomy. The investigation of the psychological im-plications of mutilation of such symbolic organs revealed ideation center-ing on the themes of delivery (Id wish of giving birth) and castration (Super-ego wish). As for delivery, the metaphor of abortion or miscarriage was produced by the patient since the cellular tissues removed would be an allegorical "three month fetus." We are well aware of the symbolism of castration involved in cases of abortions and miscarriages. Celia's associations disclosed guilt due to the sexual enjoyment of her friend Bruce. After years of deprivation with Michael, Celia's sexual involvement with Bruce on the one hand, her father transference with her therapist on the other, surfaced strong infantile yearnings, and with them punitive forces. It seems to us that the tumor fulfilled simultaneously the cravings of an Id impetus and Super-ego needs. As her relationship with her therapist was becoming oedipalized, and her liaison with Bruce unhampered and pleasurable, infantile longings for pregnancy by her father were activated. The tumor was the fantasized fetus, the result of a fantasized incest.

Georg Groddeck, whose understanding of somatization was far-reaching, illustrates the somatic impact of the wish for pregnancy:

> Nearly twenty years ago a wen developed on my neck. At that time I did not know what I do now, or think I do. In any case, I went about the world for ten years with this thickened neck in the full belief that I must bear it to the grave with me. Then the day came that I learned to know the It and realized—no matter how—that this wen was a fantasied child. You yourself have often wondered how I managed to rid myself of the monstrous thing without operation, without treatment, without iodine or thyroid. My view is that the wen disappeared because my It learned to understand, and my conscious mind also, that I am just as other men in having a bisexual nature and life, and that it is unnecessary to emphasize this fact by means of a swelling.[3]

The neck, a tubular byway, a zone of passage for blood (arteries and veins), air (trachea) and food (esophagus), a glandular region (tonsils, thyroid, lymphatic glands), because it functions as a transit area, became a substitute for a uterus and a Fallopian tube. The culprit organ in Celia's case was the reproductive organ.

Celia described her gynecologist as "a rough man with the manners of a butcher." Group members were shocked to learn that Celia had kept him as her physician for more than fifteen years. This gynecologist was representative in this patient's unconscious of the executioner who will perform the hysterectomy-castration. The group therapist and the members advised her to seek another opinion before the drastic decision of surgery. Celia visited a second doctor who opposed any surgical intervention, qualifying the tumor as a benign growth. It has been observed, in my work with patients with a predilection for somatization of their inner conflicts, that their preference is marked for doctors who over-diagnose the illness, offering radical solutions (surgery, over-medicalization). Given a choice between a moderate medical opinion and a drastic one, they select the more extreme one. It seems to us that their choice is in the service of the Suepr-ego which is a collector of injustices.

Partial Mutilation as Sacrifice

C'est avec crauté que se coagulent les choses.*
Antonin Artaud,
Le Théâtre et Son Double⁴

The Case of Stephen

This case we are about to present is startling in its content and far-reaching in its implications. Stephen was a thirty-year-old college instructor of Romance languages. His father, a Sephardic Jew of North African background, made his living as a Rabbi, a *mohel* (circumciser) and a *chochet* (ritual slaughterer). Due to paucity of means, until the age of eighteen Stephen's sleeping quarters were relegated to the parents' bedroom. At the age of eighteen, Stephen immigrated to the United States with his family. The event which is of interest to us is the following. While in treatment with his first therapist, whom he described as "pontifical" (let us recall that his father was a Rabbi) Stephen complained of a wart which had located itself on his penis. Our patient was emotionally involved with a married woman, Amanda, a person he particularly enjoyed sexually. Stephen was advised by his therapist to have the wart removed surgically. A urologist he visited did not recommend any surgical interference. The patient insisted and the urologist, against his best judgment, acquiesced. The operation provided extreme levels of anxiety. A few months later, the patient terminated treatment with the therapist on the ground that he, the patient, was misunderstood. He joined group therapy with a male therapist who had been highly recommended. In need of individual analysis, the patient asked his group therapist, whom he admired greatly, to recommend an analyst. Stephen started individual couch analysis with a female therapist. Six months later the wart reappeared at the same location where the preceding one had been located. Alarmed, the patient began the exploration of such a repetition. Oedipal material surfaced. Stephen described the guilt experienced at the recollection of memories of an incestuous nature. Stephen had been prone as a child to inflammations of the tonsils (symptomatic and symbolic organs). Each crisis of tonsillitis gave him the privilege of sharing the parental bed with his mother. He recalled nocturnal erections with his mother at his side. The patient wondered if the wart was some form of punishment on the guilty organ. This urgency for a surgical operation on his penis, in spite of the physician's advice, made him

* Things coagulate with cruelty." Antonin Artaud in the chapter entitled "Le Théâtre et la Pesta" (Theatre and the Plague), after a study of outbreaks of the plague in history, endows the epidemic with metaphysical proportions. He speculates that the plague purged civilizations that were suffering from a sense of guilt. The disease broke the social structure and all impulses were loosened. When the plague arrived hysteria was unbridled.

think of the possibility of a wish to have his organ severed at the hands of his father, a ritual slaughterer and a circumciser by profession. Fragments seemed to fit in this psychic puzzle.

In a private interview, his group therapist recommended to him a urologist who used surgery only as a last resort. The new doctor treated him with an ointment. After the second visit, the wart wilted. The patient realized that he had found in his group therapist a benevolent father. A few months later, Stephen ended his liaison with the married woman.

Analysis revealed that Stephen's relationship with Amanda had awakened his incestuous feelings toward his mother. Castration wishes were activated. During his treatment this rather articulate and sophisticated patient displayed ample materials to substantiate his wishes for castration. He would awake in the middle of the night and imagine a man hiding in the dark an axe in hand ready to sever his head. Stephen identified with the poultry his father used to slaughter for Yom Kippur, the Jewish Day of Atonement. The psychic situation was exacerbated by the fact that his first name was originally Isaac and not Stephen. The patient recalled that his father would often narrate to him the Biblical story of Isaac led to the altar to be sacrificed by his pious father Abraham. This name Isaac was given to him by his father, a fact which evoked a sense of dread. His father as a ritual slaughterer, whom he interpreted as a sacrificer, and a circumciser, did not help the situation. To escape the destined slaughter that almost was, Isaac changed his first name to Stéphane, which he later anglicized to Stephen.

An analysis as to the causality of the change divulged remarkable associations. The name Stéphane was adopted from the poet Stéphane Mallarmé whose poem "Pour un Tombeau à Anatole" (For a Tomb to Anatole) had particular significance for our patient. In this piece the poet predicts the death of his seven-year-old son who was taken by an illness two years following the publication of the poem. For Isaac, our patient substituted Stéphane, the name of a father who foresaw the death of his son. Identification with the aggressor was the Ego defense, an attempt to correct fate and re-establish a sense of security.

Thus in this case it is in our understanding that the penal wart was the execution of a wish to amputate the organ which experienced in a literal way erotic gratification with an incestuous partner.

In our research we have found substantial data to corroborate our theory concerning the wish for organ mutilation and the realization of that wish. The next case to be presented is extracted from the literature.

The Case of Mr. G.

In a paper entitled, "An Occult Conversion Reaction Superimposed on a Facial Nerve Lesion," Dr. Ira S. Halper describes the presenting problem of a twenty-eight year old writer and director, Mr. G.:

His acting career was [aborted] by parotid surgery at the age of nineteen. He expected merely the removal of a cyst, and was shocked when he awoke to find one side of his face paralyzed. During the year following the operation, Mr. G. has some spontaneous return of function which then stabilized. He accepted his paralysis without question. He did not perform the exercises recommended by his doctor, and he never investigated the possibility of corrective surgery.[5]

The patient's resistance to the amelioration of his facial condition seems to indicate some unconscious gains in the service of the Super-ego. After a few months of psychoanalytic teatment the patient began connecting with oedipal material. Dr. Halper summarizes the psychic events of this period:

After six months of treatment Mr. G. began to deal directly with Oedipal material, connecting his isolation from his wife with his fear of adult sexual relationships and relating his sexual fears to his relationship with his mother. The following is a fragment of a dream reported during this period: Mr. G. was walking with a girl, and they met an older woman he knew at the radio station. Her nickname was Mom. The girl disappeared: Mom invited him to her apartment for coffee. His wife was there, and they left behind Mom's back.[6]

"Mom invited him to her apartment for coffee" suggests an incestuous seduction. The oedipal temptation is presented as an oral metaphor. The paralyzed oral area clearly indicates the cathected situation of that particular territory. "Common hysterics use their pregenital zones in a genital way" Fenichel observed.[7] We find a direct application of this premise in this case. We are prepared to speculate that the oral region which had been genitalized by the patient had met its punishment twice: first in the tumor which necessitated the unpleasant act of surgery and, second, in the paralysis which followed. Dr. Halper disregards the psychogenic possibilities of the tumor and concentrates on the paralysis which followed the removal of the cyst.

Involuntary movements appeared at the paralyzed corner of his mouth, Dr. Halper noticed. The situation improved with an increase of voluntary control of the paretic side of his face. Dr. Halper writes:

He recalled that the operation put an end to his aspiration to be a leading man on the stage. He associated acting with sex and remembered risqué jokes he used to tell as a master of ceremonies in high school. He wondered if his paralysis represented punishment for something he felt guilty about; he recalled his father's opposition to his acting.[8]

Later in his paper Dr. Halper recapitulates his patient's dynamic process:

In short, Mr. G. superimposed a conversion reaction on surgical trauma on the facial nerve. He unconsciously interpreted the operation as punishment for incestuous wishes toward his mother. . . . By means of the paralysis, Mr. G. protected himself against the dangerous consequences of his Oedipal desires.[9]

We are in agreement with the first premise of this paragraph; as to the second we find it to be inadequate. In our view, Mr. G.'s tumor and its surgical removal, as well as his refusal to exercise his paralyzed side, are part of the chastisement. In our hypothesis, the removed cyst is the castrated testicle. We are prepared to speculate as well that the paralysis which followed is in fact an erection of the paretic side mimicking the phallic "hard on." This is in line with our theory of the juxtaposition of Id impulses with Super-ego counter-measures active in a definite symbolic zone.

The patient's history being available to us, some data of great richness concerning certain events in the patient's biography sophisticate our case and broaden our primary thesis. We are informed by Dr. Halper, that when Mr. G. was twenty-one, while working in a summer stock company which included a group of homosexuals, he had a religious conversion and became a devout Christian. At this point Mr. G. surrendered the stage and turned to writing.

We interpret Mr. G.'s conversion as an escape from his reawakened homosexual feelings and his shelter with the sublimated unearthly male divinity. Spiritual intercourse was more acceptable to his Ego than the homosexual one. His turning to writing, a more personal and quasi-isolated activity distant from the exhibitionistic stage, is another attempt to escape his stimulated homosexual impulses. In the light of these interpretations we propose the following—that the surgical removal of the cyst was perceived by the unconscious as a symbolical intercourse and delivery in the hands of male surgeons: i.e., intercourse, in the penetration of needles and scalpels in the oral cavity, a genitalized zone as we have demonstrated; a delivery, in the symbolism of the cyst growing in the oral-anal uteral cavity as the fantasized fetus.

There are similarities with the cases of Celia and Mr. G. in the pregnancy fantasies figuratively realized. Symbolization is the defense of the Ego refractory to the idea of acting out fully the impulses of Id and Super-ego. Acting-in remains in these patients the last resort in their resolution of their inner crisis.

Freud considered homosexuality to be a defense against the dread of the incestuous situation and George Devereux considered homosexuality to be the product of oedipal repression.[10] These two views are certainly compatible with our understanding of Mr. G.'s actions. Our theory of fantasized pregnancy in the case of Mr. G. is supported by interest in the stage. The word "delivery" is spoken of an actor's verbal production on stage. We remember that he used his oral zone as genitals which dared "risqué jokes." We find of great interest Dr. Halper's sentence: "His acting career was aborted by parotid surgery at the age of nineteen." The participle "aborted" selected to describe the situation shows that Dr. Halper was subliminally aware of the unconscious meaning of the development of the oral cyst as fantasized fetus, although he does not explore this thesis. Acting, which was the main interest of Mr. G., who had performed on stage in high school, is equated in this instance with sexual intercourse. This equation explains the patient's cyst and paralysis as obstacles which in Dr. Halper's words "put an end to his aspirations to be a leading man on the stage." His father, another "leading man," was, as he recalled, opposed to his acting.

To recapitulate this interesting case, Dr. Halper treated the paralysis successfully using the oedipal model. The patient was able to verbalize (oral "act") his wishes. His psychotherapist supported and encouraged his "verbal acting" in the analytic relationship.

We have been intrigued by the title of Dr. Halper's paper. The introductory word "Occult" finds no elucidation in the course of the monograph. If by "occult" we mean the etymological Latin word *occultus* from *occulere* (to conceal, not to reveal), we could safely state that this particular conversion hides indeed in it the fruit of a metaphorical intercourse. If by "occult" we understand "related to supernatural agencies and their effects"—as the dictionary seems to indicate—we could hardly underestimate the unconscious forces at play and their manifestations on the facial region of this patient, the victim and subject of these repressed wishes activated and propelled with an inner vengeance that defies the limited concept of homeostasis as it is narrowly defined by science.

In this paper we have attempted to illustrate what we might define as a psychotization process which depicts the individual as a pulsating and expanding organism. The purpose of somatization in these patients is a complex enterprise to turn structure into process, stasis into ex-stasis, to convert the inner sclerosis into a flux. This psychic undertaking, unacknowledged by a vigilant Ego, is forced to overflow into the body which is the concrete manifestation of the self, the self made visible. The Ego's blocking actions, its opaque resistance, its obduracy to recognize inner ambivalent and contradictory impulses precipitated somatization was not a tragedy but a strategy. In other instances it is fatal. The reason these three patients survived this psychosomatic challenge is to be attributed to the strength and exuberance of their life impulses threatened and defied by their death wishes. The reproductive wishes were the strongest in front of a harsh Super-ego.

The psychotherapists who treated these patients appeared to us as consciousness-brokers who intuitively focussed on the oedipal drama which was unfolding in the backstages of consciousness. Following oedipal lines they surfaced the incestuous plot which bound psyche and soma in sacrificial throes. These patients, victims of their own destined fate, scripted for mutilation, encountered in their analysts benevolent healers who were tuned to the patient's inner executioners. The sentence was appealed and emotional bail (anguish, partial amputation) was paid to the exacting conscience.

Notes

1. Freud, Sigmund. "Inhibitions, Symptoms and Anxiety." Standard Edition, Vol. 20. London: Hogarth Press, 1968, p. 128.

2. Ferenczi, S. *Further Contributions to the Theory and Technique of Psychoanalysis.* (1926) N. Y.: Basic Books, 1953.

3. Groddeck, Georg. *The Book of the It.* N. Y.: Mentor Books, 1961, p. 22.

4. Artaud, Antonin. *Le Théâtre et Son Double.* Paris: Gallimard, 1964, p. 157.

5. Halper, S., M.D. "An Occult Conversion Reaction Superimposed on a Facial Nerve Lesion." *Psychosomatics,* Vol. VII, Sept-Oct., 1966 (5), p. 311.

6. Ibid., p. 312.

7. Fenichel, Otto. *The Psychoanalytic Theory of Neurosis.* N. Y.: Norton, 1945.

8. Halper, op. cit., p. 312.

9. Ibid., p. 313.

10. Devereux, George. "Ethno-Psychoanalytic Consideration on the Notion of Parenthood." *L'Homme,* July, 1965.

6 Wilhelm Reich's Cancer Biopathy

Robert A. Dew

Introduction: An Overview of Reich's Work

Although Reich began with an extensive classical training in natural science, medicine, and psychiatry, his research was to carry him into hitherto unknown territory. As a pioneer, he had to fashion his own guiding theoretical concepts and terminology. For us to understand and evaluate what he says about cancer, it is essential that we see it clearly within the context of his life's work. Indeed, Reich's remarkable conclusion that the cancer disease is linked causally to a disturbance of sexual functioning came after almost twenty years of work in the biological investigation of sexuality. To the reader unacquainted with new and revolutionary concepts, such a conclusion would seem incomprehensible and preposterous. It is therefore imperative that we orient ourselves as to the substance and direction of Reich's thinking leading up to his involvement in the cancer problem. We shall restrict ourselves, however, to work which directly impinges on this problem. Our review is in no way comprehensive.

Wilhelm Reich was born in 1897. His early years were spent on his parents' farm in the easternmost part of the Austrian empire. Encouraged by a private tutor, he soon became interested in and familiar with the natural history of plants and animals. He began the study of medicine in Vienna in 1918 and was soon drawn to Sigmund Freud because of his interest in sexology. Reich proved so brilliant in his grasp of psychoanalysis that by 1920, two years before his graduation in medicine, he had become a practicing analyst and member of the Vienna Psychoanalytic Society. He presented numerous papers which were regarded as major contributions to psychoanalytic theory. In 1922 Freud selected him as first assistant physician at the Psychoanalytic-Polyclinic and then in 1924 appointed him to the teaching staff of the Psychoanalytic Institute.

Reich soon established himself as an innovator in psychoanalysis. He concerned himself in the teaching seminars with the causes of psychoanalytic failures, and began to see that the major obstacles to getting well were the patients' latest resistances. He shifted his emphasis from simply interpreting material as it came up in the sessions to noticing *how* the patient presented the material. He pointed out to the patient *the way he behaved* and exposed the attitudes themselves as a manifestation of the underlying resistance. This technique evoked considerable affect and with consistent use broke down the resistances. Not only did it bring out the painful and theretofore repressed feelings and memories, but it also affected changes in the patients' character and way of living. Moreover, this approach was to prove of immense value as a research tool in the subsequent exploration of the neuroses. Reich called it *character analysis* and dealt comprehensively with its theory and application in his book, *Character Analysis,* which was first published in 1933 after over a decade of clinical experiences.

His review of cases also impressed upon Reich that the difference between success and failure in treatment lay not in the duration of the analysis but in the ability of the patient to establish a satisfactory sex life. This was entirely consistent with Freud's original postulation that if somatic sexual excitation or libido is blocked from perception and discharge it is converted to anxiety, which in turn gives rise to the neurosis. This brought into focus the idea that sexual disturbances were not only *symptoms* but were in fact the underlying *cause* of the neurosis itself. Reich was the first to formulate this theory of a sex-economic basis for the neurosis and presented it in 1923 in his paper, *Genitality from the Standpoint of Psychoanalytic Prognosis and Therapy.* He qualified this concept in 1924. At the Psychoanalytic Congress in Salzburg he proposed the idea that sexual stasis or blockage is not merely a matter of a lack of sexual *activity* as had been previously thought but rather a *specific* disturbance in the discharge of sexual excitation which affects the capacity for gratification. It was revealed that the major source of health was the capacity to surrender *completely* to the total convulsion of the body and momentary loss of consciousness that characterizes the full orgasm. This capacity permits the total discharge of sexual excitation and results in the experience of gratification. Reich called it *orgastic potency.*

The orgasm theory was of critical importance not only because it supported Freud's earlier idea, but, more significantly, it implied that the libido was something *real.* Further, the gratifying orgasm had to be more than nature's inducement to procreation but served as a vital mechanism for the discharge of libido energy. The one function of the orgasm is therefore as a regulator of the energy household of the body. The neurosis on the other hand then had to be a manifestation of chronically *undischarged* libido energy which was retained due to orgastic *impotence.* Reich reasoned that if dammed up libido was converted to anxiety as Freud said, it was then crucial to the therapeutic process to understand how this conversion occurred, i.e. so that it might be reversed.

Clearly, from many clinical experiences it was evident that sexual excitation and anxiety were intimately connected with the vegetative or autonomic nervous system. Reich came to understand and subsequently demonstrate experimentally that it is not a matter of an "interconversion" of libido and anxiety but, rather, that they represent vegetative excitation in *opposite directions*. This was later formulated in the concept of the *vegetative antithesis,* in which sexual excitation or pleasure are seen as vegetative excitations outwards toward the erogenous zones and skin (periphery), whereas in anxiety it is away from the skin toward the center, i.e., the region of the heart and diaphragm—the solar plexus. From the point of view of the movement of the libido energy, pleasure represents an *expansion* and anxiety, a *contraction*. "It became increasingly clear that the overburdening of the vasovegetative system with undischarged sexual energy is the fundamental mechanism of anxiety, and thus, the neurosis." (2, p. 111).

There was no doubt from the character analytic work that with the dissolution of the neurotic defensive character attitudes the emotions "came out." With these breakthroughs the patient experienced relief from anxiety and marked vasomotor changes. These are typified by a shift from the sympathetic excitation associated with anxiety, e.g., pallor, cold perspiration, tachycardia dilation of the pupils, etc., to increased parasympathetic excitation, e.g., pinking up of the skin, warm perspiration, slowing of the heart, and pupillary constriction. Thus the coming out of the emotions is associated with a moving outward of vegetative excitation toward the skin surface, i.e., in the same direction as in sexual excitation. Their expression takes place by virtue of an expansion toward the surface and a discharge in muscular and vasomotor activity—hence the sensation of relief of inner tension (anxiety). Reich found that repression was not only associated with anxiety and its attendant sympathetic autonomic manifestations. Indeed in many cases anxiety was not always prominent. But along with the character attitudes there was a *bodily rigidity* which the patient often felt and which Reich recognized as widespread spasms of the musculature. This *muscular armor* as Reich called it is, significantly, associated with heightened sympathetic autonomic tone. Reich found that, by working directly on the spasms, anxiety would appear and/or increase and that the release of affects and vegetative changes would be expedited. The muscular armor therefore served to bind the vegetative excitation and prevent its reaching the surface. With the release of the energy from its fixation in these defenses, pleasurable erotic *streaming* sensations would be felt. These sensations Reich believed were the direct perception of vegetative currents. As the armorings were dissolved, these sensations became more and more intense, in most cases eventually producing a reaction of terror. Reich was convinced that all the resistances, all the defenses from first to last led to and had at their roots this terror. He called it *orgasm anxiety.* The end stage of treatment consisted of getting the patient to overcome his fear of the sensations and become accustomed to them. For obvious reasons, Reich now called the system of treatment, *character analytic vegetotherapy.*

In 1927 Reich's book, *The Function of the Orgasm,* was published. His consistent application of the orgasm theory and its theoretical consequences had by 1928 created a rift between himself and Freud. Freud had already given up many of his own earlier theoretical principles. In 1920 he had postulated the death instinct as a force equal to the sexual instinct. Reich, later, through his character analytic work was able to refute the idea of the death wish. For Freud and the psychoanalytic movement, the libido had long ago become an empty abstraction. Reich, convinced of the physiologic reality of the libido sought to overcome the experimental difficulties in objectifying it. In 1933, with Hitler's ascendency, Reich was forced to leave Germany. He was literally one step ahead of the Nazis. Driven first from Denmark and then Sweden he was, in 1934, able to find sanctuary in Norway at the invitation of the Institute of Psychology at the University of Oslo. By 1935 he had succeeded in designing and constructing a device for measuring and recording small changes in electrical potential at the surface of the skin and mucus membranes of human subjects. Over the next two years he accumulated and compiled compelling evidence that not only confirmed the libido as a real energy but also the essential validity of the orgasm theory and the vegetative antithesis. Concurrently, he began the work which was to lead him directly to the study of cancer.

Having found and recorded in the skin electrical-potential experiments objective evidence of his subjects' streaming sensations, Reich sought to determine if such streamings did not also occur in the cytoplasm of single cells, i.e., that the vegetative streaming is a function general to all life. This was in fact confirmed in his microscopic observations of amoebae in their natural habitat of vegetation rotting in water. What was totally unexpected was that protozoa appeared to develop from the products of the dying and disintegrating vegetable matter. As the grass decayed it swelled with fluid, lost its color, and broke down into tiny bead-like vesicles which piled up, became enveloped by membranes, and developed into organisms indistinguishable from those already free in the solution. Of course what he found would have been (and still would be) considered heresy according to accepted biological precepts which say that life developed eons ago and that subsequent life evolved from that remote event. Reich acquired time-lapse motion picture equipment and painstakingly filmed the entire process. He then began to examine many different materials, organic *and* inorganic, to see whether or not if made to swell in water they too would break down into vesicles which would then give rise to organisms.

Realizing the implications of this research he repeated these experiments literally hundreds of times. In order to exclude bacterial contamination he autoclaved his preparations and observed strict sterile technique. To his surprise he found that many substances including earth, charcoal, and pulverized iron yielded vesicles but only those from the autoclaved earth—under certain conditions—could be made to organize into protozoa. Reich concluded that life forms must be arising continually in nature in this manner. He called these vesicles "bions," postulating that they represent a transitional form—a stage between non-living and living matter. He found out several years later that a contemporary of Pasteur's—Henry Bastian—had already discovered and written about these vesicles, presenting evidence that they could give rise to yeasts and bacteria (19). In 1938 Reich published his book, *The Bion,* an account of the experiments in biogenesis and bions.

1939 was a momentous year. Freud died in London. Reich spent the Norwegian winter in his laboratory studying bions prepared from ocean sand. These bions proved to have remarkable properties. Despite the confinement of winter, he and his co-workers became deeply tanned. Reich developed a conjunctivitis from looking at the bions through the microscope. The atmosphere of the laboratory seemed highly excited. Metal objects in proximity to the preparations became magnetized, and organic materials such as cotton and rubber gloves were found to put a charge on the electroscope when brought near it. When the lights were turned off, blue-gray, fog-like light formations and flashing pinpoints of light became visible in the room. Photographic plates with or without lead shielding became fogged.

Frightened by the possibility of radioactivity, Reich sent a bion specimen to a physicist who found "no evidence of radiation." Reich was reassured, but he knew he had to be dealing with some kind of radiation. In order to confine and study the radiation, he built a metal-lined cabinet for the bion preparations. The light phenomena within the cabinet seemed intensified. He built another cabinet and to his surprise found the same phenomena even without the sand bions. This radiation energy seemed to be "everywhere." He believed that in their preparation the sand bions were releasing sun energy absorbed by the sand, and that this was permeating the laboratory. A rubber glove left in bright sunlight also charged the electroscope. Another glove, left on the skin of the abdomen charged the electroscope in the same way. It seemed to Reich that the energy was at once everywhere and yet, at the same time in the living organism, i.e. an organismic energy. Because of this and its discovery as a consequence of the investigation of the orgasm he called it *orgone.*

We can then see how the orgasm theory of 1924 had led Reich to the vegetative antithesis, to the objectifying of the libido energy, to biogenesis, and finally to the orgone energy in 1939. Each step followed logically upon the last. As a result of his observations of the development of protozoa from the bionous disintegration of grass, it occurred to him that cancer cells might arise from living tissue by the same mechanism. This he was subsequently able to prove by direct observation and, further, to capture on film with the time-lapse motion picture technique. Since the cancer cells developed from dead or dying tissue, it occurred to Reich that their very development depended upon the reduction or loss of the orgone or life energy from the tissue. By combining the sand bions with their powerful radiation with the cancer cells it was found that the cancer cells were destroyed. These findings not only confirmed the mechanism by which cancer arises but pointed the way toward a method of treatment. Injecting cancerous mice with the bions resulted in prolonged survival over the un-treated control animals. This work was published in 1939 under the title, *Bion Experiments on the Cancer Problem.*

This exciting and vital work had to be interrupted when Reich was forced to immigrate to the United States. For two years he lectured on medical psychology at the New School for Social Research in New York. He founded the Orgone Institute, treated patients, and trained physicians in the technique that he had now come to call *medical orgone therapy.* In the meantime he resumed his research at his home in Forest Hills. While on vacation in the clear, dry atmosphere of Maine in 1940, he was able to make the observations which confirmed the existence of the atmospheric orgone energy. The first atmospheric *orgone energy accumulators* (ORAC) were built and became important tools for research in orgone physics and the biological effects of the energy. Most important to us in the present context is that Reich was able to duplicate the prolongation of life of cancer-prone mice by treating them in the accumulator instead of injecting them with bions. Autopsies of sacrificed animals showed that tumor tissue could be destroyed and the carcinomatous process delayed. This implied that the ORAC did concentrate the energy from the atmosphere with the effect of increasing the charge in the mice. In 1941 he began the treatment of human cancer patients with the ORAC.

In his eighteen years in America he left an astonishing record of ac-complishments in his studies of the biological, physical, and meteorological aspects of the orgone; he established the foundations of the new science of orgonomy.

A Definition of the Biopathy

Reich considered cancer to be the result of the premortem putrefaction of tissues devitalized by the loss of bioenergetic (orgonotic) charge. The devitalized cells disintegrate into bion vesicles from which the cancer cells organize (cancer biogenesis). This is identical to the origin of the protozoa from rotting vegetable matter; in fact Reich called these protozoa the "cancer" of the grass. It is the cause and nature of this process of devitalization which concerns us here. Reich regarded the development of the cancer cell and tumor as but one phase—a relativley *late* phase—of a general or systemic disease which he termed the *carcinomatous shrinking biopathy*.

The term *biopathy* connotes a revolutionary concept of disease of which cancer is but one example. This concept rose directly out of Reich's work on Freud's libido theory of neurosis. It not only explains the origin of the psychoneurosis itself but also establishes the relationship between the emotional disorders and the diverse physical (somatic) disorders commonly referred to as "psychosomatic" or "functional." The term "psychosomatic" is generally understood to signify a *somatic* disturbance which arises from antecedent *psychic* conflicts. To Reich *both* the somatic and the psychic disturbances are seen to have a common biopathic root of which the psychic and somatic are simply different manifestations. The biopathy is then a unified concept of disease presupposing an underlying fundamental disturbance of natural functioning.

> Under the term *biopathies* we subsume all those disease processes which take place in the autonomic life apparatus or simply, in the plasmatic system. There is a typical basic disturbance of the plasmatic system which—once it has started— may express itself in a variety of symptomatic disease pictures all of which have in common: *a disturbance of the biological function* of plasmatic pulsation in the total organism.
>
> Sexual stasis represents a fundamental disturbance of biological pulsation. Sexual excitation, as we know, is a primal function of the living plasma system. *The sexual function has been shown to be the productive life function per se.* Thus a chronic disturbance of the sexual function must of necessity be synonymous with a biopathy.
>
> The stasis of biosexual excitation may manifest itself basically in two ways. It may appear as an emotional disturbance of the psychic apparatus, that is, as a neurosis or a psychosis [*psychic* biopathy]. But also directly in a malfunctioning of the organs and express itself as an organic disease [*somatic* biopathy].
>
> The central mechanism of the biopathy is a disturbance in the discharge of biosexual excitation. (3, pp. 128–130)

This disturbance is what Reich referred to as *orgastic impotence*. Its bearing on the etiology of the biopathy must be clearly understood. We must first clearly differentiate between healthy and disturbed genital functioning.

Reich's peers had objected to his emphasis on sexual problems as a cause rather than just symptoms of the neurosis. They insisted that they could point to any number of neurotics with "normal" sex lives. *Potency* was then (as it is nowadays) assumed to be normal if a man were able to carry out the sex act, that is, with erective and ejaculatory capability and the woman with a clitoral climax. In general, *sexual activity* was not differentiated from *genital functioning*. It was this difficulty which led Reich to set aside previous assumptions regarding "potency" and to scrutinize genital health more closely. In the ensuing four years of clinical work, the Orgasm Theory was formulated and consolidated; sexual "potency" came to be clarified and redefined.

Genuine *orgasm* is not synonymous with *ejaculation* or *climax* (a peak in excitation) but does involve them as prerequisites or concomitants. *Orgasm* itself is a phase of sexual intercourse in which there is a sharp rise in genital excitation to acme associated with the onset of *involuntary* pleasurable* contractions of the total body musculature which begin in the pelvis and genital apparatus. It is associated with a clouding or momentary loss of consciousness.

Orgastic *potency* consists of the capacity to give in to these contractions without inhibition, permitting the flow of biological energy and the discharge of all built-up sexual excitation.† It is in this specific circumstance that *complete satisfaction* is achieved. In neurosis these criteria are never completely met. Phantasies, sadistic or masochistic impulses, disgust, wariness, all more or less disguised, are inevitably present to one degree or another; they divert full concentration from the genital sensations. The body usually stiffens against the excitation, e.g., the breath is held, the buttocks squeezed, and the copulatory movements harsh or forced. This reduces sensation and prevents surrender to the involuntary movements. In short, in neurosis there is avoidance of the full orgasm. As a consequence some portion of the energy is retained. As Reich puts it, "The energy source of the neurosis [psychic biopathy] lies in the differential between accumulation and discharge of sexual energy" (2, p. 88).

What, one might ask, is the basis for the inability to surrender? This question was answered only after years of character-analytic investigation. In treatment, all resistances were found to have as their ultimate point of focus a terror of being overwhelmed by orgastic genital sensations. This often first appears in the form of a *fear of dying* or of catastrophies of various kinds, e.g., fatal illness. In all cases, a fear of *sexual intercourse* eventually develops. Reich called this *orgasm anxiety;* he explains it in the following way:

> If sexual excitation is checked, there arises a *vicious circle: the checking increases the stasis of excitation, and the increased stasis diminishes the ability of*

---

* Ejaculation can occur even in an unsatisfactory sexual experience.

† The reader may wonder just why this build-up takes place. Where does the surplus of energy come from? Why is the orgasm mechanism even necessary? As Baker explains it, "In the normal course of events, more energy is built up than can be used. Energy is stored in the body like money in a bank for emergency situations. During such emergencies as battle, worry, or exhausting work, this excess energy is used up and the organism is asexual. In ordinary circumstances, however, energy keeps piling up, so that the organism would have to grow continually or would eventually burst unless some mechanism were present to discharge the accumulated energy after it had reached a certain level. This level of energy is known as the "lumination point," and in the healthy individual is experienced as sexual excitement." (14, p. xxii)

the organism to decrease it. Thus, the organism acquires a fear of excitation, in other words, sexual anxiety. This sexual anxiety, therefore, is caused by an external frustration of instinctual gratification, and is anchored internally by the fear of the dammed up sexual excitation. This is the mechanism of orgasm anxiety. It is the fear of the organism—which has become unwilling to experience pleasure—of the *overpowering* excitation of the genital system. *Orgasm anxiety forms the basis of the general pleasure anxiety,* which is an integral part of the prevailing human structure.

It usually shows itself as a generalized fear of any kind of vegetative sensation or excitation at the perception of these. Since joy of living and orgastic pleasure are identical, general fear of life is the ultimate expression of orgasm anxiety. (2, p. 136)

If we accept the idea that the dammed-up energy due to the orgastic blockage underlies psychic and, as we are suggesting, somatic disequilibriums, we must then explain how the stuck energy in fact causes the disequilibrium.

Biological Pulsation: The Orgasm Formula and the Vegetative Antithesis

Reich first saw the orgasm as a mechanism of discharge for the surplus biological energy; the relaxation of tension as a consequence of orgasm is experienced subjectively as a complete sense of relief. More detailed consideration of the phenomenon disclosed that the sequence of psychic and somatic events follows a four-beat formula which, naturally enough, he termed the *orgasm formula:*

1. *Mechanical tension:* erection, due to engorgement of sexual organs with blood ⸻►
2. *Electrical* charging:* generalized pleasurable excitation which through sexual friction becomes focused and heightened in the genitalia acme ⸻►
3. *Electrical discharge:* onset marked by a clouding of consciousness followed by involuntary orgastic muscular contractions of the genital apparatus which are transmitted to the entire body ⸻►
4. *Mechanical relaxation:* detumescence of sexual organs, emotional somatic sensations of relief, gratification.

Briefly:

Mechanical tension ⸻►Electrical charging ⸻►
Electrical discharge ⸻►Mechanical relaxation.

---

* When the orgasm formula was first conceived, Reich had assumed that the biological energy was bioelectricity, and, subsequently, he demonstrated its presence with an electrical detector: hence, "electrical" charging. Later, after discovering the orgone, he termed this stage "energetic" (orgonotic) charging.

Reich's theoretical leap at this point and the one which led him from sexology into pure biology was to perceive the orgasm formula as a general formula for the function of *pulsation* in the living.

It is abundantly evident that all physiologic functions are pulsatory—exhibiting *expansion* and *contraction* phases—each with its own particular period. In the formula: *mechanical tension* ————→ electrical charge corresponds to expansion while electrical discharge ————→ *mechanical relaxation* equal contraction. In other words the entire sequence taken together constitutes a single *pulsation* (expansion-contraction). A consideration of the functioning of various autonomic viscera confirms the generality of this form of pulsation. For example,

> The tension-charge process governs the cardiac function, also, in the form of an electric wave which runs from the auricle to the apex. Prerequisite for the beginning of contraction is the *filling* of the auricle with blood. The result of the charge and discharge is the propulsion of the blood through the aorta due to the contraction of the heart. (2, p. 251)

Starling's "law" of the heart can therefore be seen as having an *energetic* basis. An identical mechanism may be seen in the function of the intestine and bladder and in the cellular division following the fertilization of the ovum. One may therefore perceive cell division as an orgastic function. The *orgasm formula* indeed *is the life formula itself*, i.e., this form of pulsation is the sine qua non of biological (living) functioning.

In complex organisms it is the autonomic nervous system which permits *unitary* pulsatory functioning (expansion-contraction) throughout the organism by means of the antithetical actions of the parasympathetic and sympathetic apparatuses. In protozoa and other microorganisms without an organized nervous system these functions are mediated strictly by chemical substances such as ions, e.g., K^+ and Ca^{++}, H^+ and OH^- which form *antithetical pairs*. In other words, chemical substances can take the place of a nervous system in the plasmatic system of a protozoan.

Functionally, this *vegetative antithesis* directly relates the vegetative activities of the multicellular organism—man—to those in the single cell—amoeba. In the amoeba the putting out of the pseudopodia is an expansive process which is functionally identical to pleasurable sexual expansion, erection, in the human. The withdrawal of pseudopodia and assumption of a spherical configuration, as say in the presence of a strong electrical current, prodding with a filament of glass, or lowering the temperature, is in the amoeba a contraction in the deepest sense identical to the behavior of a human being in a state of anxiety and *unpleasure*. In the human the expansive process is associated with an overall greater excitation in the parasympathetic apparatus, contraction with the sympathetic. Optimum health implies a free, full alternation of expansion and contraction in the total organism. This pulsation is what relates the individual cell, tissue, or organ function to the function of the entire organism. Conversely, the chronic disturbance in the orgastic discharge must ultimately affect the individual cells. As energy builds up, the increasing tension ceases to be pleasurable and the human organism contracts down just as in the amoeba; but in this case the *unpleasurable stimulus comes from within*. The contraction takes the form of muscular armoring and chronic increases in sympathetic autonomic tone (see below). In other words, the organism, unable to discharge the energy in orgastic clonisms, *is threatened with a sensation of bursting,* a threat against which it contracts.* Some of the energy is discharged in neurotic behavior. However, this in itself fosters even more tension and anxiety. Eventually there are discharges which take the form of *somatic disease.* Both the neurosis and the somatic disease are therefore forms of a spontaneous, *partial* discharge in the face of chronic orgastic sexual stasis. Emotional and sexual excitation, denied natural expression, come out in internal autonomic discharges. In asthma and peptic ulcer, for example, the major symptoms are due to parasympathetic discharges. Cardiovascular hypertension and paroxysmal supraventricular tachycardias represent sympathetic discharges.

The Bioelectric Skin Potential: Objectifying the Libido

The orgasm theory and vegetative antithesis formed the conceptual and theoretical basis for the science of sex economy. One had, for the first time, an understanding of what constitutes health. On the pathological side, the way was indicated toward an understanding of purely psychic and psychosomatic disease. What was sorely needed was objective physiologic experimental confirmation of the orgasm formula.

In simple terms, it became necessary to determine if, in the course of sexual excitation, the genitalia and erogenous zones would exhibit a rise in bioelectrical charge. In 1935, a year after the publication of his paper, *The Orgasm as an Electrophysical Discharge,* Reich had completed the experimental design for this demonstration.

The apparatus consisted essentially of electrodes, amplifier, and oscillograph which were designed to detect, amplify, and record changes in electrical potential on the surface of the skin and mucous membranes in human subjects. The technical premise was that the human organism is essentially a complicated salt electrolyte, colloidal electrolyte, and membrane system; the skin in its electrical function expresses a unitary function

---

* The theme of bursting or dissolution in one form or another actually comes up in the treatment of most of our patients. Reich found it to be at the center of the disorder of *masochism.*

related to the bioelectric totality of the organism in the same way as does the cell membrane to the cell's interior. From over two years of work involving exhaustive control studies, we may present only the essence:

1. Mechanical congestion of a sexual organ, e.g., *mechanical tension or erection* may be present without any rise in skin potential *unless it is associated with subjective pleasurable erotic streaming sensations*. Thus, sexual excitation is functionally identical to *charging* of the erogenous zone; for the pleasure sensation to be *perceptible,* in addition to erection, an increase in charge is required. Furthermore, it was determined that the *psychic intensity* of the pleasure experience corresponded to the physiologic quantity of the potential. It must be added that severely emotionally blocked or armored subjects showed little or no bioelectric reaction. Emotionally healthier individuals sufficiently free of blocks to experience preorgastic sensations or streamings were able in many instances, on the basis of subjective feelings, to accurately describe the tracings appearing on the apparatus in an adjoining room.

2. The three most important circumstances in which a negative electrical response at the periphery (skin or mucosal surface) is obtained are:

   a) *The peripheral orgastic discharge,* in which all the charge built up prior to acme is discharged to the outside (provided there is no sexual stasis as exists in neurosis).
   b) *Anxiety,* in which there is a fall in potential to *below* the unexcited or *resting* potential.
   c) *Death,* in which there is extinction of the source of the charge.

3. There is an autonomic or vegetative center. From the clinical work in removing the muscular armor, it was clear that control of vegetative excitation—emotion, sexuality—was achieved by the inhibition of respiration. The chest is held in chronic inspiration in an attitude of anxiety. When this armor is relieved, the emotions are powerfully expressed, and the sensation of streaming is first experienced. Reich's postulation was that the muscular armor compresses the abdominal contents, thereby inhibiting impulses from the largest of the autonomic ganglion, the solar plexus. He concluded that the autonomic ganglia and nerves and the body's membrane-electrolyte biosystem are the sources of the energy of the emotions and means of transmission of the excitation between interior and periphery. This found confirmation in the bioelectrical experiments in the following way:

   a) Deep *inspiration,* or the Valsalva maneuver or direct external pressure over the epigastrium causes a sharp drop in potential in this location.
   b) Upon *expiration,* the potential rises slowly to the previous level.

This variation in charge at the epigastric surface with the phases of respiration is reduced or absent in individuals who are strongly blocked emotionally or suffering from severe muscular armoring.

The importance of these findings is manifold. First, it shows that *pressure exerted at the organismic interior,* e.g., an inspiration, causes a decrease in potential at the *surface.* This presupposes the continuous generation of a field of excitation between the center and the periphery. Furthermore, it is obviously not transmitted by known neutral pathways alone but by any of the innumerable fluid-membrane interface systems between the center and the periphery.

Taken in their entirety, the findings in these experiments are far-reaching in their implications. Clearly, the orgasm formula had been dramatically confirmed, and for the first time it was possible to objectify and quantify *psychic subjective* sensations in terms of charges and direction of charge. Thirdly, the validity of the vegetative antithesis is demonstrated: the processes of excitation in pleasure and anxiety give rise to currents of energy in *opposite* directions, namely, toward the periphery and toward the center. The energetic processes in sexual excitation and in pleasure are seen to be identical to the charging of the cell surface in the mitosis of cell division and are thus identical to the life function itself. Anxiety on the other hand, as the fundamental functional antithesis of sexuality, is therefore related (but not identical) to death. In death, the energy source is extinguished; in anxiety, the energy is withdrawn from the periphery (away from the world, toward the self) and dammed up in the center creating the subjective sensation of oppression, but the *source* of the energy is still alive and reexpansion remains possible.

The bioelectric experiments proved the libido to be a real, measurable biological energy rather than just a metaphor. Sex economy was thus put on a solid physiologic footing. The neurosis could no longer be regarded as only the result of unresolved *psychic* conflicts and infantile fixations. Rather, the conflicts and fixations, by means of the armor, become anchored in the body creating disturbances in the normal handling of the energy, i.e., discharge. Psychic and somatic processes are inseparable inasmuch as they have the same energy source and exhibit corresponding excitations with respect to the direction of charge. The cerebrum, heretofore regarded as the center of the nervous system, in reality is subservient to the autonomic center, which is the source of the energy. Indeed, rational organismic behavior does not require a cerebrum since organisms without this structure may still behave purposefully. The cerebrum *integrates, enhances,* or *inhibits* but is not the sole source of instinct. Both psyche and soma therefore operate on the basis of biological law. The *pathologic* psychosomatic structure is the result of a conflict between social and biologic (instinctual) functions.

The importance of the confirmation of the orgasm theory and the vegetative antithesis in the present context is that the link between the psychic and somatic-vegetative processes is clearly established. One must be able to understand the relationship between emotional and cellular function; otherwise the relationship between sexual stasis and cancer is incomprehensible. The emotions represent a spontaneous movement of energy of which the sexual orgastic function is the most comprehensive; in repression this movement is blocked and the energy held by the muscular armor. The unimpeded movement of this energy, the process of charge and discharge that produce biological pulsation typify and sustain the life process per se. Reich in fact came to view the life process as a specific manifestation of a primordial energy.

The Muscular Armor

Character analysis made it clear that the defensive character resistances were not merely a "state of mind" of the patient. Emotional and sexual excitation were found to be held back directly by *chronic muscular spasms.* For each character "attitude" there proved to be a corresponding *muscular* attitude by which it is represented. Invariably it was found that there were childhood experiences in which strong emotions such as hatred, anxiety, or love were suppressed by mechanisms which directly affected vegetative functions such as holding the breath, tensing the muscles of the neck, shoulders, chest, abdomen and pelvis, etc. In short, the tightening of the muscles represents the *somatic* aspect of repression and is responsible for its continuation.

While the tightening in the musculature initially takes the form of acute voluntary *holding,* the circumstances which induce it, by repetition and reinforcement, may ultimately produce *chronic involuntary spasms.* By blocking dangerous vegetative (emotional) sensation, acute anxiety is at first reduced but at the expense of motility and spontaneity. The muscular armor enables one to be "good," to be "nice" rather than angry, calm and controlled rather than anxious, aloof, and cold against forbidden love and sexual excitation. In fact,

> Every muscular rigidity contains the history and meaning of its origin. . . . The neurosis is not only the expression of a disturbed psychic equilibrium; much more correctly and significantly, it is the expression of a chronic disturbance of the vegetative equilibrium and of natural motility. (2, p. 267)

Thus, the vegetotherapeutic treatment of muscular attitudes is interwoven in a specific manner with character analysis, which it supplements (but does not replace). As the character and muscular armor are functionally identical, they are often mutually dissolvable, i.e., a character attitude may be dissolved through the dissolution of a muscular armoring or vice versa. Destruction of the muscular armor therefore requires the same systematic handling as the character defenses; it is neither a matter of exercises nor mere massage, nor is it in any way a haphazard, arbitrary affair.* Its removal permits a concentration of vegetative excitation which in breaking through often produces the memories of the circumstances which led to it. Reich found that the armoring occurs in groups of muscles which work as a functional unit, that is, one which is capable of producing (or repressing) a complete emotional expression. These groups are called *segments*. Like the sections of an earthworm, the segmented armoring is oriented on planes perpendicular to the long axis of the body. It is along this axis that the streamings are felt as the armoring is dissolved. There are seven clearly defined segments: ocular, oral, cervical, thoracic, diaphragmatic, abdominal, and pelvic. The arms and legs are appendages of the thoracic and pelvic segments respectively.

Muscular armor functions to prevent the breakthrough of emotions and vegetative sensations, absorb the energy of the instinctual drives, and ultimately block orgastic surrender which in the armored individual is experienced as a terror of dying. It is associated with a preponderance of sympathetic autonomic tonus (sympathecotonia) and hence has the potential for creating an autonomic disturbance of the viscera within the segment. This finding is of extreme etiologic significance in cancer and the "psychosomatic" diseases; the muscular armor constitutes the link between the repression of emotions and the disturbed organ physiology in these disorders. Of cardinal importance in this regard is the effect on the respiratory apparatus.

The *inhibition of respiration* through armoring of the diaphragm and thorax forms the central physiologic mechanism for the suppression and repression of emotion. Clinical observation shows time and again that there is not one neurotic who does not exhibit some disturbance of respiration, namely an inability to expire fully, deeply, and evenly in a spontaneous and unforced manner. Commonly the chest is held in an inspiratory posture, an attitude associated with anxiety, which has the following effects:

a) Emotion and sensation are blocked directly by the armor itself.
b) The generation of biological energy is hampered by the effects on oxygenation and metabolism itself.
c) A third effect (alluded to earlier) is the damming up of energy in the vegetative centers which interferes with the generation and spread of vegetative excitation.

* Many so-called "body therapies" make use of mechanical exercises and/or massage. These have no pedagogic relationship to vegetotherapeutic technique; they usually derive from a misunderstanding of it. Most frequently some fragment of Reich's technique is lifted out of the context of sex economy and utilized in a distorted, often violent manner. As long as the entire structure of concealing and defensive attitudes is not systematically uncovered and eliminated, the release of genuine affect or natural spontaneous movements cannot occur except fortuitously. They can only be forced or simulated.

The Discovery of the Orgone

The postulation of a specific "life" energy was not original with Reich. He was very much influenced by natural philosophers and scientists such as Aristotle, Driesch, Bergson, Kammerer, and finally Freud, who had suggested such an entity. However, the concept had been continually lost in a miasma of metaphysics and mysticism or rejected entirely by mechanistic science which attempts to reduce life to an electrochemical machine. Reich himself, with his considerable classical background, operated until 1939 on the assumption that the libido energy was bioelectric in nature. Obviously there is electricity in the organism in the form of charged colloidal and ionic particles. Electrical events are clearly evident in the physiology of muscle and a multitude of physiochemical processes. But Reich's extensive clinical, theoretical, and experimental contact with the phenomena of vegetative functioning pointed to serious inconsistencies in an exclusively electrochemical-mechanical theory of life. To cite just a few: Electromagnetic energy travels at the speed of light; the movement of the biological energy, e.g., as seen in the excitation curves of the skin potential experiments is exceedingly slow. The *form* of biologic movement is slowly undulatory as in the cardiac and respiratory cycles or peristaltic waves of the gut. This slowness cannot be explained on the basis of high electrical resistance in living tissue; an electrical stimulus applied to the body produces an instantaneous, involuntary response. What is more, electrical stimulation produces unnatural, uncoordinated, and functionally meaningless contractions. It is difficult to conceive of an emotion or an expressive organismic movement of the body as a product of an electrical current. We experience electrical stimulations subjectively as alien. Our senses fail to respond to the electromagnetic waves as say, a radio or television receiver which operates with these energies.

As we have seen, the orgone energy was first discovered in the sand bions. The bions appeared to be the source of an energy which had at one and the same time the qualities of radiation, static electricity and—as was found in the bioelectric skin potential experiments—bioelectricity. Subsequent studies were to show that it could be manifest as visible light, heat, and—under special circumstances—in the Geiger counter. Yet, in his almost twenty years of work with it, Reich proved that it was neither electromagnetic or nuclear. Microscopically the energy is evident as a vivid, radiant, blue-white field around bions and red blood cells. It is particularly brilliant around leukocytes and in other cells as the "radiation" of cell division or mitosis. The sand bions were capable of immobilizing and killing bacteria and ameboid cancer cells at distances of up to 10 microns. This phenomenon was believed due to an unique property of the energy: the capacity for a *reversed potential* or, simply, the flow of energy out of a weaker toward a more highly charged system.

Reich was dealing with an unknown energy a manifestation of which is life itself. It appeared to be present in the atmosphere. Living organisms therefore live in an "ocean" of the very energy from which they ultimately derive. They take up the energy by respiration, direct absorption, and nutrition. The basis for this absorption is the energy's affinity for organic substances which retain it and the flow from the lower to the higher (organismic) potential. A surplus is built up periodically, reaching a certain tension at which the energy spontaneously luminates; this lumination produces the urge to mate. The resulting orgastic convulsion discharges the energy and relaxes the tension. The process of tension-charge thus initiates not only the orgastic pulsation of the entire animal; in addition, each individual organ or cell forms an energetic system which is governed by this orgasm or life formula. If the function of pulsation is sufficiently interfered with, the organism loses its capacity to charge, and the structure and function of its tissues are irrevocably altered (i.e. degeneration).

Cancer Cell Formation: The Discovery of the T-Bacillus

In his study of cancer tissue in the live state, Reich found that it disintegrates into a tiny (0.25 micron) bacillus-shaped bion. Believing it might have a connection to the origin of the cancer cell, he sought to isolate and cultivate it. Injected into healthy mice these bions proved rapidly lethal: hence the name T (for *tod*—the German word for death) bacillus. With smaller doses the mice survived longer but went on to develop cancerous growths. These findings raised the exciting possibility that a "specific agent" of cancer formation had been discovered.

Things proved quite a bit more complicated, however. T-bacilli were found to be culturable from a wide number of sources including *healthy non-cancerous blood and tissue*—in fact from the degeneration and disintegration of any living *and* non-living protein. Furthermore, when innoculated into healthy blood or tissues they induced bionous disintegration of these cells. The large, blue strongly radiating bions which resulted, then had the effect of agglutinating, immobilizing the smaller T-bacilli, *and destroying their biological activity*. Sterilized cultures of the large bions obtained from healthy tissues or prepared from charcoal if allowed to degenerate in turn gave rise to T-bacilli.*

---

* The T-bacilli are not to be confused with the gram-negative bacteria such as B. proteus and others which often complicate terminal cancer. These bacteria are morphologically and biologically distinct from the T-bion. Reich refers to them as "rot" bacteria because they appear to be by-products of the bionous disintegration of devitalized tissue and blood. It is significant that pure cultures of these bacteria when they deteriorate may give rise to T-bacilli. This suggests that the T-bion represents a more advanced state of degeneration. Perhaps T-bions disintegrate further into virus-like particles.

To summarize:

1. Cancer cells degenerate into T-bacilli.
2. Healthy tissue and blood or inorganic material undergoing bionous disintegration at first yield large radiant bions which, in turn, also degenerate into T-bacilli.
3. T-bacilli induce bionous disintegration in living and non-living protein.
4. The large blue bions and the T-bacilli are antagonistic.

These observations seemed incomprehensible until it was realized that all of these events are a function of a change in orgonotic charge. The bions result when healthy tissue begins to lose its vitality or bioenergetic charge (orgonotic potency). The bions, in turn, as they lose their charge, degenerate into T-bacilli. Cancer cells, because of their initial lower orgonotic vitality (being organized out of bions), may break down directly into T-bacilli. Sufficient numbers of T-bacilli, being extremely toxic, induce normal cells to break down into bion vesicles. These vesicles, having a higher charge, neutralize the T-bacilli by drawing off their remaining energy. The direction of the breakdown is ultimately toward the T-bion unless the energy is replenished. The validity of this concept was demonstrated in *reverse* in an ingenious experiment in which T-bacilli placed in filtered serum from healthy blood swelled up under direct observation into large blue bions. Reich concluded that the T-bacilli from the spontaneous disintegration of poorly charged tissues constitute the specific stimulation for cancer cell formation by first inducing bionous disintegration in other cells. Recalling the antagonism between the resulting bions and the T-bacilli we can preceive this as a defensive reaction of the organism but one which is *pathological* in that it is at the expense of the healthier cells. The subsequent organization of the resultant bions into cancer cells then takes place by itself. The cancer cell and the tumors which develop may be seen then as a *result* and not a *cause* of the cancer disease.

For these reasons Reich regarded the cancer cell as less significant than the tissue damage which precedes its development. Though aware of the mechanical dangers of growing tumors, he was more concerned about the depletion of the patients' energy in combatting the cancer cell and the T-bacilli into which it disintegrates (3, p. 228). By itself the cancer cell is relatively weak biologically, a fact which forms the basis for its susceptibility to chemotherapy and radiation therapy. Reich makes the case that the "wild" mitotic activity of the cancer cell is in fact a product of its orgonotic weakness and its own cellular orgastic disturbance. In the deepest biological sense, the accelerated cell division is a manifestation of the cell's own nuclear "anxiety," and anxiety which is largely absent at the surface, *viz*. the cancer patients chronic emotional calm and resignation (3, pp. 190–192).

Cancer: The Shrinking Biopathy

Reich contended that the origin of the cancer cell has eluded conventional cancer research because—in both a literal and figurative sense—of the way the researchers *look* at things. For example, the blue bion vesicles from which the cancer cells organize and the T-bacilli into which the cancer cell disintegrates cannot be seen in fixed (killed) and stained tissue sections. They are seen only in living preparations. Secondly, with magnifications of less than 2000x the observations of which he speaks cannot be appreciated. Without examining living preparations at very high power the intermediate stages of cancer cell development could not have been discovered. Conceptually, the *approach* to the genesis of the cancer cell is blocked because of a rigid and unqualified denial of the natural organization of protozoa out of dying or non-living substances and the adherence to the idea that all present-day life *must* come from pre-existing spores or air germs. Lastly, medicine and biology have a largely *mechanical* orientation which not only looks for causes in individual cells, organs, *dead* tissues, and chemicals but grind up the living to find out how it works. Thus while many small details are discovered, the overall functioning that determines these details is often lost.

This last bias is most significant because it underlies the failure to recognize the role of a disturbed sex economy not only in cancer, but in any of what are considered the psychosomatic diseases (somatic biopathies). A pivotal point in Reich's cancer research is therefore the realization that the cancer cell does not develop directly out of a healthy cell but in fact from devitalized tissues which are the consequence of a general systemic illness: the *carcinomatons shrinking biopathy*. This systemic disease is associated in most cases with a chronic and gradual loss of vitality in the organism—often over a period of many years. The loss of vitality is a specific response in turn to the chronic disturbance in sexual functioning (sexual stasis) and may be manifest most notably in the emotional life of the prospective cancer patient. Reich, I believe, was the first to understand the significance of *the deep underlying emotional and characterologic resignation* which could be detected in most cases *before* the development of any tumor. In this sense the cancer patient may be quite distinct from those with other biopathies. Reich, for example, compares them to patients with hypertensive cardiovascular disease in the following way:

> In the cardiovascular biopathy . . . the sexual excitation remains alive, biologically, physiologically, and emotionally. That is, the biological core of the organism, the autonomic life apparatus, continues to produce energy to the fullest extent. The organism, in its state of contraction, reacts to this [the underlying stasis] with outbreaks of anxiety or anger and with somatic symptoms such as hyperthyroidism, diarrhea, tachycardia, etc.
>
> In cancer, on the other hand, the biological core reduces its energy produc-

tion. Thus, as time goes on, the excitations and emotions become weaker and weaker. . . . Functionally speaking, an eruption of anxiety or anger is still a *discharge* of energy, pathological as it may be. Chronic emotional calm, on the other hand, must correspond to a depletion of energy in the cell and plasma system. . . . Affects are the expression of biological cell excitation. (3, p. 177–179)

Reich observed that cancer characters exhibit predominantly mild affects and went so far as to say that he had never seen a cancer patient with violent emotions or explosions of anger.* Most typically they show characterologic resignation. Here again Reich expresses it in very biological terms:

> Let us think of the biological, physiological, and psychological functions in terms of a wide circle with a center ("core"). The shrinking of the circle periphery then would correspond to the characterological and emotional resignation. The center, the core, is as yet untouched. But the process progresses toward the center, the "biological core." This biological core is nothing but the sum of all plasmatic cell functions. When the shrinking process reaches this core, then the plasma itself begins to shrink. This coincides with the process of weight loss. But long before the plasma function is directly disturbed, the peripheral physiological and character functions are disturbed: first the ability to establish social contact, to enjoy life and pleasure, the ability to work, and then plasmatic excitation and pulsation.
>
> When . . . the peripheral character resignations have progressed to the biological core, when, thus the production of impulses in the cells itself is effected, we are dealing with the process of biopathic shrinking. (3, p. 180–181)

External respiration in cancer patients is severely disturbed. Though Reich found such disturbances in all neurotics, that found in association with cancer is particularly serious.† It is Reich's contention that this leads to impaired *internal* respiration at the tissue level. This is supported by the findings of an increased tendency toward anaerobic metabolism in cancer tissue and the metabolic acidosis sometimes seen in terminal cancer. The combination of disturbed respiration and muscular armor (which have their roots in a deep fear of sexual excitation) are seen as major factors in the genesis of the cancer cell. The biological weakening and devitalization which results in the tissues also leads to an increased susceptibility to carcinogenic stimuli. This Reich believed lay at the heart of the "disposition"

---

* Reich's assertions regarding the emotional character of cancer patients have been supported by others in the more recent literature (21, 22, 23). We should point out that despite the seeming extremity of this view, Reich himself repeatedly stressed the danger of being dogmatic or mechanistic. He was aware that cancer patients will sometimes develop and even succumb to cardiac or hypertensive disease. He reminded his students that even in cancer the organism does not give up entirely without a fight, i.e., plasmatic excitations. He also warned that the characterologic resignation may be deeply concealed and difficult to detect. This may reflect the patients' defense against a deep awareness of the dying process even before the diagnosis of the condition.

† As we are speaking of it here the impairment has nothing to do with secondary mechanical effects of tumors such as pleural effusions or pleuritic pain.

toward cancer—a belief which was consistently confirmed in his clinical experiences with these patients.

Spasms of the musculature and decreased orgonotic charge are felt subjectively as "being dead" and are associated with functional disturbances and symptoms. As examples Reich cites spasms of the uterus in frigid women which he says have no other function than to block sensations of sexual excitation in the vagina. These spasms produce menstrual disturbances, uterine polyps, and fibromata and underlie the degenerative changes which may culminate in uterine cancer. Likewise, spasms in *annular* musculature are believed to be a major factor in the frequency with which malignancies develop in the throat, near the entrance and exit of the stomach and near the anus. To repeat, the spasms prevent the biological energy from charging these sites with their highly susceptible mucosae and glands (3, pp. 132-134). The armor thus directly impairs the vitality of the tissues—that vitality being a function of its energetic charge and freedom of pulsation. It therefore not only plays a role in the overall proclivity toward cancer but also in the sites of the primary tumor and its metastases. With the respiratory inhibition it forms an integral part of the shrinking process.

Another significant manifestation of shrinking in cancer is that of *pain*. Cancer pain is often difficult to handle and sometimes not easily comprehensible from a purely mechanical standpoint. These pains are sometimes described as "drawing" or "pulling" in quality. Seen in the context of the shrinking biopathy they may become understandable. First, Reich challenges the idea that the nerves are merely immobile, passive transmitters of impulses:

> In the metazoan, the contraction and expanding ameba continues to exist in the form of the contracting and expanding autonomic nervous system. This autonomic system is nothing but organized [and specialized] contractile plasma. Thus, the emotional, vegetative, autonomic movement is the immediate expression of the plasma current. The prevalent concept of the rigidity of the autonomic nerves is incompatible with every single phenomenon of biophysical functioning, such as pleasure, anxiety, tension, relaxation, and the sensations of pressure, pulling pain, etc. On the other hand, the contractility of the autonomic nervous system, which forms a functional and histological unity ("syncytium"), explains in a single manner our subjective plasmatic sensations. What we experience as pleasure is an expansion of our organism. The autonomic nerves, in pleasure, actually stretch out toward the world; the whole organism is in a state of vegotonic expansion. In anxiety, on the other hand, we feel a crawling back into the self, a shrinking and tightness. What we experience here is the actual process of contraction in the autonomic nervous system.
>
> The orgasm we experience as an involuntary expansion and contraction; this reflects the actual process of expansion and contraction in the total plasma system. The pain in cancer patients reflects the fact that the autonomic nerves retract from the diseased region and "pull" on the tissues. The expression of "pulling" pain describes an actual process." (3, pp. 142-143)

The cancerous shrinking biopathy may be viewed as a *chronic* process having its roots in the origin of the neurosis and, hence, early in life. Its obvious outward manifestations, e.g., tumor, cachexia, etc. represent a late state in its course. Clearly, this biopathy cannot be viewed as having a mechanical inevitability. Spontaneous recoveries, though uncommon, have been documented. Each individual has his own peculiar capacity to fight the shrinking process. Nor does every cell or organ surrender to it in a mechanically uniform manner. Certainly its course and development must be influenced by such vicissitudes as personal losses or disappointments. Deprived of some critical outlet for self-expression, for pleasurable expansion, the process of resignation may be precipitated or hastened.

That the shrinking biopathy may have its beginnings as early as intrauterine life is obvious from the occurrence of congenital and infantile cancer. Here biological pulsation has been severely compromised long before genital sexuality is even a possibility. One thinks of the vigorous fetal clonisms in this connection—the "kicking" that every pregnant woman feels. Fetal pulsation must be affected within a spastic maternal uterus, and the fetus or infant itself will reflect in its vitality and future responses the effects of living and growing in that environment. Reich believed that such factors should not be overlooked in considerations of heredity in cancer.

Reich's Orgone Therapy of Cancer (1941-1945)

It will be recalled that the effect of the bions on the T-bacilli formed the basis for the experimental treatment of cancer in mice. Many months of work were required to show that the primary mechanism underlying the success of the bions in destroying tumor tissue and prolonging life was that of charging the cancer-prone mouse's bioenergetically weakened erythrocytes. It is the mouse's own erythrocytes which help to destroy the cancer cells (3, p. 253).

The *untreated* mouse dies using up the available charge of its erythrocytes in combatting the disease. In the *treated* mouse this is deferred by providing additional energy from the outside, i.e., via the charged bions. Until the winter of 1939-1940, the existence of the atmospheric orgone energy was unsuspected. After its discovery in the summer of 1940 the experiments were repeated utilizing the atmospheric orgone accumulator instead of injections of bions. Not only was this far more convenient, but the results were superior. Further, it opened the way for treating human subjects without the risks of injecting foreign (albeit sterilized) substances but, instead, by recharging them directly with the atmospheric orgone energy. Between 1941 and 1945, Reich treated and followed fifteen cases of cancer, including malignancies of the brain, breast, stomach, adrenal, ovary, rectum, bladder, and esophagus. Thirteen were diagnosed in hospitals and two by Reich himself. Two had had previous X-ray therapy. All had metastases, advanced cachexia and were considered incurable by conventional methods; they came to Reich as a last resort.

Diagnostic Considerations in the Cancer Biopathy

As we have seen, the difference between health and cancer does not lie solely in the absence of T-bacilli, but in the *orgonotic* charge of the organism. In health the capacity to destroy the T-bacilli is vigorous, while the tendency of the blood and tissues to break down into T-bacilli is very slight. In the shrinking biopathy disintegration into T-bacilli occurs easily and rapidly.* The conclusion is that the potential for putrid disintegration and cancer is *universal,* but is effectively dealt with so long as the blood and tissues are strongly charged with the orgone or life energy. The carcinomatons shrinking biopathy is in reality a premature and accelerated form of a natural process—that of death and decay. The cancer cell arises out of decaying tissue in an as yet living host.

Reich's approach to the biopathies, developing as it did, spontaneously transcended the boundaries between psychiatry, medicine, and biology. In each case a standard medical history and physical examination were obtained. Appropriate laboratory and X-ray studies were used to evaluate the patient and the effects of treatment. But, in addition the following were of vital interest:

1. Patients were evaluated in terms of their emotional health which, naturally, included a history of sexual functioning. Character analytic vegetotherapy was used as an investigatory as well as a therapeutic tool.
2. Tissues and excretions were examined in the *live* state and at *high power* for evidence of T-bacilli, abnormal cell forms, and bionous disintegration.†
3. Blood was examined periodically to ascertain its biological resistance to disintegration—the Reich blood test.

---

* One can see here the core of validity to the immunologic concept of cancer which says that the difference between cancer and non-cancer is the capacity for immunologic differentiation i.e. the individual who does not develop cancer is the one who "recognizes" the cancer cell as immunologically "foreign." In healthy individuals, the blood, tissues, and excreta must be allowed to disintegrate over extended periods before T-bacilli are obtained. "Immunity" lies in the stronger orgonotic charge of the organism. The relationship between the *orgonotic* potency and the *immunologic potency* of the lymphocyte is probably highly significant.

† These may be evidence *before* the Papanicolou preparations are positive.

The precise significance of the Reich Blood Test in the various somatic biopathies remains for future research to determine. Its meaning with regard to the bioenergetic state of the organism in general and in relation to cancer is clear and worth some elaboration.

As we have seen from the discussion of the vegetative antithesis, the blood vascular system is a major mechanism of organismic pulsation. Under high magnification (2000–5000x), the erythrocyte itself can be seen to pulsate vividly. If exposed to adrenergic stimulation the red cell contracts. In the chronic sympathecotonia of the cancer biopathy, the erythrocyte is already contracted. If the disease has progressed to the phase of shrinking, a fresh specimen may reveal many of the erythrocytes to have a rounded up or assumed a spherical configuration, as well as other distortions of shape; bionous disintegration may already be extensive. The energy field around each cell is narrow, and the blue color inside the cell periphery is pale, reflecting a low energy charge. Even before the development of a clinically visible or palpable tumor, the patient's erythrocytes will be seen to desintegrate rapidly, predominantly into T-bacilli. In advanced cases, blood inoculated on bouillion will produce a growth of T-bacilli in days to weeks. This appears as a thin, green-blue margin at the periphery of the culture medium; it has a characteristic ammoniacal odor. Autoclavation of the blood produces a friable clot which on microscopic examination reveals mostly T-bacilli. These are the essentials of what Reich termed the "T-reaction" of blood.

In healthy vigorous blood the erythrocytes appear ovoid and expanded with a wide vivid field and an intense blue coloration within the periphery. They disintegrate into the large blue, highly radiant bions but they do so after enduring intact for thirty minutes or longer. A significant number of cells will survive autoclavation in a recognizable state of preservation, the remainder breaking down into large bions. Grossly, the clot which forms exhibits good cohesiveness; these are the major features of the B-reaction. Strongly charged cells have the capacity to immobilize, agglutinate, and kill T-bacilli as well as bacteria; however, in the process the cells' disintegration into bions is accelerated. The red cell is thus destroyed in the process of combatting the T-bacillus in identical manner to the tissue cell (see Origin of the Cancer Cell above.)

Certain conclusions arose from experience with the Reich blood test which should be emphasized:

1. The RBC appears to reflect the level of energetic charge of the total organism as well as its capacity to hold that charge. Even in vigorous individuals, extreme fatigue or emotional depression may modify the typical B-reaction, e.g., produce faster breakdown, but they do not produce the fullblown T-reaction of the shrinking biopathy. One may therefore expect infinite gradations between the extreme B or T-reactions.

2. The test allows one to monitor the most important parameter in the

course of the cancer disease as well as evaluate the response to orgone therapy: the state of charge.

3. The test supports the postulate that the biological energy normally functions to hold the organism together or, conversely, that the energetic stagnation and depletion which result from the loss of pulsation leads to an accelerated disintegration of the cells. The test may explain the anemias sometimes seen in cancer in which hemorrhage and bone marrow infiltration cannot be implicated. In reversing the T-reaction in the blood, depressed hemoglobin values were found to rise. While the hemoglobin is not a criterion of the biological vigor of the blood, its improvement in these cases derives from the reduced tendency of the erythrocytes to disintegrate prematurely. It is now well known that the erythrocyte life span may be reduced in cancer. One explanation for this is that it is an angiopathic hemolytic effect due to circulation through the abnormal vasculature in the tumor mass. However, the finding of the T-reaction in the erythrocytes even *before* a tumor develops suggests that this is not necessarily the case.

4. The T-bacillus is inextricably involved in the cancer process. The T-reaction is typical of an advanced cancer biopathy; it "is often present *before* any symptoms of anemia, and can betray the cancer process long before the development of a palpable or visible tumor" (3, p. 32). It reflects bioenergetic (orgonotic) depletion.

Procedure

Reich believed that a genuine *cure* of the cancer disease implies the capacity to attack the processes of shrinking and putrefaction—in effect a premature *dying* which begins with the chronic sympathetic tone typical of all biopathies and progresses to a generalized T-reaction recognizable in the blood. Since the shrinking biopathy may long precede the appearance of the tumor, the diagnosis of the local tumor (regardless of the presence or absence of metastases) always comes very late in the disease. The process of putrefaction and its causes are untouched by local tumor therapy.* The task for a real cure becomes that of enhancing orgonotic charge, expansion, and pulsation in the organism—in brief, to further the B-reaction and decrease or reverse the T-reaction. The following table, modified from Reich, contrasts these two reactions across a spectrum of vital functions (3, p. 244–45). One may appreciate the reality of his assertion that the cancer problem is identical with the infinitely difficult problem of the biological connection between life and death. Of course, in actual experience most pa-

* In this connection one can see a further rationality to the recent immunotherapeutic approaches such as B.C.G. and interferon. One might view these treatments as a shift in emphasis in the direction of the cancer as a *general* disturbance rather than equating the disease with the tumor itself.

TABLE 6-1. Comparison of B- and T-Reactions

	B-REACTION	T-REACTION
1. Total Organism	Elastically erect Tonus good. No spasm and clonisms Capacity for pleasure	Shrunken. Flaccid or hypertonic Spasms and clonismus Feeling of weakness Incapacity for pleasure; Pleasure anxiety
2. Skin	Warm, glowing, good turgor; capacity for warm sweating	Cold, clammy, pale poor turgor, tendency toward *cold* sweating
3. Musculature	Relaxed but capable of alternating tension and relaxation; strong: absence of muscular armor	Chronically tense or flaccid and atrophic; obesity may be common; general musculature armor
	Lively peristalsis Facial expression lively variable	Constipation, hemmorrhoids; face rigid, mask-like; expression of dying
4. Blood	See Reich blood test above	
5. Cardiovas- cular System	Pulse regular, quiet and strong	Pulse irregular, abnormally fast or slow, weak: hypo or hypertension.
6. Tissues	Vigorous turgor	Poor turgor, shrinking bi- onous structure or rapid bionous disintegration in KCL
7. Eyes	Bright, lively pupillary reactions.	Dull, "far away" expression Pupil reactions sluggish; pupils often dilated; eye balls protruding or sunken
8. Respiration	*Full* respiration with pause after expiration; free pulsation of thorax; ca- pacity for genital pleasure sensations after each ex- piration	Inhibited, incomplete expira- tion, pause after *inspiration*. Fixation in inspiratory atti- tude (anxiety); no genital pleasure after expiration
9. Orgasm	Regularly occurring, full body convulsion; no sexual stasis	Absent or disturbed
10. Orgone energy field around organism	Wide, variable	Narrow or absent

tients exhibit some manifestations of both reactions, but on the whole one or the other predominates. The therapeutic problem is that of reversing the "slow living death," a living death which is in no way meant as a metaphor.

Reich's approach consisted of full-scale orgone therapy* including:

1. *Daily patient use of the orgone accumulator:* Unfortunately space does not permit a full discussion of the orgone accumulator. Its design came from Reich's efforts to confine the radiation from the SAPA bions, thereby making it easier to visualize and study. For the treatment of human cancer, the enclosure was made large enough to accommodate a seated patient.

2. *Character-analytic vegetotherapy:* Before treatment is begun on any kind of patient one obtains an *historical* evaluation of the patients' overall functioning, past and present, including a medical review. This initial interview ascertains the patient's symptoms and, most importantly, his suitability for therapy. A biophysical examination is conducted to determine the location, extent, and severity of blocks and the patient's reactions when they are challenged. All these facets of the history and biophysical exam contribute to the diagnosis and prognosis.

The therapeutic work is generally begun *farthest* from the genital: the head, working downward as each segment is cleared. The purpose is to gradually accustom the patient to the increasing excitation as the armorings are removed. The deepest sexual conflicts and hence the greatest anxiety are bound up in the pelvic blocks and thus they are the last to be dealt with. The technique consists of three components:

a. *Freeing up respiration.* This gets energy moving and increases excitation to the level of making contact with the emotions. In itself, freer respiration will overcome certain blocks and uncover others; the spontaneous expression of affect simply with respiration is a common experience.

b. *Attacking the muscular armor directly.* This is accomplished by direct pressure on spastic muscles near their origins or insertions. This causes maximal contraction and then relaxation: if the patient is prepared by adequate respiration, the relaxation is accompanied by a release of emotion. Pain is neither the purpose of nor the "prime mover" in this procedure. One may in many instances dissolve the armor by simply *having the patient do the right thing at the right time,* e.g., making faces, screaming, punching or kicking the couch, rolling the eyes, winking, or even smiling. Each segment is dealt with in a particular manner, at the same time allowing for individual requirements.

c. *Character analysis.* By exposing and overcoming the negative transferance, resistances are eliminated and a *genuine* positive transferance become possible toward the end of treatment. In this way the patient can become more open and helpful in the therapy.

---

* In present day usage, orgone therapy is functionally identical to character-analytic vegetotherapy.

Results and Conclusions

Reich's experience with cancer was more extensive than the fifteen cases reported here. He deliberately chose the worst cases for his account in *The Cancer Biopathy* so as to discourage the impression that the orgone therapy was a "cure-all"—That it could "cure" cancer under any circumstances. Indeed, it was an understanding of the *failures* which proved more instructive. In the series cited, the course of treatment ranged from two to eight months with the following result:

1. In all cases there was relief from pain, permitting reduction or elimination of the use of morphine and other analgesics.
2. In all cases there was a decrease in the size of the tumors and a general improvement in condition. Breast tumors disappeared in all those cases so afflicted.
3. In four cases there was recalcification of metastatic lytic bone lesions on follow-up films.
4. In three cases there was prolongation of life; in six, there was prolongation of from 5–12 months beyond expectations with a distinct improvement in the quality of life.
5. In six cases the process of shrinking was arrested by clinical and Reich blood test criteria. Six patients were able to resume working.
6. Five of the surgically inoperable cases were alive and in tolerably good to good states of health two years after treatment.

If one considers that these patients were near death at the outset, that no dangerous drugs, irradiation, or surgery were used and the essential simplicity of the treatment, the results are indeed astonishing and unprecedented. Nevertheless, Reich consistently emphasized that destruction of the local tumor and the T-bacilli would still only constitute *symptomatic* treatment. The shrinking biopathy had to be mastered, otherwise, the possibility of a relapse would always exist. The problem which occurred repeatedly in his experience with cancer patients was that of a particularly severe reaction to the therapeutic process of expansion. Sexual and characterologic resignation are at the foundation of the shrinking biopathy; all of the patients showed a striking lack of libido. As treatment succeeded in recharging the organism, sexual excitation again became possible, but in an organism biophysically still incapable of tolerating it; his characterologic disease, furthermore prevented the patient from doing anything about it.* Just as the patient appeared to be breaking through toward health there would ensue a violent, unforeseen physical collapse.

---

* The prevailing sex-negative social attitudes often provided the final blow. In some instances, despite obvious improvement in the patients, the hostile attitudes of relatives and physicians interfered with treatment.

All the hard-won gains in functioning would seem to evaporate. A shock-like state, a loss of equilibrium, and *a profound terror of falling* would cause the patient to take to his bed. Subjective and objective clinical impressions were that the patient was *dying*. Reich called this "falling anxiety" and attributed it to a sudden withdrawal of energy from the periphery of the organism—in effect an acute anorgonotic attack. Falling anxiety and anorgonia may occur to some extent in any biopathy as a consequence of severe pleasure anxiety, but unlike these other conditions, in cancer it is an ultimate expression of the shrinking process and the organism is often unable to recover; death may actually result. Regardless of the manner in which it presents, it is a major obstacle to complete cure. For this reason Reich predicted that the prevention of cancer would prove easier than curing a fully developed case.* The prognosis in cancer thus improved to the extent that the capacity for emotional and sexual excitation survive in the patient, i.e., the capacity for pulsation. Put in another way: a certain minimum of vigor in the organism must be required if it is to be capable of accepting and holding a charge. A simple experiment illustrated this:

Grass infusions placed in the orgone accumulator showed little or no protozoal development whereas normally they grow to abundance in two to five days. If an older disintegrated infusion is placed in the accumulator, the growth of the protozoa is not influenced. In order to prevent or eliminate protozoal or bacterial development, a viable orgonotic system capable of being charged is necessary.

The Situation Today

It is important to reemphasize that Reich did not claim to have cured cancer, at least according to his own rigorous criteria. His claim *is* to have comprehended the essential causes and central mechanisms of the disease, thereby opening the way to a genuine cure. The orgone therapy was remarkable in that it reversed for a time a premature dying process; certainly by conventional medical standards some of these cases would have been called "cures." Tumors, metastases and anemias were eliminated, the quality of life considerably improved and life itself prolonged. Furthermore this was accomplished in large part through the disturbingly simple expedient of utilizing a naturally occurring atmospheric energy. In most of the cases cited, however, the patients ultimately succumbed to their disease or to a related complication. The reasons for this lie in the nature of the shrinking process and its ramifications. The marked tendency for the

* The seriousness of this problem can only be appreciated by reading Reich's cancer cases. I cannot convey here the emotional impact of these narratives. I would venture to say that no serious cancer researcher who can conceive of an emotional cause in cancer should fail to review them.

cancer patient to fall apart at the point of breakthrough of strong genital excitation carried with it the danger of an accelerated course and death. Another problem which Reich identified but was not fully able to overcome was the finding that in both experimental cancer-prone mice and human subjects death had been shown to occur in some cases because the liver, kidneys, and reticuloendothelial system were unable to cope with the products of tumor breakdown. The excretory systems were literally choked with debris from destruction of the tumor, i.e., the successful treatment of the tumor could have a fatal outcome. For this reason he could see a role for limited surgery in the orgonomic treatment of cancer. Surgical elimination of tumor mass might also serve to remove a drain on the patients already depleted bioenergetic resources. Obviously removal of the tumor may be absolutely essential in those cases where it endangers a vital function.

There are other considerations. Since the time of Reich's original work in cancer and orgone physics, over three thousand nuclear devices have been detonated in the earth's atmosphere and crust. There are many nuclear power plants operating; the sources of high-voltage electricity and electromagnetic radiation have multiplied. This has had a profound effect on the atmospheric orgone which penetrates everything and from which there is no shielding. Nuclear and electromagnetic energies cause an irritation of the orgone which makes it behave in an abnormal way. The effects of this interaction have been fully described by Reich (20). In certain respects these effects on humans resemble low-level radiation sickness, e.g., irritability, loss of equilibrium, nausea and vomiting, diarrhea, etc. The atmosphere shows signs of hyperexcitation, e.g., increased tornado activity, hurricanes, earthquakes, and extremes of weather such as droughts. Reich termed these "Oranur" effects.* These effects may also have something to do with the absolute increase in the incidence of cancer noted by epidemiologists. In recent years there have been strong indictments of the pollution of the air and water in the epidemiology of cancer. Reich, for example, was able to demonstrate the generation of T-bacilli from soot and noted the possible connection to the coal tar cancer produced experimentally in mice. A good argument could be made for the overwhelming of the organism, particularly if its orgonotic strength is "borderline," by respired and ingested carcinogens.† The controversial issue of low-level radiation is

---

* *Oranur* is a term derived from the Orgonomic Anti-Nuclear Radiation Project, an experiment Reich began in 1950 to determine if the orgone energy could be used as an antidote against nuclear radiation sickness.

† By our definition a carcinogen is any exogenous chemical, physical, or radiating agent which is capable of inducing signifcant bionous disintegration of tissue. However, we would say' that in ordinary circumstances the orgonotic vigor of the organism would be a major determinant as to whether or not the agent would prove carcinogenic in any particular individual. The B or T proclivity is a major determinant of carcinogenicity.

an interesting case in regard to radioactive pollution. Those who argue that it causes cancer and leukemia cite the positive correlation between the incidence of these disorders and the history of exposure. Their opponents point out that only high level radiation dosages have been proven to cause leukemia, and that the long latent period between low-level exposure and the onset of the disease mitigates against it as a causal factor. Reich found that a powerful Oranur effect can occur with a relatively small source of nuclear radiation* in the presence of a high orgone charge, e.g., the orgone accumulator. Furthermore, the irritation of the orgone continues long after the source is removed and the effect is propagated through the atmosphere. Mice kept in or near accumulators, but at considerable distance from the radioactive source (e.g. in a separate building), died with leukemia in the Oranur experiments. These findings could prove highly significant in the resolution of the problem of low-level radiation.

Even more important right now is the comprehension of cancer as a disease of our society and civilization, because this is the key to its *prevention*. If the role of the disturbed sex economy in this and the other biopathies continues to be ignored, then in our view hope for their prevention would appear dim. It is evident that, despite the current lively and widespread interest in Reich, his concepts have been largely misunderstood, distorted, and even derided. Ironically, the most destructive criticisms often come from those with no firsthand knowledge of his work. A calm, thorough consideration of Reich's work would reveal him to be a serious, brilliant, highly diversified and qualified scientist. His findings in the etiology and treatment of cancer deserve the most careful scrutiny and development.

There are some encouraging signs. The *aura,* which is identical to the orgone energy field around living subjects, has been visualized by Kirlian photography and other mehtods. It has also been detected with field meters. Recent findings in astrophysics have raised questions about the "emptiness" of space. Reich believed that the old idea of the "ether" is closer to the truth: the atmosphere and outer space are filled with the orgone. There is more and more data from independent sources accumulating which support a wide variety of Reich's discoveries. And, of course, there is the present volume which indicates that clinicians and researchers are willing to consider seriously an emotional causation in cancer. In time we may come to appreciate the full richness of Reich's legacy.

Bibliography

The following bibliography in no sense includes a comprehensive listing of Reich's work. It will provide the reader with complete treatments of sub-

* In the Oranur project Reich used a 1 mgm radium needle.

jects only touched upon in the present chapter. While the "Basic Antithesis of Vegetative Life" is dealt with in references 4 and 5, the original paper (written in German in 1934), which has been translated into English and serialized in volumes 1 and 2 of the *Journal of Orgonomy,* is much richer in detail and development. The same applies to the translation "The Experimental Investigation of the Electrical Function of Sexuality and Anxiety" (1937) and "The Bions" (1938), which are alluded to in references 2 and 3. These serialized translations will be found to be highly informative, particularly to those interested in the details of equipment, protocol, and methodologic approach to the experiments. They are not, however, intended to replace the discussions to be found in volumes 1 and 2 of *The Discovery of the Orgone.*

1. REICH, W. *Character Analysis.* New York: Noonday Press, 1962.

2. REICH, W. *The Discovery of the Orgone:* Vol. 1, *The Function of the Orgasm,* New York: Noonday Press, 1961.

3. REICH, W. *The Discovery of the Orgone:* Vol. 2, *The Cancer Biopathy,* New York: Orgone Institute Press, 1948.

4. REICH, W. "The Basic Antithesis of Vegetative Life" (part 1), *Journal of Orgonomy* 1:4–22, Nov. 1967.

5. REICH, W. "The Basic Antithesis of Vegetative Life" (part 2), *Journal of Orgonomy* 2:5–23, Mar. 1968.

6. REICH, W. "The Orgasm as an Electric Discharge," *Journal of Orgonomy* 2:117–131, Nov. 1968.

7. REICH, W. "Experimental Investigation of the Electrical Functions of Sexuality and Anxiety" (Part 1), *Journal of Orgonomy,* Mar. 1969.

8. REICH, W. "Experimental Investigation of the Electrical Functions of Sexuality and Anxiety" (Part 2), *Journal of Orgonomy* 3:132–154, Nov. 1969.

9. REICH, W. "The Bions: An Investigation into the Origin of Life" (Part 1), *Journal of Orgonomy* 10:5–56, May 1976.

10. REICH, W. "The Bions: An Investigation into the Origin of Life" (Part 2), *Journal of Orgonomy* 10:156–171, Nov. 1976.

10a. REICH, W. "The Bions: An Investigation into the Origin of Life" (Part 2, continued), *Journal of Orgonomy* 12:6–15, May 1978.

11. REICH, W. "The Bions: An Investigation into the Origin of Life" (Part 3), *Journal of Orgonomy* 11:4–14, May 1977.

11a. REICH, W. "The Bions: An Investigation into the Origin of Life" (Part 3, continued), *Journal of Orgonomy* 12:149–165, Nov. 1978.

11b. REICH, W. "The Bions: An Investigation into the Origin of Life" (Part 3, continued), *Journal of Orgonomy* 13:5–30, May 1979.

12. RAPHAEL, C. M., and MACDONALD, H. E. "Orgonomic Diagnosis of Cancer Biopathy." A compilation based on a course on cancer given by Wilhelm Reich, M.D. at Organon, Rangely, Maine, during July and August, 1950. *Orgone Energy Bulletin* IV:66–125, April, 1952.

13. BAKER, E. F. *Man in the Trap,* New York: Macmillan, 1967.

14. ROSENBLUM, C. F. "The Temperature Difference: Experimental Protocol," *Journal of Orgonomy* 6:61, May, 1972.

15. ROSENBLUM, C. F. "The Electroscope" (Part 1), *Journal of Orgonomy* 3:188, Nov. 1969.

16. ROSENBLUM, C. F. "The Electroscope" (Part 2), *Journal of Orgonomy* 4:79, May 1970.

17. ROSENBLUM, C. F. "The Electroscope" (Part 3), *Journal of Orgonomy* 10:57, May 1976.

18. BAKER, C. F. "The Electroscope" (Part 4), *Journal of Orgonomy* 11:35, May 1977.

19. BASTION, H. C. *The Origin of Life.* G. P. Putnam's Sons, New York. The Knickerbocker Press, 1911.

20. REICH, W. "The Oranur Experiment;" First Report (1947-1951). *Orgone Energy Bulletin* III: 185-344. October 1951.

21. BAHNSON, C. B.; and BAHNSON, M. G. "Denial and Repression of Primitive Impulses and of Disturbing Emotions in Patients with Malignant Neoplasms." In *Psychosomatic Aspects of Neoplastic Disease,* edited by D. M. Kissen and L. L. Jeshan, p. 42-62. Pitman. London, England, 1964.

22. GINGERELLI, J. A.; and KIRKNER, F. J., editors. *Psychological Variables in Human Cancer.* University of California Press, Berkeley and Los Angeles, 1954.

23. LESHAN, L. "Psychological States as Factors in the Development of Malignant Disease: A Critical Review." *Journal of the National Cancer Institute,* vol. 22, pp. 1-18, 1959.

7 Exploring the Relationship Between Personality and Cancer

Stephen A. Appelbaum

In the last three years I have worked in psychotherapy with some twenty-five cancer patients in order to explore the possible relationship between personality and cancer, and if possible to arrest or reverse the cancer. Until recently nothing had prepared me for this task, neither formal academic training, clinical experience, or a culture that encouraged the study of the relationship between personality and cancer. I do remember, as a graduate student, reading about such a possibility. For example, a psychologist was able to predict from the Rorschach test whether a patient would have slow-growing or fast-growing tumors (Klopfer, 1957). Like many others I was temporarily intrigued, but then put it aside in a sort of "ho-hum, that's interesting" compartment of my mind. The proximal cause of my finally pursuing the personality-cancer relationship was a patient's developing cancer in the midst of two suicide attempts. This juxtaposition reminded me that I had heard, and again filed away for future reference, the story of a local patient having overcome cancer by means of psychological treatment. Such treatment included the recognition that cancer could be caused or maintained in order to solve emotional problems, that cancer could be a suicidal equivalent. This patient had used, in conjunction with the recognition and working through of that idea, a meditation-visualization procedure, the whole approach put together by Carl Simonton, a radiation therapist, and Stephanie Simonton, a psychologist.

I probably would not have remembered and used that information if in recent years it had not had a cultural context, an atmosphere that encouraged pursuing a treatment modality for cancer that for many people seems unlikely, if not bizarre. This supportive culture began in the 1960s, as part of the counterculture revolution of those times and includes, along

This work was generously and graciously supported by the Menninger Foundation.

with many new ideas applicable to just about all of our institutions, an alternative medicine often called "holistic medicine."

Many of the differences between conventional and holistic medicine bear directly upon the personality-cancer issue. In conventional medicine the major responsibility for treatment is given to and accepted by the physician. The patient comes with symptoms, and the physician assumes the task of diagnosing and treating those symptoms. The interpersonal mode is between subject and object, the physician doing something to or for the patient, who accepts what is done to or for him. In conventional medicine the focus is on the body. The mind, if attended to at all, is split off into the specialty of psychiatry. The word "holistic," as applied to the new medicine, reflects the understanding that the organism, the person, functions as a unit—body, mind, and spirit are conceived of as one. Thus, feelings, imagination, creativity, values, ethics, are all implicated in illness. Practitioners of conventional medicine often overlook many of the ways that mind can influence body, such as through meditation, visualization, biofeedback, or positive thinking, while holistic medicine explores and exploits these procedures. In conventional medicine hope for the future lies in new inventions, drugs, surgical techniques. In holistic medicine reliance is placed on old wisdoms, herbs, homeopathy, naturopathy, and Oriental medicine. In conventional medicine, despite its heavy empirical bent, practitioners try to implement their stated belief in the need for research and experimentation before application. Practitioners of holistic medicine are more frankly empirical, more willing to try anything. Conventional medicine is more hierarchically organized, its wisdom is held apart, as through the use of technical language. In holistic medicine, information is made freely available; indeed the patient is encouraged and relied upon to acquaint himself with knowledge about his illness and sometimes to contribute to that knowledge. In conventional medicine illness and cure are central, and medical forces are brought into play mainly in response to pathology. In holistic medicine illness is conceived of as one in a series of wide-ranging problems in living; medicine is enlisted both to prevent illness and to improve the quality of living even in the absence of clinical pathology. In conventional medicine causes are largely conceived of in physiological terms, while in holistic medicine causes rooted in self and behavior are dealt with. In conventional medicine consciousness is in the body, a function of the brain; the body is superordinate, and its boundaries are physical and observable. In holistic medicine the body is a subordinate expression of consciousness; the body may die but consciousness may go on. Instead of being solid, physical and boundaried, the body is a congealing of energies that are in constant flux, and its energies transcend observable boundaries, as can be seen in Kirlian photography.

Holistic medicine is one of the many expressions of the "consciousness-raising," or "human potential" movement, such names denoting crystallized ideas and practices of the counterculture. In general, the counter-culture is characterized by rebellion, revisionism, questioning of all establishments, and openness to all ideas alternative to conventionally established ones. Providing an invitation to speculation, imagination, and novelty, it is thus receptive to the personality-cancer relationship. The counterculture is characterized also by hope, a belief that our limitations are self-imposed, that we systematically minimize our potential for wisdom, health, physical feats, and ultimately happiness. We do this, in part, by turning over responsibility to other people and fixed systems of thought, thus overlooking our own capabilities, which if exploited, can create new realities, can transcend conventional expectations. In principle, then, there are no hopeless situations, no incurable diseases.

My participation in the human potential movement came about through my wish to learn about the psychotherapeutic arm of the counterculture, the new or alternative psychotherapies. For over four years, in-between my duties at the Menninger Foundation, I studied and experienced a panoply of these therapies, the record of which is *Out in Inner Space—A Psychoanalyst Explores the New Therapies* (1979).

In general the Simontons believe that undue stress interferes with the immune system, thus allowing the growth and proliferation of cancer cells that are ever-present in the body. By the same token, good feelings, coincident with a lessening of stress, increase the efficiency of the immune system and enable the body to destroy cancer cells. A detailed explication of the work of the Simontons is now available in their book, *Getting Well Again* (1978). Their approach can be divided into two parts. The first is a meditation-visualization procedure based on yoga. The person is assumed to have the capacity to control functions usually regarded as beyond conscious control, and to create the reality he wishes for through visualizing it while in the altered state of consciousness called meditation. The Simontons provide cancer patients with a cassette tape which guides them through a meditation procedure that includes encouraging the cancer patient to visualize the cancer being destroyed by the body's defenses.

Several kinds of meditation have been shown to change physiological readings in the direction of greater efficiency of bodily functions, which plausibly aids the body in fighting disease (Benson, 1975). The contribution of imagery to health is not yet as well substantiated, though there are many anecdotal reports and observations of changes in the direction of health as the apparent result of creating mental images. I know, for example, a chemotherapy patient who believes that she has avoided losing her hair through systematic imagery of her hair remaining full. I know of a woman who created the image of herself reacting with distaste towards sweets, and losing a good deal of weight as a result.

The second part of the Simonton program stems from the belief that cancer represents an attempt to solve life problems, a last-ditch despairing alternative to what seems an otherwise hopeless situation. It follows, then, that treatment of cancer should include a psychotherapeutic attempt to enable the patient to develop other and better solutions to problems in living, thus reducing stress and encouraging health-producing good feelings.

As of January 1, 1978, the Simontons offer the following statistics: Of 139 patients (20 of the original sample of 159 were lost to follow-up evaluation) 55% (76) died; 22% (14) of the living 63 show no evidence of disease, 19% (12) show tumor regression, 27% (17) have their disease stabilized, and 32% (20) show new tumor growth. 51% (32) have resumed all their previous activities, 25% (16) resumed three-quarters, 9.5% (6) resumed one-half, 9.5% (6) resumed one-quarter, 1.5% (1) resumed less than one-quarter, and 3% (2) are hospitalized. The living patients have exceeded two times the national average for living after diagnosis (24 as against 12 months). Even those who died lived 1½ times longer than the national average. The patients included in these statistics were all judged medically incurable before coming to the Simontons, so changes for the better could not likely be ascribed to previous medical treatment.

These statistics have to be read in the light of some special considerations. Patients who seek out unconventional treatments, who are willing to apply themselves to the Simonton program, are likely to be "fighters," more highly motivated than the general run of patients. Many physicians have informally observed that highly motivated patients tend to do better than depressed or compliant ones. This informal observation seems to hold true particularly with cancer patients, among whom it seems that nice guys finish last. The Simonton patients are better educated and are from a higher socioeconomic class than the general population. They therefore may be better physically cared for and nourished than the general run of cancer patients.

There is much in the Simonton approach that could be called "placebo," or "suggestion." In contast to many impersonal, strictly medical contexts, Simonton patients receive much personal attention in an atmosphere of warmth and optimism. The assertion that people have control over their illness, though shocking at first to some patients who feel they are being blamed for their illness, carries with it the recognition that if one caused his or her disease, then one can overcome it. Borrowing heavily from Gestalt therapy, transactional analysis, learning theory, and the application of conscious intention, the Simonton approach maximizes the mobilization of energy and effort while paying relatively less attention to matters outside of awareness, to the unconscious. While the relatively short time of psychotherapy made available to Simonton patients may prevent them from working out emotional distress and unconscious conflict, the very shortness of time may serve to muster all available capabilities quickly (Appelbaum, 1975). In so doing it may maximize an inspirational, placebo effect.

As I observed the vicissitudes of the Simonton patients, I often thought that if a little psychotherapy was helpful, would more psychotherapy be more helpful? I wondered whether more thoroughgoing work, over an extended period, with the unconscious, defenses, resistances, and character attitudes might possibly resolve conflicts in cancer patients, as occurs in non-cancer patients, and effect the disease.

I began my association with the Simontons by way of telephone supervision of the patient who temporally combined cancer and suicide attempts. I went on to participate in their training programs, including a week spent with them and their patients in their live-in therapeutic retreat, finally intermittently participating with them in the presentation and teaching of their work. On occasion I offered seminars to them and their staff on the psychoanalytic point of view. Their interest in that approach crystallized the issue as to whether one kind of psychotherapy characterized by a particular set of conditions would be more or less effective in the treatment of cancer patients. What that boiled down to, practically speaking, was how effective I, as a psychoanalyst working mostly in private practice, would be in applying the basics of the Simonton treatment as amended by myself. And so it was that I began treating cancer patients with psychotherapy. What had seemed almost unthinkable a few years previously was now a reality. What the dimensions of that reality were I hoped to find out.

Could what I resolved to do be considered an outcome study, an attempt to answer the question whether the general Simonton approach to the treatment of cancer, as implemented by myself with attendant differences, would result in cure? Hardly. In order to answer such a question, certain rules would have had to be observed: If one were to generalize about all cancers, then all cancers would have to be worked with. The dozens of cancers, after all, have differences in prognosis, course, possible etiology, and more. The number of people treated would have to be sufficiently large in each category to minimize the possibilities that results were merely chance. Diagnoses would have to be unequivocally established, as would indices of improvement or cure. Possibly therapeutic influences other than what I was doing would have to be controlled, as for example, the effects of conventional medical treatment. If there could not be a matched control group whose outcome could be observed to be different from the experimental group, then at least the expectations for the experimental subjects, serving in effect as their own controls, should be clearly established medically. To give the method an adequate try the patient should be treated as often and as long as would be optimal. Should the patients be cured, and influences other than the putative psychotherapeutic procedure be controlled, knowledge would be greatly enhanced if one could parcel out the various possible aspects of the procedure that might have made the difference—the interpersonal relationship, insight, extension of hope, suggestion, the placebo effect, the relative contribution of meditation-visualization, and other aspects of psychotherapeutic work. Those patients whose disease was arrested, reversed, or seemingly eradicated would have to be judged after a sufficient time so that the durability of such changes could be established. Should patients appear to be getting worse, a sufficient time would be required in order to establish whether their decline would continue.

In my work none of these conditions was adequately attended to, and so it would be erroneous to draw hard-and-fast conclusions as to the outcome of my therapeutic approach, its effectiveness in curing cancer, and by implication the accuracy of the theory on which it is based. Rather, this exploration falls in the tradition of the amassing of observations providing conditions for hypotheses, and the gathering of whatever evidence is available under the circumstances with regard to building up some sense at least of the efficacy of the procedures.

Having said all this and after reflection, I must acknowledge that I was able only intermittently to maintain the implied scientific objectivity and dispassionateness. Rather, I wanted very much to believe in the effectiveness of a psychological approach to cancer, for mankind in general and all the more so for my patients as I involved myself in their struggles. Such wishes and feelings, and the consequent dangers of excessive disillusion and excessive enthusiasm, needed to be guarded against in the evaluation of therapeutic attempts.

The "selection of patients" (a rather formal term for a totally informal process) came about in a variety of ways. Some patients heard me speak on the subject, some read about it in *Out in Inner Space,* some were told about my work and interest by friends and occasionally by their physicians, several were referred by the Simontons. Those who followed through showed, by definition, a degree of motivation, perseverance, and probable capacity for hope.

Some patients never followed through. There can be many reasons for their not doing so, including the lack of "face validity" of the procedure for many people, the sharp divergence in such an approach from what has become conventional in the treatment of cancer, and probably the negative attitudes of friends and physicians. Yet the way they managed the situation made what is to me a convincing impression that, as with many suicidal people, their commitment was to hopelessness and despair, a yielding to lethality. If that impression is true, then it lends support to the assumption that the commitment of some cancer patients is to self-destructiveness, and by that token they find ways to avoid possibly helpful procedures. Typically such patients offered a tissue of rationalizations about why they could not pursue the treatment. Their attitude often seemed eerily out of joint with the reality of their situation.

One example of such an interaction is detailed in *Out in Inner Space* and in "The Refusal to Take One's Medicine" (Appelbaum, 1977). The man discussed there by his own reckoning was at the end of the time allotted to him, and yet his difficulties simply making and keeping an appointment were like those that might interfere with, for example, a date to play tennis. Here is a note that I dictated about another such patient following a phone conversation with her: Mrs. R. said that she had gotten my name from somebody, but she did not remember who it was. She told me that she had esophageal cancer, and had been given six to seven months to live. She asked whether it was true that I was associated with the work of the Simontons. When I told her that I was, she wondered how long in advance she would have to wait for an appointment. I said that I could see her the next day. Then she raised the question of money. I told her my usual fee, but added that for certain cancer cases I would charge much less. She insisted on knowing exactly how much I would charge, even for the first appointment. I assured her that I would charge only what she could afford, that we ought to meet and see what was what, and go from there. She insisted that she know the fee, although she said that her son told her it was "tacky" to discuss money with a doctor. I asked whether she had gotten the Simonton tapes, and she had not, although she knew about their availability. She said something about doing the tapes herself, and I thought she meant she wanted to duplicate my tapes, and I agreed to this. However, what she really meant was that she wanted to design her own tapes, so she turned down my offer of even lending her the Simonton tapes to listen to. She said that she would call me if she "needed a lifeline." I suggested that from what she had told me she needed a lifeline right now. She politely responded to that, but was adamant in saying that she was going to take care of things herself. I never heard from her again. For all I know she recovered from cancer, but I doubt it. I have come to recognize blandness, vague *non sequiturs,* seemingly drummed-up objections such as she displayed among those patients who seem bound and determined to avoid help and to succumb. Another man, from a distant city, returned a tape by mail on which the Simontons explained their work saying that it was broken upon arrival. Indeed a bit of plastic was broken off the cassette, but it played perfectly well. One can only surmise that he took advantage of the damage not to listen to the tape.

It is no surprise to any clinician that a number of patients have marked resistances as well as reality circumstances that preclude their proceeding with psychotherapy. But this group of patients seemed homogeneous in the quality of their disinclination to pursue psychological treatment. They gave me the feeling that I was grasping at thin air, trying to walk up an icy incline with nothing to hold onto. The Simontons and others have noticed what they call "nose dive," the rapid and unexpected demise of some patients when they are first apprised of the possibility that they have some say-so about their disease and that there may be a way of dealing with their disease involving their own thoughts and feelings. The patients cited here might be considered extremes of that group of people who will not be dissuaded from their adoption of cancer as a "solution." I am reminded, chillingly, of two youthful cancer patients, one adolescent who said inferentially but clearly that she could not contend with the challenges of growing older, and another latency-aged child who said flatly, "I am not going to get older."

From 1978 to 1980 I worked with 24 patients. They included eight males and 16 females. Seven patients were in their sixties. (Carl Simonton believes that emotional issues play less a role with patients over 60, as factors related to physiological aging become more determining. It also could be that people of that age tend to suffer many losses—of other people, opportunity, skills—and thus are increasingly subject to hopelessness.) Four patients were in their fifties. Seven were in their forties. Five were in their thirties, and one was an eight-year-old.

While at the Menninger Foundation, I saw in psychotherapy and monitored the meditation-visualization procedures of four patients, for extended periods of time, 163, 103, 60, and 36 sessions each. After leaving the Foundation for teaching and private practice, I worked with another 21 patients, two of whom are with me at the time of this writing, the remaining 19 of whom were seen from one session through 69 sessions. Eight of these 19 were seen only from one to four sessions, stopping for a variety of reasons. The remaining 11 patients were seen from eight to 69 sessions. Such variability does not offer much opportunity for generalizations on the basis of number of sessions.

A way of grouping the patients that is more clinically meaningful to me than simply the number of sessions is the degree to which the patients came to grips with the emotional conflicts that plausibly related to their developing or maintaining their cancer. Seven patients did that to a considerable degree, sometimes very quickly and despite the relatively few times that I saw them. Four patients were intermediate in this regard, and four never got to the point of connecting their personalities and motivations with their illness. Of the seven whom I thought I knew best, and with whom I could make the clearest inferential connections between their personalities and cancer, the two whom I saw most often are still, some three years later, free of disease. However, their cancers are such that it would not be necessarily expectable that they would have recurrences, and one in particular was also aggressively treated by non-psychological means. One whom I saw only a dozen times also took the Simonton program. She has defied medical predictions of longevity and recovered bodily functions thought to be irremediably paralyzed by her brain tumor. The remaining four of the seven are, for me, heartbreakers. I experienced with them the kind of clarity and therapeutic movement, the desired blend of insight and feelings along with a warm but task-oriented relationship, that one strives for in all psychotherapies. Moreover, they were beginning to translate their intrapsychic changes into changed behaviors, often with gratifying results, before their death.

The lesson I learned from these four patients is that such therapeutic experiences as we had are not identical with amelioration of cancer. As with psychotherapy in general, cure or change need not be isomorphic with internal consistency of theory. It did indeed happen that the operation seemed a success yet the patient died. However, that melancholy result need not be the rule. Are 69, 36, 20, and 12 sessions respectively sufficient to promote and maintain such physiological changes as may be necessary to reverse or cure cancer? How many sessions *are* necessary? And to answer such a question one would have to take into consideration the kind of cancer, the virulence of it, and its stage of development when the treatment began, among other things. It would be a lot to ask that cancers should be reversed in a relatively few hours of psychotherapy and a brief program of meditation when, for example, the cancers had already recurred, when there were active metastases (in the instances of my patients from lung, ovarian, and bowel cancers,) and other dread stigmata of a likely lethal disease. I learned there was no such magic, and I learned that no matter how rational I tried to be I wished for such magic.

Of four patients whose degree of insight and therapeutic movement was in the mid-range, one, a latency-aged child, continues to do well after 60 sessions; he has had continued chemical treatment. Two patients, one with lung cancer and one with indeterminate original site seemed to do well, but then suddenly sickened and died. The remaining one is doing well at this writing, but at the moment it is not long enough after her mastectomy, which precipitated her coming to see me, to judge.

Throughout the literature there frequently surfaces the observation that many cancer patients have considerable difficulty with the management of aggression. "Management of aggression" is a terribly general way to put it, and one can justifiably respond that most neurotics, if not most people, have more or less difficulty in the management of aggression. I have, however, come to experience a particular pattern and quality of this difficulty in a good many of these patients. In as many as 14 of the 24, with two more leaving a tendency in that direction, I am satisfied with regard to the following: The intolerance of these patients for anger in themselves, their fear of the fantasied repercussions of the expression of such anger, and the consequent submissiveness in the service of controlling such anger are excessive, clear, dominating, and determining of much of their behavior.

This difficulty acknowledging, contending with, and expressing aggression often showed itself strikingly in their visualizations, during meditation, of the white cells supposedly attacking the cancer cells with the aid of their medical treatment. One patient, for example, instead of visualizing an attack had the white corpuscles "washing over" the cancer. I drew the patient's attention to his having used such a loving image instead of an attacking, destroying image. The next image that he used was of the white corpuscles getting out their knives and cutting and dicing the cancer cells. I asked him to draw the image, and the knives were nowhere to be seen. "I just left the knives off," he said. Another patient could not bring herself at first to use words like "attack," or "destroy," and used images of clowns, as if to playfully minimize the destruction explicit in the task. These patients seemed to be protecting rather than destroying their cancers. Such intolerance of anger fits with the often stated informal observation of hospital and other medical personnel that the patients who succumb fastest to cancer are the nice ones, the agreeable, compliant, submissive ones, those who smile through their tears. The irritable, contentious patients do better. Thus the hypothesis of inhibited aggression set forth by others (Field, 1963; Bacon, Renneker and Cutler, 1952; Greer and Morris, 1975) receives additional support here.

Speculatively the hypothesis of inhibited aggression seems to trade on a kind of hydraulic conception of aggression, with blockages in its outward expression resulting in inner-directedness in the form of attack on one's self. When mortality rates for the fifty leading causes of death in the United States were correlated with an "anger-out" and "anger-in" dimension, the anger-out dimension correlated with hypertension while anger-in related to leukemia and aleukemia lymphatic neoplasms. (Field, 1963). Inner-directed attacks may be physical, as in the development of cancer, and they may take the form, as with many of these patients, of a constricted, "masochistic," often joyless and frequently unnecessarily burdensome way of life. One patient allowed herself to be physically manhandled and held accountable for a trifling incident that happened more than a decade previously. Another slaved away in a never-ending attempt to please family members, especially her mother, at great cost to herself, agonizing over the responsibilities that she had difficulty apportioning to others. Another kept finding ways of undercutting and minimizing such good fortune as would come her way. Still another uncomplainingly assumed excessive work responsibilities and blame, explaining her behavior with tortured rationalizations. Another patient had so rigidified the need to be agreeable that he found himself automatically, unthinkingly, nodding his head in agreement even before I had finished making a statement.

I administered a battery of psychological tests to eight of these patients, and a ninth had the same battery administered by another psychologist. In previous researches (Appelbaum and Holzman, 1962, Appelbaum and Colson, 1968) an association had been demonstrated between the so-called color-shading Rorschach test response and suicide in hospitalized psychiatric patients. The color-shading response is one in which the person defines a response in part because of its color and in part because of some characteristic such as texture based on the shadings in the color. Suicide in these researches was defined as any overt attempt, as well as completed suicides. Among my non-hospitalized, and in a way non-psychiatric, cancer patients there was only one who gave such a response. However, every one of the nine did have an "experience balance" that was weighted on the color side. The "experience balance" is a ratio of seeing people in movement ("M" response) as compared to using color to define a response. It has been taken to reflect the relative contribution to the personality of thought as against feeling, the capacity to establish ideational controls over overt behavior as against allowing behavior to take place without the delay occasioned by thoughtful processing, and as reflecting whether the personality is generally more introverted or extroverted. An experience balance that is inflated on the color side (with due regard to the amount of such inflation and other factors) can be taken to reflect one of the following: (1) labile often tempestuous moods, (2) an inclination to take unreflective, impulsive actions, and (3) something to do with organic illness, either hypochondriasis, psychosomatic disease, or organic disease without a psychological component (if there is such a thing). The theory underlying these three meanings is based on the way supposed energy is discharged—in feeling, in behavior, or "into the body." The last fits with a number of researches that generally have posited inner and outer as dimensions of existence, related them to various diseases, and located cancer as a disease reflecting the inner-directed dimension. The "anger-in" relationship to cancer has already been cited. In other research, cancer patients were shown to make more flexor figure drawings than controls, while hypertension patients made more extensor ones than controls. (Harrower, et al., 1975) The finding of inflated color responses relative to "M" responses implies the usefulness of a psychotherapeutic emphasis on freeing thought. If patients are inclined toward discharge somatically in the relative absence of ideational processing, then it is plausible that as repressions lift and ideational processing is allowed more free rein, less discharge should take place to the inside, somatically. The relative inhibition of free thought, as reflected in the low "M" responses of the cancer patients, fits with the tendency of such patients to inhibit their aggressive-assertive potential, the discharges into the body being an alternative forced upon them by way of their fear that overt expressiveness might reveal their anger.

There has been speculation that cancer, or exacerbation of it, can be a resistance to erotic aspects of the transference. With one of these patients I considered just that inference. This patient had remarkably strong convictions that she had to please her husband, and especially not make him jealous, attitudes that fit with her general inhibition of sexual and aggressive impulses. Despite such inhibitions she developed a good working relationship with me, and after thirty or so sessions began to show a few mild indications of having sexual fantasies about me. While she usually dressed in such a way as to minimize her attractiveness, to one session she wore an attractive red outfit that enhanced her appearance. In the course of that session she offered indications of a new-found strength to stand up to her husband. That was the last time that I saw her out of a hospital bed where she went not long after with a fatal recurrence.

Because all patients did not overcome their cancer as a result of my psychological work with them does not mean that the ideas set forth by Simonton and others are incorrect. By the same token, if the patients had all gotten better that would not in and of itself prove the theory either. For reasons already enumerated, my work could hardly be considered a proper study of outcome. However, the association of cancer with inhibition of aggression, and of cancer with heightened affect discharge in a context of ideational inhibition imply that, indeed, personality characteristics do play a role either in the etiology or course of cancer. That being so, the call for imaginative, controlled experimentation with psychotherapy as a cure is clear.

I can only hope for general agreement that the possibility of a personality-cancer relationship will be considered too important to be left for the kinds of investigations that have thus far mostly been made. It is not a task for solitary *ad hoc* investigations, for psychotherapists of only one persuasion or one level of skill working with an uncontrolled selection of patients with various types of cancers in various stages and subjected to various medical treatments being treated psychologically for widely varying amounts of time. It seems to me that conventional medicine, and we as a society, should take advantage of the free laboratory, and inviting context, provided by holistic medicine. There is now enough evidence to justify concerted coordinated expenditure of social resources, an amalgamation of the contributions of culture and counterculture. The two cultures are, after all, both interested in human potential.

References

APPELBAUM, STEPHEN A. (with Phillip S. Holzman). "The Color-Shading Response and Suicide." *Journal of Projective Techniques,* 26 (1962):155–161. Reprinted in *Handbook of Rorschach Scales,* Lerner, Paul, ed. New York: International Universities Press, 1975.

———. (with Donald B. Colson). "A Reexamination of the Color-Shading Rorschach Test Response and Suicide Attempts." *Journal of Projective Techniques and Personality Assessment,* 32 (1968):160–164.

———. "Parkinson's Law in Psychotherapy." *International Journal of Psychoanalytic Psychotherapy,* 4 (1975):426–436.

———. *Out in Inner Space—A Psychoanalyst Explores the New Therapies.* New York: Doubleday/Anchor, 1979.

————. "The Refusal to Take One's Medicine." *Bulletin of the Menninger Clinic,* 41(6) (1977):511–521.

BACON, CATHARINE L., RENNEKER, RICHARD, and CUTLER, MAX. "A Psychosomatic Survey of Cancer of the Breast." *Psychosomatic Medicine,* 14(6) (1952).

BENSON, HERBERT. *The Relaxation Response.* New York: William Morrow, 1975.

FIELD, PETER B. "Mortality Rates and Aggression Management Indices." *Journal of Health and Human Behavior,* 4(2) (1963).

GREER, S. and MORRIS, TINA. "Psychological Attributes of Women Who Develop Breast Cancer: A Controlled Study." *Journal of Psychosomatic Research,* 19, 147–153.

HARROWER, MOLLY; BEDELL THOMAS, CAROLINE; ALTMAN, ANN. "Human Figure Drawings in a Prospective Study of Six Disorders: Hypertension, Coronary Heart Disease, Malignant Tumor, Suicide, Mental Illness, and Emotional Disturbance." *The Journal of Nervous and Mental Disease,* 101(3), 191–199.

KLOPFER, BRUNO. "Psychological Variables in Human Cancer." *Journal of Projective Techniques,* 21(4) (1957):331–340.

SIMONTON, CARL; SIMONTON, STEPHANIE MATTHEWS; CREIGHTON, JAMES. *Getting Well Again.* Los Angeles: Tarcher, 1978.

PART III
The Role of the Practitioner

The new understanding that the cancer patient has intense psychological stresses and needs associated with the contraction and treatment of the disease is reflected in the changing role of the practitioner. Patients are no longer content to obediently follow physician's prescribed treatment regimens without consideration of their emotional needs. Further, patients have made it clear that adequate treatment includes addressing issues that had previously been avoided: how do sexual partners make adjustments when surgery has removed or impaired the sex organs? How do we feel about our own death and the death of someone we love? Is it permissible to feel angry at the person who is dying?

A number of practitioners who were interviewed for the preparation of this book noted an interesting phenomenon: their practice seems to have fewer cancer patients than one would expect proportionate to the numbers of people contracting the disease. This suggests that cancer patients may be a special subset of the population, and that one descriptive variable for them is a reluctance to enter into psychotherapeutic treatment. It is perhaps for this reason that practitioners not specifically trained in psychotherapy have assumed a dual role of physical caretaker, as well as psychological counselor.

The first chapter in this section, written by Richard Renneker, explores how a psychiatrist can be active in both the medical and physiological treatment of the cancer patient. Harold Searles, specifies the role that the psychoanalyst can play in the exploration of the unconscious of the cancer patient. The last chapter in this section, written by Jane Goldberg, explores the intense transference relationship that develops between the patient and physician, and how the treatment ministrations may come to acquire symbolic meaning.

8 Cancer and Psychotherapy

Richard E. Renneker

This chapter has emerged from thirty years of interest in and working with cancer patients. The first seven years were spent as director of a research project that investigated possible psychosomatic factors in cancer of the breast.[1,2,3,4,5] This project was conducted at the Chicago Institute for Psychoanalysis and was psychoanalytically oriented. Four analysts (myself included) attempted analytic therapy with four patients who had recently been surgically and radiologically treated for cancer of the breast. Our efforts were unsuccessful as regards cancer return. Over the subsequent twenty-three years, I have worked psychotherapeutically (not psychoanalytically) with twenty-one other patients with active cancer of various types. I have consistently altered my methods and thinking according to the results or consequences encountered in each therapy. All patients were concomitantly being cared for by other physicians: surgeons, chemotherapists, and/or radiologists. The following is a brief account of those experiences, as regards the evolution of my psychotherapeutic methods and psychodynamic thinking.

Bidirectional Interactions Between Emotions and Cancer

The modern concept of health and disease is multicausal. It includes healthy and disturbed psychological and emotional states as partial and potential mediating agents. These contribute to raising or lowering the threshold of host resistance to disease through their physiological, biochemical, and endocrinological effects upon the functioning of immunological systems. This concept also applies to cancer, although there is still considerable disagreement about the validity of such an application. On the other hand, there is a rapidly growing body of literature that espouses such a connection. It is not my purpose here to review the pro and con literature regarding the concept that psychological-emotional factors can either act for or against cancer. Interested readers can refer to two recent and extensive reviews of the field provided by Constance Holden[6] and

131

Lawrence LeShan.[7] Much research remains to be done before the antagonistic beliefs of the "pro" and the "con" advocates can be resolved. A quotation from the Holden article neatly sums up the situation:

> Elmer Green of the Menninger Foundation, a leading biofeedback researcher, says, "the placebo effect is where it's at." Says Green, "Everybody knows there is such a thing as a placebo effect but they don't think about what it is." "Obviously," says Green, "it is an activation of the body's self-regulatory mechanisms produced by the individual's expectation. The most startling example of this effect is manifested in the rare cases of sudden remission from cancer. No one knows what causes them, but according to NCI's Bernard Fox, investigators have found that 'very powerful belief' is the common factor in such cases. Potential research has been greatly impeded by the fact that biochemists don't know about psychology and psychologists don't know about biochemistry. Thus we have psychotherapists at one end of the spectrum and mouse researchers at the other and no communication between them. These types, in addition to specialists in epidemiology, genetics, environmental carcinogens, and clinical oncology, will have to be brought together in team efforts if scattered hints are ever going to become merged in a fuller picture." . . . Clearly it is going to be awhile before biochemical research establishes the role of the mind in precipitating cancer, or of that ill-defined but potent factor—'the will to live'—in mobilizing physical defenses once the disease has set in.

I am on the "pro" side of the dispute. I am also a firm believer in and practicer of the pragmatic portion of the Medical Model, namely, the traditional habit and freedom of physicians to utilize promising therapeutic modes long before they have been understood and validated by scientific research. I am referring here to the therapeutic mode of trying to help patients fight their cancer psychologically.

A pertinent question posed by the concept of bidirectional relationships between emotions and cancer is how many psychiatrists are working with cancer patients in their fight for life?

Psychiatrists and the Psychotherapy of Cancer Patients

During the period of 1975 to 1979 I personally interviewed 250 members of the American Psychiatric Association about their experiences with cancer patients. Nearly all were friends and acquaintances who were familiar with my interest in the psychotherapy of such patients. The mean average years in practice for this sample was 17.2. I asked them the following questions and got the following responses:

1. Have you ever worked with a patient who had cancer?
   YES: 235
   No: 15

2. If so, approximately how many?
   TOTAL: 1018
   MEAN AVERAGE PER PSYCHIATRIST: 4.3

3. Were your therapeutic efforts directed toward helping them cope with their emotional reactions to having cancer?
   YES: 235

4. How many patients have you worked with?
   TOTAL: 1018

5. Approximately how many therapy hours did you spend with each patient?
   RANGE OF THERAPY HOURS PER PATIENT: 1 to 42
   MEAN AVERAGE PER PSYCHIATRIST: 9.2

6. With how many of those patients were your therapeutic efforts also directed toward helping them fight their cancer psychologically?
   NUMBER OF PSYCHIATRISTS RESPONDING AFFIRMATIVELY: 13
   TOTAL PATIENTS: 21

7. Approximately how many therapy hours did you spend with each patient?
   RANGE OF THERAPY HOURS PER PATIENT: 5 to 42
   MEAN AVERAGE PER PSYCHIATRIST: 12.4

8. How many cancer patients were referred by physicians who were not psychiatrists?
   NUMBER REFERRED: 0

9. How many cancer patients were self-referred or referred by non-physician friends of the patient?
   SELF-REFERRED: 13
   FRIEND-REFERRED: 27

10. How many of your cancer patients were already in psychotherapy when they developed cancer?
    TOTAL: 978

Discussion of the Above Statistics

There are three significant findings that are reflected by this sample of 250 psychiatrists:

1. The 235 psychiatrists who had an opportunity to help their 1018 cancer patients adjust to cancer worked to do so in every instance. They devoted an impressive 9.2 hours per patient in their endeavors. I say "impressive" because another survey of 50 cancer surgeons taken by myself during the same time period disclosed a mean average of 1.4 hours per patient "helping them to adjust to their cancer." More about this later.

2. Only 13 of the 235 attempted to help 21 patients fight their cancer psychologically. This strongly suggests that the remaining 222 psychiatrists were unaware of the possibility, uninformed as how to proceed therapeu-

tically, emotionally unwilling, or did not believe that it represented a genuine alternative. Furthermore, the mean average hours per patient devoted to the cancer fighting process was only 12.4 *vs.* 9.2 for the cancer coping. In addition the range of therapy hours per patient for the "coping" and the "fighting" was 1 to 42 *vs.* 5 to 42. A dubious difference. Perhaps some of the psychiatrists failed to differentiate the hours spent "coping" from those spent "fighting"? In any case, 12.4 "fighting cancer" therapy hours per patient is decidedly subminimal.

3. In my opinion, perhaps the most significant fact is that none of the 1,018 cancer patients were referred by non-psychiatric physicians.

These findings strongly suggest that (1) Psychiatrists do include within their range of normal therapeutic activities helping cancer patients cope emotionally with their cancers; (2) very few psychiatrists (5.5 percent) feel this way about helping patients fight their cancers psychologically and then only subminimally so; and (3) psychiatrists, apparently, are not regarded by most cancer therapists as either feasible or useful therapeutic agents in the coping-fighting processes.

After processing the data I realized my questionnaire had been incomplete. I had failed to get information to answer questions that came to me during and after the data processing. Did the therapist feel that the coping with and/or fighting cancer therapy periods had been sufficient and successful? What criteria did he use for reaching this decision? How many of the psychotherapies were terminated or continued after the cancer coping-fighting periods were over? If terminated, who made the decision and upon what grounds? Did the therapist feel uncomfortable or uneasy in working with his/her patients who had cancer? If so, in what ways? If the ongoing pre-cancer therapy was terminated after the coping-fighting period, did the therapist feel some sense of relief? Were there any significant correlations between the number of pre-cancer therapy hours and the number of coping-fighting therapy hours; the number of pre-cancer therapy hours and coping-fighting therapy hours as regards a therapist's relatively positive or negative feelings about each patient and, also, the patient's diagnostic category?

Therapist Reactions to Cancer Patients

One might wonder, while reading the above post-survey questions I raised, as to their points and relevancy. Both considerations can be best answered by asking, *Why didn't you include those questions to begin with?* The answer comes clearly and immediately. I have treated 22 cancer patients in both their coping and fighting periods. Incidentally, I do not differentiate in my therapies between coping and fighting. Both begin in the beginning and both continue throughout. The dominant emphasis is upon fighting.

Fighting is immediately a way of coping. Periodically more therapeutic energy and attention has to be devoted to helping the patient cope with his/her disturbed reactions to the course of the cancer, to the non-psychological cancer therapy modalities being utilized, to clarification of the non-psychological cancer therapist's utterances and attitudes and, also, to patients' reactions to utterances and attitudes of family and friends. Never, however, when these periods occur does one let up on the emphasis upon active fighting. I have just digressed in order to make the point that fighting and coping are continuing factors in the psychotherapy of a cancer patient and that fighting is the predominant mode of coping.

The relevancy of my experiences with 22 cancer patients to "Why didn't you include those questions to begin with?" is that I have *never* worked with a cancer patient without periodically becoming aware that I am experiencing disturbing emotional reactions to the cancer and the possibility/probability of the patients death. This has been recurrently disquieting to me because, since my initial traumatic experience with the patient in the Chicago Institute for Psychoanalysis project, I have never begun the psychotherapy of a cancer patient without hoping that *this time* I will not be upset by the fact of cancer and the possibility of death. *This time* has always turned out to be erroneous. Yet I suspect that when I begin with cancer patient 23, the identical process will reoccur. Is there no end to it? For me, I assume not. Nonetheless, I continue to hope—not expect. The differentiation is critical: "hope" is the possibility and "expect" is the probability. I do believe that hope "springs eternal" and is basic to humanness so long as one ceases expecting in the face of all evidence to the contrary. I believe that the informational-emotional correlation between cancer and death is still universal and will continue to be so until the multimodalities of cancer therapies reduce the threat of death from cancer to an almost zero statistic. Furthermore, not only did I experience periodic disturbing emotional reactions in all the cancer therapies, but also, on all of those occasions when psychotherapy was terminated by death from cancer, my grief reactions and feelings of failure were always mitigated to some extent by secret feelings of relief that "it" was finally over. This might strike one as a rather bizarre and psychopathological reaction, or else as a rather natural one. I believe it to be the latter. For in almost every instance in which I have shared my "relief feeling" with fellow cancer psychotherapists, cancer specialists, internists, etc., their response has been the same: "me too," or words to that effect. I believe just about all physicians of every kind would probably agree that therapy of a cancer patient almost inevitably has it's rough emotional moments. It also has it's rewards.

Now to return to the question, *Why didn't you include those questions to begin with?* Because I was still defending my "unrealistic" hope that it is possible to work with cancer patients without becoming emotionally upset. This in spite of the almost absolute evidence to the contrary accumulated from my own experience, the literature, and communications with fellow cancer therapists. A further irrationality in the matter is the fact that I regard myself as an excellent methodologist. This has been confirmed by significant others. Certainly the original questionnaire did not demonstrate such an ability. Yet I did not recognize this until the data-processing phase. Embarrasing indeed. In the years when I was exclusively an analyst (I gave up psychoanalytic therapy in 1958), I would have categorized the defense of my unrealistic belief as a persistent defense against recognizing a chronic countertransference reaction. Now I see it as a natural and inevitably recurrent human response: to the conscious-unconscious meanings associated with cancer, to the extreme suffering and pain of a fellow being, to intimate, ongoing proximity to potential or impending death, and to the predictable ego distress associated with feelings of helplessness.

Some Cs-Uncs Meanings Associated with Cancer

The basic meanings of cancer are all threatening. The threat of:

1. Death
2. Pain
3. Disfigurement
4. Helplessness and hopelessness
5. Disruption of interpersonal relationships (i.e. family and friends).
6. Economic disaster
7. Loss of control of the body and the self—and thus, loss of the normal capacities to function
8. Idiosyncratic things relatively specific to the individual

Most of the above threats are obvious and require no further explanation. They generally apply only to the patient and not to the therapist. However, the threats of death, helplessness and hopelessness, loss of control of the self, and the "idiosyncratic things" are relevant to and involved in therapist reactions. The list of the major threats (others could have been included) makes it easier to understand why helping the patient to cope with his/her cancer can rarely be a short-term task (1.4 hours per patient for the surgeons and 9.2 hours per patient for the psychiatrists). Adjusting to cancer is long-term, ongoing, and periodic. The problem is acutely, chronically there, so long as the cancer is, and periodically for years thereafter. After all, isn't it somewhat beyond the realm of reason to assume that anyone could actually and effectively cope with so many coexistent threats to the self and to one's world as it was before? Certainly there are periods, usually brief, when one is unaware of the threats. Cancer therapy, however, is usually relatively long-term, emotionally traumatic, replete with unexpected intervening variables, and tends to physically deplete and exhaust the patient.

Death as a Threat to the Therapist

Most cancers are statistically tied to the possibility or probability of death. Most psychiatrists are more or less aware of these figures. If not, they will likely check out the latest statistics for the type of cancer that their patient has. The threat of death to his patient is usually and initially both challenging and stimulating to a psychiatrist. It reactivates a keener sense of physicianship, as well as memories of clerkships, interning, and residencies. This is one of the initial rewards secured from working with a cancer patient. It begins that way, but if the cancer patient's clinical condition worsens, then something else is added—proximity to dying and death. Surgeons, radiologists, and chemotherapists are familiar with this and protect themselves emotionally through limiting their personal involvement with the patient. For example, the mean of 1.4 hours devoted to helping the patient "cope." Another example is the surgeon who was so "certain I got it all out" (radical excision of a maxillary cancer) that after the hospitalization he told his patient, "no need to see me again for three months." The patient was dead in five. The latter instance goes beyond natural self-protectiveness into an area of neurotic defensiveness. In the light of his past experiences with such cancers he could have said, "I hope that I got it all out" (accompanied by a wry smile), but never with certainty that he "got it all out." His unwarranted belief was as neurotic as my believing that "this time I will not be upset by the fact of cancer and the possibility of death."

Empathy and identification are important therapist tools within the therapeutic process. Empathy is a therapist's free use of feeling into the patient's material so that he can understand it better. This represents a partial identification of the free moveable portion of a therapist's ego with various ego states and experiences of the patient.

These processes essential to the therapist can be seriously hampered by his reaction to a terminal cancer patient. We say it is impossible to imagine ourselves dead. So also is it impossible to freely lend ourselves to dying through indentification. In the Chicago Project we instinctively resisted or stopped the further investment of ourselves when we sensed that it was truly hopeless (i.e., barring a miracle of sorts). This was self-preservative, since it decreased the degree of personal investment "lost with the patient's death," which would subsequently have to be regained through mourning. There was also an economic motive. The urge to recapture one's investment before death. This was like the desire to leave a sinking ship in time with all one's valuable possessions—easier for the company representative to take along the gold bullion than to have to dive for it later. In our desire to "cure" the patient as well as to protect ourselves, we periodically lapse into omnipotent beliefs about our own abilities, in spite of knowledge and experience to the contrary. So, therapist reactions of natural self-protectiveness and periodic episodes of self-defensiveness can be expected. Each psychotherapist who has an opportunity to work with a cancer patient should first ask himself, "How relatively comfortable or conflictfully threatened do I feel when I think about cancer and my own dying and death?" If the response is strongly threatening, then I believe that both he and the patient would be better off if he immediately made a referral to a colleague.

The kind of terrible emotional impasse humans are capable of getting into is illustrated by an experience I had with the husband and family physician of a thirty-two-year-old mother of two small children who had been "successfully" treated for cancer of the cervix. She concealed her history of cancer during the three months of office psychotherapy. She then called to cancel her next two appointments because she had to "go into the hospital for a check-up." Two weeks later she phoned and asked if we could continue the therapy through "home visits," since she was "confined" to the house under orders from her family physician. On my first house call she told me the history of her "past cancer." I found her to be unnaturally, for her, apprehensive and euphoric. She explained that a biopsy had been done. No recurrence of cancer had been discovered: "How lucky I am." Instead, a different gynecological "problem" had been revealed that would be readily treatable through "home confinement." Of course I was suspicious, and called the family physician when I returned to my office. He said that she had a return of the cervical cancer, previously treated by radium, and that it was hopeless. He became quite agitated and angry when I inquired as to the clinical basis for his conclusion of "hopelessness." He stated categorically that "she will die as soon as possible and I will not allow her suffering to be prolonged by surgery or chemotherapy." It seems that two members of his family had "suffered painful, lingering deaths caused by cancer therapy," and he "would never allow that to happen again." "In fact," he said, "if I ever develop cancer I'm just going to blow my brains out." I arranged a conference with the husband for the next day. He was wholly in accord with the physician. She was not to be told that she had cancer and was to be kept inside her home until she died. I pleaded with him to call in a cancer specialist for another opinion, an assessment of the cancer stage, an explanation of the available therapeutic modalities, and a projection as to what her possible life expectancy might be if cancer therapy was initiated. He refused, saying that his mother "had suffered and died from cancer." A cancer specialist told the family that the mother had a 20 to 25% chance of a five-year "cure," if she began therapy right away. He informed them that it would be a costly process. Since the father and the five adult children could not come up with a decision, he told them to think it over and call him within two days. They anguished into the night. The father refused to commit himself either way. Finally, my patient's husband "took the matter in hand" and announced that, since no one else could make the decision, he would. No cancer therapy. Mother would be kept at home, narcotized, and "allowed to die in peace." The mother was never consulted, and that's what was done.

The husband told me that I could no longer see or talk with his wife. He would remove the phone from her room. There was, however, one possibility. Would I sign a paper, to be drawn up by his attorney brother, in which I would guarantee not to tell her that she had cancer? Unfortunately, I agreed. In the meantime I checked her hospital record and learned full-body x-rays were negative and there were no signs or symptoms suggestive of metastasis. The record also stated that she had been experiencing pelvic pain since just before she began psychotherapy. I called a cancer colleague at Sloan-Kettering and described the clinical picture. He said that she had a "fairly good" prognosis if surgery was performed immediately, but her chances for survival would drop to 17 percent if metastasis occurred. I relayed this information to the physician and the husband. To no avail. I made frequent house calls for one month, arranging to arrive in the evening when the husband would be at home. Thus, I continued seeking approval from him to make a full disclosure of the facts to his wife and leave the decision up to her. He was adamant. I experienced the terrible interpersonal artificiality and sterility of cancer concealment.

During the first week she made several guarded remarks which were indirect ways of asking the question, "Do I have cancer?" Each time I was evasive, suggesting that she ask her physician directly, and if she was not satisfied, to call in a consultant. I gave her several names and numbers to call. Her physician said, "no cancer," and she refrained from calling a consultant because she was certain that doing so would anger her husband. She never asked me again. She was on enforced bedrest, which precluded going downstairs to have dinner with the family. She had around-the-clock nurses to give the morphine which had been started in the hospital. More morphine was required as the pelvic pain increased. An ugly situation developed toward the end of my third week of visiting. I had noticed a decided increase and intensification in her manifest signs of pain over a four-day period, and when I asked her about it she triumphantly told me that now she was starting to get better. The physician had given her a lecture to the effect that the pain was all in her head. She was becoming a morphine addict. And now, she said, was the time to get control of herself and to get well through refusing the morphine injections "when the nurses try to give them to you." She had been doing just that for the past four days. I told her the pain was real and to resume the injections. She readily agreed. I told her to find out what was causing the pain and that I would set up a four-way telephone conference between myself, the husband, the physician, and a renowned cancer specialist in New York, but she was not to say anything about this to her husband until I gave her the go-ahead sign. She readily agreed. I cleared it first with the man in New York and then somehow I managed to talk the other two into participating. I was exhilirated, but I should have known better. I showed up at the appointed time and place agreed upon for the phone conference: they didn't. I met with her mother and sister, explained the situation, and asked them to tell the patient about the cancer and her, as yet, favorable prognosis. They refused. Finally, I made the horrible mistake of calling the husband and warning him that on the next day I was going to make a full disclosure to his wife about the cancer unless he did so himself on that very evening. When I arrived the following afternoon there was an armed guard stationed at the locked gate to their driveway with specific instructions to keep me out. I dashed back to my office and called her. Both house phone numbers had been discontinued and, obviously, private numbers substituted. I consulted an attorney and found that I had nowhere to go. Four months later I received a phone call from a triumphant sounding husband, who informed me that his wife had just returned from the hospital and this time they had found metastasis to the lung. Then he hung up.

Helplessness and Hopelessness as Threats to the Therapist

Subjective helplessness is the feeling-belief of being unable to help oneself. Objective helplessness is the feeling-belief of being without external help or aid. A combination of the two results in hopelessness. The *American College Dictionary*'s definition and differentiation of hopeless, despairing, despondent, and desperate perfectly reflects my thinking:

> They all describe an absence of hope. Hopeless is used for a feeling of futility and passive abandonment of oneself to fate: "hopeless and grim he still clung to the cliff." Despairing refers to the loss of hope in regard to a particular situation whether important or trivial; it suggests an intellectual judgment concerning probabilities: "despairing of victory, despairing of finding his gloves." Despondent always suggests melancholy and depression, it refers to an emotional state rather than to an intellectual judgment: "despondent over ill health; she became more and more despondent and suspicious." Desperate conveys a suggestion of recklessness resulting from loss of hope: "as the time grew shorter he became desperate." Desperate may apply either to feelings or to situations: "the case seems hopeless but is not yet desperate; a desperate remedy." Despairing and despondent may apply only to feelings.

Hopeless, despairing, despondent, and desperate come into play in all therapists with some cancer patients, in very many cancer patients depending upon the state of the cancer process or their belief about it, in all severe depressive states, or periodically and to varying degrees in lesser depressions. It is important for psychiatrists to be aware of these probabilities if we are considering working with a cancer patient or one in a depressed state. We must examine ourselves to determine whether our personality structure contains a tendency toward pessimism and depressive mood reactions. If the answer is yes, then the patient should be referred to another psychotherapist. I have my most consistent therapeutic successes with depressed patients. They usually comprise most of my practice. In thirty-five years of being a psychiatrist I have to date never had a suicide. I believe this record is largely due to the ways I am as a person. I am optimistic about myself, life, and the patient. I am predominantly "up." My "down" periods last hours: never days. I believe this quality of "brief downness" is directly related to my active usage of what I call the "principle of multipossibilities." In essence it means that there are more roads to Rome than anyone could ever dream of. Thus, if I experience a disappointing setback in life or in working with a patient, I quickly turn to the principle of multipossibilities. There *are* more ways of retackling the problem than I have ever dreamed of, and so I initiate the active process of finding them. I have learned never to stop short of identifying three different possibilities. For me, there is something remarkable about forcing myself to reach that number. Not infrequently the first three possibilities are not easy to find, but if I persist to that point then frequently something exciting occurs. More possibilities come easily and quickly. They start to flow. My habit is to stop at eight and to begin examining the choices laid out before me. I do this because, usually, many of the choices logically complement each other and fit together to form a *plan* of action. Some of the choices are ones that have been forgotten. I do not feel frustrated if I cannot come up with any possibilities at the moment, because I *know* from experience that they will come: from myself in time, from asking other persons (including the patient), or from consulting articles and books. I recommend trying the process if you have not yet discovered it for yourself.

What do I mean when I talk about helplessness and hoplessness in a psychotherapist who is working with a cancer patient? In the Chicago Institute project we began with feelings of hopefulness, therefore we did not feel helpless. Our hope was based in the potential of psychoanalytic therapy to positively effect both the patient and the cancer. As it became increasingly clear to each of us in his own time that our analytic therapies were neither feasible nor effective, we began to feel relatively helpless and hopeless. We attempted to sustain hope in various ways of experimenting with modifications of the parameters of analytic method. We increased or decreased the number of therapy hours per week. We tried two or three sessions on the same day. We increased the frequency of our interpretations and altered the nature of those interpretations. As our "experiments" failed, the cancer recurred or worsened, and we began to feel increasingly helpless and hopeless. This occurred for various reasons:

1. We were ignorant about the disturbing emotional reactions that would occur if the cancer progressed, thus we were not forewarned as to what to expect.

2. We made the mistake of basing all of our hope in the efficiency of analytic therapy and had not thought out in advance any alternative plans of action.

3. We failed to differentiate treatment of the patient from treatment of the cancer. We are out to treat the cancer through facilitating changes in the patient, and we did not recognize, until too late, that our primary goal was to arrest or cure the cancer. Unrealistic and irrational? Yes, but that's the way we were and that's what happened. Our orientation was that we were fighting the cancer, rather than fighting it *with* the patient. Our growing feelings of helplessness and hopelessness about achieving *the* goal carried over to feelings of helplessness and hopelessness about helping the patient. We were not prepared in advance to help the patients cope with the multiple emotional problems of terminal cancer, and so we did a poor job of it.

4. We made the error of becoming disturbed because we were disturbed. After all, we each liked to think of ourselves as having been "well analyzed." The idea just never occurred to us that our reactions were natural and predictable within the given context and situation. An unnecessary double disturbance. How irrational and stupid it seems from this distance. Yet that's the way it was. But it doesn't have to be.

Loss of Control of the Self as a Threat to the Therapist

The expression, "eaten up by cancer" is incorrect but still popular. The disease progresses by cellular multiplication, invasion, and metastasis; not by "eating up" the host. This expression does, however, reflect the association of cancer with primitive, destructive oral impulses out of control. The manifest dream content of cancer patients not infrequently contains threats from carniverous animals, fangy monsters, armies of menacing crabs, etc. These reflect not just an externalization of an internal threat (i.e. cancer), but also of a different kind of inner threat—the loss of self-control and the eruption of ego alien impulses. The patient feels physically out of control of the self. This feeling easily carries over into anxiety over potential loss of control of the psychological-emotional self. Something inside is physically out of control, so watch out for the controlled, repressed, psychic things within. Cancer is not just a threat to physical life, but is sometimes experienced as though it were a threat to one's self-control system and therefore to one's identity. Previously stabilized ego boundaries threaten to dissolve and to be replaced by troublesome ego alien impulses and behaviors.

The therapist too can react in a similar fashion through his therapeutic identification with the patient. He is dealing with a process outside himself (cancer) which is uncontrolled and primitive. To the degree that he is identified with the patient, the process is now inside himself and is then reacted to as anxiety over his own primitive impulses and their control. His reaction is somewhat like the reactive anxiety of some first-year medical students when thrown into close contact with primitive biological material.

Idiosyncratic Threats to the Therapist

These are specific conscious or unconscious meanings given to the fact of cancer and impending death that represent idiosyncratic threats for individual therapists. Two examples will suffice:

1. Therapist Transference Reactions to a Cancer Patient

A psychiatrist and friend of mine had been treating a much older male patient for about one year. The man was then discovered to have a terminal cancer. The therapist continued seeing the patient, off and on, for over a month. He became increasingly upset about the situation and finally talked it over with me. It seems that the patient's condition had reactivated some old guilty, conflictful feelings about his father and about his own behavior during the terminal phase of his father's death from cancer of the same type. His anxiety and depressive reactions had reached the point at which he felt he had to cease and desist, both for his own sake and that of his patient. He transferred the case to me. The fact that neither of my parents died of cancer probably makes it easier for me to work with patients of either sex. Obviously, a similar situation could develop if the patient is a woman and a therapist's conflictful feelings centered on a mother who died of cancer.

2. Unconscious Therapist Response to Specific Fantasy of Cancer Patient

Eissler[8] describes the identification problem of the dying patient. The feeling is "I feel different from the healthy. I am removed from them. I am lonely. I want contact. I wish the therapist too had cancer, then we could truly share this experience together. We could be close and I could use his strengths for this last phase."

In the Chicago Project we observed a therapist response to exactly such a patient need. One analyst developed an obsessive preoccupation with the idea that he had cancer. He was an exceptionally intuitive, sensitive, therapeutically oriented analyst who keenly felt his inability to reach and help his patient. His "symptomatic" reaction represented an attempt to narrow the distance between himself and the dying patient. It was thus an unusual emergency measure of the unconscious in response to his frustrated and great therapeutic drive.

Psychotherapy of the Cancer Patient

The particular life situations and personality features associated in the literature with cancer patients are remarkably few and consistently noted. These are held to be higher in incidence than either the general population or in comparison with other preselected categories of patients. These are:

1. cold and remote parents
2. denial and repression of negative emotions, particularly anger
3. lack of self-assertiveness and self-fulness
4. helplessness and hopelessness
5. despair and depression
6. inability to cope successfully with a severe emotional loss.

As a rationale and aid for my psychotherapy of cancer patients I combined these elements into a psychodynamic schemata.

Discussion of the Schemata

1. The Three Parent-Child Combinations

A. These are parents whose basic attitude is one of intolerant judging and negative misunderstanding of most of the temporarily disturbing child behaviors that are inherently normal within the various phases of child development. Such things as temper tantrums, defiance, determined pursuit of pleasure principle behaviors, etc. In short, it is intolerance of any behavior that displeases the parents because it is contrary to their values, standards, principles, and expectations.

Behaviors deviant from the parents expected "norms" are consistently and severely punished. Thus, the child is "home-broken" at an early age. The parents can love the child very much indeed. They are acting out of their love for the child and simply following the mold within which they were raised, or believe they should have been. These parents are not necessarily "cold," but they do tend to be inhibited in their expressions of positive feelings, both physically and verbally, toward each other and their

The Schemata

Nature of three parent-child combinations

Suppression and repression (denial) of anger etc., and rebellious behaviors

Acceptance of coping mechanism of compliant submissiveness

Progressive inhibition of and failure to develop habits of active selfness and self-assertiveness

Progression into defended habit pattern of indiscriminate niceness, as a basic security system and source of identity

System is basically frustrating, but frustration is attenuated by

System becoming relatively rewarding and stabilized through intervention of a particular life situation

Survival of a "secret self" and development of partial means of satisfying one's concealed human needs and wants

Deterioration or loss of the stabilizing life situation

Intensification of niceness in quest to find a replacement

Increased reliance upon secret self-gratifications as coping measure

Inability to find a replacement for the deteriorated-lost life situation, in spite of repeated attempts. As frustration mounts, anxiety and beginning helplessness enter the picture

If a life situation replacement is found, or if new self-active habit patterns are superimposed over the ineffectual niceness ones—then restabilization occurs and the psychological-emotional symptoms disappear

As time lengthens and continued efforts to reestablish the urgently needed security life-situation fail— strong feelings of subjective and objective helplessness develop; also hopelessness.

Diminishing importance of secret means of securing partial satisfaction

(NOTE: People vary tremendously as to the length of time spent within the above two stages. It depends upon the number of efforts made, the presence of other coping measures and the resiliency of their ability to regain a basis for renewed and temporary hope. Eventually though, as all efforts at reestablishment are in vain and as their emergency coping measures fail—then

Progressive disruption of normal biological functioning with increased proneness to inception of disease— including cancer

there is the onset of despair, depression and loss of the "will to live": "What is there to live for"? They continue to attempt to mask their emotional state from others, but cannot do so for themselves.

At this stage secret self-gratification is perceived as "worthless", or almost so children. These children feel "secure" so long as they are believing and thinking within both parents' value systems. Their rewards are the absence of angry disapproval reactions and the reception of monosylabic positive remarks, pats on the head and facial expressions of approval.

B. A variation of the above is a situation in which one parent specializes in complying with the rigid, intolerant, unforgiving, and dominant other-parent demands in order to keep peace. Compliance means passive, uncomplaining submission to the demands of the dominant "security" parent. A child can identify with this submissive parent and internalize the same system; which will, often, persist throughout adulthood.

C. The other variation is a parent combination that shares egocentricity, omnipotence, and a dislike and resentment of parenting in general and parental responsibilities in particular. These are the "unloving" parents who are prone to fly into fearful rages over any child behavior that displeases them. The child feels unloved, misperceived, and neglected. Children in such circumstances frequently develop a personality structure characterized by shyness, feelings of low self-worth, inadequacy, and unwantedness; the child attempts to be invisibly unobtrusive and focused on the critical and constant need to be nice at all times. While their goals are essentially similar to most of the children covered by parent-child situations A and B, their difference lies in the gratefulness exhibited when they receive the rare scraps of "like" and "approval" from their parents.

2. Pathological Niceness Syndrome (PNS)*

The individuals who grow up within any of the three parent-child combinations without rebelling and successfully carrying through the revolution will enter adulthood suffering from pathological niceness. Niceness contains some of the finest human qualities, if the behaviors reflective of those qualities are appropriate to the context and *if* they are made by choice and not by habit. The pathological type of niceness is a form of promiscuity: indiscriminate niceness. Such a person is out to be "nice" even if it ends up hurting the self and/or the other person. Its expression does not involve freedom of choice, since there is no opportunity for making the decision to be "nice." It is the expression of an automatic habit pattern. It is a statement about the self: a virtue. It can also be that person's sole means of coping interpersonally—of seeking security, love, admiration, respect—through selfless ways of pleasing others. In short, the "nice" person's self-identity is in the minds of other people, not within himself. The paramount goal of each "nice" behavior is to avoid being disliked. The secondary goal is to be liked.

---

* The expression *Pathological Niceness Syndrome* (PNS) contains the meaning of cancer personality feature 2: denial and repression of negative emotions, particularly anger; but also much more, as will be apparent in the following.

This means that displays of anger or any other negative emotion associated with displeasing people are out! So also, is self-assertiveness and direct asking and actions in behalf of one's own wants and needs.

The internalization of "niceness" as one's identity and as the dominant way of coping with life inevitably produces consequences. The personality emerges as compliant, submissive, passive, selfless, and overly anxious to please. There acrues not only a profound inhibition of active selfness and self-assertiveness, but also a downright failure in their development. Since degree of self-confidence is based on the actual record of one's effective or ineffective functioning in each life area, these persons suffer severely from lack of self-confidence. Of course they can realistically afford to be proud of certain abilities—intellectual, physical, sexual, job functioning, etc.—but even these feelings can be immediately undercut by some other person's negative judgment, warranted or not. Besides, whatever confidence they find from their ability to please others is rather treacherous and uncertain, since they continue to experience their inability to please all of the time.

They learn to "adjust" to the continuous self-deprivations and self-denials inherent in this system by endlessly saying to themselves and others, "Oh, I don't mind," "I don't care," "It's ok," "it doesn't bother me," etc. But they do "mind," "care," and they are "bothered." Periodically, and progressively so, they begin to realize that virtue is so infrequently responded to in kind, and also, that most self-centered people readily believe altruistic statements and tend to take the "nice" person's behavior for granted.

3. The Secret Self

Fortunately or unfortunately, in spite of all the energy and work that goes into creating, executing, and defending the mode of "niceness," a secret self-fulness survives. This concealed portion of self-identity provides some self-satisfaction through fantasies, dreams, and vicarious identifications with self-assertive, self-declarative, self-doing friends and fictional film characters. This secret self occasionally seeks to express itself through indirect, convoluted, vague verbalizations of the "nice" person's real feelings, wants, and desires. "Nice" people are so expert at accurately deciphering the indirect askings of others that they erroneously expect to receive the same in kind. They fail to grasp the fact that such communications are generally ineffective, because they are only rarely understood. The secret self is both a friend to the self and also a threat to the "niceness" security system. Therefore, it tends to remain private and isolated with the self. I agree with LeShan that mobilization and actualization of this relatively dormant part of the self-identity is fundamental in the psychotherapy of most cancer patients.

Incidentally, many "nice" people do manage to break out of their dismal habit pattern. They learn to recognize the ineffectiveness of the system and to superimpose over it patterns of self-assertiveness and taking action in one's own behalf. Even in such an instance, the old "niceness" habit remains lurking under the surface and is easily reactivated by life events. I believe that, probably, no one ever completely rids the self of such long-lived habit patterns. They will return. They have to be identified and labelled as enemies of the self, so they can be more readily recognized and immobilized when they inevitably reappear. This is a basic principle to teach a patient in all psychotherapies, particularly with cancer patients.

4. Helplessness and Hopelessness

In a prior section I defined *subjective helplessness* as the feeling-belief of being unable to help oneself, and *objective helplessness* as the feeling-belief of being without external help or aid. A combination of the two results in *hopelessness.* Let's consider the applicability of subjective and objective helplessness to the cancer patient's situation. Before doing so, however, I must introduce the antithetical concepts of *subjective and objective helpfulness,* so that we can explore some of the logical interrelationships between them—particularly as they apply to the cancer patient. Subjective helpfulness is the feeling-belief of being *able* to help oneself, whereas objective helpfulness is the feeling-belief of being *with* external help and aid. Obviously, the combination of the two should produce *hopefulness;* which is exactly what we strive to instill within cancer patients.

Subjective helpfulness is composed of the abilities to think for oneself, to be self-assertive, and to take action in one's own behalf. Most patients undergoing surgical-medical cancer therapies are in the opposite state of subjective helplessness. Thus, the only thing standing between them and hopelessness is objective helpfulness: the feeling-belief of being *with* external help and aid. Cancer therapists and therapies are the sole sources for instilling and facilitating that critical feeling state of being *with* external help and aid. I call it a critical feeling state because it is the only thing that stands between them and hopelessness; unless of course they have a powerful belief in the actuality of God and the possibility of "miraculous" intervention.

It should be clear from the above exposition that the degree to which cancer patients experience objective helplessness or objective hopefulness is entirely dependent upon the amount of trust and confidence vested in their cancer therapists. This is a very important point because the extent to which they feel trust and confidence, or the relative lack thereof, in the cancer therapy modalities utilized is almost always in direct proportion to the degree of trust and confidence that they place in each of their cancer therapists. After all, how many cancer patients have enough knowledge about these modalities to evaluate them for themselves?

If you accept that the combination of subjective and objective help-lessness produces hopelessness and the combination of subjective and objective helpfulness produces hopefulness, then two principles and two primary goals of cancer psychotherapy become immediately apparent.

1. Principles:

a. Prevent or undercut either subjective or objective helplessness to secure a state of relative hopefulness.

b. Prevent or undercut both subjective and objective helplessness to secure a state of full hopefulness.

2. Two primary goals of cancer psychotherapy:

a. To prevent or undercut the inevitable development of subjective helplessness in the Pathological Niceness Syndrome (PNS) cancer patients, by devising and teaching them various active ways and means whereby they can be self-helpful in their own behalf—within the ongoing process of their cancer therapies. This represents the beginning of a new life pattern of self-assertiveness and taking actions for themselves and about themselves. This involves such therapist activities as helping patients prepare lists of questions pertaining to everything they want to know (at the moment) about the surgeon's training and experience, the type of cancer, the number of such cancers he has operated upon and, the percentage of results obtained, as well as his prognosis for this particular patient. The patient is instructed to go over the list with the surgeon, reading whichever items he feels like, and whenever he doesn't understand something or encounters vagueness to ask for clarification. In our next session we go over the questions asked and unasked, as well as the information received and not received. Inevitably lists follow lists. Most surgeons hate this technique and tend to regard the patient as "difficult," "troublesome," or "neurotic." Being aware of this tendency in advance, I call the surgeon before the first list arrives. I explain to him that the lists are my idea and that his spontaneous full answers to the questions will help the patient greatly in coming to feel himself as being *part* of the process, rather than simply the *object* of the process. I tell him that his open, complete, and patient answering of the questions will assure him of having a patient who will feel the deepest trust, admiration, and confidence in him, and who will undoubtedly rave about him all over town. I ask him to set aside an extra half-hour for the patient's next visit, or as long as he thinks will be necessary. I advise him that there is no reason to be vague, evasive, or uncomfortable during the question-answer session, since I have already instructed the patient to ask only those questions on the list that he really wants information about at this time. I also warn him that there will be more lists. I continue calling him in advance to warn him of the impending arrival of another list. Sometimes we have time to talk about the last session. Sometimes he asks questions, and I have the opportunity to try and help him better understand the patient and my methods and goals. If the surgeon answers clearly and to the point, the lists rapidly cease. In their place comes an occasional question that arises out of some special contextual happening. It might be something as simple and important as the surgeon's altered tone and facial expression as he examines the patient or looks at some new x-rays. What I promised the surgeon about the patient's future attitude toward him does hold true if he effectively carries out his portion of the interpersonal exchange. Most surgeons have accepted the situation and cooperated. A few became angry and arrogant. They said in effect, it's none of your business and I won't answer the questions, no matter what they are about. They said things like "patients don't need information, it just gets them upset and causes trouble." Each time this has happened I give the patient the names of two different surgeons and ask her/him to consult both of them and to ask each one whatever questions on the list that they feel like asking. Then they may pick the one they liked the most and felt the most comfortable with—and continue therapy with him. I again explain the critical importance of feeling trust and confidence in the cancer therapist. Of course I give them the names of two men I have had positive experiences with in this regard. And of course I call both men and inform them of what has happened and what is needed. This procedure has worked to our mutual satisfaction on all such occasions. The factor of choice once more puts the patient into the position of having to make his or her own decision.

b. To prevent or undercut the development of *objective helplessness* in the Pathological Niceness Syndrome (PNS) cancer patients. In order to make this point more comprehensible, I feel that I have to repeat a few things already said before. The degree to which cancer patients experience objective helplessness or objective hopefulness is entirely dependent upon the amount of trust and confidence vested in their cancer therapists. This is a very important point, because the extent to which they feel trust and confidence, or the relative lack thereof, in the cancer therapies utilized is almost always in direct proportion to the degree of trust and confidence that they place in each of their cancer therapists. What is the source of those positive feelings of trust and confidence?

The process begins with their feelings about the person or entity who supplied the name of the cancer therapist into whose hands they place their life. It can be the family physician, a spouse, a relative, a friend, an acquaintance, a newspaper, a magazine, a hospital, or a cancer medical center. The important issue is that, hopefully, they ask or use only those sources of information for whom/which they feel respect. This feeling carries over into the initial meeting with the cancer specialist. It is good to begin with a choice that is based in one's own positive self-appraisal of someone or something. It is bad to begin with a choice that has been made by someone for whom one has little or no respect, trust, or confidence. Unfortunately, such is frequently the case for those cancer patients possessed by the Pathological Niceness Syndrome (PNS). It is especially unfortunate because the cancer therapist becomes shrouded in negative transference feelings before they even meet. The positive or negative basis that determines who they originally see is of particular significance because it usually sets a pattern for their subsequent behavior and attitudes throughout the cancer therapy. If they make their decision from active freedom of choice, they will probably continue to exercise that same freedom of choice throughout. If they make their decision out of a habit pattern of submission to unliked authority figures, they will probably continue to do so. The latter probability is partially due to the dominant and critical priority placed by most cancer therapists, the American Cancer Society, and the press upon the importance of speed of intervention, once cancer has been diagnosed. This deprives him of the opportunity to see as many cancer therapists as are necessary; that is, until he finds one who instills within him those essential feelings of trust and confidence.

The point here is that if the cancer patient does not respect, trust, or have confidence in his cancer therapist, then the same set of attitudes is carried over to distrust of the cancer therapy modalities prescribed by the negatively invested therapist. This is a classical position of objective helplessness combined with subjective helplessness-hopelessness. It should be avoided at any cost.

Stabilized Life Situation and Loss Thereof

Should the "niceness" person succeed in finding a life situation which provides sufficient rewards for the niceness, then they experience a period of relative stabilization. This situation can be a job, a friend, personal relationships within a neighborhood, a house, a spouse, etc. The happiest thing that can happen to such a person is for them to form a lasting relationship with someone who has the same system. This is not a common event, since a "niceness" person usually most admires very self-centered persons who are certain of themselves and their own opinions, who are unaware of their own relative lack of sensitivity to the feelings and needs of others.

Loss of the stabilizing life situation and the inability to replace it leads to increasing frustration, intensification of the niceness, and the secret self activities. The more often the cycle is repeated without sufficient satisfaction, feelings of helplessness begin to develop and eventually depressive mood states make their appearance. Continued failure to establish another security life situation brings feelings of subjective and objective helplessness. These in turn rather quickly bring on feelings of hopelessness, despair, and masked depression.

I believe that earlier on in this frustrating cycle of failure to either initially find that life situation, or to replace it, there begins a progressive disruption of healthy biological functionings. And by the time they reach hopelessness, despair, and/or depression and loss of the will to live their biological malfunctionings are reflective of the malfunctioning psychological-emotional state. There is presently far insufficient evidence to fully warrant this belief, but I hold it anyway.

This, theoretically, for me is the psycho-socio-biological context within which *some* cancers appear. I do not believe that all cancer patients fit into such a picture. I do believe that some do. I have no idea what percentage of patients are involved, but I suspect that they are in the minority. I feel this way because I have seen so many cancer patients who do not fit into the life and personality picture described. In addition, it is immediately obvious that the life history and personality patterns identified in the literature are to be found in a variety of other psychosomatic illnesses and disturbed emotional-behavioral conditions, in particular the neurotic and psychotic depressive states.

The Total Cancer Population upon Which This Chapter is Based

I have seen a total of fifty-six cancer patients in my private practice. The twenty-two mentioned earlier were the ones who stayed for coping/fighting cancer psychotherapy. They all shared the Pathological Niceness Syndrome (PNS). Probably, the presence and action of the PNS itself was part of why they accepted my recommendation for psychotherapy. I believe, however, that their acceptances were chiefly due to the *shock of self-recognition* that they experienced when early in the first session, after taking the clinical history of the cancer, I then immediately proceeded to describe to them the nature of their early and late life experiences centered in the development and perpetuation of the PNS—without first securing any personal life history. This includes many specific and descriptive examples of how they probably felt and feel in different life stages and situations and the probable limited ways in which they had attempted (ineffectively) to cope, plus the kinds of consequences encountered. I observe their kinesthetic reactions to my postdictive account of their life history, inner feeling states, modes of communication and coping—then stop and wait for their verbal reactions. These are strong expressions of amazement, and long excited detailed accounts of verifying situations that illustrate many portions of what I have recounted to them. The main impact and result of this method, when it fits for a specific patient, is that they feel understood. The excitement reflects an immediate resurgence of hope that perhaps something different might be learned and tried—a something different that might lead to positive changes in themselves and in their lives. This technique, when successful, is dramatic and rather shamanistic, since it seems slightly magical to some;

but above all it quickly institutes a feeling of confidence and a powerful belief in the therapist as someone who can probably help, because he understands and therefore must know what to do about this particular problem.

Of the thirty-four other patients who did not remain for therapy, only four had the Pathological Niceness Syndrome. The thirty-two-year-old woman cited earlier in the clinical anecdote was one of those. She had become progressively hopeless in her relationship with her husband and her inability to cope with his righteous certainties and his predominant gloomy outlook on life and their relationship. She came to me to help her find new ways of coping, and if they failed, to support her in the wish to get out of the marriage and with her children. This was an instance of relationship deterioration after the first few years of "blissful," defended illusions, into progressive helplessness and hopelessness about the formerly "secure" life situation. The other three (two men and one woman) who rejected my recommendation of what LeShan calls "crisis therapy" did so for the same reason. They got caught up in their PNS reaction to the disapproval of their spouses, who strongly believed that the "idea" of psychotherapy for a cancer patient was downright "foolishness" or charlatanism. The mean hours spent with those four patients was 12.6. It would have been considerably less if I had not persisted and brought the spouses into some of the conferences. Since those experiences, I handle the matter differently. Now, if I get the impression in the initial session that the spouse might be opposed to psychotherapy, I immediately ask the patient not to reveal anything about the first five therapy hours to anyone, including the husband or wife. I say, "Tell him/her that the sixth hour will be a joint session. I will then summarize the inherent problems, the rationale, the procedure, and answer all questions. Please abide my request. There are important reasons for making it. First of all, it will take that long for you to understand, digest, and reflect upon what we will be talking about. Your past interpersonal record suggests that perhaps you have never made a significant life decision or taken an important and desired life action without basing it upon the opinion and approval of others. Now is the time to begin a new phase of your life, one characterized by self-assertiveness and self-actions determined by yourself. It is *your* life. The challenge is can *you* make up *your* mind *yourself* about what you want to do or don't want to do. Whichever way you decide, the critical issue is that you make the decision by yourself." This procedure, of course, applies only to the patients with the Pathological Niceness Syndrome (PNS).

The other thirty cancer patients I saw only briefly, or periodically for help in coping. Twenty had relatively early cancers and ten were terminal: "six months or so to live." All were undergoing various forms of cancer therapy. These individuals had none of the psycho-emotional or life situational features outlined earlier, and I told them so. My postdictive reconstructive "speech" was reacted to with amusement, tolerance, and annoyance; or as one person succinctly put it: "Doctor, you are talking about somebody else." Most of these patients were already actively fighting for their life, in their own ways. I respected those ways and told them so. Overall, I was impressed with the differences in this group from the PNS group. Denial was minimal. They were, generally speaking, coping well in their adjustments to the problems generated by the fact of cancer. I helped them with whatever problems they did present. They were relatively quick to learn and to try different modes of coping. Seventy-six percent had seen two or three cancer specialists before selecting a therapist. I was impressed with the trust and confidence manifested toward their cancer therapists. I was also impressed with how many had maintained their sense of humor, in spite of the cancer. Some described periods of hopelessness, but they were transient. Depressed mood was clearly post-cancer in onset and not out of control. In general, I found them to be well above my version of the average person for self-assertiveness, communicative spontaneity, emotional expressiveness, an active sense of humor, and the relative absence of neurotic difficulties in their life histories. The mean hours per

TABLE 8.1.   Statistics for the 22 Fighting/Coping Psychotherapy Patients

Site of Cancer	Number	Sex		Dead	Alive	Mean yrs. Clinical Prognosis	Mean yrs. Survival Time	Mean # Psychotherapy Hours
		F	M					
Breast	11	11	0	3*	8	5.9	14.4	178
Leukemia	1	0	1	1	0	1	3	142
Maxilla	1	0	1	1	0	3.5	5 mos.	35 (3 mos.)
Melanoma	2	0	2	1	1	2.4	6	108
Pancreas	1	1	0	1	0	1.5	5	150
Prostate	4	0	4	1	3	6.8	12.6	172
Thyroid	1	0	1	0	1	7.5	25	135
Stomach	1	0	1	1	0	7.5	15	161
Totals	22	12	10	9	13			3,485

* My Chicago Project patient, nine months after psychotherapy had begun, developed a recurrence with axillary node involvement. A radical mastectomy was performed. Psychotherapy continued on for three more years with no signs of recurrence. One year later she was killed in a commercial airline crash. My traumatic reaction was to the recurrence. My grief was over the plane crash. My mixed secret relief and frustration was because now I would never know what would have happened if the crash had not occurred.

patient with this group was 17.7. I know that eight of the ten terminal ones are dead. The other two are still alive three and five years later. I have no follow-up on the remaining twenty.

The average clinical prognosis for all twenty-two patients is 5.2 years and the average survival time is 12.2 years. All patients were treated, off and on, with the various cancer therapy modalities. Much of this treatment went on during the span of each psychotherapy. I do make a practice of continuing my therapy for at least three months beyond cessation of the other cancer therapies. I had only one opportunity to begin therapy with an obviously terminal patient. The one with the maxillary cancer and the clinical prognosis of 3.5 years, who died 5 months after surgery. I worked with him during the last three months of his life. Seven other patients became terminal, and I continued working with them through home and hospital—until the end.

The Truly Terminal Patient

My methods and goals in such a circumstance vary considerably depending upon the individual and the particular nature of that person's current life situation. It goes something like this:

1. I shift from fighting/coping to coping/fighting. I stress the high probability of death, while finding means of keeping alive at least a spark of hope. I focus on the intercurrent coping problems, figure out what can or might be done about them, then work at seeing that it is tried or accomplished if possible.

2. I make regular and frequent visits to see the patient. It is highly supportive for him to know that he is not forgotten. I keep after the family to do the same. I urge them to urge his friends and liked relatives to drop by as frequently as possible.

3. I contact the family physician and the cancer therapists and inquire about their plans for medical management and the frequency of their visits and phone calls to the patient. If both radiation and chemotherapy have been discontinued, I urge the chemotherapist to initiate placebo injections represented as a promising new drug that thus far has had no uncomfortable side effects. I bring the spouse, or critical relative, into this decision and tell them the truth about the placebo, as well as making them aware of the possibility of a "placebo effect." I warn them never to tell the patient about the placebo. If the chemotherapist refuses to do this, I then try the family physician. If he refuses, I do it myself or turn it over to a nurse, if there is one in attendance. I monitor the patient's pain and the narcotic orders. I make certain to inform the physician-in-charge immediately if the pain outpaces the narcotics.

4. I discuss death and dying with the patient. I make sure that all his affairs are in order. I ask to see his will and read it aloud to him to make certain that he hasn't overlooked somebody or something.

5. I tell the patient, "Well, sure there is a high probability of death, but in the meantime let's see what we can do to make each one of your remaining hours and days as full of as much enjoyable life-doings as is possible under the circumstances. I review with him the things in his life that he has enjoyed. For example, if it is cards, I get the family to arrange as many card games as he desires, or/and play with him myself. If it is sports, music, ballet, or a favorite TV program, then I get the family to make a weekly TV schedule just for him and composed only of *his* favorites. If I find out that he has not watched a particular favorite, I give him gentle "hell". If it is marijuana, I ensure that he has an adequate supply and someone to roll them if he can't. If the family is up to it (emotionally), I ask them to eat all their meals *with* him and in his room, if he is not ambulatory. (If they are too uptight about doing so—forget it.) If it is his favorite things, I find out what they are and get the family to fill his room (walls and surface spaces) with as many of them as he desires, etc., etc.

6. I draw him out about the greatest experiences of his life and join in with my own. I also draw him into discussions of the current events and issues that I know, or discover, he is the most interested in.

7. The bottom line, I suppose, is that I do "take over" to see how much life and living can be brought into the patient's life, that might not have happened if I had not gotten into action.

8. I encourage the patient to speak up at once, or as soon as possible, if any of the aforementioned measures are experienced as unpleasant or as too much: "Whenever you are too tired, not feeling up to something, or just not enjoying it—say so—and it's over for the day, or as long as you want it to be."

9. In particular, in my sessions with the patient and with the family alone, I try to draw out of them any positive or appreciative feeling, thought or opinion, that has never before been communicated to the person concerned. If it is a family session, I send them right to the patient's room "to get it off your chest right now." I usually add: "The way it came out here is just perfect, so don't bother to think anymore about how you are going to put that something into words." If it is the patient, and if the person concerned is in the house or outside in the hospital corridor, then I will repeat the same speech and hustle out to send that person into the patient's room while he is still feeling it and ready to speak.

I do not know if my fighting/coping psychotherapies actually contributed something to my patient's survival time, and if so to what degree. *They* felt it did. I like to believe that *maybe* the psychotherapy had something to do with it, but one has to stop there. However, with the terminal-phase patients, I *know* that I helped in many specific and measureable ways. And *that's* a great feeling!

The Growth and Development of My Therapeutic Orientation and Methods

The critical experiences that altered my thinking and methods occurred during the period of 1956–1960, when I was the methodologist and co-ordinator of the Therapeutic Process Project conducted at Mt. Sinai Hospital, Los Angeles, California. I spent four years observing five psychoanalytic psychotherapies. There were three analyst observors of each therapy. The methodology was designed to make our project the first scientifically controlled investigation of psychoanalytic therapy. The project was a dismal failure. The data were either not processed, or if processed and written up, banned from publication by the Project Committee on Publication. The committee consisted of myself and the three analytic therapists. Unfortunately, a majority vote determined publication. Among other casualties of the "banning procedure" was a brilliant and original book by Arthur Brodbeck that contained the processed data and findings derived from following fifteen psychological measures extracted from transcripts of the total hours of one therapy. They were constructed to focus on variables concerning the nature of therapist-patient verbal interactions and changes in therapy. They were also designed so that they could be meaningfully interrelated. One paper was published. It described the methodology (most of which did not occur) and supplied the "first finding" of the project: the therapists, except for the first few hours, were described as not anxious or bothered by being observed by three of their peers. Nothing could have been farther from the actuality of the data. I think that much of the time they believed they were not "bothered" by being observed. They *had* to believe it in order to continue. I think all observers were enriched and/or shaken up by their observings. I *know* I was.

What I learned from those observational experiences drastically altered my thinking about therapy and my methods of going about it. I learned through identifying twenty "things" in the therapeutic process that seemed to me (and still do) to be definitely anti-therapeutic. After listening to several of my own therapy tapes I discovered that I too had the same "horrible twenty" running through my therapies. So I began experimenting in my own therapies with ways of controlling for some of those anti-therapeutic behaviors and with ways of substituting different therapist functionings in place of the others. I will confine myself here to discussing only those "anti-therapeutic" therapist behaviors (and my modifications of them) that I consider most relevant to, and critical in, the psychotherapy of cancer patients.

Seven Anti-therapeutic Therapist Behaviors and Attitudes

1. The "sick" patient and the "healthy" analyst

Traditional psychotherapy is problem-oriented and focused on "what's wrong with you?" It pays very little attention to "what's right with you," or to the relative lack of problems. In the project, this consistent focus on the patient's neurotic problems was counterbalanced by the analysts' tacit attitude of "I don't have any neurotic problems" (because they never admitted to any) and thereby increasingly moved the therapist into a superior position and the patient into an inferior one. Such a concentration on the "sick" areas, combined with ignoring the healthy areas, distorts the clinical picture on the negative side and causes some patients to believe that they are "sicker" than they thought. This results in a lowered self-image and increased dependence upon the therapist.

2. Therapist model for patient identification

The therapists did not provide a realistic, human model for patients to identify with, if patients chose to. They failed to provide any personal information about their beliefs, values, standards, life philosophies, and experiences. Instead, they tacitly set up a model of "the way to be is like me: normal, healthy, always right, all-knowing, patient, tolerant, and endlessly persevering in putting up with your neurotic resistance against recognizing and accepting the absolute correctness of my interpretations." And that is predominantly what "resistance" turned out to be in the project: patient failure to agree with an analyst. It was often verbalized by therapists in almost exactly that way: "Why do you resist me?" or, "Why do you resist believing me?" Unfortunately, there were very few occasions upon which a therapist appeared to seriously consider the possibility that his interpretation might have been in error, could have been based upon something the patient never said (a not infrequent occurrence), might have been too global, non-specific, and not tied into behavioral data or was simply so poorly phrased that it just did not make sense or was illogical in and of itself. What a model for identification!

3. Transference interpretations

Therapists' transference interpretations of remarks made by a patient about the therapist often precluded them from recognizing that the remarks

accurately reflected an analyst's active, rampant countertransference behavior or an anti-patient therapist attitude.

4. Therapist's need for agreement

One therapy was terminated when the patient stopped months of "resisting" and suddenly began agreeing with all of the analyst's statements. The
patient did a lousy job—facially, tonally, and verbally—of trying to make
his obviously phony agreements sound genuine. While the therapist did not
recognize what was happening, two of the observers did. The psychological
measure used to process the transcripts picked up the patient's maneuver
and documented it clearly and exactly. This case was supposed to be a successfully concluded psychoanalytic psychotherapy, but the book of the psychological measures said otherwise. No wonder it was banned!

5. Therapist's lack of respect for patients

The therapists' prevailing attitude toward the patients was that of a benign,
all-knowing parent talking down to a stubborn child, or to one who was
relatively unintelligent. The more often I observed the therapists' failure to
treat the patients as fellow adults and their thinly veiled annoyances with
the patients for having different opinions than themselves, the more I
gained a greater and greater respect for the patients. How patient they were
with the therapists. How hard they tried in so many ways to be understood.
How gentle, tolerant, or silent they were about various gross misunder-
standings by the therapists. How imaginative, careful, and persistent were
their efforts to get the therapists back into trying to understand them as
they actually were, as opposed to the ways the therapists "knew" they
were.

6. Therapist's failure to provide the patients with appropriate appreciation feedback

Each therapist obviously enjoyed positive statements made by his patient
about the therapist himself, but they rarely responded in kind.

7. Therapist's distortions

I gained a healthy disrespect and distrust of therapist's memories—my own
included. Comparing the transcript of the hours with the therapist's one to
two hours of post-hour dictations allowed me to see many kinds of distortion processes and patterns of distortion. The therapists tended to change
the content of the hour to fit their interpretations within that hour. This
unconscious process probably became the basis for their future certainties

about the fitting-correctness of many non-fitting-incorrect interpretations. I came to the conclusion that one major function of the memory process is to provide us with evidence (whether nonexistent or scrambled to fit) for what we already believe. That is why I run a sound recorder in most of my therapy hours, as a means of checking out the evidential basis for any particular interpretation.

The Therapeutic Principles and Methods Extracted from the Anti-Therapeutic Therapist Attitudes and Behaviors

Instead of listing and describing these separately, I am going to use the device of putting it all together into a theoretical ''speech'' given to a cancer patient during our first session. Actually, this is a misrepresentation, since I do not lay it all out at one time, but bit by bit over the first five hours, as it seems appropriate to the context: how urgent the patient is to talk about the cancer and the self, or to secure information as to what the cancer psychotherapy will be like. The ''speech'' follows.

''I will describe my version of what is required from *both of us* in order for this psychotherapy to be effective. I cannot promise you that the therapy will effect the cancer, but I believe that such is possible. We are both aware of the cancer and *we* will fight it *together*. We are both aware of the odds for life or death. We will work *together* to try and increase the odds for life. If death from cancer does occur, I will be *with* you till the end, if you so desire. In any case if you work *with* me in the ways to be described, I will help you to learn active ways of being and doing that will be of real value for you in coping with the various emotional problems that are associated with having cancer and cancer therapy. I promise that these ways of being and doing will cause you to feel better about yourself and your life and living in the future; whether it be for a normal life span, or shorter.

''I have worked with eighty-six cancer patients over a thirty-year period, helping them to cope. Twenty-two of those patients worked with me at fighting their cancer by learning how to be more active and assertive in their own behalf. (Then I show them the statistics regarding those patients and answer all questions they have about the figures.) Incidentally, I have discovered through experience that I work best with only one cancer patient at a time, so if you decide to go on with me—you are the *one*.

''I have already described to you in general, before you told me about yourself, your personality makeup, your feelings about yourself, and some aspects of your life experiences. The goals of our therapy *together* will be to help you like yourself instead of disliking yourself, to feel yourself as an active force in life rather than a passive, nice person who is dedicated to being nice to others. *We* will emphasize the lifeful joys of living and the importance of effective functioning. You see, I believe that the first three letters of function were put there knowingly, because that's what *fun* really is: the feeling derived from effective functioning in any area in which one has ability and confidence. I will help you to learn how to function effectively—interpersonally and for yourself. As you experience the positive differences in outcome and the positive feelings that occur, then you will begin to gain confidence in your self. The more such experiences you have, the more self-confidence you will feel.

"*Our* therapy will be based in the simple fact that our beliefs determine our behavior. Thus, if I believed the best way to get along in the world was to be nice to just about everyone else, because this would prevent me from being disliked and cause me to be liked instead, then I would certainly do my damnedest to do just that. Of course, this would involve giving low priority to my own needs, wants, feelings and opinions, because a nice-nice person focuses exclusively on the needs, wants, feelings, and opinions of other people. If this actually worked—wonderful! Unfortunately, *we* humans are so constituted that *we need* and *have to have,* self-full satisfaction of our own needs, wants, feelings, and opinions—as much as is realistically possible. The "satisfaction" of satisfying other people just does not substitute or make up for the lack of satisfaction of our own self. Some of the finest human qualities and behaviors are embodied in the concept of nice, but only if they are appropriate and in balance with our own needs. If we set out to make niceness our self-identity, then we have made it a virtue. Actually, it can be categorized as a form of promiscuity: indiscriminate niceness.

"Now for 'simple fact' number two. Just as our beliefs determine our behaviors, so also do the results or consequences of our behaviors reaffirm or challenge our beliefs. If the results attained by our behaviors reaffirm the underlying belief, hurrah for the belief and the behaviors resulting therefrom! However, if the behaviors produce consequences, then the underlying belief responsible for those behaviors has to be identified, reexamined, altered, or discarded. We usually do not do this for quite a while, since another quality of our humanness is a great reluctance to change our beliefs. Therefore, we often never identify the belief; instead, we work harder at the ineffective behavior pattern, thinking such things as 'I wasn't nice enough, or in the right ways'; and so it goes. Unfortunately, usually the same or different consequences occur and continue to be rationalized away. Keeping this going too long is both nonadaptive and maladaptive. I am going to help you replace nonadaptive habit patterns with effective ones. This means the underlying belief responsible for an ineffective behavior pattern has to be identified and modified, or discarded and replaced with a different belief that will logically lead to different behaviors.

"Our therapy work has to be based upon what I call Open Communication. This, ideally, means a free flow of spontaneous information from me to you and from you to me. Information about anything either one of us feels is relevant at the moment. In fact, anything you feel curious about or want to know *is* relevant. To achieve this we have to verbalize the feeling in the form of a request or a question. Thus, anytime you would like any information from me about myself, my life record and experiences, my feelings, my thoughts, my opinions, my values and beliefs, my prejudices, my neurotic areas, my healthy areas, what I think or feel about you or a behavior of yours—ask—and I'll tell you exactly what comes to mind. It will be the truth as nearly as I know it to be. I guarantee to tell you anything about myself, but nothing about another person or patient. I know from experience that you will not feel free to exercise this right, so you will have to work at doing so, because you will find that any such request of me will be of great importance to both of us and to the therapy. On the other hand, I respect your privacy, because you have guarded it so carefully throughout your life. So anytime I ask for information you don't feel like supplying, that's ok with me.

"We will both try to practice a sense of mutual respect and concern about each others' feelings and humanness. In normal life events I consider other people's feelings as important as mine and mine as important as theirs. In this situation, however, I regard your feelings as more important than mine, since you are the one who is in one of the most difficult situations imaginable: having cancer. So, please work at getting your feelings out, no matter what you think my feeling reaction might be.

"Let's try to be as spontaneous, direct, and interactive as possible. Actually that's incorrect. Don't worry about me. I'll be that way because that's the way I've taught myself to be. What I actually meant was—please, *you* work hard at being more spontaneous, direct, and interactive as possible.

"I believe strongly in the value of humor in life and in psychotherapy. The way I go about them, they are relatively the same. Life is trying to be understood and to understand. Most of us work hard at both aspects. What is so sad or ridiculous, depending upon one's orientation, is that we very often fail to be understood or to understand. If we accept this as what commonly happens to us, then we can learn to appreciate being understood or achieving understanding as special, positive happenings. If we don't take being understood and understanding for granted, then we won't be frustrated by failure—since only an expectation is frustrated, not hope. We can be understood and we can understand, but usually only if we accept both as exceedingly difficult processes that gradually emerge from learning about effective and ineffective modes of communicating. We mean to communicate and to understand—effectively and exactly. If you can accept that these are relatively uncommon occurrences, then you can laugh at yourself for once again feeling hurt by failure in either direction. We have a choice about how to treat our unintended absurdities: laugh or cry. I prefer laughing. Understand though, I will never find anything humorous about cancer or any of its implications. This doesn't mean that we can't laugh about some of my behaviors and experiences and those of others—including your own. Everything isn't cancer connected. We need the periodic lightness of humor and laughter to distract ourselves and to discharge the tension, anxiety, and heaviness feelings that build if one thinks consistently only about cancer. (I then describe the principle of multipossibilities.) And while I'm on the subject of multipossibilities let's make a contract to accept our inevitable human differences of opinion. We will have some interesting discussions while exploring our many reasons for thinking and believing differently about the same thing, but for our own sake let's try not to convince the other one that "my" opinion is the right one. A waste of time, since frequently both opinions are correct and parts of a whole. One difference of opinion that isn't even worth discussing is our differing memories about something that happens, or is said, during this or any other therapy hour. Memories are necessary, inevitable, and not to be trusted, since one of the major functions of memory and perception is to provide us with evidence for what we already believe. Disagreements based on differing memories are rarely resolved, because we tend to have unwarranted confidence in our perceptions and our memories.

There are things that I have more knowledge and experience about and there are some things I can do better, but the same applies to you as regards me. I am here to share those knowledges and experiences with you and to teach you about any of those doings, and I will expect the same from you.

One last point before we begin working. I take for granted that everyone, in every day, manifests at least one neurotic behavior. In other words, a perfect neurotic-less behavioral day would be a rarity, or a misperception. A neurotic behavior is a behavior that has failed in its goal and caused consequences to the self or someone else and has been repeated more than three or four times. One reason we have such trouble recognizing them is that often we stupidly feel badly about being less than perfect. We tend to feel that we have failed. Actually, real failure lies in not recognizing a neurotic behavior, because then it can go on and on. Success is when we do recognize one in action or after it has happened. A real triumph, because recognizing it gives us the opportunity to stop it by using our conscious powers of intelligence, knowledge, and multipossibilities. We can then substitute a different or new behavior in its place. We can stop a neurotic behavior almost any time we recognize it, but it will be back. Old negative habits never die, they just disappear for indeterminate time periods as they become replaced by new effective habit patterns. We will label such ineffective old habit patterns as enemies of the self. Accept their return in certain stressful situations as natural humanness, but accept also that they can be immobilized and replaced if one learns to recognize their reappearance.''

Summary

1. Prerequistes to Cancer Psychotherapy

A. A psychotherapist must have prior knowlege about the range of coping problems with which cancer patients are confronted.

B. A psychotherapist must have prior knowledge about the probable inevitability of his experiencing disturbing emotional reactions to helplessness—hopelessness, identification with the cancer patient, and to dying and death.

C. The personality and life history of a psychotherapist are probably critical factors in determining whether or not he should attempt fighting/coping psychotherapy.

D. A psychotherapist must have prior knowledge of the available assumptive psychodynamics and life history patterns of "cancer patients," as contained in the literature.

E. A psychotherapist must have prior knowledge of the therapeutic orientations, principles, methods, and procedures utilized by others in their fighting/coping therapy efforts.[7,10]

2. Therapeutic Orientation, Principles, Goals, and Procedures for PNS Cancer Patients

A. Therapeutic orientation: the Schemata.

B. Principles and Goals:

1. Fighting is the predominant mode of coping.
2. Replace subjective helplessness with subjective hopefulness.
3. Replace objective helplessness with objective hopefulness.
4. Help the patient to recognize the PNS, its origins, its manifest patterns of behavioral expression, its ineffectiveness and the psychological, interpersonal, and biological consequences that ensue therefrom. Label the PNS as *the enemy of life and self.*
5. Familiarize the patient with the concept of mobilizing host resistance.
6. Help the patient to develop new habit patterns of cognitive, verbal, and behavioral self-full self-assertiveness; making and carrying into action decisions made from choice and in one's own behalf, and in spite of what other persons might say or think.
7. Development of a warm human relationship through open communication. A relationship emergent from a pre-agreed upon and carried-out

contract of bidirectional, absolute truthfulness.* One that produces mutual understanding and acceptance of and respect for each others' feelings and humanness propensities.

8. Practice and teach the principle of multipossibilities.
9. Identify and reinforce the positives in the patient through appreciation reactions: immediate descriptive feedback of any positive therapist reaction to something the patient has said or done in the past or present. These appreciation reactions identify what the therapist is reacting to and why he values it.
10. Encourage externalization of the "secret self" verbally and behaviorally.
11. Counteract negative self-image statements by asking the patient to enter into a contract whereby each negative statement about the self *has* to be followed by a positive one (i.e., a quality, perception, thought, doing, life experience, etc.)
12. Be active in establishing an operational relationship with the operational oncologists, the immediate family, and the "closest" friend.
13. If there has been a loss or disruption of a critical life situation that previously had provided stabilizing rewards for the PNS, then actively explore the exigent possibilities of replacement or a mending of the disruption.
14. Expect both new and old coping problems to appear throughout therapy.
15. If the patient is "terminal," shift to coping/fighting. Be active, imaginative, and aggressive in helping with the coping problems and in ways and means of keeping some hope alive.

Notes

1. Renneker, R. and Cutler, M. (1952), "Psychological Problems of Adjustment to Cancer of the Breast." *J.A.M.A.,* 148:833.
2. Bacon, C., Renneker, R. and Cutler, M. (1952), "A Psychosomatic Survey of Cancer of the Breast." *Psychosom. Med.* 14:453.
3. Renneker, R. (1957), "Psychological Impact of Cancer." *Year Book of Cancer.*
4. —— (1957), "Countertransference Reactions to Cancer." *Psychosom. Med.* 19:409.
5. —— et al, (1963), "Psychoanalytical Explorations of Emotional Correlates of Cancer of the Breast." *Psychosom. Med.* 25:106.
6. Holden, C. (1978), "Cancer and the Mind: How Are They Connected?" *Science* 200:1363.
7. LeShan, L. (1977), *You Can Fight for Your Life.* New York: Jove Publications.

* The placebo maneuver with the terminal patient is the one exception.

8. *The American College Dictionary* (1959). New York: Random House.

9. Eissler, K. R. (1955), *The Psychiatrist and the Dying Patient*. New York: International Universities Press.

10. Achterberg, J., Simonton, O. C., Matthews–Simonton, S. (1976), *Stress, Psychological Factors, and Cancer*. Forth Worth, Texas: New Medicines Press.

9 Psychoanalytic Therapy with Cancer Patients

Some Speculations

Harold F. Searles

Upon being invited in March of 1978 to contribute a chapter to this book on the psychotherapeutic treatment of cancer patients, I reacted with a kind of self-depreciation concerning my potentiality for making a contribution to this subject that went far beyond my realistic lack of credentials as an authority on this subject. It was quite true that, during the thirty years of my work as a psychoanalyst and psychoanalytic therapist, I had worked with no greater number of cancer patients, or relatives of cancer patients, than had any other analyst over a similar time span.

But far beyond this realistic basis for modesty, I reacted initially as though I had scarcely ever before heard of cancer. This naïveté I soon recognized to be grounded in counterphobic denial. Upon starting to question this denial of essentially any experience whatever concerning cancer, I promptly recalled that, throughout my childhood and youth, I implicitly and quietly assumed that I would die, one day, of cancer, as had each of the only two grandparents I had known. It is only since each of my parents has died, during my adult life, of coronary-artery disease that I have been relatively inclined to assume that this, rather than cancer, will be the mode of my eventual death. I am not speaking here on any informed, medical-statistical level, but only on a kind of personal-superstitious one.

So, in short, my initial naïve response to the invitation to contribute a chapter was based less upon any realistic lack of relevancy of this subject to my life and work than upon my unconscious reaction to it as being all too relevant. In addition to my attempt to maintain under repression my long-time fear of death from cancer, there are additional determinants of my denial-based, subjective naïveté which will be touched upon in my further speculations here.

I react violently against the idea that cancer is potentially curable through psychological means. My own subjective infantile-omnipotence has tyrannized my life to such an extent, and the relief I have gained from its partial resolution has been so welcome, that such an idea is anathema to me. My late training analyst, Ernest E. Hadley, found a place in his classically analytic approach for teasing, and on occasion addressed me as "God Searles" in his highlighting of my subjective omnipotence. My papers on my psychoanalytic therapy with schizophrenic patients discuss, repeatedly, the repercussions of these patients' strivings for omnipotence, and their rekindling the therapist's comparable strivings in the course of his attempts to help them. In the latter phases of my training analysis which, incomplete though it was (as, I have come long ago to realize, are all analyses), had enabled me to undergo a great deal of personality change in many regards, I gained a clear sense of the basic unknowability of the precise ingredients which had gone into, and were going into, such changes. I felt that unconscious changes were at work, deep within me, which were as far beyond my predominantly obsessive-compulsive orientation as though they were powerful currents, deep in an ocean, whose workings were barely perceptible on the ocean's surface. The fact that I felt able, to the extent that I did, to give myself up to these currents during the later years of my analysis represented, for me, a tangible and most memorable (even though partial) resolution of my erstwhile grandiose need to know and be in intellectual control of everything.

My feeling concerning this present subject, further, is that we cannot arrogate to ourselves such benignly omnipotent power (i.e., the fantasied power to be able to cure cancer through psychological means) without taking upon ourselves, in the same process, a comparably omnipotent power for malignity. That is, if we hold ourself capable of curing cancer by psychological means in the patient with whom we are working, then we must hold ourself capable, as part of the bargain, of having caused the cancer in the first place, or of being able to do so in future patients. This corollary may not at all follow scientifically—although I believe it would—but at least it would follow in our reasoning on a primitive-superstitious level. If we are going to take the powers of a benign god into our hands, we cannot do so without at the same time taking upon ourselves the power of a diabolical god also.

I surmise that relatively few medical psychoanalysts, as compared with non-medical psychoanalysts, are prone to attribute to psychoanalytic therapy a potentially omnipotent effect upon bodily physiology and anatomy. But one of the vignettes in my personal experience has to do with a medical psychoanalyst, the late Frieda Fromm-Reichmann. Since childhood I have had nearsightedness which limits my vision to 20/200; that is, without glasses I must be within twenty feet of a sign, for example, which a person with normal vision can read at two hundred feet. It never occurred to me, during my training analysis, that this condition would be altered by the analysis, nor was it. Some years after my analysis was over, Frieda commented to me, in full seriousness, looking at my thick-lensed glasses,

"I don't see why Hadley didn't help you to get over your myopia." Tact is something in relatively short supply on my part, and I have always felt, since then, a quiet pride that I was able to muster sufficient courtliness not to utter the retort which came to my mind, "And I don't understand why your analyst didn't help you to grow a couple of feet more." Frieda was four feet, ten inches in height; I cite Bullard (1959) here, in my exactitude. Frieda's capacity for tenderly empathic psychotherapeutic relatedness was world-renowned; but her assertiveness, equally important to her therapeutic success and well known to her colleagues, was comparably formidable.

The cruelty of any such omnipotent self-expectations as Frieda's comment to me implied should be noted here. I recall, for example, a psychoanalytic patient of mine who was bitterly disappointed in herself, and much less so in me, at finding that she was unable, through various psychological attempts including her years of analysis with me, to cure her uterus of fibroids; she had to resort to surgery. One could argue that, had she had an analyst who fully shared her deep conviction that such results were analytically achievable, these might have come about. But I have had, for one lifetime, all too much of such omnipotent self-expectations.

I regret that, as can already be seen, this paper must rely more upon speculation and less upon solid clinical experience with the subject, than the reader (as well as I) would wish. But it does seem to me that there are striking similarities and many close analogies between this subject and psychoanalytic therapy with schizophrenic patients, a clinical field with which I have had much experience.

Chronic schizophrenia, like cancer, is malignant, inspires a kind of superstititous awe in the populace, and causes the sufferer to be regarded as someone set apart from his fellow human beings. A sense of secrecy and shame tends to surround the condition and the person who suffers from it, much as used to be the case with tuberculosis decades ago. The concept of "process schizophrenia," which I do not find meaningful, is particularly analogous to cancer. "Process schizophrenia" is a term which connotes, by contrast to "reactive schizophrenia," that the patient is afflicted with a schizophrenic process which is of a basically unknown and unknowable, but essentially hereditary, physico-chemical nature, and which proceeds on its innately malignantly chronic course essentially irrespective of outer reality, for it is held to be of a self-determined nature, rather than in the nature of any reaction to the person's psychological environment.

The reader may ask why, then, if I regard even "process schizophrenia" as potentially amenable to, or at least ameliorable by, psychotherapy, why do I not regard cancer likewise? I have no convincing answer for this, and can only plead that, at least for me, there are limits which one must find for one's aspirations and self-expectations. I am sure that a factor here is that my psychoanalytic therapy with schizophrenic patients, although effective to a degree and not infrequently inspiring to me, was also sufficiently limited as to leave me with much disappointment as to my capacities for that work, such that it is not at all a matter of my having demonstrated to myself that I can conquer chronic schizophrenia, and am filled with confident zest for taking on cancer next. I am, instead, a badly bruised veteran of long wars of—in too many, although by no means, all instances—dubious outcome.

In my earlier writings (Searles, 1965), I have described that the therapist, in working with the chronically schizophrenic patient, tends to come to identify with the schizophrenia which is afflicting the patient. He tends to do this partly out of the frustration of his attempts to rescue the patient from the illness; then, out of his helplessness-born vindictiveness (all greatly intensified by the extent to which his infantile-omnipotent aspirations have been rekindled in the course of this challenging work), he tends to feel at one with the patient's illness, in a spirit that at least *this* is something which is capable of affecting the change-resistant patient. I have seen this same phenomenon in my teaching-interviews with seriously depressed patients who have made one or more suicide attempts. That is, I find that such a person is, not surprisingly, difficult to interview, and often, in fact, so extremely ungiving and walled-off to my attempts to work with him that I find myself, time and again, so exasperated at feeling unable to make any emotional impact upon him that I keep bringing him back, time and again, to narrating the details of his nearly successful attempt to kill himself.

In a relatively recent paper (Searles, 1976) I hypothesized that the symptoms of any patient in psychoanalytic therapy, irrespective of his diagnosis, need in the course of the therapy to become transitional objects for both therapist and patient in order for the therapeutic process to achieve a relatively full resolution of the symptoms. In the instance of patients whose illness is so formidable as chronic schizophrenia, suicidal depression, or cancer, it can be seen that it is a most challenging task for the therapist to become aware of his own identifying so deeply with the patient's illness. This kind of experience requires him to make contact with and to integrate early-childhood images of himself as being non-humanly destructive. I would fully assume that, in any therapist's long-time psychoanalytic therapy with a cancer patient, the therapist inevitably and necessarily would go through a phase of feeling identified with, and being perceived by the patient essentially as, the cancer itself.

The plea to be rescued, as that plea is conveyed by the schizophrenic patient at any rate, has in it a kind of spuriousness, for behind it there is a largely unconscious cherishing of the schizophrenic mode of existence, and with this a determination not to let the therapist rob him of this. To what extent this is true in one's work with cancer patients, I can do little more than conjecture.

If the therapist is well known to have a special interest in some particular field, whether it be schizophrenia or cancer or whatever, it is inevitable that the patient will feel under a demand to feed that special interest of the therapist. It is commonplace for me, for example, to find patients dredging up some uncharacteristically weird bit of their experience and serving it to me for my presumed delectation in a spirit of ill-concealed contempt for my own presumed craziness. It seems to me that anyone who specializes to a degree in some particular clinical area must be alert to the psychodynamics involved in this kind of thing. It brings in the whole question of goal-oriented psychoanalysis and psychoanalytic therapy, which is well beyond the attempted scope of my paper. But I make mention of this matter as a way of introducing the topic of the demands, real and projected, by which the patient comes to feel oppressed in the work.

Incidentally, the topic of the therapist's special interest in cancer has involved for me, as I have thought about it, the discovery of an additional determinant of my initial disinterest in the invitation to contribute a chapter to this book. When I was a child, my father had a men's clothing store in a village in the Catskills, and a couple of stores up the street was a variety store owned by a middle-aged couple. My mother used to spend much time there, sitting with the proprietor's wife and, usually, two or three other women of similar years, and gossiping until the cows came home. My memories are from a time when I was perhaps five to seven years of age. As I heard it, silently from the fringe of things, nearly all their chatter devolved into two main themes: sex and cancer. They all seemed to share as lascivious an interest in discussing the cancer of some inhabitants of our village as in discussing the latest evidence of an affair or an illegitimate pregnancy. My father and his friends, by contrast, while much given to recounting the latest sexual jokes they had heard, showed no unusual interest whatever in cancer. In short, in terms of my childhood experience, cancer is a subject about which a woman, but not a man, possesses a lively interest.

The cancer patient who, in addition to undergoing formidable medical and surgical procedures, is involved also in psychotherapy, must tend to be assailed by doubts as to how this psychotherapy can possibly be a contribution to his life. His cancer condition tends to make the psychotherapy seem insignificant as any potentially curative, or even palliative, measure, and to make it seem, much more, as but one additional demand upon the waning energies of one who has more than enough already with which to contend. This situation tends to cast the therapist, in the eyes of both participants, as being an energy sapping parasite, equivalent to the cancer itself. To the extent that the patient projects upon the therapist his own repressed oral demandingness, such a perception of the therapist (on the part of both the patient and the therapist himself) is greatly intensified.

Another part of this complex picture is the cancer's giving vicarious expression to the oral demandingness which, so I am postulating, the patient is repressing and projecting upon the therapist. Thus the therapist, while experiencing himself as not well-differentiated from the cancer itself, may be feeling under intense demands to rescue from being devoured from cancer a patient who is massively repressing any awareness of genuine psychological dependency upon, and need for, his help. Such a patient would be attempting to wall off his repressed dependency feelings, much as he would hope that the cancer can become medically or surgically walled off and removed, and to keep these feelings projected into the therapist and walled off, as it were, within the latter.

Such a patient-therapist interaction would tend powerfully to evoke the therapist's fantasied-omnipotence as an unconscious defense against the realistic helplessness and insignificance he would tend to feel. Further, then, to the degree that the therapist becomes caught up in omnipotent goals in the work with the patient, he (the therapist) indeed is burdening, however unwittingly, the patient with essentially insatiable demands (for fulfillment of the therapist's largely unconscious strivings for omnipotence). Thus the therapist and the cancer, each in the nature of a devouring affliction upon the patient, become extremely difficult to maintain (in the experience of both patient and therapist) as perceptually differentiated, unconsciously, from one another.

As a part of this same process, in the largely unconscious experience of both therapist and patient, it will be difficult for the patient to be perceived as differentiated from the cancer. For example, the therapist tends to experience the need-denying but implicitly demanding patient as being nothing less than a malignant affliction, much as the patient naturally experiences the cancer itself.

But now, in this portrayal, it is well to give a more comprehensive picture of the importance, in working with the cancer-patient, of achieving various differentiations—not only such basic differentiations as those among the patient, the therapist, and the cancer.

Since cancer, like schizophrenia, is something the exact nature and origin of which has never been defined scientifically, and since it tends to threaten the patient with an essentially non-human status—set apart from his fellow human beings—it serves as a kind of Rorschach card not only for these people round about, but also for himself, to project into the cancer condition all kinds of unconscious threats. One of the therapist's greatest potential opportunities for deeply helping the patient is to discover, with him, the nature of these projections, and to come to distinguish clearly between them and the cancer itself. In other words, the therapist may help the patient to separate out what is the realistic physical threat to life—the cancer—from the primitive, distorted perceptions that have been added onto that, by the patient himself as well as family members and others.

There are real, external hazards to life, and we all eventually die. But it has been my experience, in my own analysis as well as in decades of working with patients with illnesses of various diagnoses, that what tends to be intolerably anxiety provoking are not these external threats *per se,* but rather the unconsciously threatening psychological contents which have been projected onto, or into, these truly external threats.

At the beginning of the work, neither the therapist nor the patient can know at all fully what the cancer represents unconsciously to the patient; but the two can work together in such a way that this becomes clearer. Hopefully the therapist can become sufficiently free from the patient's and his own urgent demands upon himself to begin to notice, and call the patient's attention to, those junctures in the sequences of the patient's associations, and of the interactions between the two pariticipants, at which either the patient's thoughts, or the therapist's own thoughts, turn once again to the subject of the cancer. In this standard psychoanalytic fashion, the two can gradually discover various of the heretofore unconscious defensive functions which the fact of the cancer (or, more precisely, the preoccupation with the fact of the cancer) is serving in the patient's psychological life.

It is realistic to hope and expect that, to the extent to which this procedure is followed, the two participants can discover, together, that the cancer has taken on, or will come to take on as the therapy continues, all sorts of psychological connotations as the symbol of covert sexual threats, murderous feelings, various primitive self-images, and so on, on the part of one or both the participants.

A number of narcissistic patients with whom I have worked have equated, in dream material and comparable material from their unconscious, their narcissism with life-destroying cancer; hence I would be prepared to find that, in working with a patient who actually has cancer, one of the unconscious meanings this has for him is the narcissistic, foreign-body, inimical-to-life area of his personality functioning. The cancer is likely to represent his unconscious denial mechanism itself, so alien to living in good access to inner and outer reality. I have already indicated that the cancer is likely to come to be seen as representative of each participant's oral, devouring, basically infantile-omnipotent demandingness.

In the course of my work with one woman whose husband had an eventually fatal cancer, it became very difficult, indeed, to distinguish between her at-times-malignant hostility toward him, and his cancer itself. I do not doubt, in retrospect, that her frequent detailing, during the sessions, of the latest medical developments in the treatment of her husband's advancing cancer, was serving to keep largely off the scene any full exploration of the more malevolent of the feelings between herself and me in the transference-countertransference context.

If I ever learn that a cancer is discovered in me, it will be a struggle for me to become convinced that this is not a curse brought upon me by reason of my malevolence, my malignancy at a psychological level, toward others, including those who have loved me. And, in turn, I shall have to do more exploring than heretofore of those reactions on the part of my mother toward me—among many more loving reactions—as being inherently in the nature of a curse, the product of an unwanted pregnancy, upon her. I have much reason to believe that I was, in conventional terms, the product of a sought-for pregnancy, and I received much love from my mother. But I knew a full measure, too, of feeling unloved, and of experiencing myself as being a basically non-human affliction to her.

It is scarcely believable to me that any mother is so thoroughly loving toward and accepting of her child as never to confront him with any of the "Bad Mother" attitudes so prominent on the parts of the mothers of schizophrenic patients. I surmise that everyone has experienced in childhood some degree of feedback from the mother giving the child to experience himself as being in the nature of a curse, the product of an unwanted pregnancy, for the mother. If the adult who was once this child now develops cancer, one of the unconscious meanings for him of this cancer is that it is a just curse for his having been such a curse upon his mother's existence.

To illustrate the need for the therapist (as well as the patient) to become able to differentiate clearly between the patient and the patient's cancer, I shall cite two experiences, by way of analogy, from my personal life; I do this partly to avoid the task of having carefully to disguise (for the preservation of anonymity) vignettes from my work with patients.

My mother, widowed at the age of sixty-four by my father's fatal coronary occlusion, herself suffered a coronary occlusion some five years later, at night during a rare visit in my marital home. She recovered from this and lived until the age of eighty-four, when she died (in 1972) during the night after a pleasant evening of bridge with elderly women friends in her home.

During my approximately semi-annual visits to her with my wife and children, the nights we spent in her home were anxious ones in her last years. When she was wakeful during the night, I was anxious lest she was having another heart attack and might die imminently. I do not doubt that death wishes toward her were part of the feelings at work in me, but only part. The experience I want to cite here was on one of such occasions when, filled with more dread than usual, I had an awesome sense that she, moving about there in her small nearby bedroom, was death itself.

The other experience, undoubtedly related in being from the same poorly analyzed area of my own psychopathology, had occurred nearly fifteen years before, and had to do with my feelings concerning Freida Fromm-Reichmann.

Frieda came to Chestnut Lodge from Germany in 1935, and a home was built for her on the grounds of Chestnut Lodge. At the time of my becoming a psychiatric resident at the Lodge in 1949, I had already had some lecture courses from her, and came fully to share in the general admiration of and fondness for her, although I was not among her intimate friends nor favorite students. I learned much from her, and she enabled me to obtain a grant which made possible the publication of my first book (Searles, 1960). Nonetheless, as will be seen, my feelings toward her were considerably ambivalent.

Although I had no occasion to know in any detail how her daily life was lived, it seemed to me that she was a lonely person, and I found it poignant—as, I am sure, did many of her other colleagues—that the title of her last paper, composed from her unfinished notes on the subject, was "On Loneliness" (Fromm-Reichmann, 1959). Frieda died in 1957 of a coronary occlusion. She died during the night, and her body was found in the second-floor bathroom of her home.

Following her death, in due course her former home was turned into badly needed office space for five members of the sanitarium's psychiatric staff, myself included. Another psychiatrist and I had offices on the second floor; mine had been Frieda's bedroom, one of the doors of which opened into the previously mentioned bathroom. I spent many evenings alone in that building working on papers, and for a considerable time—I have no recollection just how long, but probably for several months—I had a distinctly unpleasant sense (never strong enough to curtail my work, but anxious and awesome and uncanny nonetheless) that the place was haunted by Frieda's ghost, which I sensed as a hostile and menacing presence somewhere in the house. It was only as I came gradually (without any deliberate personal-analytic work devoted to the problem) to experience Frieda's "presence" as being a loving and protective one that I became free from any sense that the place was haunted by her. As I recall, in the last several years of my having my office in that building, before I left the Lodge in 1964, I had no tangible sense of Frieda's presence, one way or another.

I want to re-emphasize that I am not trying to lay claim here to having experienced psychopathology of near-psychotic degree. The setting, nearby the buildings where the patients lived, was at best a rather spooky one. Late one evening, for example, when I was working at my desk, a chronically paranoid woman burst into my office in a panic and, although she was older than I by quite a number of years, she was physically much more fit, such that I would not like to have had to grapple with her; fortunately, I did not need to.

But the haunted feeling I had experienced, relatively mild though it was, I regard as having to do with my projecting of a persecutory introject, entirely comparable with the aspect of the therapist's work with the cancer patient wherein the cancer becomes the target of projected persecutory introjects from within either or both of the two participants in the therapeutic interaction. In the instance of my just-described experience, the hostile ghost of Frieda must have been, so it seems to me, my way of experiencing my unintegrated hostile feelings (undoubtedly to a significant degree transference-based) toward her, and the hostile component of her feelings toward me. The element of my unconscious identification with her presumably was heightened by my own loneliness in that setting. Another way of thinking of it is that I was largely unconscious of how greatly I hated being relegated, as it were, to work in such loneliness. I can well believe that there must have been, in Frieda, hatred concerning the more lonely aspects of her life; but it was characteristic of her not to complain of, or openly reveal, such feelings as loneliness or unmet dependency needs.

Those two analogies from my personal experience are presented here by way of illustrating the point that, in the therapist's work with the cancer patient, the cancer can be better dealt with by the patient once his and his therapist's hateful death wishes toward one another have been dealt with as such, so that the cancer need no longer symbolize (as did, transitorily in my personal experience, my perception of my mother as indistinguishable from death itself, and my sensing in Frieda's former home a menacing ghost of her somewhere about) these threatening emotions.

I do not mean to imply that these psychoanalytic-therapy tasks, relatively easy to describe fairly succinctly, are at all easy of accomplishment. For the therapist, for example, to feel himself to be the object, prolongedly, of negative transference attitudes on the patient's part, of the degree of intensity which I am implying here, is very threatening and burdensome to him. I recall here, by way of analogy, how drained I felt in the course of several years of work with a borderline man who manifested toward me unremittingly, year after year, intense death wishes derived from his childhood experience with an intensely hated foster-father. For a therapist and a cancer patient to keep their focus upon the cancer as such could well serve as a refuge from confronting such death-wishes as that patient manifested toward me.

Relevant to this aspect of psychoanalytic therapy with the cancer patient is the whole literature concerning introjects and introjection. Marie L. Coleman's (1956) paper entitled "Externalization of the Toxic Introject" is of specific relevancy here, and there is much concerning this topic in Hanna Segal's (1964) *Introduction to the Work of Melanie Klein,* Herbert A. Rosenfeld's (1965) *Psychotic States—A Psychoanalytical Approach,* and Kernberg's (1975, 1976) recent books.

A lengthy paper of mine (Searles, 1979), "Jealousy Involving an Internal Object," contains much that is relevant to psychoanalytic therapy with cancer patients. In that paper I describe, for example, a male patient's castration anxiety and sexual impotence as being based in part upon the fact that his penis, the object of much fascinated absorption on the part of his mother during his childhood, has come to represent, unconsciously, a jealously-regarded internal object—a hated, successful rival of his for his mother's interest. His jealous hatred, turned against his penis, interferes with the sexual functioning of his penis, which he regards unconsciously as not being his own bodily organ but, instead, as being in the nature of a hated third person in the oedipal triangle.

Such psychodynamics, when looked for in the psychoanalytic therapy with the cancer patient, would make the therapist alert to the likelihood that the patient is unconsciously jealous of his cancer, the care of which is so much in the forefront of the attention of those responsible for his medical/surgical care that he, the patient himself, may tend to feel largely excluded and ignored. Unworked-through feelings of this sort, at an unconscious level, would tend to make him much less co-operative than otherwise with those who are trying to "care" for the cancer in such a way as to free him from it. Furthermore, there may develop a de-differentiation, at an unconscious level, between his own personal identity on the one hand and the cancer on the other hand, for by being thus fused with the cancer, unconsciously, he can defend himself against the recognition of his repressed jealousy toward it when experienced by him as being a separate but successful oedipal-rival, psychological object. I have already touched, earlier in this paper, upon the tendency in psychoanalytic therapy with cancer patients for each of the two participants to come to view the other as being undifferentiated from the cancer itself.

I surmise that the therapist's develoment of an irrational fear, lest the patient's cancer somehow spread by contagion to himself, would have as one of its causes these unconscious jealousy psychodynamics. It has long been a belief of mine that one can find some reason or other for experiencing envy and/or jealousy of anyone, no matter how unfortunate this other person may at first appear. It seems to me eminently likely that the therapist will have occasion to feel jealous of the patient for being the object of so much care and concern, and to feel jealous of the cancer itself for seeming, from the therapist's view, to be of so much greater significance, in the concern of the patient, than is the therapist himself.

To become quite speculative indeed for a moment, I wonder what it means to the therapist of a patient afflicted with an incurable cancer that the patient presumably knows what will be the fundamental cause of his—the patient's—eventual death. For most of us, this is one of the great unknowns. Even if one thinks of a death from cancer as being one of the least enviable among the possible forms of death, I think we human beings have a deep longing for certainty, for assuagement of our having no knowledge—most of us—as to how and when we shall die. I can imagine a therapist's envying the patient's relatively secure knowledge, as it were, of this.

The cancer patient's envy of the therapist for not being afflicted with cancer, and for being able to live for all practical purposes forever (as, I do not doubt, the afflicted patient views the therapist), are such obviously expectable aspects of psychoanalytic therapy with cancer patients that I shall not elaborate upon them. My paper (Searles, 1961) "Schizophrenia and the Inevitability of Death" contains clinical material and theoretical discussion which I am sure the reader will find relevant to the present topic.

It seems to me likely, nonetheless, that in work with cancer patients, as in work with borderline individuals, the atmosphere of the treatment situation will tend to involve a considerable element of suspense—suspense as to whether the patient's cancer will recur, or as to when the patient's death may occur. In this setting, I believe that the therapist tends to withhold himself from as full a commitment to the relationship as he might otherwise make, lest he do something, in the process of making that fuller commitment, which will upset the patient's precarious equilibrium and set in motion a chain of potentially lethal events. Such a concern on the therapist's part is a milder (but nonetheless tangibly anxious) verison of the threat which one finds to be of maximal intensity in a catatonic patient who is afraid to speak or move, lest he set in motion a chain of world-destroying events.

It is my impression that this sense of suspense which the therapist experiences although felt to be essentially *temporal* in context—the therapist dreading to make a move lest he unwittingly do something which will, for example, lower the patient's resistance to the cancer and thus cause a recurrence of it *in the future*—is basically a function of the tantalizing tentativeness, the lack of relatively full, mutual interpersonal committedness in the patient-therapist relationship *in the present moment*. This impression of mine derives mainly from my work with many borderline patients, work in which such a tantalizingly incomplete committedness, on the part of both the patient and myself, and a treatment atmosphere of unremitting, and at times intense, suspense is characteristic. From what I have been suggesting earlier, one can see that a fuller commitment on the part of both participants entails for each a fuller acceptance of one's own and the other person's humanness, and a relinquishment of grandiose and idealized images of oneself and of the other person.

There is still another in the complex of ingredients, expectable in work with cancer-patients, which I want to mention. To the extent that either participant is accustomed to relying upon paranoid defenses (and, to my way of thinking, everyone is to some degree), he is likely to find that he can experience most freely his own loving capacities in a setting of approaching separation—in a setting, specifically, wherein the patient's death is most imminent. That is, a relatively highly paranoid person finds it most difficult to experience anything in the realm of a loving sense of intimacy with someone whom he can reasonably expect to be seeing for indeterminately many years in the future; such a prospect confronts him with too great a danger of being devoured and, more basically, with loss of identity through fusion with the other person. But if he can rely upon the certainty that the relationship will not be lasting very long, he can permit himself, as it were, to care with unaccustomed depth for this other person. The popularity of love songs which have a sweetly poignant setting of separation rests in part, in my impression, upon this soothing appeal to that aspect of us which longs for relatedness, yet fears that relatedness will bring a loss of our individuality. In those songs to which I refer, the separation, or imminent separation, itself is highly libidinized.

The aspect of this chapter's topic upon which I have just been dwelling is obviously relevant to my preceding comments about the therapist's difficulties in making a relatively full commitment of himself to the relationship with the cancer patient—difficulties having to do with the suspenseful aspect of the treatment atmosphere. The aspect which I have just been discussing serves, I believe, not so much to modify the therapist's ambivalence, but to intensify it: on the one hand, the patient presents him with a rare opportunity for deeply felt relatedness at minimal long-range threat of loss of the therapist's own ego boundaries; but on the other hand, at a more mature level of ego functioning, the therapist may have reason to fear his imminent loss of this other human being. To the extent that paranoid dynamics are as appreciable in the therapist as they typically are in the borderline patient, his basic fear, here, is that he will lose both—lose the patient through the latter's death, and in the same process lose his own individuality, through his having made the mistake (so to speak) of having come to care too much for, of having developed an identity-fusion (not in actuality on the basis of a too-intense genuine caring, but as an unconscious defense against ambivalence) with the terminally ill patient.

If the therapist can experience relatively fully in awareness, however, both his hateful feelings as well as his loving feelings toward the patient, he need not long unconsciously for the patient's early death to protect him, the therapist, from the loss of himself through the loss of a patient for whom he has come to "care" too deeply. Instead, the therapist can deal with his own grief having to do with the patient's illness, and thus can help the patient, likewise, to grieve. The therapist may well become the one person in the patient's life who dares to bridge the isolation that is shutting the patient off from the world of people and making the patient feel nonhuman.

Not many years ago I attended the funeral of a physician who had died of a cancer which he himself had first detected, after he had been in analysis with me for a number of years. I admired much about this man— his medical astuteness but, far more than that, the bravery which he showed in living the last many months of his life in the clear-sighted knowledge of the danger of his imminent death. I do not recall that he ever wept openly in any of his sessions, nor—and I am reasonably sure of my memory here—did I. Even in retrospect, I believe that my grieving openly would have undermined certain necessary defenses on his part against becoming overwhelmed with grief and unable to do the many things he had to do. But I was quite able to experience grief at his funeral, and one of the things which enabled me to do so was the sense that I had not been responsible for the cancer which killed him. I can only surmise how I might feel in attending the funeral of a patient of mine who had suicided; but I cannot believe that I would experience such relatively uncomplicated grief as I felt then, for I would feel too responsible, too much to blame.

In closing, then, I want to reemphasize that psychoanalytic therapy with cancer patients tends powerfully to revive the therapist's subjective omnipotence, and to require him to come, once again, to some human terms with it. The patient's cancer is not the only malignancy with which the two participants have to reckon, for each of them—like all other human beings—possesses this potentially malignant personality aspect as well. The manner in which the therapist can cope with his own side of this problem, while accepting the help of the patient in this task, is crucial to the two participants' becoming able to work together in this cruelly difficult situation in a fashion which enables them to explore not only the feelings of love, but also the feelings of hate and of grief which the situation will evoke in them.

In summary, it is my belief that the psychoanalytic therapist cannot cure the patient's cancer. But the effectiveness of the psychoanalytic therapy will depend upon, more than anything else, the manner in which the therapist's own "cancer"—his never finally eradicated infantile-omnipotence—is treated by the two human beings involved in the therapy.

References

BULLARD, D. M., ed. (1959), *Psychoanalysis and Psychotherapy—Selected Papers of Frieda Fromm-Reichmann*. Chicago: The University of Chicago Press.

COLEMAN, M. L. (1956), "Externalization of the Toxic Introject: A Treatment Technique for Borderline Cases." *Psychoanal. Rev.,* 43:235-242.

FROMM-REICHMANN, F. (1959), "On Loneliness." *Psychiatry: Journal for the Study of Interpersonal Processes,* 22:1-15.

KERNBERG, O. F. (1975), *Borderline Conditions and Pathological Narcissism.* New York: Jason Aronson.

——— (1976), *Object Relations Theory and Clinical Psychoanalysis.* New York: Jason Aronson.

ROSENFELD, H. A. (1965), *Psychotic States—A Psychoanalytical Approach.* New York: International Universities Press.

———. (1960), *The Nonhuman Environment in Normal Development and in Schizophrenia.* New York: International Universities Press.

SEARLES, H. F. (1965), *Collected Papers on Schizophrenia and Related Subjects.* New York: International Universities Press.

————. (1976), "Transitional Phenomena and Therapeutic Symbiosis." *Int. J. Psychoanalytic Psychotherapy,* 5:145-204. Reprinted on pp. 503-576 in *Countertransference and Related Subjects—Selected Papers.* New York: International Universities Press, 1979.

———— (1979), "Jealousy Involving an Internal Object." On pp. 347-403 in *Advances in Psychotherapy of the Borderline Patient,* ed. by J. LeBoit and A. Capponi. New York and London: Jason Aronson.

SEGAL, H. (1964), *Introduction to the Work of Melanie Klein.* New York: Basic Books (new, enlarged edition 1973).

10 Medicine as Food

Exploring the Unconscious Meanings of Cancer Treatment

Jane G. Goldberg

Children all through the ages seem to never tire of listening with fear, wonder, and a certain amount of glee to the Big Bad Wolf's threat to eat Little Red Riding Hood all up. As with most myths and fairy tales preserved over time, the story must touch upon primitive and yet still relevant conflicts for each one of us.

The fantasy of being eaten up is expressed in a number of ancient myths. Ovid tells the story of Erysichton, whose punishment for his destruction of a sacred grove was an insatiable hunger finally turned against himself in an act of self-devouring.[1] Similarly, the Aztec festival of *tcoqualo* involved the killing and eating of the god Huitzilopochtli in effigy, after which it was said: "The god is eaten."[2]

Lest we think that as sophisticated inhabitants of a modern world we are free of such ancient mythical notions, let us look again. The notion of being eaten up finds a modern equivalent in the fears and fantasies associated with the dread disease of cancer. The wasting of the patient is a well-observed phenomenon in the gamut of types or sites of cancer,[3-10] and it is commonly thought that the hapless victim is being eaten up from the inside-out. It is not unusual to hear a patient say it is as though he were being consumed.

The wasting of the cancer patient suggests physiological disturbances associated with the utilization of food.[11] Weight loss is, in fact, one of the first presenting signs of cancer.[12] As such, the monitoring of weight can serve as either reassurance that the disease is not yet out of hand, or as the dreaded affirmation that the disease is devouring its victim. Eating, then, comes to have absolute and primary significance to both the cancer patient and to those surrounding him.

Infantile feeding experiences largely determine the relation one has to food, and those processes remain associated with food for the duration of life.[13] Because of the human being's unique ability to symbolize, food

182

comes to have conscious and unconscious meaning beyond nutrition. Alternatively, substances that are not strictly defined as food can come to have meaning as food. In the case of cancer, these meanings can have serious implications for the treatment of the disease.

Nutritional Needs of the Cancer Patient

While the precise nutritional needs of the cancer patient are not yet well understood, the notion of the body feeding on itself is largely a myth. The physiological representation of such a notion would be of a tumor feeding on its host. All scientific evidence available thus far indicates, however, that this is not the case. Rather, the host and the tumor have nutritional needs to ensure their respective survival, and they must compete for whatever nutritional goods are available.[14] Tumor and host are, in fact, rivals.

The phenomenon of weight loss appears to be a result of a decline in food intake. Reduction of food intake has indeed been demonstrated in animals in the laboratory.[15] It is commonly observed that cancer patients show a disinterest in and sometimes a revulsion for food, and protein in particular—most often meat.[16] It is possible that this loss of taste for high-protein foods may represent a regulatory mechanism in a biological system intolerant of large amounts of protein.[17] Recent research suggests that an additional component in the weight loss may be an increased nutritional need due to metabolic changes.[18-25]

Precise articulation of the degree to which food intake falls or nutritional needs rise may be extraneous.[26] What seems to be the central problem is that the cancer patient simply fails to eat a sufficient amount to meet his needs.[27] This failure is not a normal response. Humans, as well as other animals, normally respond to a developing deficiency by increasing food intake when the food is freely available.[28-38] To do otherwise results in depletion of vital nutrients, and ultimately in the death of the organism.

The amount of time spent eating progressively declines almost from the beginning of tumor growth,[39] though it may not be noticed until much later. Compensatory mechanisms operate initially. The decrease in feeding duration is balanced by an increase in eating efficiency,[40] so that there is no reduction of actual food intake. Eventually, however, the compensatory mechanisms fail,* and absolute food intake fails. This is probably the point at which an eating disturbance is recognized in the human system.

---

* Reasons for the breakdown in the regulatory mechanisms of food intake and utilization are still obscure. Morrison's review[41] includes the alternative hypotheses: tumor toxins,[42,43] sequestration of essential materials from the host by the tumor[44,45] autoimmune abnormalities,[46,47] associated anemia,[48] malabsorption,[49,50,51] hyperlipemia[52-55] hypoglycemia,[56] response of the CNS to spurious signals,[57-62] metabolic energy loss from excess gluconeogenesis stimulated by tumor demand for glucose.[63,64]

Whether or not there are psychological components that contribute to the loss of interest in food and the subsequent wasting of the cancer patient has not yet been determined. At some point in the illness, though, surely the physiology and psychology reinforce each other. Inability to tolerate or eliminate food due to physiological dysfunction creates psychological disturbances around eating, and may lead to psychological aversions or phobias. Should the disturbance have psychological origins, the mediating mechanisms of the neuro-hormonal, immune, and central-nervous systems will ultimately yield physiological dysfunction as well.

Once the cancer patient begins medical treatment, nutritional deficiencies are likely to occur as a result of the treatment, as well as the disease itself. Medical treatment includes the use of chemotherapy, radiation, and surgery.[65] Both chemotherapy and radiation have profound effects on tolerance for food ingestion and elimination during the course of treatment and, often, for prolonged periods after termination of treatment. Common side effects include nausea and vomiting, dysfunction of the bowels, and revulsion for food. While surgery has a less drastic effect on the ability to utilize food, patients recovering from surgery are routinely intravenously "fed" saline and sugar/water solutions. These water solutions are crucial in preventing dehydration. They do not, however, add any nutritional support to a system already weakened from the physiologic trauma of surgery. In many hospitals, recovering surgery patients who are able to tolerate solid food are offered the services of a nutrition consultant. In spite of data that suggests that eating meat may be related to the development of cancer,[66] cancer patients are routinely grouped together with the other surgery patients, and advised to eat plenty of red meat to build up their strength.

The picture is confusing. Very little research has been performed on the nutritional needs of the cancer patient. Available information is often contradictory and misleading. The cancer patient ultimately suffers from a lack of objective and useful information about how to combat nutritional deficiencies effectively.

The Original Feeding Paradigm

Psychoanalytic theory posits that all human relations have their origin in the relationship to the initial object—the mother.[67] The adult cancer patient who has been competent to make independent eating decisions for much of his life is upon diagnosis and the first manifestation of wasting suddenly transported to a realm close to infancy. It is because of the regressive aspect of being a patient whose eating habits have become of more public concern that the nature of the original feeding paradigm needs to be articulated.

While not all infants come into the world hungry, the desire for food is one of the earliest drive states the infant will experience.[68] Indeed, the entire early life of the infant is characterized by an alternation between hunger and sleep; hunger is the tension state which repeatedly interrupts the calm of sleep.[69]

The feeding situation is the infant's most intense experience of a world outside himself.[70] He does not, however, initially recognize it as such. Intrauterine life consists of a biological unity between mother and child, where the placenta nourishes the growing fetus. After birth, the infant may continue to experience this unity during the act of feeding. The mother's narcissim extends to the child, and the child accepts the breast as part of his "narcissistic milieu."[71]

The hungry infant, however, is confronted with a puncture in his envelope of narcissism. He learns quickly that the supplies he wants are external, that he must experience some frustration, and his state of unpleasure, before his needs are gratified.[72] It is thus, through the tension state of hunger and the feeding situation with the gratifying object, that the infant forms his first object relations.[73]

As the infant is compelled to recognize a world outside himself to meet his need, he finds that objects differ from each other. He learns that some objects which he puts in his mouth will satisfy his drive and thus reduce tension, and others will frustrate him and increase tension.[74] The first recognition of reality, then, is in the differentiation of whether to swallow the object or spit it out.[75] Swallowing represents the first positive instinctual behavior; spitting out represents the first negative instinctual behavior.[76] The decision to incorporate or expel is the infant's earliest judgment.[77]

The close contact the mother and infant have with each other means that there is an intense exchange of emotional communication; the feelings of the one influence and induce feelings in the other.[78] The healthy mother and healthy baby induce positive feelings in each other. The baby who eats his food cooperatively and produces normal, healthy stool gives the mother a feeling of adequacy. She feels that she is emotionally in tune with her baby, and she prides herself on her motherhood. The mother who is sensitive to the delicate balance of frustration and gratification the infant needs for maturation induces in the baby a feeling of pleasurable satisfaction with himself. He knows that he can sometimes have what he wants, and the gratification of his desire feels good. He also knows that sometimes he cannot have what he wants, or not always immediately on the asking, but he easily tolerates the frustration of either not getting or the delay of gratification. Later, with minimal ego development, he may even feel pride in himself for his ability to tolerate deprivation.

Situations can occur, however, which will prove to be overly frustrating or overly gratifying for the underdeveloped ego of the infant.[79] The mother may not be able to read the communications of the child, and in that way, not understand the infant's needs; or, the child may have an inherently weak digestive system, and the mother may be unable to alleviate the infant's discomfort. In these situations, the infant will continue to experience frustration. The mother may begin to question her adequacy. Her frustration at not being able to please the baby may turn into aggressive feelings toward the baby; the infant's frustration at not being able to be pleased will thus turn into aggressive feelings towards the mother. The infant and mother, sensitive to the emotional states of the other, may begin to experience eating as an act filled with anxiety. Eating, and those processes associated with feeding, may come to be experienced by mother and child as unpleasurable, at best, and traumatic, at worst.

The overly gratified infant who is never allowed to experience hunger will come to have expectations about what it means to be in a relationship based on this feeding paradigm. He may, then, have difficulty in moving from his state of narcissistic omnipotence to the post-oedipal object-oriented state where desires can be tolerated with ease, with or without gratification.

Fears that come to be associated with displeasurable feeding often have as their content the idea of eating, or being eaten.[80,81] The fear represents a wish to return to a more pleasurable state of unity. Eating is incorporation, where two objects come to be one. The longing can be to incorporate, or to be incorporated—a yielding of one's own omnipotence to a larger, more powerful object,[82] and this can be anticipated with either pleasure or anxiety.[83]

The object that most readily banishes the state of unpleasure is the mother's breast. As such, she comes to be experienced as omnipotent.[84] As the most important object in the infant's world, she is the object on whom fears of incorporation are projected.[85] The relationship becomes ambivalent. Love and hate are both felt.

For the infant, this may be a confusing situation, and one that his underdeveloped ego cannot handle. And so, he develops the mechanism we call "splitting," by which we mean that the object is split into good and bad parts;[86,87] the good breast and bad breast.[88] The introduction of this mechanism allows the infant to tolerate the fact that his nourisher is also his controller; he is both gratified and frustrated by the same person. Separating the good and bad objects allows him to experience his normal feelings of aggression towards the frustrating object, without fear of destroying the nurturing object.

The fact that the infant continues to put objects in his mouth which do not provide physiological nourishment indicates that oral incorporation has become separated from the function of nourishment. Rather, the stimulation derived from the contact with the object is pleasurable in itself and becomes independent of the original tie to nourishment.[89] The effect of this independence is that objects can come to have symbolic significance.[90]

When the child begins to learn to feed himself, it is an indicator that his symbiotic dependence on the mother is changing to some modicum of independence.[91] Separation is, of course, an ongoing process that begins with birth, but the skill of learning to give oneself nourishment can be seen as a developmental milestone. This act can have symbolic significance in later life when the exigencies of the world demand from the adult that he maintain this self-loving, self-nourishing attribute. Later, during the oedipal phase, the equation of mother and food fades out completely and is replaced by eating attitudes determined by infantile sexual ideas.[92]

Equally important is the infant's reaction to the change from breast to solid foods, the introduction of new tastes and consistencies. Here is reflected for the first time his leaning toward progression and adventureness, where new experiences are welcomed, or a tenacious clinging to existing pleasures, where every change is experienced as a threat and as deprivation.[93] Whichever attitude dominates will have consequence in later developmental roles.

The symbolic equation of mother equals food helps us understand battles around food between mother and infant. The mother may experience every refusal of food as a personal rejection of her maternal care.[94] The child may act out his emotions through eating: he may refuse to eat following a traumatic separation from the mother (rejection of the mother substitute), or he may overeat (treating food as a substitute for mother love). Often, when these situations develop, a noncathected or differently cathected person (nursemaid, friend) may be substituted as the maternal figure in the feeding situation and have more success than the mother.[95]

Parallel to the developmental sequence from mother feeding to self-feeding is the sequence which involves the control, modification, and transformation of the urethral and anal trends.[96] Because body products are highly cathected with libido, they are precious to the child and surrendered to the mother as gifts of love.[97] They are also cathected with aggression, and can be used as weapons through which anger, rage, and disappointment may be discharged. The gradual process of toilet training will proceed uneventfully and untraumatically if the mother retains her sensitivity. She will need to sympathetically mediate between the environmental demand for cleanliness and the child's anal and urethral tendencies.[98]

The Feeding Paradigm in Cancer: Medicine Is Food

Cancer, and the usual concomitant medical treatment, is a regressive experience. Severe psychological reactions have been noted and they include immobilization, depression, anxiety, paranoid responses, feelings of inferiority, aggression, isolation, increased dependency, suicidal thoughts, feelings of rejection, withdrawal, denial, and obsessive preoccupation.[99,100,101] The cancer patient may already be fixated at early developmental stages as the psychosomatic literature suggests, and this itself may play a role in the development of the disease. But even without this conceptualization, the contraction and treatment of the disease sets up situations which necessarily induce regressive feelings in the patient. It is not uncommon for patients to say "If I have to die, I want to do it with dignity," "I couldn't bear to be a burden to my family." Such statements reflect the deep, unconscious material that is touched by the implications of the disease, and the strength of the desire to not allow themselves to be affected by these regressive tendencies.

The typical cancer patient will initially feel quite helpless in the face of his life-threatening disease. He feels that his body is out of conscious control, and that he does not have the internal resources to reverse the progression of the disease.[102] This feeling of helplessness parallels the state of biological helplessness he felt as an infant, where he was dependent on his mother to provide the supplies necessary for life sustenance. It is with these pre-oedipal feelings already activated that the cancer patient seeks help in fighting for his life.

Cultural tradition defines the physician as the person from whom the patient can expect the most help. The physician has superior knowledge and tools that are otherwise unavailable to the patient. All hope for cure is placed in the hands of the physician, and he comes to be endowed with omnipotent powers.

The omnipotence ascribed to the physician parallels the experience the infant has of the mother. Relative to the child, the mother is intensely more powerful. In this regard, the doctor/patient relationship is a structural recreation of the original mother/child relationship.

Evidence of this phenomenon can be garnered from observations of the affective responses of patients and their families toward the physicians. Some patients who have been informed of a poor prognosis will, even in the face of contrary evidence, still maintain the firm belief that their doctor will find a way to save them, or that medical science will make the necessary advancement in time.

The illusion of the cancer patient that he is being eaten away by the disease has its roots in this projection of omnipotence. Despite the horror of the progressive nature of the disease, the fantasy of being consumed is not always met with dread. The fantasy may include the idea that one will be eaten whole, as Jonah by the whale, and spit out without bodily injury. Or, the idea of yielding to a larger, more powerful force may suggest an intimacy that is thrilling, like the threat of the Big Bad Wolf: "All the better to eat you with, my dear." Some patients, upon diagnosis, have expressed relief that the long-dreaded event has actually come to pass. These patients may willingly submit to the will of the cancer. The release from the struggle to ward off the feared event may be pleasurable. Some patients are pleased to finally have a good enough reason to give up self-destructive behavior (smoking, working until exhaustion, late night partying), and use the cancer as an excuse to reverse life patterns.

Because incorporation destroys the object, however, it gives the aim of incorporation an ambivalent character.[103] Accompanying the feeling of pleasure are feelings of anxiety as well. The cancer patient fears the consuming nature of the cancer, and awaits his own eventual destruction with dread.

The patient does not, however, limit the power of incorporation to the disease. Treatment, as well, ravages the body and can come to be experienced as intensely devouring as the cancer. Chemotherapy and radiation destroy healthy cells as well as the diseased cancer cells. The feelings associated with the threat of this new object powerful enough to devour will largely determine the patient's participation in his treatment program.

The physician's devotion to treating the patient parallels the mother's commitment to providing life-sustaining nurturance to the child. Like the mother, he comes to represent life itself. Because his medicine is what will give his patient life, the medicine comes to have the symbolic meaning of food. The patient, like the child, hopes to share in the omnipotent powers of the superior object. Incorporation of the omnipotent figure, or its psychic equivalent of introjection, is the mechanism by which this transfer of power will take place.

On the level of the unconscious where symbolism has power, it makes no difference whether the medicine is ingested orally or whether it is given through body absorption (radiation and injections of chemotherapy) or cutting (surgery). In conditions of regression, all sense organs are conceived as mouth-like.[104,105] Objects are not looked upon as individuals, but rather only as food or providers of food.[106]

Incorporation has the effect of uniting the person with the object. The magical notion of communion, that one can assume the vital power of a desired object through the eating of the object, has wide historical precedent.[107] In many cultures the flesh and blood of dead men are eaten and drunk to inspire the qualities those men personified.[108] Bushmen refrain from feeding their children the heart of a jackel lest they become timid.[109] The cancer patient, too, hopes, then, that in eating the foods of the physician he will acquire the power the physician has come to represent—triumph over death. The patient whose childhood history included feelings of pleasure and safety in the hands of a seemingly omnipotent mother will cooperatively submit to the ministrations of this new omnipotent figure.

With or without the pleasurable anticipation of the beneficial effect of the medication, the physiological reality of treatment remains unchanged. Drug therapy is the administration of a known toxic substance to the body. It is done on the premise that the toxicity of the cancer is more damaging to the system than the toxicity of the drug. Radiation can be lethal. Dosage is carefully adjusted so as not to kill the patient through the cure.

The body responds to the medication/food as though it were undigestible. Spitting out is the body's instinctive response to bad food. The common side effects of the treatment are attempts by the body to reject or eliminate toxic material.[110] Thus, awareness is dual. The conscious agreement to ingest a poison violates the body's awareness that it is being fed bad food and impedes its instinctive reach for nutritional substances.

The body's response to these toxins activates unconscious feelings around the digestion and elimination of food which may have long since been mastered. For the adult whose childhood history showed no significant feeding disturbances, the inability to take in and release food in socially appropriate ways will introduce new fears, accompanied by feelings of shame.

Despite the fact that it is the physician who is feeding the patient these toxic foods, this awareness is generally kept from conscious knowledge. In the service of protecting the omnipotent figure, the patient acknowledges only gratitude for the physician's persistence in treatment and professional skill in applying his techniques. The patient does not acknowledge feelings of aggression toward the object, despite the fact that the physician is the source of the toxic food.

The patient is able to effectively protect the physician from his aggression by resorting to the mechanism of splitting. Good and bad breast are perceived by the infant as separate and unconnected entities. Similarly, the cancer patient who needs to maintain a good/bad object split is unable to integrate the fact that a good doctor is giving bad food.

The relationship to the doctor/food-giver may now become highly ambivalently charged. On the one hand, he is the hoped-for sustainer of life; on the other hand, his food/medicine is poison to the body. The situation replicates the early love/hate relationship to the mother. Dependence on the nurturing object makes discharge of aggression toward the object an impossible solution. The repression of aggression becomes psychologically toxic, just as the medicine is physiologically toxic. While the body may retain instinctive power to attempt discharge of toxicity, the mind may not. The build-up of psychological toxicity may mean that the relationship to the physician/food giver may, in time, become as toxic to the patient as the treatment.

The fantasy of omnipotence and omniscience is doomed to failure, then. The food turns out to be not only bad-tasting, but turns against the body. Further, the power of the cancer more often than not proves stronger than the power of the medicine. The cancer grows. The patient is left with the ravages of the disease and the treatment.

As the power of the food/medicine diminishes, so too is the omnipotent position of the physician in jeopardy. Franz Alexander noted that it is only in the dark that we see ghosts.[111] Most cancer patients become familiar with the various aspects of the disease. They become proficient at de-mythologizing the very particular language of the medical profession. They become acquainted with the statistics predicting the probable course of the disease. They learn lessons in the physiology of their own bodies. In addition, the physician comes to be seen in a more humanized fashion. He is revealed to be vulnerable and mortal.

Concomitant to the de-mythologizing of the physician's power is a consequent evocation of aggression. The aggression is aroused by the thwarting of the dependency needs.[112] Patients who have stripped away their own omnipotent projections from the physician may blame him for anything from poor diagnostic procedures, unforeseen complications, the inability to find effective medication, to the imminent death itself. The dramatic increase in malpractice suits suggests that the manifestation of this phenomenon is rapidly becoming a cultural practice.

The Feeding Paradigm in Psychoanalysis: Words as Food

The effectiveness of psychoanalytic technique depends on the analyst's ability to aid the "transferring" to the analyst early object feelings (object transference), or, in the case of pre-oedipal patients, self-feelings (narcissistic transference).[113] Once this transference has occurred, the patient has the chance to relive early developmental sequences with a new parent object. Inadequately mastered phases can now be successfully mastered under the more sensitive and more therapeutic parenting. The psychoanalyst is sensitive to the maturational needs of the patient, and times his interventions so that they help to move the patient along the developmental process.[114]

The analyst's words to the patient are experienced by the patient as food.[115] Insofar as his interventions are successful in enabling the patient to grow (the growth now is emotional rather than physical), his words are, indeed, symbolic food. The analyst, like the good mother, is careful to dole out his food, achieving a delicate balance between frustration and gratification.[116]

The ideal maturational process in psychoanalysis would proceed consistent with the ideal maturational process in original infancy. The patient moves from a position of dependence to independence, where he learns himself the proper amount of food he can contain, and can even instruct the analyst as to what this proper amount is (self-dosing). He learns impulse control (feces and urine retention), and he learns proper and constructive release of impulses—both positive and negative (elimination of feces, conceived of as both gifts and as weapons).

As with the original maturational process, so too in psychoanalysis is the ideal sequence rarely, if ever, achieved. Resistance to growth is witnessed. Within the context of the transference, the resistance to change is worked through.

Cancer and Countertransference

The effects of the disease and the possibilities of treatment alternatives induce feelings in people close to the patient. Rarely is the choice of treatment the decision of a single person. Rather it typically reflects a group decision made by the patient and those responsible for his care. Thus, the feelings induced in those surrounding him become vitally important.

The kinds of feelings induced depend on the state of the disease and the implications of treatment, as well as the cancer victim's coping mechanisms. If the cancer is considered not terminal and easily treated, the feelings induced are likely to be concern and compassion. As with the mother who is able to successfully relieve the baby of his discontent, the friends and relatives of a cured (or, to be cured) cancer patient will have a feeling of adequacy. While they will not take responsibility for the actual cure, they will pride themselves on their ability to be nurturing and loving in a crisis. They will feel that their competence is reflected in their ability to have secured adequate treatment for the patient.

The feelings induced by a terminal patient are, of course, quite different. Here, the parallel is to the colicky baby for whom it seems nothing can be done to relieve his suffering. In the face of such impotence, one begins to feel helpless and hopeless. The cancer patient too may share these feelings of helplessness and hopelessness.

The feelings the analyst develops for his cancer patient are not unlike those feelings induced in the friends and relatives of the patient. The analyst who has worked with terminally ill patients becomes acutely aware of these induced countertransference feelings. He may not have the time needed for a prolonged analysis. He may feel that time is working against his patient and his work. He may feel panic, wish that he could do something for his patient faster than the analytic process allows. These feelings parallel the mother's feelings toward her sick infant. She does not like to see her child ill, and wishes to rectify the situation as quickly as possible.

As it is inappropriate for the mother to allow her anxiety and pain to invade the infant's coping mechanism, so too the analyst is taught to not act out on these induced countertransference feelings. The patient who is caught up in his own panic will need a therapeutic agent who can be solid and objective in the face of dire circumstances. Resistance, as always, is material for working through—and here, the resistance work may be the patient's resistance to his own imminent death.

The transference the patient develops will influence the analyst's countertransferential reactions. The cancer patient in a panic may turn to the analyst in hopes that the analyst can effect a cure. The analyst may feel the weight of this expectation, and feel inadequate to the task. What has been recreated is the paradigm of the ill child and the mother who feels that she has neither the knowledge nor skill to cure the infant. She turns, then, to the doctor who is trained to cure. Like the mother, the analyst may feel the need to share the responsibility of cure. He may turn to a supervising analyst, or he may attempt to work it through in his own analysis. Or, he may come to share with the patient the hopes in a medical cure, doubting his own ability to deal with the disease in a curative way and, thus, shifting the responsibility of cure to the medical practitioner.

Hopelessness and impotence are felt by those surrounding the patient, most typically when these are the feelings of the patient. The cancer patient who manifests an anal coping mechanism evokes very different kinds of feelings. Anger and aggression can be induced to the extent of wishing the patient would die more quickly. Cancer patients can use their illness in a passive-aggressive way. They can make demands that exceed the limits of human capability to fulfill; they can be troublesome and quarrelsome and argue that nothing is ever done the way they want it. For some, the onset of the disease is a natural fulfillment of their already entrenched position in relationships. The disease may be experienced as a relief, because there is now concrete evidence for rationalizing their mode of interaction. This attitude usually reflects an unconscious blaming of another person for the disease. The demands for care-taking are used as weapons of revenge.

The analyst recognizes that such a patient is involved in an anal-sadistic power struggle, like the baby who defecates in his diapers at precisely the times that are most inconvenient for the mother. The mother, or analyst, may think: "This person is going to be the death of me." The thought is accurate for it is indeed the intent of the patient/infant to cause a great deal of misery and trouble to the caretaker. The feeling of wanting to kill first to avoid being killed arises in the care-taker as a natural self-preservative defense. The analyst who can tolerate the patient's anal-sadistic power struggle may provide him with the first opportunity of being allowed to be demanding and argumentative without fear of killing through aggression. Analytic sessions may become scenes of angry vituperatives, but the patient will leave the sessions feeling relieved and understood.

Cure: Medical and Psychoanalytic Definitions

Cure, as defined by the medical profession, means a cancer-free diagnosis for five years subsequent to termination of treatment.[117] The high recidivism rate, often beyond the five-year period, makes the medical definition particularly problematic. The disease seems, at times, to represent more of a fluctuating phenomenon than an ever-increasing growth pattern. Remission suggests that the disease is highly volatile.

The definition of cure for the analytic patient, on the other hand, is more demanding. It requires that cure immunize the patient against future deterioration.[118] While there may be temporary reggressions during treatment, paralleling the temporary remissions of the cancer patient, ultimately the cure becomes permanent.

Cure in psychoanalysis consists of the patient comi
that his dependency was a once, but no longer needed cc
The process parallels the original feeling paradigm, in th
breast-feeding, where the infant is totally dependent on tl
sustaining nurturance, to self-feeding, where the growir
experience his own adequacy in providing the needed
himself. As the mature adult has sufficiently incorporated
to become a mother to himself, so too has t' ured anal
ciently incorporated the analyst so that '   ~w
himself.

Some cancer patients get well, tempe
tion, or permanently. The cure may be e
logical treatments, alternative treatme
tice, any combination of treatments,   al
research does not yet tell us definitiv   .he
healing process. The growth or rem.   ., to
be unpredictable. Medical treatment, at ι.   ɔears
somewhat more resemblance to a hit-or-miss ɡ.   to an
actual science. There is no way of foretelling which treaι..   e effec-
tive in which body system, nor how long efficacy, once achieveu,   ill maintain itself. Researchers and doctors are increasingly refusing to make predictions as to the life-expectancy of the patient and for the anticarcinogenistic effect of the treatment.

Curing Cancer Psychoanalytically

The psychoanalyst attempts to cure his patients through the tools of transference and resistance analysis.[119] The aim of the transference technique is to bring the universe of conflicts into the therapeutic relationship.[120] Typically, the analyst becomes the primary transference object onto which fantasies, ideas, and feelings are projected.[121] The establishment of a negative transference is recommended in the treatment of neurotic and psychotic patients in order to aid the patient in the free verbalization of all thoughts and feelings—negative as well as positive.[122]

The treatment of cancer patients differs in some respects from the usual analytic process as the establishing of a prolonged negative transference early in treatment may be contraindicated. The slow analytic working through process is out of pace with the speed with which his life processes are deteriorating. During the time it takes to work through an intense and prolonged negative transference, the patient may die.[123]

The immense amount of toxic material accumulated, however, suggests the importance of discharge. The tendency the patient has to project omnipotence onto a healing agent enables him to defend against the aggression that is concomitant with dependency needs and with the inevitable failed expectation.

The initial task in the analysis is to facilitate expression. While this catharsis is not ultimately curative, it is a necessary step in removing emotional blockages that interfere with the progressive flow of verbalization.

The cancer patient who is receiving medical treatment as well as psychotherapy will develop a relationship with his physician which has intense transference elements. The physician may be seen at various points in the progression of the disease as the omnipotent and idealized embodiment of cure, or, more negatively, as the god failed. The analyst may not, then, represent the primary transference figure. Even more, the power of the food (words) of the analyst may pale compared to the power of the food (medicine) of the physician.

In such cases, the transference is split between two objects.[124] When splitting occurs, the analyst regards it as a resistance to allowing all thoughts and feelings to develop toward the single object of the analyst.[125] A patient who employs this mechanism may choose the physician to be the bad object—the dispenser of poison food which creates havoc for his body. The psychoanalyst may then come to represent the good object—the dispenser of nutritional food which gives him the strength to endure the other. Splitting enables the patient to discharge aggression against an absent object without fear of retribution.

Where the attribution of good is to the physician and bad to the psychoanalyst, the cancer patient who has not yet established a strong positive transference will generally not stay in the psychological treatment. The omnipotent transference to the physician is on the other hand so profound that the patient will insist on medical treatment regardless of his negative reactions to the physician or the treatment. Because cancer is typically thought to be a strictly physiological disease, the cancer patient does not expect the psychoanalyst to cure him of his cancer. The diluted transference, without dependency on the analyst for cure, makes the relationship fragile, and one that is likely to dissolve if the patient's negative feelings toward the analyst are too intense. The analyst must compensate for the loss of attachment that a stronger transference would provide by being sufficiently gratifying to keep the patient in treatment.

A cancer patient in medical and analytic treatment will have thoughts and feelings associated with the relationship between the two transference figures. These fantasies may be related to early experience of the parents' relationship. A patient in a good/bad object split will fantasize that the good object shares his hatred for the bad object. Where the analyst represents the good object, sessions can be spent on discussions about the inadequacies of the physicians, how cold and mechanical they are.

The patient who is helped to master the developmental phase necessitating the good/bad object split will be able to tolerate love and hate feelings toward the same object. At this point in the analysis, the analyst can actively work to facilitate the verbal discharge of aggression towards the analyst, the object who remains present. Primitive feelings of disappointment, anger, and hate will be revealed. The analyst welcomes the release, knowing that the patient's ability to connect his feelings of aggression to his words means a high level of ego integration, and is essential to the cure.[126]

When the patient has been enabled to verbalize positive and negative feelings within the context of the transference relationship, he will have made a significant move from his position of dependence to a stand of independence. At this point, his relationship to his physician will change as well. He may request at this time that analyst and physician work as a team in his treatment plan. He will actively participate in his treatment. Defenses of compliance or rebellion will be dropped, and he will enter into a truly cooperative relationship with his physician. He will want to know, prior to administration of treatment, the implications of the treatment. If he plans to continue his daily activities during the course of treatment, he will anticipate the possible interference of toxic side effects. He will try to secure the doctor's cooperation in planning treatment at times that will minimize interference. This patient will be able to make rational and realistic decisions about how he wishes to live and if necessary how he wishes to die.

Curing Oneself: Food as Medicine

Patients who seek cure outside established western practice—medical or psychological—represent a growing minority. They may choose to treat themselves with substances which have not been approved by the FDA or AMA and which have been labelled quack remedies. The recent battle for the legalization of laetrile* suggests the intensity of the movement.

The battle for the right to exercise freedom of choice of treatment is not

---

* A non-toxic food substance made from apricot pits. The author is not promoting the use of laetrile as an anti-carcinogen. The struggle for its legalization is of interest as evidence of a movement by a number of people toward assumption of the right to treat themselves. The battle is unusual because no substance used to combat disease has previously been made available through state legislation. The normal channel for such action is the FDA. Whether laetrile can be approved for use on the state level is an issue which has not yet been settled.

without psychological overtones. In struggling against branches of a government which does not want to feed its citizens substances which have no proven worth, these cancer patients are recreating the original mother/ infant separation. The child, as he grows into independence and realizes himself as an entity separate from mother, becomes aware that he does not like all the foods she feeds him. As he explores his environment, he may find that she has withheld foods from him that are pleasing to him. So, too, with cancer patients seeking methods alternative to orthodox treatment. The bureaucratic structure becomes the target for release of aggressive impulses, as with patients in orthodox treatment where the doctor or analyst may serve this same function.

Some patients using alternative treatments seek cure through the careful and selective use of food. Here the symbolic meaning of food, as in medical or psychological treatments, is by-passed. The notion that food itself promotes natural, healthy growth is a literal return to the paradigm of mother/ food as physiological nourishment for the growing child. The memory of parental care in providing food for proper nurturance is evoked. Food is no longer chosen for taste or convenience, but is selected for health-giving properties.

The patient who believes that proper nourishment from food will be palliative is re-instituting the movement from maternal nourishment to self-nourishment. Food, insofar as it is thought to have curative powers, comes to be understood and experienced as medicine.

Cultural factors make the practical aspects of following a self-selected treatment regimen very different from carrying out a doctor's orders. Medication prescribed by a doctor is gotten from a drugstore or administered at a hospital. The patient's responsibility is to be at the right place at the right time. If he is unable to drive, dependency on others is exaggerated by the need to rely on friends or relatives for transportation.

The nutritionally minded patient does not have it so easy. While he may be initially dependent on a nutritionist for guidance, he quickly learns that food is a kind of medicine that he must do some work for. He must learn to prepare foods in a new way; processed foods containing toxic chemicals and preservatives are eliminated; unsprayed raw and cooked vegetables must be found and fresh vegetable and fruit juice prepared.*

The ease with which the cancer patient can adjust to his new diet may have its origins in his initial ability to handle feeding transitions.

Curing oneself means that the patient has moved from his initial, helpless position to a profound understanding of his role in creating and perpetuating the circumstances in his life, and to the newly found ability to be able to move actively and constructively toward health. He has learned to "feed" himself. He can regulate his own food intake and elimination

* Programs for the nutritional treatment of cancer have not yet been experimentally tested in humans, though clinical evidence is available.[127-129]

rationally on the basis of his physiological needs, and independent of his conscious and unconscious fantasies about food, and irrespective of his relationship to the provider of the food.[130]

Notes

1. Ovid, *Metamorphoses,* translation by Sir Samuel Garth, Heritage Press, New York, 1961, lines 738–878.
2. Frazer, J. G., *The New Golden Bough,* edited by J. H. Gaston, Criterion Books, New York, 1959.
3. Bignall, J. R., "Bronchial Carcinoma: A Survey of 317 Patients," *Lancet,* 1955, pp. 786–790.
4. Ewing, J., *Neoplastic Disease: A Treatise on Tumors,* 4th edition, W. B. Sanders, Philadelphia and London, 1940, chapter 1.
5. Hardy, J. D., "On the Cause of Death in Cancer: Systematic Effects of Non-endocrine Tumors," *Surg. Clin. N. Armor.,* 42, 1962, pp. 305–334.
6. Harnett, W. L., "A Survey of Cancer in London," British Empire Cancer Campaign, London, 1952, p. 26.
7. Hoffman, F. L., *The Mortality of Cancer Throughout the World,* Prudential Press, Newark, N. J., 1915, p. 44.
8. Klipstein, F. A. & G. Smarth, "Intestinal Structure and Function in Neoplastic Disease," *Am. J. Digest Dis.,* 14, 1969, pp. 887–899.
9. Rosenberg, S. A.; H. D. Diamond; B. Jaskowitz, and L. F. Craven, "Lymphosarcoma: A Review of 1269 Cases," *Medicine,* 40, 1961, pp. 31–84.
10. Warren, S., "The Immediate Causes of Death in Cancer," *Am. J. Med. Sci.,* 194, 1932, pp. 610–615.
11. Morrison, S. D., "Control of Food Intake in Cancer Cathexis: A Challenge and a Tool," *Physiology and Behavior,* 17, 1976, pp. 705–714.
12. Ibid.
13. Freud, A., *The Writings of Anna Freud,* vol. VI, *Normality and Pathology in Childhood and Assessments of Development,* International Universities Press, New York, 1965.
14. Dedrick, S. J. and E. M. Copeland, "Nutritional Concepts in Head and Neck Cancer," In *Neoplasm of Head and Neck,* Year Book Medical Publishers, Chicago, 1974, pp. 325–337.
15. Mider, G. B.; J. Tesluk; and M. J. Morton, "Effects of Walker Carcinoma 256 on Food Intake, Body Weight, Nitrogen Metabolism of Growing Rats," *Acta Unio. Int. contra Carcinum,* 1948, pp. 409–420.
16. De Wys, W., "Working Conference on Anorexia & Cathexia of Neoplastic Disease," *Cancer Res.,* 30, 1970, pp. 2816–2818.
17. Kelley, D. K., *One Answer to Cancer,* Valenkel Press, Kansas, 1974.
18. Midor, G. B.; L. D. Fenninger; F. L. Hasen; and J. J. Morton, "The Energy

Expenditure of Rats Bearing Walker Carcinoma 256," *Cancer Res.*, 11, 1951, pp. 731–736.

19. Bramante, P. O.; A. S. Nunn; M. C. Steiner; and D. E. Teaulieu, "A Method of Quantification of Oxygen Consumption of Tumor-Bearing Rats," *J. Appl. Physiol.*, 18, 1963, pp. 216–220.

20. Fenninger, L. D. and G. B. Mider, "Energy and Nitrogen Metabolism in Cancer," *Adv. Cancer Res.*, 2, 1954, pp. 229–253.

21. Morrison, S. D., "Partition of Energy Expenditure Between Host and Tumor," *Cancer Res.*, 31, 1971, pp. 98–107.

22. Morrison, D. D., "Limited Capacity for Motor Activity as a Cause for Declining Food Intake in Cancer," *J. Natn. Cancer Inst.*, 51, 1973, pp. 1535–1539.

23. Pratt, A. W. and F. K. Putney, "Observations on the Energy Metabolism of Rats Receiving Walker Tumor 256 Transplants," *J. Natn. Cancer Inst.*, 20, 1958, pp. 173–187.

24. Waterhouse, C.; L. D. Fenninger; and E. H. Kentmann, "Nitrogen Exchange and Caloric Expenditure in Patients with Malignant Neoplasms," *Cancer*, 4, 1951, pp. 500–514.

25. Williams, M. W.; C. S. Williams; and G. R. DeWitt, "Activity, Weight, and Oxygen Consumption of Hyperthyroid Mice Bearing Sarcoma 180, *Life Sci.*, 5, 1966, pp. 545–594.

26. Morrison, 1976, p. 707.

27. Ibid.

28. Brobeck, J. R., "Food and Temperature," *Recent Progr. Horm. Res.*, 16, 1960, pp. 439–466.

29. Mayor, J.; N. B. Marshall; J. J. Vitale; J. H. Christenson; M. B. Mashayekhi; and F. J. Stare, "Exercise, Food Intake and Body Weight in Normal Rats and Genetically Obese Adult Mice," *Am. J. Physiol.*, 177, 1954, pp. 544–548.

30. Carlisle, H. J. and E. Stellar, "Caloric Regulation and Food Preference in Normal, Hyperphagic and Aphagic Rats," *J. Comp. Physiol. Psychol.*, 69, 1969, pp. 107–114.

31. Morrison, S. D., "Feeding Response to Change in Absorbable Food Fraction During Growth of Walker 256 Carcinoma," *Cancer Res.*, 32, 1972, pp. 968–972.

32. Smith, N., R. Pooland and H. Weinberg, "The Role of Bulk in the Control of Eating," *J. Comp. Physiol. Psychol.*, 55, 1962, pp. 115–120.

33. Middleton, W. R. J. and G. R. Thompson, "Mechanism of Steatonrhoea in Induced Hyperthyroidism in the Rat," *J. Lab. Clin. Med.*, 74, 1969, pp. 19–30.

34. Silverstone, H. and A. Tannenbaum, "Influence of Thyroid Hormone on the Formation of Induced Skin Tumors in Mice," *Cancer Res.*, 9, 1949, pp. 684–688.

35. Cole, H. H. and G. H. Hart, "The Effect of Pregnancy and Lactation on Growth in the Rat," *Am. J. Physiol.*, 123, 1938, pp. 589–597.

36. Morrison, S. D., "The Total Energy and Water Metabolism During Pregnancy in the Rat," *J. Physiol.*, 134, London, 1956, pp. 650–664.

37. Slonsker, J. R., "The Effect of Copulation, Pregnancy, Pseudo-pregnancy, and Lactation on the Voluntary Activity and Food Consumption of the Albino Rat," *Am. J. Physiol.*, 71, 1925, pp. 362–394.

38. Wang, G. H., "The Changes in the Amount of Daily Food Intake of the Albino Rat During Pregnancy and Lactation," *Am. J. Physiol.*, 71, 1925, pp. 736–741.

39. Morrison, S. D. and N. F. Coffey, "Feeding Activity and Feeding Efficiency as Distinct Modes of Change in Food Intake," *J. Appl. Physiol.*, 34, 1973, pp. 268–270.

40. Morrison, 1976, p. 706.

41. Ibid.

42. Nakara, W. S., "A Chemical Basis for Tumor-Host Relations," *J. Natn. Cancer Inst.*, 24, 1960, pp. 77–86.

43. Sylven, B., "Factors Produced by Tumors Cells Which Contribute to the Death of Cancer Patients," *Carlo Erba Foundation Lecture Series*, Feb. 26, 1969.

44. Mider, G. B., "Some Aspects of Nitrogen and Energy Metabolism in Cancerous Subjects: A Review," *Cancer Res.*, 11, 1951, pp. 821–829.

45. Moreschi, C., "Beziehungen wischen Ernabrung and Tumorwachstum," *Z. Immunita Forsch.*, 2, 1909, 651–685.

46. Anderson, M. R. and H. N. Green, "Tumor-Host Relationships," *Br. J. Cancer*, 21, 1967, pp. 27–32.

47. Pikovski, M. A. and Y. Zifroni-Gallon, "Peculiar Gamma G in Tumor Cells and Depletion of Antibody Forming Organs in Tumor-Bearing Mice," *Nature*, 218, 1968, pp. 1070–1073.

48. Prince, V. E. and R. Greenfield, "Anemia in Cancer," *Adv. Cancer Res.*, 5, 1958, pp. 199–290.

49. Berndt, H., "Malabsorption in Cancer of and Outside the Bowel," *Digestion*, 1, 1968, pp. 305–310.

50. Dymock, I. W., "Malabsorption and Structural Changes in the Small Bowel in Relation to Malignant Disease Outwith the Alimentary Tract," In *Malabsorption*, edited by R. H. Girwood and A. N. Smith, Williams & Wilkins, Baltimore, 1969, pp. 269–279.

51. Wiseman, G. and F. N. Ghadially, "Biochemical Concept of Tumor Growth, Infiltration, and Cachexia," *Br. Med. J.*, 11, 1958, pp. 18–21.

52. Haven, F. L. and W. R. Bloor, "Lipids in Cancer," *Adv. Cancer Res.*, 4, 1956, pp. 237–314.

53. Liebelt, R. A.; A. G. Liebelt; and H. M. Johnston, "Lipid Mobilization and Food Intake in Experimentally Obese Mice Bearing Transplanted Tumors," *Proc. Soc. Exp. Biol. Med.*, 138, 1971, pp. 482–490.

54. Posner, I., "Abnormal Fat Absorption in Tumor-Bearing Rats," *Proc. Soc. Exp. Biol. Med.*, 98, 1958, pp. 477–479.

55. Stewart, A. G. and R. W. Begg, "Systemic Effects of Tumors in Force-Fed

Rats. III. Effect on the Composition of the Carcass and Liver and on the Plasms Lipids," *Cancer Res.,* 13, 1953, pp. 560–565.

56. Shapot, V. S., "Some Biochemical Aspects of the Relationship Between the Tumor and the Host," *Adv. Cancer Res.,* 15, 1972, pp. 253–286.

57. Baille, P.; F. K. Millar; and A. W. Pratt, "Food and Water Intakes and Walker Tumor Growth in Rats with Hypothalamic Lesions," *Am. J. Physiol.,* 209, 1965, pp. 293–300.

58. Liebelt, R. A., et al., 1971.

59. Liebelt, R. A.; G. Gehring; L. Delmonte; E. Schuster; and A. G. Liebelt, "Paraneoplastic Syndromes in Experimental Animals Model Systems," *Ann. N. Y. Aud. Sci.,* 230, 1974, pp. 547–564.

60. Nathanson, L. and T. C. Hall, "Lung Tumors: How They Produce Their Syndromes," *Ann. N. Y. Aud. Sci.,* 730, 1974, pp. 367–377.

61. Theologides, A., "Pathogenesis of Cachexia in Cancer: A Review and Hypothesis," *Cancer,* 29, 1972, pp. 484–488.

62. Theologides, A., "The Anorexia-Cachexis Syndrome: A New Hypothesis," *Am. N. Y. Acad. Sci.,* 230, 1974, pp. 14–22.

63. Gold, J., "Proposal Treatment of Cancer by Inhibition of Gluconeogenesis," *Oncology,* 22, 1968, pp. 185–207.

64. Gold, J., "Cancer Cachexia and Gluconeogenesis," *Am. N. Y. Acad. Sci.,* 230, 1974, pp. 103–110.

65. Israel, L., *Conquering Cancer,* Vintage/Random House, N. Y., 1978.

66. Eckholm, *The Picture of Health: Environmental Sources of Disease,* Worldwatch Institute, Wash., D. C., 1979.

67. Freud, S., "The Dynamics of Transference," *Collected Papers II;* Institute of Psychoanalysis, Hogarth Press, London, 1924.

68. Fenichel, O., *The Psychoanalytic Theory & Neurosis,* W. W. Norton, N. Y. 1945, p. 35.

69. Ibid.

70. Ferenczi, S., "The Problem of the Acceptance of Unpleasant Ideas," *Further Contributions to the Theory and Technique of Psychoanalysis,* Institute of Psychoanalysis, Hogarth Press, London, 1926.

71. Hoffer, W., "The Mutual Influences in the Development of Ego & Id: Earlier Stages." *The Psychoanalytic Study of the Child,* 7, 1952, pp. 31–41.

72. Freud, A., 1965, pp. 70–71.

73. Ferenczi, S., 1926.

74. Freud, S., "On Negation," *Int. J. of Psychoa.,* 6, 1923.

75. Fenichel, 1945, p. 38.

76. Ibid.

77. Ibid.

78. Escalona, S., "Emotional Development in the First Year of Life." In Smilton Senn, *Problems of Infancy and Childhood,* translations of the Sixth (1952) Conference, Josiah Macy, Jr. Foundation, Ann Arbor, Mich.

79. Fenichel, S., 1945, pp. 65–66.

80. Fenichel, S. "The Dread of Being Eaten." *Int. J. of Psychoa.*, 10, 1929.
81. Freud, S., "The *Problem of Anxiety,"* Norton, N. Y., 1936.
82. Fenichel, 1945, p. 64.
83. Grabor, G. H., Die Zweisrlei Mechonismor der Identifizierung. *Imago,* 23, 1937.
84. Fenichel, 1945, pp. 62–63.
85. Ibid., p. 39.
86. Freud, S. "Splitting of the Ego in the Defensive Process." *Int. J. of Psychoa.*, 22, 1941.
87. Kerberg, O., *Borderline Conditions and Pathological Narcissism,* Jason Aronson, N. Y., 1975.
88. Klein, M., "The Origins of Transference," *Int. J. Psycho-Anal.,* 33, 1952, pp. 433–438.
89. Fenichel, 1945, pp. 62–63.
90. Ibid., p. 49.
91. Freud, A., 1965, pp. 75–77.
92. Ibid., p. 71.
93. Ibid., p. 71.
94. Ibid., p. 71.
95. Ibid., p. 72.
96. Ibid., pp. 72–75.
97. Ibid., p. 73.
98. Ibid., p. 74.
99. Abrams, R. D. and J. E. Finesinger, "Guilt Reactions in Patients with Cancer," *Cancer,* 31, 1951, pp. 474–482.
100. Kline, N. S. and J. Sobin, "The Psychological Management of Cancer Cases," *JAMA,* 146, 1951, pp. 1547.
101. Simmons, H. E., *The Psychogenic Theory of Disease: A New Approach to Cancer Research,* General Welfare Publications, Sacramento, Calif., 1966.
102. Schmale, A. H. and H. Iker, "Hopelessness as a Prediction of Cervical Cancer," *Social Science and Medicine,* 5, Pergamon Press (England) 1971, pp. 95–100.
103. Fenichel, O., 1945, p. 64.
104. Fenichel, O., "Ueber Respiratorische Introjecktion," *International Zeitschrift fuer Psychoanalyse,* 17, 1931.
105. Fenichel, O., "The Scoptophilic Instinct and Identification," *Int. J. of Psycho-Anal.,* 18, 1937.
106. Fenischel, O., 1945, p. 63.
107. Slater, P., *Microcosm,* John Wiley, N. Y., 1966, pp. 62–63.
108. Ibid.
109. Frazer, J. G., 1959, pp. 464, 466.
110. Sackman, R., personal communication.

111. Alexander, F. and T. M. French, *Psychoanalytic Therapy,* Ronald, N. Y., 1946.

112. Mills, T. M., "Authority and Group Emotion." In *Interpersonal Dynamics,* edited by W. G. Bernnis, et al., Homewood, Ill., Dorsey, 1964.

113. Spotnitz, H., *Modern Psychoanalysis of a Schizophrenic Patient,* Grune & Stratton, N. Y., 1969.

114. Spotnitz, H., *Psychotherapy of Preoedipal Conditions,* Jason Aronson, N. Y., 1976, p. 16.

115. Spotnitz, H., 1969, p. 61.

116. Ibid., p. 68.

117. Israel, L., 1978, pp. 5–9.

118. Spotnitz, H., *Psychotherapy of Preoedipal Conditions,* Jason Aronson, N. Y. 1976.

119. Freud, S., "The Dynamics of Transference," *Standard Edition,* 12, 1912, pp. 97–108.

120. Greenson, R., *The Technique and Practice of Psychoanalysis,* vol. 1, International Universities Press, N. Y., 1967, pp. 151–155.

121. Ibid.

122. Spotnitz, H., 1969, pp. 38–39.

123. Meadow, P., personal communication.

124. Goldberg, Unger J., "Working with the Split Transference," *Modern Psychoanalysis,* 3, no. 2, 1978, pp. 217–232.

125. Ibid.

126. Spotnitz, H., 1969, pp. 114–115.

127. Gerson, M., *A Cancer Therapy: Results of 50 Cases,* Durt, N. Y., 1958.

128. Nolfi, K., *My Experience with Living Food.*

129. Tresillian Fere, M., *Does Diet Cure Cancer?,* Thorsons, Wellingborough, Northampshire, 1976.

130. Freud, A., 1965, pp. 69–70.

PART IV
Group Treatment

Group treatment was postulated as a viable method of psychotherapy by early practitioners in the field. It is theorized that group psychotherapy provides an experience in socialization and in the formation of many potentially therapeutic relationships, unlike individual psychotherapy where the relationship is limited to one therapeutic agent. The general acceptance of group treatment within the therapeutic community has had profound implications for the practice of psychotherapy; therapy is now accessible both to more patients and to a wider range of patients.

Various kinds of group treatment with cancer patients have been formed, with reports of successful outcomes. Some have sprung up spontaneously, while others have been formed purposefully; some have leaders who are medically trained, and some have no leaders at all; some include the cancer patients, some the patients and their families, and some the cancer patient and health care workers; and some include the cancer patient in on-going group psychotherapy with non-cancer patients.

Group theorists usually identify two broad kinds of groups: (1) those concerned with a task; and (2) purely therapeutic groups. Group treatment of cancer patients reflects this same division.

Purely therapeutic groups are more likely to have varied group composition. While narcissistic identification with others like oneself may be a prelude to successful group treatment, it is seen as important only in the early phases of treatment. The emphasis here is not so much on the specificities of the commonalities of the disease. Rather, the cancer patient is one member who has a disease, or symptoms, which may not be overtly related to the difficulties of the other patients. This situation is a closer approximation to the real-life circumstances of the cancer patient, where he or she is surrounded by people who do not have the feelings concomitant with having a life-threatening disease. Lou Ormont, in Chapter 11, utilizes this model of a purely therapeutic group and gives examples of how cancer patients have used the group situation both constructively and destructively. Lena Furgeri (Chapter 12) presents her experiences with groups and speculates that the development of cancer in a psychotherapy patient may be an unconscious attempt by the patient to sabotage the treatment, and thus defeat the therapist.

Groups comprised strictly of cancer patients are usually concerned with the specific task of helping the patient to be more comfortable with his disease. The concept of homogenous group composition is borrowed from the precedent of self-help groups, of which Alcoholics Anonymous is the most visible and successful model. Such groups offer the person acceptance, understanding, and the comfort of being with others who are like himself. The involvement in the group can be emotionally intense and can help create a whole new way of life to rival the sense of discomfort and lack of empathic understanding the cancer patient experiences in the outside world. The McCloy and Lansner article (Chapter 13) is a vivid description of the psychodynamics of a cancer task group.

11 Aggression and Cancer in Group Treatment

Louis R. Ormont

Every practitioner is familiar with examples of what J. B. Cannon called the "wisdom of the body." The patient with a somatic problem knows without knowing. The unconscious holds vast stores of information which it communicates heiroglyphically and indirectly. This information may remain meaningless if untranslated and yet manifest itself in bodily reactions.

The thesis that emotions and cancer are related is neither novel nor startling. For centuries, the role that grief, frustration and despair play in neoplasms has impressed many outstanding physicians. In 1870, Sir James Paget,[1] the greatest oncologist of his day, wrote that deferred hope, disappointment, and deep depression were followed by an increase in cancerous tissue. Others—Cutter,[2] Hughes,[3] Snow[4]—went beyond positing a correlation; they were convinced that "mental depression" was the direct cause of a cancer.[5]

These clinical observations lay fallow because there was little physicians could offer their patients beyond reassurance, a regimen of diet, rest, and relaxation.

The treatment challenge was taken up by the cellular specialists. With microscopes, x-ray machines, and chemicals, they attacked the malignancies. Great advances were made in the local destruction of neoplasms. The total organism within which the cell resided with its neural and hormonal systems received scant attention.

However, each time they identified a specific cause-effect relationship, specialists found they had to account for some annoying fact. For example, their research demonstrated that tobacco was directly implicated in lung cancer. Yet only a small fraction of the addicted smokers developed a malignancy.

The specialists attacked the problem anew. Every year they stumbled on additional precipitants of lung cancer. Why, with so many people exposed to so many different kinds of irritants, did so few develop lung cancer?

Early in the twentieth century, theoreticians began an energetic search for a framework that would account for the bewildering array of facts. The result was the hormonal-immunological theory.

This construct starts with the assumption that the body is always turning out defects—due to faulty constitution, viruses, or pollutants. Fortunately, its defense system has a way of detecting maverick mutants and destroying them. But stress disrupts this detection and protection process; the body cannot correct the imbalanced physiology. The defective cells are free to reproduce themselves at random. This theory was supported by the observation that a cancer patient has weaker immunological defenses than the average person; his body cannot quickly and effectively destroy defective cells.

During the 1950's, Hans Seyle[5] and others mustered enough data to support the contention that emotional tensions may act as stressors. Such emotional states as depression and disappointment can exhaust the adrenal gland, it is no longer able to produce the hormones the body needs to prime the immunological response. If the exhausted gland does manage to send out signals, they are inadequate or misleading.

At this point, any of a number of carcenogenic precipitants can set off a toxic train of reactions. The overstressed system cannot monitor mutant cells or neutralize invading substances. Parasitic penetration, chemical and pollutant contamination, or ionizing radiation can do deadly damage to the vulnerable cellular tissues.

This finding was corroborated by experiments on healthy subjects. Cancer cells died when implanted under the skin of vital and vigorous subjects [Boyd, 1957].[6] Even if these subjects did develop foci of neoplasia, they contained them and held them in check. It appeared, therefore, that the nineteenth century surgeons were right. Emotions do influence the body's defenses.

However, long before the physiologists constructed their immunological theory, psychotherapists were observing and writing about the psychological implications of organic disease. Therapists had noted that the tendency to somatize develops early in life. Persistent stress during the developing years or a psychic trauma could lead to a life-long tendency toward organic expression of tension.

But psychoanalysts had hit-and-miss results with their efforts to reverse the tendency to channel tensions into the body. Investigating and analyzing the emotional states of despair, hopelessness, and their noxious cousins did not guarantee desirable results.

It emerged that an underlying drive was being neglected: aggression. But knowing this fact and doing something about it were two different things. Psychoanalysts had a method of treating the effects of disordered love but not the effects of primal rage. Even uncovering this hatred was often a formidable task. Patients tenaciously held on to their acceptable social feelings.

Should the rage well up, many therapists found it difficult and frightening to confront the patient, and with good reason. First of all, an angry-speaking patient could turn into an angry-acting one. Secondly, the patient's hatred induced unacceptable counter-hatred in his therapist. The prevailing opinion was that psychotherapy could do little with irrational anger. Psychiatrists resorted to palliative drugs to keep the obstreperous patient calm. Failing that, the patient was committed to an asylum.

A new set of constructs with new attitudes was needed. Sparked by the insights of Winnicott (1958)[7], Searles (1967)[8], Alexander (1953)[9], Rado (1956)[10], and Spotnitz (1976)[11], investigators began to use their own feelings to investigate what patients were experiencing. They used these feelings to reconstruct the past, which, their patients could not recall. With these feelings they penetrated deeply into the embalmed years—from birth to age two. The early psychological stimulus and physiological responses were directly related to each other. Psychosomatic patterns could be pinpointed and studied. They illustrated that people's fantasy life, distorted self and body images, primitive defenses, and unmet maturational needs played a critical role in the development of schizophrenia and organic illness.

The developmental pieces began to fall into place. Either through inherited predisposition or defective mothering, certain children are especially vulnerable during their earliest years. They cannot convert drives and tensions into identifiable feelings. Their psyches can only express these tensions along the most primitive paths of communication—through body language, symbolic gesture, frozen attitudes, and the like.

The thwarting and frustration that these people experience eventually culminate in all shades of aggression. But it is a rage that cannot be expressed. In their minds, this aggression is capable of destroying the people they need for survival.

Finding no outlet for this aggression, they turn it against themselves. Such a redirection of energy raises further havoc with the way the body functions. Our physical being becomes the target of every unexpressed and unacknowledged negative feeling. Our denied drives become expressed as physical symptoms, which can range from a canker to cancer.

Research Evidence of the Somatic Effects of Aggression

The ravaging effects of unexpressed aggression have been observed by many researchers.

Cobbs (1954)[12] found that conflicts around the discharge of activity were high among those with cancer-susceptible personalities. Passivity inhibits the release of anger, even under dire conditions.

Bacon et al. (1952)[13] found a facade of pleasantness in many women with carcinoma. This masked an inability to deal effectively with their aggressive impulses—as well as those of others. The victims felt resigned to an inverted expression of rage in the form of "passive suicide."

Kissen and Eysenck (1962)[14] found that certain people who tended to "bottle-up" emotional difficulties also tended to contract cancer.

LeShan and Worthington (1955)[15] observed that cancer-prone personalities tend to push down feelings of hostility rather than bring them to the surface and work them through. They suggested that this tendency lowers resistance to a malignancy.

LeShan (1966)[16] noted again that one condition predisposing to cancer was the inability to use aggression as a self-protective tool. Envy, jealousy, competition, and resentment are squelched. The person, unable to find an interpersonal outlet for these emotions, comes to feel lonely and unloved.

Goldfarb et al. (1967)[17] connected this inability to express hostility with the "hopeless-helpless syndrome." Because the victims think their condition unsalvageable, they allow themselves to sink into a bottomless despair. Electroshock therapy, aimed at clearing up the depression, often led to a remission of the neoplasm. They concluded that depression affects the immunological system. Depression is classically defined as aggression directed at oneself.

Simonton and Simonton (1975)[18] confirmed that a predisposing condition for cancer was a marked tendency to hold back resentment. They also noted such correlates of stunted aggression as self-pity and a poor self-image.

Mode of Attack

Such findings lead us to ask: How can psychosomatically entrenched aggression be approached, released, and resolved?

Modern psychoanalysts, especially Spotnitz (1969),[19] offer an approach to the problem. First they deal with the way the person defends himself against the awareness and release of aggression. Then they help him redirect this raw energy away from his body, discharge it verbally, harness it at the service of his ego, and creatively sublimate it. This procedure can be applied in any of a variety of treatment modalities. In group therapy we make certain modifications. One is the use of the members as co-therapists.

There are several significant steps the therapist might take. To begin with, we mobilize the group's interest in a member's defense against aggression—the particular way a member wards off awareness of his unacceptable feelings. The aggression is not our initial concern: we are seeking out his *protection* against knowing he has it. This is no light task. As researchers discovered, cancer-prone people seem to be anything but hostile. They appear even-tempered, genuinely concerned about the comfort of others, friendly, and sometimes bordering on the heroic in their compassion.

Therefore, we spend our early contacts looking for, sensing out, or intuiting the ways a group member denies, represses, or avoids the feelings he senses are present. This may call for a free-floating, detached attention to his behavior or appearance. To the world he may seem no more than compliant, forbearing, or indifferent.

Having identified a member's particular survival mechanism, we do not jump in to change it. Instead, we silently study it. We observe, for example, when he uses his compliant response, how he repeats it, and the different forms it takes under different conditions.

Next we get confirmation concerning the mode of defense used. Other members are asked if they observed the pattern. When does it tend to be used? Can it be described?

After this, we mobilize the group interest in making the member aware of the defense. Members are encouraged not to hammer at the pattern but simply to apprise the person of this piece of his behavior.

We are now in position to separate the covert behavior from the underlying feeling. We encourage an investigation of all possible clues. Why did the member bite his lip and say "yes" when insulted outright? We pay detailed attention to subtly expressed attitudes, to intonation and to facial reactions. Sometimes the feeling emerges as soon as the defense is examined.

Often we have to show how the emotional state passes through the person's barriers. We watch for subliminal signs of leakage. Does the patient sense that his eyes are narrowing while the lower part of his face smiles? Is he aware that there is an edge of anger in his "helplessness?" Are there two messages being expressed at once?

With the softening effect of awareness, the inner world of the member comes to the fore. Now he may admit to inner torture. The despairer openly despairs; the griever grieves. Throughout this stage the member is encouraged to experience the unacceptable feeling.

All the while the members are training him to communicate his experience in words as fully as possible. Words are preferred, as an advance over "skin talk" and other, more primitive methods. Verbalizing establishes new neural pathways, outlets for inner stimuli, and opens up the way for fresh thoughts and ideas.

We want the member to direct his charged words toward a nonrecriminating person in the group—one who will not punish or provoke guilt. The ideal target, of course, is the group analyst. His attitude and response can go a long way toward detoxifying devastating feelings.

While the member is struggling with these feelings, he may not acknowledge, or even know, that they are a cover for underlying aggression. Some members—especially prone to organic tension—need a form of communication that will reflect their own emotional state. These reflections help the member to maintain his identity while permitting him to allow all his feelings their place. In reflecting, the analyst uses joining, mirroring, extending, role-reversal, devil-advocating, or out-crazying.

The analyst should use the group to do the work. In the following example, the analyst evoked the rage by mirroring it and used the group to mirror it further.

To a complaining woman, the analyst complained that she was taking up too much time with her woes. How could anyone get a word in edgewise? The woman took exception to this implied criticism. She contended she was complaining only because she had a lot to complain about. What was wrong with the analyst? She proceeded to find fault with him. When he addressed her complaints, reflecting her attitude, she would let loose a stream of criticism. The other gorup members found the explosions a welcome change from her beseeching behavior. They caught the spirit of the analyst's reflection and began mirroring the member's behavior. Explosive confrontations went on for weeks. What Norman Mailer called "hatred that had never breathed the air of open rage" gave her a sense of personal elation and freedom.

With the aggression made manifest, the analyst encourages the group to investigate the feeling. Our purpose is to uncover erroneous ideas supportive of those emotional states and to plumb the foundations of negative feelings. Aggression can emanate from many sources—from frustration, rejection, abandonment, or counterphobic fear.

Members can help one another learn to tolerate all shades of aggression. They may encourage a new attitude toward it. Ideally, a patient learns to function effectively no matter how intense his irritability may be. Members never let him overlook his intolerance of it. So what if you are mad? Why can't you still speak in a civilized way? What makes you think you have to go into action or use four-letter words? We also have available other methods of intervention such as exploration, suggestion, education, and trial-and-error. Relying on them, we enable the patient to develop leniency toward his own aggression.

We can also relate present patterns to the climate of the patient's early life. The group itself may speculate about the relationship between a freed feeling and a physical symptom in a member. If the member himself cannot discover the crucial connections, the analyst can help him reconstruct the events of his formative years. The analyst can make use of the member's behavior in putting together a picture of his past. The group members, at this stage, become able to help the patient see his own aggression as valuable energy. Within the group setting, they can aid the patient to transform and refine it. For instance, they may show him how to convert anger that was previously destructive into socially acceptable wit; they thus cultivate his new-found ability to put his aggression at the service of his best interest.

With the loosening and release of repressed feelings, made possible by the group's response and understanding, there occurs an enormous redirection of energy. The physical symptom loses much of its psychic charge.

Then, as the feelings find verbal outlets, begin to abate in intensity, and behavior changes, the malignancy seems to lose its virulence.

The Utilization of Group Therapy

Traditionally, the patient who seeks help has done so through individual analysis. This has certain obvious values. There is no better arrangement for searching deeply into the meaning of motives. However, this modality sometimes leaves the therapist with little leverage. His only ally is the patient, who oscillates between defying, drifting from, and denying all attempts to help him experience his emotions. The analyst is often rendered ineffective by the psychosomatically prone patient.

Group therapy has special advantages for working with the organically ill. Ulcer and colitis clubs have been notably successful in alleviating serious pathology. Though this writer has never conducted a group composed exclusively of cancer victims, it is conceivable that a shared setting could achieve the same results.

Group therapy offers a number of advantages so far as prevention is concerned, as it can exert pressure on the neglectful or self-destructive member.

In the following case, the group exercised its influence none too soon.

Some months after a hysterectomy, a woman in group mentioned in passing that she had abdominal discomfort and occasional bleeding. When questioned by certain members, she mentioned that she had not been back to see her gynecologist since the surgery. She brushed away their concern, construing her discomfort as a natural after-effect of her operation. She countered their every question with some seemingly plausible explanation for her torpidity.

However, one alarmed member would not be put off by her evasion and opened up each session with a prodding inquiry. She would promise to look into the matter but did not do so. The member observed, "You probably think something serious is going on. You are wishing it will go away by itself—counting on magic." The prodding member piped in, "I know what's wrong with us. We've been recommending that you go to a doctor. We should have pushed for a magician." A sharp exchange ensued. The next session she reported she had visited her gynecologist and a biopsy was scheduled. There was a malignancy, which, fortunately, was discovered in time.

The members had brought to her awareness the intense nature of her denial. Though she fought the group's reaction to her postponements, she had managed to glimpse the ludicrous nature of her own, endless rationalizations. It was not only this insight but also the release of her own anger that propelled her into taking care of herself. The value of the group was unmistakably evident in this case.

The sensitivity of a group enables it to provide early warnings and to repeat them. The patient with an incipient neoplastic growth is often reluctant to take the initiative in concern with his own health. There is a latent fear that the malignancy is already too advanced to be contained.

Even when the stress is not mentioned by the person, its vibrations can be felt by those who are attuned to the person's unconscious processes. Once these members become alerted to some smouldering crisis, they display uncanny skill in sifting out significant cues. Through their partial identification with the victim, they can often detect the faintest tremors of tension. One member may suspect the tension because of a particular side-effect, another perceives it from a very different angle. For instance, the first discerns it in a dream, the second through its effect on an interpersonal exchange. If at times a member dashes off on a false lead, sooner or later another member is likely to call a halt and return the group to the basic track.

The following case illustrates the resilience of a group in its own pursuit.

A member presented the dream that termites were constructing a great hill on the plains of Africa. He kept tearing the hill down, but the insects persisted in rebuilding it. The group saw themselves as ants, constantly raising objections to his grandiose vocational schemes. They saw the dreamer as the undaunted builder of castles on the sand. Hearing this, the patient who had the dream lamented loudly that it was true: they were always fouling up his plans. There was a noisy interchange in which some of the interpretations went far afield.

Then a member, a woman with a borderline streak to her personality, expressed a more ominous view of the dream. She felt the hill was *inside* the dreamer. The termites were cells and were out of control.

At this, the dreamer blurted out that he did have a "funny sore" on his inner thigh that was not healing. A member asked if he had had it looked into. No, he had no physician. He would go to specialists with each body complaint. This was not specific enough. Members assailed him for holding such a negative attitude. By the end of the session he agreed to get a complete physical check-up from an internist. A lymphona was found, which could be contained.

By its understanding, empathy, and suggestion, a group can exert enormous effect. It provides an antidote to isolation. Perhaps its greatest asset for the organically ill is that it provides objects toward which the patient can direct strong feelings. The patient receives supportive acceptance within the group while he works through his conflicts. The consistency with which many members see that a person is doing is likely to provide him with a convincingly accurate picture.

On the other hand, the group's inherent weakness is its focus on the here-and-now at the expense of the highly pertinent there-and-then. This makes it difficult to relive a past experience intensely. Group does not provide the unlimited psychological space to a member which might enable him to explore his inner world. There is always a communal pressure, no matter how slight, to "get on with it" or reach some desired emotional response. The most restrictive aspect of group is its need to limit members to one part of the total talking time.

The ideal solution for the somatically vulnerable patient would be to reap the best of the two therapeutic worlds: that is, to enter conjoint therapy. While the patient is in individual treatment with one therapist, he attends a group with another therapist. In this approach his distortions, emotional communications, and behavioral manifestations are viewed from many angles and perspectives. The tendency to somatize tensions is carefully monitored under varied conditions.

No matter how organic the origin of the disease, the writer's assumption is that the process is inevitably accompanied by psychological and emotional stress. This position is holistic: it maintains that all functions, healthy or diseased, psychological and physiological, are intimately intertwined with one other. There is no point at which one ends and the other begins; rather, each affects the other.

A Note of Caution

The most evident limitation of the author's experience with cancer is his exposure to a population of only 38 cases, collected during a period of nearly 30 years. There were eight "cures," nine remissions, whose outcome is still in abeyance, 10 incomplete or prematurely terminated cases, and 11 failures. The types of carcinoma ranged from liver cancer to lymphoma.

The writer did not find a specific personality pattern that matched a specific type of malignancy. For example, cancer of the bowels was not a necessary correlate to an anal retentive character structure. Nor could a characteristic course of treatment be pinpointed. Every case followed a path different from the others. The only thing common to them all was the therapist's approach: an intensive study, analysis, working through, and resolution of the defenses against the verbal communication of buried aggression.

Also, since the writer's practice has been essentially with groups, the material is presented solely from what was revealed in the shared setting. The only way of corroborating what a group member reported was to see if his communications and actions in the group supported or confirmed it.

Despite enthusiastic endorsements and fervent testimonials from recovered patients, the writer cannot say there is any hard evidence that group psychotherapy—by itself—was the single curative agent; for in addition to chemotherapy, surgery, and radiation therapy, there were many other interventions being attempted at the same time.

A tightly controlled experiment would, of course, be impossible to conduct. When other therapeutic interventions were introduced—either by the group member or his medical specialists—the writer did not feel it his prerogative to interfere with them.

Two Case Histories

With these reservations in mind, let us consider several cases. We may learn most by comparing our successful outcomes with our unsuccessful ones. First, a case which had a successful outcome.

When her marriage fell apart, a woman, then thirty-five years old, began group treatment. Her self-effacing manner won ready acceptance from the others. She liked them. When she would present a problem that concerned her children or her job, she always found them helpful. They, in turn, appreciated her sensitivity and concern for them.

After about a year, she discovered a lump on her breast and went to a specialist. It turned out to be cancer. She was shattered by the news. So were the members, who rallied to her support. They seemed to suspend all other matters, in order to discuss the specialist she was seeing, the hospital she was to enter, her fear of mutilation, and the medications she was taking. They took seriously her doubts and left nothing untouched if it involved her anxiety over the cancer. In addition, they demanded that she mobilize her strength. They took instant exception when she spoke of "conserving energy" through passive acceptance of her condition or total dependence on some authority.

Her post-operative prognosis was only fair, and chemotherapy was instituted. It was physically debilitating and seemed to weaken her resolve. Once again, the members rallied to buoy up her spirits. For example, to help her bear her acute apprehension, a member taught her techniques for relaxation. She learned to utilize them well.

Before long she saw the group as the only stable force in her life. The members knew everything; she knew nothing. Life seemed composed of group meetings with breathless pauses in between. She became deeply dependent upon them and experienced a profound need to do the right thing for their approval. When they did approve, she felt loved and hopeful. She lived by their suggestions and according to their directions.

Still, the doctors indicated the malignancy might be spreading; further treatment was indicated. She fell into a state of desperation and became greedier than ever for the group's advice. However, the members were experiencing mounting frustration. Though she would follow their suggestions to the letter, she ignored the spirit behind what they said. They began to see her as doing everything to please, to feel good, to calm herself, but nothing to improve her lot.

Her response to their dissatisfaction caught them by surprise. Instead of contritely agreeing as usual, she became offended. She countered that the members were smug and unfair to her; none of them had a sense of what it was like to face death.

With the analyst's help, she began to fight for more attention. After each hostile encounter with a member, she could recall incidents from her past, and how she felt about them; most of these had previously eluded her.

She remembered that throughout her marriage she had been on the phone for hours with her mother, who played a dominant role in her life. Not surprisingly, her husband fretted about this and felt neglected. Finally he insisted that she break with her mother. Somewhat relieved, she did. But she immediately replaced that relationship by commencing a telephone life with her nanny three thousand miles away. Her husband was furious and told her he would leave her if she did not stop her overreliance on other people. In an effort to save the marriage, she stopped the calls. But she could not stop over-reaching and complying when anxious, and the marriage soon ended.

Recalling these incidents, she realized that being good had not given her much—a realization that appeared to deepen her despair. She had been living a charade. But another group member pointed out that she had been her own architect. She retorted, "What do you know about life? You've never even had a husband or children!" As this slipped out, she felt a pang of guilt. How could she have said such a thing? She apologized profusely.

However, the members were made of sturdier stuff than she expected. They confronted her in return. One person wanted to know "What's the big deal? Can't you say anything you want to say?" Their acceptance of her anger reduced her need to turn it on herself. She felt free to criticize them. And the offended members felt free to fight back. When the session ended, she was feeling exhilarated. Emboldened in the following sessions, she hurled stinging insults at the members, and being the object of their vehemence did not daunt her. One session after another was marked with acrimonious skirmishes. A member protested to the analyst, "The pussy cat's turned into a tiger!" Indeed, it did appear that all restraints had been broken. Her wild ideas and lack of verbal control bewildered everyone.

At one point, when her assault on another member was especially harsh, the analyst intervened. He told her that she was not there to attack people. This outraged her. Who was he to tell her what to say? He asked her to turn the question into a statement. She told him to drop dead. She would do what she wanted to do. He replied that he would do what he wanted to. And at the moment, he was thinking of asking her to leave. She stared at him in shocked silence. The rest of the session she sat sullenly.

Distressed, she opened the next session with a complaint. Didn't the analyst know that what she was doing in group was helpful to her? She was taking better care of her children than ever: she was cleaning her house—indeed, her whole life seemed better in hand. If she could not be her rotten self, how could she continue to work in group or even live? He told her she could be anyone she wanted to be as long as she stuck to the contract: identify her feelings, put them into words, tell others why she had them.

This structure was too much for her. She ignored his words and regressed to petty complaining. She spent most of the next session on a mistake that had been made in her electric bill. She wanted the group's advice on how to handle it. Many gave their practical opinions and she seemed grateful. But then, a member questioned why she invested so much in a trivial matter. As she continued to talk about it, the group brought out that her thinking was burdened by concepts such as "must," "should," and "have to." As before, they found themselves up against her severe super-ego. But this time they knew there was more to her. They barraged her with questions. Who wanted her to do what? Suppose she refused? What would her preference be? Why wasn't she pursuing it? They refused to accept any self-demeaning rationale for her helplessness.

In this atmosphere, she soon recaptured her emerging freedom and confidence. Now, however, she was much more cooperative and less combative. For the first time, she showed some conflict-free curiosity about the physical details of her condition. She attended health conferences; she read copiously; she pursued a number of off-beat approaches in treating the carcinoma.

Soon she found a doctor who specialized in nutrition. Spreading her medical records in front of her, he explained in detail how cancer develops and progresses. He showed her actual pictures, slides and specimens of diseased tissue. When she came to him with techniques she had learned elsewhere, he was always interested. They talked about the seriousness of her condition. Several such conversations helped her discharge accumulated tension.

One technique she used effectively was visualization. It consisted of picturing healthy lungs. The physician helped by explaining how people breathe and what would interfere with it. This put her in intimate touch with the malignant process. She began to "think its death." Another exercise was to picture the cancer in her mind's eye as an octopus with a thousand tentacles. She visualized her "healthy cells" chopping away at them, gnawing at each tentacle. This exercise was followed by peaceful scenes of meadows through which she would go for a stroll with the group members. In her mind they told her that all was well and she could relax.

She described these healing exercises to the group. The members encouraged her to write them down in a journal. She began one, enlarging upon her fantasies and relating them to her malignancy. Occasionally, she read excerpts to the group, and members offered their impressions.

Though her real life appeared to be at a stalemate, her mind was a cauldron of activity. One session she came a half-hour early and eagerly waited for the group to arrive. She announced that she had a dream. In it, the world was as flat as a pancake in a frying pan. With a skillet she flipped it over. Some members seemed to know at once the dream's message. It was time for a change. They encouraged her to talk about the options open to her. Others helped her clarify what she wanted to do, and what could be done. An immediate decision was to quit her job, which had put constant pressure on her.

With this done, she phoned her estranged husband. He had moved to another city. She told him she wanted him to come back; she needed him. When he wavered, she decided to go off to see him. She spent three days persuading him that things were different. With misgivings, he returned on a trial basis. He made the provision that he himself visit her group to be sure the members knew the "true story." She might appear an independent person in public, but at home she played helpless and was excessively needy. He was reassured to discover that the group was already aware of these traits in her. And he appreciated their standing invitation to return when he wanted to.

That experience was crucial for their relationship. Until then, they had been on somewhat formal terms with each other; they had handled disagreements mainly by not dealing with them. Now there were spats, but there was also plenty of physical affection. The two of them gave up their concern over coming across to their neighbors as an "All American couple."

To her it ceased seeming necessary that she do everything by herself. With the group's help, she overcame her fear of asking for her husband's co-operation with daily chores, such as helping with the Friday shopping; she dropped three friends who were "more of a drain then a gain;" she joined a new church and took an active role in its art program, teaching a drawing class. Her husband supported her search for a part-time job and felt more comfortable about her resumed relationship with the nanny. He also helped her cultivate and maintain an independent attitude toward her mother.

She was no longer a victim of the desperate need for others. When the old passivity crept into her talk in group, the members were quick to point it out.

She developed a strong conviction that the total treatment was succeeding. Indeed, her enthusiasm took on a missionary drive. In hospitals, offices, wherever she met sick people, she urged them to assume a more optimistic attitude. Her vitality communicated itself to others.

Within this patient's mind, it would seem, lay the inherent power to inhibit the progress of her own malignancy. She rid herself of burdensome emotional baggage and established firm pathways for the future discharge of her energies, and thus freed her body to mobilize its weapons against the proliferating neoplastic material. Her revitalized system restored the natural order of physical functioning. It reestablished its capacity to cope with the malignancy through the immunological system. Medically, her prognosis went from guarded to excellent.

In this case, every step in combatting the neoplasm was marked by a bout with her aggressive impulses. Whenever her anger—overt or covert—was overlooked, her therapeutic movement ground to a halt. In various ways the group offered her a corrective opportunity to direct toward them the noxious attitudes that she formerly repressed, denied, contained, rationalized, or directed toward herself. She was permitted to be "bad" without being punished.

It may be that once they settle for a static state of existence, the bodies of certain people rebel against it. There is an inborn drive to move forward. If the body cannot break through the entrenched patterns, it redirects its basic drive into cellular tissue on a primitive level. The result is cancer.

Naturally, it is an open question as to how or why the neoplasm started. There may be a connection between the loss of needed objects—mother, nanny, husband—and the later onset of the carcinoma. What reversed the malignant process is an even more intriguing question. The patient's physicians attributed the improvement largely to chemotherapy; the group members saw their own understanding of the patient as curative. One even had the idea that it was a diet he had urged on her. The woman herself put a different construction on the cause. "Pain and death—these were my real motivators. And in a way my allies. They pushed me. It was the cancer or me."

Our failures are, of course, many and baffling. Yet some of our defeats would seem to illustrate the importance of getting in touch with one's own aggression. We seem to be hamstrung when the patient fails to develop an awareness of his hostility, is unable to release it, and thus cannot utilize it.

Sometimes we have the impression we are helpless spectators of a tragedy that plays itself out before our eyes. We experience our efforts as futile when the toxic effects of unexpressed aggression unfold before us.

A young actress held her father in awe. But his sudden death from cancer of the brain seemed hardly to affect her. She went off to attend his funeral and returned within the week. On the surface this seemed odd. He had encouraged her singing and acting career and given her money to further it, and she seemed very appreciative. But in another respect, her relief was understandable. She had to call him regularly. He wanted to know every detail of her professional career but would express great discontent with its progress. When he visited her, he was critical of her friends, her apartment, and her appearance. His carping was threatening to her. It implied that he might cut off his financial support. Of two areas he knew nothing: her group experience—which she paid for by teaching singing—and her uneven love life.

She entered group because of her penchant for turning chance attractions to men into compulsive involvements. These would last until the affair foundered on the rocks of distrust—about six months later. She seemed sure the object of her love would sooner or later disappoint her, and indeed, at some point she would come across indications confirming her fears. At once, she would find the man wanting on a number of scores. In dissatisfaction, she herself would break up each relationship.

When members questioned her about the last of these, she replied that there had been nothing to the involvement in the first place. But she felt bitter and generally disillusioned, and these feelings manifested themselves elsewhere in her life. Within the next six months she suffered a number of professional reversals, one of which was mortifying. She almost landed and then lost a lead in a musical that opened to smash reviews. This epitomized a career in which she had repeatedly been the stand-by for some recognized star, never quite making it herself.

A few weeks later, she developed hoarseness. Being prone to hypochondriacal reactions in the face of reversals, she had remedies on hand and resorted to them. But this time the rasp worsened. Friends and group members urged her to see a physician. Always on some pretext, she kept postponing the visit. Finally, when she could no longer speak above a whisper, she consulted one doctor, and then several others.

Her vagueness and hesitancy confused the members. One insisted on knowing exactly what took place. Apparently, she had told each doctor that she did not want to know the "fancy name" of her ailment. All she wanted was a prescription. If she did not like the import of what the doctor said, she tuned him out and ignored his recommendations. She was discontent with all of them.

A member told her of a relative with a rare tropical disease, who could get no help from local doctors. He had finally cleared up the malady by going to a medical center for a "read-out and treatment." This tale sparked interest. The rest of the group prevailed on her to enter a well-known clinic, where a number of specialists would examine her and then consult among themselves. Reluctantly, she went—at the tail end of a vacation to the Bahamas.

The clinic made the differential diagnosis of malignancy of the throat, involving the thyroid, pharynx, and surrounding tissues. Because there was a familial history of neoplasms, and the growth had already metastasized, her prognosis was poor. The news of her condition devastated her. Upon returning to New York City, she closeted herself in her apartment and would see few people. She systematically restricted the arena of her life, pulling the social drawstrings so close together that she became virtually alone. She dropped out of acting classes, theatre going, and travel. Even her teaching, to which she was unswervingly committed, suffered. She missed appointments, rejected new students, neglected to return phone calls.

Members were able to get her to attend group by picking her up on the way to the analyst's office, bombarding her with reminders, and alerting her answering service. During the sessions, she would question fate. Why her? What did she do to deserve it? It was not fair. There was no rhyme or reason to life. There was little give-and-take with the members. But they kept confronting her with her self-pity and preoccupation. She began to make some contact with them and in the real world, as well.

Her reconstituted daily routine consisted of seeing doctors, talking to a few friends on the phone who were ever peppering her with novel medical nostrums. She studied pamphlets and literature she picked up at the health food stores. There were missions to Bermuda, Mexico, and the Phillipines, seeking healers. Just over the horizon there must be a new technological discovery or drug. She undertook a desperate search for anything that offered hope.

In a health food store she ran into a former member. He had left group a year before to go on the road with a show but had never returned to treatment. They had been attracted to each other, and she made it clear back then that she was quite fond of him. Naturally, he was distressed to see the disordered state she was in. He took her to dinner, had her apartment cleaned, demanded she take physical care of herself—even set appointments at beauty parlors for her and brought her to the best clothing stores. He tossed her nostrums out of the window, insisted that she go to physicians he personally checked out, and forced her to attend group sessions regularly. He lectured to her about her self-neglecting habits, encouraged her in every way to live in the moment, and actively rejected her script of doom. He called the group analyst. After a consultation with him, he decided to see what he could do "to at least put the pieces together."

Initially this man had reminded her of her father, and now he actively behaved like him.

She began to mobilize an impressive amount of energy to deal with her problems. At each session she would arrive before the members, often with an agenda which she had rehearsed with her new lover. Her voice—though cracked and wavering—came across clearly. Members gave her space, sensing her courage and fragility. She made it clear that she did not want to hear what *they* thought would be helpful—only what *she* thought would be helpful. They sympathetically restricted their responses to telling her what she wanted to know.

Within a few sessions she revealed that she hated her voice. It had forced her life along restrictive lines. She felt her singing was instrumental in her father's death. He once had aspirations to be on stage and had hoped she would fulfill them, but she had let him down.

A member suggested another possibility. The reason she had never reached stardom in her singing was that her father would have taken credit for it. It would not be her achievement. Because she would not recognize her anger toward him for forcing her to live out his aspirations, all she could feel was guilt. After a long silence she broke into body-wracking sobs.

With this insightful experience, she became more accessible to group influence. For the first time she began to show a lively curiosity about her buried self. Everything became possible. It was possible that she had ambivalent feelings toward her father, that the growth might be the organic equivalent of mourning, that hating the cancer only paralyzed her, that dashing after folk remedies was just another avoidance of feelings— substituting hope for despair. She began to consider that her self-blame might be an evasion of her anger at the world, that her cancer was not a punishment for sexual liasions or for her deceiving her father, and that if anything, her father might have muddled up her life (an idea she found freeing). Each time she discharged some anger, her guilt lessened.

With drugs, diet, and buoyed by the concern of the group and the insistence of her lover, she took a turn for the better. This development was aided by treatment with a hypnotherapist who helped calm her many paralyzing fears. Her vigor returned. Her voice regained part of its original timbre. She felt an awakened interest in the theater and returned to teaching.

Then a disguised calamity descended on her. Her father's will was read. Provision had been made for her to receive a half-million dollars. Instead of celebrating the news, she nosedived into grief again. With that descent went every sign of her emerging resentment to her father. Compounding calamity, her brother contested the will. Because he embodied aspects of her father, she could not bring herself to effectively counter his legal legerdemian. Group members were unable to activate any anger toward him.

Her boyfriend was equally frustrated by her passivity. An acting job on the road opened for him. He wanted her to come along. But she was too deeply immersed in self-recriminations to respond. They had a quarrel. He broke off the relationship and left the city.

With her staunchest ally gone, her shaky defenses fell apart. Though she did not deny she had a role in the rupture, she complained about her own state. She had been abandoned and felt vulnerable with her lover gone. But her primary cry had to do with her inability to do anything constructive.

Under group pressure she called a highly recommended lawyer. He was briefed by a member who told him about the extenuating circumstances under which he had to function. But she undermined the lawyer's efforts by not consulting him or keeping him abreast of developments. When her brother arrived in person, she capitulated to his demands.

The rasp returned to her voice. She reported a series of dreams to the group in which various kinds of snakes were throttling her. Their recurrence distressed her, and the group's interpretations had no effect on changing them.

Her dreams ended when she found a new figure to lean on. He was a young cancer specialist with definite ideas about the course of treatment. First, he instituted a radical form of radiation. Secondly, he prescribed a strict regimen of rest and sleep. He was firmly opposed to anything that might tax her reserves.

He had serious reservations about psychotherapy. In several phone conversations the analyst was careful to describe the group treatment as an adjunctive approach. The specialist still felt it was stressful. After all, she had been in treatment for some time and no remarkable changes had occurred. He ruled out the psychosomatic factor in her disorder. But he said he would not interfere with her therapy as long as she was "enthusiastic" about it.

She was definitely not enthusiastic about anything. Often she would fail to appear at the therapy sessions. When members managed to get her there, it was again difficult to stimulate any interest in the on-going exchanges. No one could lift her out of her listless state. Several wondered why they expended themselves trying to get her to a meeting since they had so little effect on her.

The more helpless she felt, the more convinced she became that her specialist was omnipotent. He filled the role well. He was never at a loss for a new medication. He told her exactly what to do and how to do it. He was unconcerned with her secret yearnings or murmurred whims.

Her attendance in group became even more erratic. If a member's call happened to find her in, she would answer flatly. It seemed as if all her medical appointments were scheduled at exactly the hour the group met. Members felt they were combatting a suicidal surrender. There was no fight left in her. It was as if the clock in her world had stopped ticking. She died soon afterwards.

We may speculate about the psychogenic causes of this failure, by contrasting it with successful cases. From the group dynamic point of view, there was minimal interaction between the patient and the rest of the members. Her interpersonal involvement with them tended to be shallow. She could cut off her own feelings as easily as she could cut off the other members.

Her behavior was explicable in transferential terms. She treated the group the same way her father treated her mother. She was fond of the members but they were not in any way central to her life. Initially, what kept bringing her back to the group was bewilderment over one unfortunate affair after the other. Later she returned to the group to deal with the malignancy. Never did she investigate in depth her relationships with the members. For the most part, she was aloof and artificially even-tempered.

The loss of her father had been overwhelming; the replacement was revitalizing. The former member who entered her life had afforded her a temporary spur toward health. He provided her with support, admiration, and he ministered to her narcissim. She was at her best when he was in her life. With him, she had learned to articulate her negative feelings. When he left, she lost touch with this important part of her emotional life.

There is no doubt that the mechanism of denial can be protective. It limits the input that can penetrate a person's insulation barrier. But there was so much denial in this patient that at times it was difficult to pinpoint what she was actually experiencing, particularly her negative feelings. Her uncommon social charm, when closely studied, appeared to have a plastic quality.

On the outside, she appeared poised and intact; on the inside there was chaos. The two sides seemed not to be in communication with each other. When her mechanisms of repression, displacement, and rationalization failed her, she retracted her ego boundaries, and withdrew into isolation.

If we assume the development of the cancer had something to do with her inability to deal with her aggression, the death of her father certainly set into motion a process that was as insidious as it was deadly. While her father lived, she at least had the tenuous possibility of surfacing her latent hatred and directing it toward him.

Once he died, the anger had nowhere to go. She could not mobilize it in the service of separation; her grief returned her to a state of helpless fusion with him. This dilemma forced her to turn her aggression against herself. The inwardly directed anger may have furthered complete collapse of the immunological system. Very possibly, it was not the pain of parental abandonment that set off the cancer, but rather her denial of enormous rage at being abandoned.

Identification with her father, followed by introjection of his image, may have been a precipitating factor in the malignancy. She had lost part of herself with his death, and had been unable to substitute another emotional object for him. Perhaps her body made a final heroic effort to regenerate this part of her lost self, sought to recover that part through the prolific growth of tissue. Some archaic pattern may have been set in motion, a tendency that existed before the central nervous system could organize, control and regulate the organism as a whole. From this point of view, we might view cancer as an expression of a deeply regressed urge—as a drive to regenerate a psychologically amputated part of the self.

Naturally, de-differentiated cellular tissue cannot possibly replace a missing human being, an object of feeling. The effort was doomed to failure. Lower forms of life, such as the salamander, can, under stress, amputate a part of themselves and regenerate it later. The attempted reproduction by a human being under stress would, by analogy, be expressing itself through a neoplasm. However, as with any such speculation, this one leaves a number of questions unanswered. For instance, many people with cancer do not report the loss of a vital object, nor could such a loss be traced.

Another powerful factor would seem to be the patient's heredity. This is not to say that a person is marked for a malignancy. The majority of people so predisposed do not develop one. In fact, there seems a powerful potential in human beings to rise above their encoding, and this too invites the thesis that psychic factors are involved.

This patient's predisposition was doubtless stimulated by an expectation of the inevitability of cancer. It may have put her body into a state of prolonged resignation. This would be similar to the phenomenon known as the "anniversary syndrome," wherein a person gets the same illness or meets the same fate on the same day or date as a parent.

What does seem clear is that her malignancy coincided with the failure of her ego-coping dynamisms in the face of trauma. This coinciding of the onset of her disease and the deterioration of her defense mechanisms is at best an observation. If she had been able to keep in touch with her aggression and utilize it in life-preserving decisions and actions, would there have been a different ending to her case? Possibly. With further refining of our theory and technique, we may some day be able to answer this question.

Conclusion

It may prove valuable to regard cancer less as a disease than as a disorder in the body's biochemical signals. To alter these signals is to produce an impact on the body's immunological defenses. It would follow that any form of intervention designed to restore the body to physical health must use more than physical means.

Since emotions dramatically influence the biochemical system, one way of providing immunotherapy is by giving psychotherapy to patients. It should be flexible and interactional in content, constantly undergoing modification to satisfy the patient's needs.

It would seem that one effective way of meeting these needs is by group therapy. The primary aim of such treatment would be analysis and resolution of resistances to verbal communication. Its emphasis would be on the resolution of the patient's unwillingness to experience and to express negative feelings toward people important in his group life. With this accomplished, efforts can then be made to convert the freed energy so that it can be utilized in the self-assertiveness that defines our personalities and makes our lives productive and satisfying.

Notes

1. Paget, J., *Surgical Pathology* (2nd ed.), Longman's Green, London, 1870.

2. Cutter, E., "Diet on Cancer," *Albany Medical Annals,* July–Aug. 1887.

3. Hughes, C. H., "The Relations of Nervous Depression to the Development of Cancer," *The St. Louis Medical and Surgical Journals,* May, 1887.

4. Snow, H., *The Reappearance of Cancer After Apparent Extirpation,* J. and A. Churchill, London, 1870.

5. Selye, H., *The Stress of Life,* McGraw-Hill, N.Y. 1956.

6. Boyd W., "The Spontaneous Regression of Cancer," *Journal of Canadian Association of Radiology,* 8, 45, 1957, 63.

7. Cobb, B., "A Social-Psychological Study of the Cancer Patient," *Cancer,* 1954, 1–14.

8. Bacon, C. L., Renneker, R. and Cutler, M. "A Psychosomatic Survey of Cancer of the Breast," *Psychosomatic Medicine,* 14, 1952, 453–460.

9. Kissen, D. M. and Eysenck, H. G., "Personality in Male Lung Cancer Patients," *Journal of Psychosomatic Research,* 6, 1962, 123.

10. LeShan, L. and Worthington, R. E., "Some Psychologic Correlatives of Neoplastic Disease: Preliminary Report." *Journal of Clinical and Experimental Psychopathology,* 16, 1955, 281–288.

11. LeShan, L. "An Emotional Life History Pattern Associated with Neoplastic Disease," *Annals of the New York Academy of Sciences,* 125, 1966, 780–793.

12. Goldfarb, O., Driesen, J. and Cold, D., "Psychophysiologic Aspects of Malignancy," *American Journal of Psychiatry,* 123, June 1967, 1545–51.

13. Simonton, O. C. and Simonton, S. "Belief Systems and Management of the Emotional Aspects of Malignancy," *Journal of Transpersonal Psychology,* 7(1), 1975, 29–47.

14. Spotnitz, H., *Psychotherapy of Preoedipal Conditions,* Jason Aronson, 1976.

12 Cancer as a Treatment Destructive Resistance in Group Therapy

Lena Blanco Furgeri

Several years ago, during the course of therapy, a patient developed cancer and died. Subsequently, the therapist wrote a paper which discussed the course of the illness and how the group helped the patient, whose name was Jim, to face death (Furgeri, 1978). Although the patient had been helped to face death, he had become physically ill during therapy. The question of why the patient, a physically healthy man at the start of therapy, developed cancer plagued the therapist. Slowly, it began to appear that the treatment had failed; the operation had been a success, but the patient had died. As this thought began to take hold, the therapist recollected how patients seem to develop symptoms or illnesses as they are making drastic shifts in their lifestyles. When some patients are on the verge of major breakthroughs, usually involving separations from old patterns or systems, a serious mishap or hospitalization may occur.

Appelbaum (1977, p. 511), in "The Refusal to Take One's Own Medicine," discusses Freud's remarks on the purpose of symptoms: "They are needed to maintain equilibrium between two preemptory sides of a conflict, while often permitting the disguised fulfillment of unacknowledged wishes." It is the intent of this chapter to discuss the hypothesis that the development of cancer or tumorous growths during the course of treatment may be a form of treatment destructive resistance, or, as Spotnitz defines it: "any pattern of behavior that, if permitted to continue, would break off treatment" (1976, p. 145). For example, patterns connected with accumulated frustration and aggression tend to be expressed through lateness, nonpayment of fees, cancellation of appointments, and not talking. As the patient progresses and becomes more sophisticated, the resistance can take more subtle forms not easily contained within the analytic situation and become more difficult to deal with. The patient may begin to neglect the body by tiring it; engage in hazardous health activities such as smoking, excessive eating, or drinking; or use various family members to express the resistance. The patient's dietary habits are a crucial consideration because food is related to the primary relationship to the nurturing figure, the mother. As stress is experienced, the reaction is often reflected in the variation of food intake. Garma upholds the view that psychosomatic symptoms such as a peptic ulcer are integrally related to the early relationship and represent the "internalized evil mother" (Ammon, 1979, p. 92). The stress accompanied by not caring for oneself appropriately can lead to illness because an unfit body tends to break down under stress (Appelbaum, 1979; Selye, 1976; Reich, 1973).

The therapeutic framework that embodies the guidelines or treatment contract is crucial to the patient's health and ego development. Langs defines the therapeutic framework as the "frame," which is "a metaphor for the implicit and explicit ground rules of psychotherapy or psychoanalysis" (1979, p. 540). In *The Bipersonal Field,* Langs discusses how the development of illness during the course of treatment may be related to the nurturing process. He does not refer to "explicit or direct efforts to behave in a mothering or supportive manner" but rather to the "analyst's and therapist's basic stance of maintaining ground rules and boundaries, and in offering the patient a proper and sound therapeutic hold" (1976, p. 406). He elaborated on this concept in *The Therapeutic Environment* by adding that "one factor in somatic symptoms is disturbance in ground rules and the therapeutic hold" (1979, p. 66). Usually a change in structure such as the therapist's vacation can elicit reactions from relief to abandonment depression on the part of the patient.

Given these observations, is it possible that, in developing cancer and similar symptoms, patients are expressing a treatment destructive resistance? Is it possible that the development of cancer and related symptoms in a formerly physically healthy patient in actuality may be an unconscious means of resisting the therapy and/or the therapist? Will the patient, unable directly to express feelings regarding the treatment and such a crucial variable as a change of frame, somatize?

The thought that Jim had used cancer as a means of terminating treatment was highlighted when the therapist observed firsthand how group therapy had helped a woman in her therapy group to affect the cancerous process. It seems possible that Jim's illness, cancer of the liver, was unconsciously aided and abetted by members of the group who helped the therapist to fail, while Celia, another patient who developed uterine fibroids and was in a different group, was helped to cope in a more constructive manner. Ammon hypothesizes that the symptom carrier in the group "representatively acts out the unconscious conflicts of the group . . . and as a result fulfills an important function in relation to group homeostasis and cohesion" (1979, p. 236). Group members may serve as alternative therapists, transference objects, and symbolic introjects—and, consequently, can be helpful or harmful.

A treatment destructive resistance tends to manifest itself differently in group therapy than in individual therapy because group members have an opportunity to see each other on the outside. The urge for outside contact affects the treatment because it tends to promote subgrouping, which is destructive to group process. The application of boundaries such as no outside contact, no touching during the session, discussion of appropriate diet, and exercises to enhance good body maintenance tends to elicit a great deal of verbal expression of the resistance rather than nonverbal manifestations such as acting out or somatizing. Having no outside contact as part of the treatment contract enables members to be more open and direct with their aggression and in many ways decreases the possibility of treatment destructive resistance. Members can openly display their feelings about the contract and their frustrations in relation to it. The instructions or ground rules tend to arouse mixed feelings in members, particularly anger, and a skilled therapist is able to manage these feelings and destructive impulses as they are verbalized and to work them through.

Since Jim, as well as the other patients who developed symptoms, were in group therapy, the impact of group process including the roles of the group members and the therapist will be discussed. Jim's cancer of the liver and the mastectomy undergone by Faith, another patient, can be seen as failures in treatment related to the eagerness of the therapist to "cure." Cancer patients tend to induce rescue fantasies in the therapist, and this affects the countertransference and may contribute to the ineffectiveness of treatment. Therapists may be overly enthusiastic about and energetic in their efforts to help relieve the patient of depression, anxiety, or other discomforting symptoms. Celia, the previously mentioned patient who developed uterine fibroids, and Agnes, who developed precancerous mastopathy, were helped to cope in more constructive manners.

As will be described, the patients suffered considerable trauma as they experienced real and psychological losses. Their histories revealed intense incestuous family ties. These ties were carried over into their families of procreation or into present-day life in an attempt to recreate the primal family constellation, thus avoiding their facing the original feelings of loss. They were accustomed to masochistic lifestyles and were attached to their families of origin. Jim was attached to his mother and sister, for whom his wife and daughter became substitutes; Faith was excessively preoccupied with her parents and brother and displaced many of her feelings onto her husband and sons; Celia was overly involved with her mother, father, and siblings and continued her role by serving her husband and three children, as well; Agnes was attached to her father, who died of cancer, and committed to the care of her three young sons, who had been abandoned by their father.

The patients had all been programmed into the key role of taking care of others and were, in many ways, considered the hubs of their respective systems. All of them had learned to have their needs met indirectly by doing for others so that any therapeutic recommendation geared toward their directly taking care of themselves was met with resistance. This intense resistance resulted not only from the stress involved in separation-individuation, which was never resolved, but also from the angry feelings aroused in those who were dependent on them. Since the patients were so intricately bound to the family system, any effort to influence their patterns of nurturing would have been met with an inordinate amount of pressure from those they nurtured. In addition, all of the patients accepted what was done to them, that is, the abuse, mistreatment, rejection, and abandonment, with passive resignation, denying their rage. The repressed anger in these patients toward the people to whom they were bound seemed related to their feelings of guilt.

Discussing the relationship between cancer and loss, Simonton and others before him observed that patients tend to develop cancers six to twenty-four months after a deeply felt loss. Therefore, he believed that cancer results from despair and can be seen as a variation of suicide or a last-ditch attempt to solve the problem (Appelbaum, 1977, p. 515). Another researcher has noted that tumor cells that were dormant after surgical treatment sometimes grow within a few months of bereavement (1960). According to a study at Johns Hopkins Hospital in Baltimore, breast-cancer patients who responded with feelings of anger, anxiety, and depression were likely to live longer than those who accepted their illnesses passively (Thomas, 1974). Appelbaum, in his chapter "The Will to Have Cancer and What to Do About It," mentions the LeShan study which showed that cancer patients had distancing and rejecting parents and tended to find important substitutes for those early relationships. Usually a disruption or loss of these relationships tended to be followed by cancer onset (1979, p. 339). In addition, cancer patients are frequently unable to express anger.

It is not the purpose of this chapter to prove causation but to present the hypothesis that the development of cancer and tumorous growths during the course of therapy may be induced by unresolved stress related to transference and resistance, which, in turn, can affect countertransference and counterresistance. One of the main conflicts experienced by the patient during the course of therapy is that of separation-individuation. Usually this struggle is manifested by an intense division of loyalty. The patient feels torn between old ways and patterns, which may have been self-destructive but perpetuated a bond with the family system, and newer and more constructive patterns of behavior, which enhance separation from the family system but also induce anxiety that may become intolerable. The separation-individuation process related to the struggle for identity occurs in relationship to the transference and resistance. Giovacchini in his paper "Ego Equilibrium and Cancer of the Breast," discussing separation experiences and the onset of cancer, postulates that there may well exist a relationship between "personality structure and the occurrence of invasive disease" (1975, p. 415). He discusses how the disruptions in ego states during the course of therapy are not apparent until somatic manifestations have occurred (1975, p. 424).

Group and Case Presentations

The patients were in three different groups, one clinic group and two private groups. Patients entered the groups to work on problems concerning their children, their marriages, or their own potentiation. The presentations that follow will focus on the course of treatment as it concerns the evolution of frame or treatment contract, the collusion of group members in supporting the illness or discouraging it, and individual growth related to separation-individuation.

Group No. 1

Therapy Group No. 1, the clinic group, began in 1964. Until 1971, many members came and went, and there was much acting-out behavior characterized by lateness and socializing after the group session, for example, by the members' dining, dancing, and drinking together. By mid-1971, the group acknowledged that the socializing after hours was not only diluting the therapy but was also leading to subgrouping, and they agreed to cease their outside contact. As one member stated at the time, "We're coming for the after-session rather than for the therapy."

Jim, a good-looking forty-year-old man, was with the group from its inception until 1974, when he died of terminal cancer of the liver. He entered therapy because of depression and an inability to get along with his wife. For a brief time, some joint sessions were held with his wife where she brought up grievances concentrating on the past and her dissatisfaction, which Jim accepted with passive resignation.

In the winter of 1972, when Jim began to experience stomach distress, the group was cohesive and consisted of six other members, most of whom had been diagnosed as depressive. Among the members were Clara, a Holocaust victim in her late forties whose parents and brother had died in the war and who had, like Jim, been in the group from the beginning; Carl, a young, isolated man whose family had relocated, who was procrastinating in getting his college degree and caring for himself and who, following a failed marriage, had gained weight and withdrawn further; and Celia, in her late thirties, who had come from an intact family to which she was extremely dedicated, thus binding herself to home and contributing to the trouble she already had with separation. There was also Rachel, in her early forties and an only child, who never got over the loss of her father through a sudden heart attack when she was fourteen years old and who, as an adult, was mired in depression over the recent loss of her husband in the same way while her only daughter was also fourteen. Rachel tended to whine and complain and seemed orally fixated, depending on alcohol and food as pacifiers. Amy, in her late twenties, living at home, and isolated and withdrawn except for her work, had had cerebral palsy as a child, which required repeated hospitalizations; she turned out to be the group's quietest member. And there was Sam, in his early forties, who had lost his father when he was eighteen, in the army, and unable to return for the funeral, and who tended to be the most angry group member, especially at the time of Jim's death, after which Sam left the group. As for the therapist, she had lost her father who died of lung cancer at the age of forty-seven; she had been completing her master's degree when she learned of his terminal illness.

As the oldest male member of the group, Jim symbolically represented a father figure, and most members were dependent upon him. Although continuously frustrated and unhappy in his marital relationship, he did make considerable strides in therapy in other areas of his life by starting his own business, attending college, and enjoying life more by doing more for himself. He also was able to deal with his feelings of loss when his daughter married and his son went away to school. His obsession with his unmarried sister who had had a mastectomy and lived with his widowed mother and daughter persisted throughout the therapy.

During January of 1971, a break in the frame occurred when a male therapist who was training to become a group therapist came to the group. Jim, one of the first group members to welcome him, was unable to express his anger directly at the intrusion of a newcomer. The group was very passive and tended to manifest its passivity through its main resistance, which was by not talking openly. This passivity tended to arouse counter-transference feelings of frustration and anger in the therapist.

It was during the winter of 1972, after the male therapist had left, that Jim started to have stomach distress and swelling of the legs. The therapist became concerned that, with the arrival of the male therapist, Jim might have begun to somatize his repressed rage, exacerbated by recent losses symbolized by his children's moving away from him. Jim had surgery for an intestinal obstruction and returned to work and to the group, feeling better at first. But early in 1973 he started to report general malaise and nausea, and then said he had chronic hepatitis. He talked of how he trusted the group and asked them for help.

Toward the end of 1973, Jim reported that he had cancer of the liver. The group members became visibly upset, most with tears in their eyes, but sat silently. When asked about their feelings, they did not want to talk because they did not want to upset Jim. He became slightly irritated and said, "I don't want pity." Jim said he wanted to keep coming to the sessions for as long as possible. The therapist was somewhat concerned about the silence, reminding the members of the group contract about "talking" (Ormont, 1969).

When Jim felt unable to continue coming to group sessions, it was decided that sessions would be held at Jim's home. After two of these sessions, however, the therapist noticed a rigidity and tension in the group. Celia was finally able to express resentment about visiting with Jim on group time, since part of the session was invariably devoted to that, and it was agreed to add a half-hour group session at the office.

When Jim died, the therapist asked the group members to write brief comments about what the death meant. Although asking the patients to write their comments was another variation of the frame—the contract was to express all feelings and thoughts verbally—the exercise actually facilitated talking among the patients. It led them to express verbally their feelings about Jim's death, the therapist, and the group that they had not expressed before. The patients' written comments indicated that the illness had value for them in terms of secondary gain because it brought them closer together. The illness, which can be viewed as an unconscious somatic expression of aggression aimed at distancing, had perpetuated contact and closeness in a defensive way. To complicate the matter more, the illness had brought about a further variation in the frame that provided little outlet for the expression of aggression: The home visits denied the group the opportunity to be angry at either the patient or the therapist and gave Jim no opportunity to feel his rage at being deprived.

Carl was the only patient who alluded to some feelings of anger. He said:

> Jim's death affected me strongly. I was close to him in many ways. I had come to depend on him. In some ways I thought of him as a father. Jim's death had an effect on the structure of the group. He made peace with a lot of things in his life but was never able to handle the relationship to his wife. Maybe dying was the only way he could accomplish this. This seemed to have had an effect on the older members of the group. Many came to the decision that this group or any group could not help them and left. At no time previously had so many people left in such a short time.

Carl was clearly hinting that the course of treatment had somehow affected the illness. The therapist herself had been coping with her feelings of separation and loss exacerbated by the earlier loss of her father. In fact, the whole group became involved in an intense relationship with the ill father upon whom they had come to depend. The feelings of impotence and helplessness seemed to have been activated by Jim's illness, as shown by the written comments, but all of the members seemed to repress their feelings of rage. Anger is usually a taboo feeling, but even more so in relation to a dead or dying person. As a result, it seemed that many group members could do nothing but act on their feelings by leaving. The group members, including the therapist, had not resolved feelings of loss that had occurred in early childhood. Their repressed aggression, therefore, fed into the transference resistance.

As frequently occurs in therapy, this therapist's interventions were influenced by countertransference issues. While the therapist had been studying for her master's degree, her father had been in the throes of cancer, and she learned that he would die. Now, as a doctoral student, she faced a parallel situation in Jim's cancer, his progressively worsening condition, and his death. The therapist had not fully worked through her feelings and resistance to her own aggression. As a result of the countertransference resistance, she was oblivious to the life-threatening symptoms as a clue to the resistance going on in the treatment. Because of the countertransference, the therapist had attempted a "framework cure" through an inappropriate modification of the ground rules (the sessions in Jim's home) in an attempt to alleviate the symptoms (Langs, 1979, p. 541).

After Jim's death, several outspoken, active men joined the group, and the tenor of the group changed radically from one of passivity to one of more involvement and interaction. Rachel, Celia, and Carl remained members of the group, and Faith joined in September of 1974.

Faith initially came to individual treatment for herself with this therapist at the clinic in 1966 when her son was showing schizophrenic symptoms. A tall, stately woman, Faith was extremely anxious and a compulsive talker. For years she had taken abuse from her disturbed husband who would lash out at her with invectives and grab her by the throat. She was a chronic latecomer, and, when the therapist finally confronted her on her treatment destructive resistance, she was surprised. "Therapists are supposed to understand and not mind such things," Faith had said.

Handling the lateness directly helped Faith to manage more effectively other areas of her life. Her relationship with her husband improved; she began to spend more time with him and to travel with him. In addition, her children began to do better. In the middle of 1974 Faith discovered a cyst on her breast and found a renowned breast surgeon to take care of her.

Through her years in therapy, Faith was becoming less dependent on her family and yearning for more contact with others. As a result, she decided to join the group. Since her husband was resistant to paying, it was agreed that she would not come to group in the fall unless she started to work. In September she called, stating that she had gotten a job and was ready to join the group.

Soon, Faith's husband started to abuse her again. With group support, she finally was able to get an order of protection. The court ordered joint counseling, which she and her husband attended. During this time, however, Faith encountered a number of additional crisis situations. Her husband was hospitalized with a cardiac condition; her son left town for college; and, both her parents died within one month of each other. Though the group members felt a great deal of ambivalence toward Faith, who was skillful in provoking others to experience her helpessness, frustration, and hostility, Faith did receive group support for her losses, and this seemed to be life-affirming.

Throughout therapy, the patient maintained an idealized relationship with her therapist, sending cards, notes, and good wishes for every occasion. During January of 1978, the therapist terminated her services at the clinic and a male therapist, whom Faith knew and had contact with, took the therapist's place. Several months later, the first therapist received a call from Faith, who was in the hospital. She seemed high as she reported that she was going to be operated on, and that there was a good possibility that it would be a mastectomy. To the therapist's amazement, the patient sounded euphoric. As the therapist listened to this almost manic high, she got the vague feeling that here again she had in some way let the patient down. When the therapist called following the operation, the patient confirmed that she had undergone the mastectomy and said that further surgery was being considered. The therapist listened half-stunned as the patient talked extensively of how good she felt and of everyone's surprise at how well she had taken the whole thing.

It seems to this therapist that here again a variation in the frame—the therapist's leaving—had subjected the patient to another loss on the heels of many previous losses and may have influenced the course of her illness. Faith terminated with her group soon after surgery, but continues to write to this therapist. In a most recent communication, Faith said that everyone was fine, putting herself last. Her inability to accept the loss of the original therapist probably made it more difficult for her to remain with the new therapist who had replaced her.

Group No. 2

Celia and Carl, members of Group No. 1, decided to join Group No. 2, a private group as well. Celia believed she was not getting enough from the one group, and that more interaction with others would help alleviate the strong attachment she still had to her family of origin. Celia entered Group No. 2 in 1974 and remained in it until 1980, when she developed a fibroid tumor.

When Celia joined Group No. 2, the members, ranging in age from twenty-two to fifty, were intelligent, educated, sophisticated, and upwardly mobile. The female group members consisted of Myra, in her early thirties, once very depressed and unable to keep a steady job, who had succeeded in buying her apartment and finding a job she liked, and then began to work toward developing a more satisfying intimate relationship; Kate, successful professionally, who had come to the group because of an inability to have a close relationship and who had since gone onto graduate work, begun to live with a man she planned to marry, and become content; Abby, in her fifties, who had come because her young adult son was apathetic and not functioning well and who, when he successfully completed college, returned to graduate school herself and began to achieve happiness in her marital relationship; Pearl, who had raised four children and then decided to leave suburbia, including an unhappy twenty-year marriage, and who, though depressed, struggled with feelings of isolation and loneliness to make a life of her own; and Jane, who, though abandoned in childhood, managed to stabilize herself professionally and was finishing school and learning how to take care of herself.

The male members of the group included Alex, a handsome man in his late forties, very successful professionally, who had married for the third time but who, because of an unresolved relationship with his father, was unable to achieve happiness in his new marriage; Ron, a young, anxious man who was struggling against containing many feelings of rage that resulted from a childhood of intense deprivation, who had decided not to work for a while to discover what he wanted to do; Shawn, a depressed, isolated young man who had managed to get his college degree and was looking for work in his field; and Rick, a man in his early twenties who had been severely rejected by his parents, but who was making a life for himself in his field and learning how to relate more effectively to others. All members of the group had been in individual therapy, and the group as a whole was cohesive and well functioning, with its members committed to growth and group process. All had a direct and open relationship with the therapist.

Celia, a young attractive woman, first came to individual therapy with this therapist in 1964 because her oldest son was stealing. She had another son and daughter and was devoted to the home. She used this commitment to the family as a means of concealing her fear of taking her place in the world. She had always been extremely attached to her father and family, and, as the oldest daughter, had borne much responsibility. During her adolescence, she had been homebound with rheumatic fever. In her late teens, she met her husband, later marrying him when she was twenty years old.

As the problem concerning her son was being resolved, it became apparent that there was a great deal of difficulty in the marriage. Celia realized that most of her unhappiness and depression were related to this. In addition to caring for her home and family, Celia began to reach out and to work part time. This interest in matters outside the home and family tended to place more tension on the marital relationship, and Celia's husband decided to leave her, something Celia had great difficulty accepting.

Celia kept hoping for a reconciliation by going for joint counseling and attempting to speak with her husband, but he rejected her at every turn. In the meantime, her oldest son married, and as the other children grew, Celia developed more outside contacts and finally decided to seek a divorce, although reluctantly. At this time, her mother developed cancer and died. Subsequently, Celia changed to a more satisfying job and met a man she liked.

One outstanding feature about Celia was her tremendous resistance in therapy throughout the years. The therapist, who formerly would intervene actively, now permitted Celia to sit for a considerable time in group without speaking. Gradually, Celia started to talk, expressing an inordinate amount of rage about not getting enough and not being helped. She started to be more assertive in the group and actively asked for what she wanted.

Before the summer break, another patient, Abby, who had done a great deal for herself and who had been a role model for Celia, terminated. During the summer, the therapist was on vacation and sessions ceased. The loss of a cherished group member coupled with the break in treatment and "abandonment" by the therapist seemed to affect Celia's ego strength, and she felt compelled to contact her ex-husband. She did so, and the usual approach-avoidance pattern between them resulted.

When the sessions resumed in September, 1979, Celia began unaccounted for vaginal bleeding. In discussing the presence of a fibroid tumor, she said: "Part of me is saying, don't have fun—don't have fun. I feel part of me wants to give in to it, and I feel a pulling from the part not wanting to give in to it." She went on to explain that she was not happy at her new job and was thinking of returning to school, something she had long resisted. Once the presence of the fibroid was confirmed, she talked about how difficult it was to contact the doctor who was to help her with her diet, because the line was always busy.

This group, unlike Group No. 1, was more sophisticated and not so regressed. The members became angry regarding Celia's illness, mobilizing themselves toward a more militant stance. Pearl, for example, who was usually silent in group, became active, talking about a cyst that she had developed on her breast the previous year. She had become angry at this intrusion, she said, and decided that she did not want to be bothered with it. The growth, she announced, had disappeared (Appelbaum, 1977).

Celia said she had some understanding of why this was happening to her and wrote the following:

I feel that my fibroid tumor is starting to grow because I'm starting to feel my "self." The stress of growing and separating is creating a thickness or mass so that it won't be so painful. I believe that it goes way back—it's like my Achilles heel. I can recall that at fourteen years old, I started to have irregular-type bleeding, and the doctor telling my mother, "Don't worry, she's not pregnant."

Celia started to discuss the possibility of termination because she wanted to use the time for herself and stop traveling to the city. This request was an indication of her increased ability to speak up for herself and take care of herself in an appropriate way. She worked through termination feeling good about it; she had finally succeeded in getting a job she wanted, was returning to school, and was remaining with her other group, which was closer to home. In the final session, she engaged the therapist in a very personal and intimate manner, so much so that the whole group was very touched at the feelings expressed between the two women as peers.

Group No. 3

Group No. 3 was an all-women's group in which one patient, Agnes, developed a cancerous mastophathy and two other patients, Gertrude and Anastasia, developed symptoms as well. What is different about a women's group is the high level of anxiety due to the absence of males, the absence of competition for males, and the presence of homosexual feelings. The group members were most reluctant to talk about sex or their feelings about men and tended to be problem-focused.

In February, 1976, when the women agreed to have a male therapist who was training for group therapy come to group, there were eight members. Gertrude, the group's newest member, was a thin, anxious, twenty-one year old who had come for treatment because she could not bear to see couples touching or kissing. Raised by a harsh mother who had favored her brother, Gertrude, who was once very unhappy at home, had started to date, graduated from college, moved out of the house, and found a good job. Anastasia, an obese twenty-seven-year-old woman who had been an only child, came to individual therapy in 1966 because of her son's stuttering. A woman who had to leave high school due to pregnancy, whose parents moved into her home with her and her husband, and who had children ranging in age from one to nine, Anastasia arrived depressed and overwhelmed. During therapy, she got her high school equivalency diploma, began college, and worked part time to pay for therapy, which her husband was adamantly against and for which he refused to pay. During the same period, her father died of cancer and her mother moved to another state. She was withholding in group to the point of exasperation. Agnes came to individual therapy in 1967 at the age of thirty, having been abandoned by her husband and left with pre-school children. Though compelled to move to her parents' home and go on welfare, she did manage in time to become a skilled worker. She entered the group in 1971, the same year that her father, to whom she had been extremely attached, died of cancer, which led to her concern about her mother's dependency. Resentment about dependence on the therapist persisted throughout therapy, as did her anger and ambivalence about the fee.

The remaining members of the group were Edwina, a forty-seven-year-old black woman, raised by her grandmother in extreme deprivation, separated from her husband, and raising twin sons alone, who had sought therapy because of her son's disruptive behavior and become outspoken in her dissatisfaction with the group; Doreen, a forty-four-year-old woman who, like Anastasia, was quiet and uncommunicative, had come for help because of her son's stealing and was depressed as well about her sado-masochistic relationship with her physically abusive husband from whom she eventually got a divorce; Amelia, a bright but depressed twenty-six-year-old woman who had been homebound until she came to therapy, after which she started working, moved out of her parental home, and resumed her college education; Laura, a beautiful twenty-six-year-old woman who had divorced an addict-husband and remarried a successful man, who was raising a son, working at two jobs, and going to school; and Sabina, an attractive but depressed twenty-six-year-old who had come for help in 1972 because she was terrified of her homicidal impulses, against which she defended by being quiet and withdrawn, and who had become more secure, started to work, and begun a life alone after her husband left her in response to the difficulties in the marriage.

At one session, there had been a discussion regarding the new male therapist and a strong angry reaction from the patients, with one woman stating that she did not want to be a "guinea pig." These feelings were worked through, and, when the male therapist arrived, the women became preoccupied with their appearances and started to talk about their sexual feelings more openly. Anger continued toward the original therapist as some women spoke more about how they were not being helped.

In June, after the male therapist had been in the group a few months, Gertrude discovered a cyst on her breast that had to be removed. Her recent arrival in the group, the symbolic arrival of her brother (the male trainee), the joining of the original female therapist with a male—reminiscent of her mother and her father, and her involvement with a married man who had developed cancer provided more stress than she could bear. At the end of the year, when the male therapist announced that he was leaving, Gertrude fell and broke her elbow. When he actually left, she again fell, this time breaking her glasses. Her anger at being abandoned was expressed through harm to herself.

Anastasia, whose children were growing up, reacted to the male therapist's leaving with intense feelings of loss. Her oldest son was getting married. Several of her other children had entered therapy and were becoming more outspoken. Toward the end of the year, Anastasia announced that she was being hospitalized because of a cancerous tumor in her uterus. She took immediate steps to go to a doctor when she noticed the symptoms and cooperated with the therapist's recommendations. She had a double uterus that needed removal, and she had been told that this condition had been induced not only by multiple births but also by her bearing children at a young age. There was some concern and anxiety among the women in the group, who rallied to her support. When Anastasia was in the hospital, Laura sent her a book, and the others asked about her. When Anastasia returned to the group, the therapist observed how she defended against being cared for. Laura noted that she had not been acknowledged and became angry. The hospitalization over, Anastasia's main problem continued to be her weight. She decided to leave her job, with which she was dissatisfied, and enrolled in a master's degree program.

During February of 1978 the therapist terminated her affiliation with the agency that had referred the women and moved her private office. At this time, Edwina, Gertrude, and Agnes decided to terminate therapy. A year later, Agnes called but did not leave her number. When she reached the therapist, she said she was upset because a lump had been discovered, and she wanted a "second opinion." There had been many changes in her life. Her children, now grown, were leaving. In addition, she had changed to a more lucrative job, returned to school, and become involved with a man.

The following medical report was received from Agnes' physician, to whom the therapist had referred her at the time she called:

> Agnes was seen by me in June. As you know, she hit her right breast about one month ago, developed a discoloration, and noticed a lump. She was seen by her doctor who placed her on antibiotics and sent her to a breast specialist, who has been following her at weekly intervals. She has been on antibiotics ever since.

The doctor advised her to stop taking the antibiotics. The patient continued to call the therapist, but was reluctant to re-enter therapy or begin an appropriate diet and vitamin therapy. A month later the therapist received the following medical report:

> This patient has a true precancerous mastopathy, which carries a five-fold risk chance for developing breast cancer. . . . She should be on a regime of low-fat-high-fish diet and therapeutic vitamins. The other alternative is to do bilateral simple mastectomies with nipple banking and then breast reconstruction at a later date, or bilateral subcutaneous mastectomies, which we do not advise because all breast tissue cannot be removed.

Agnes called, wondering whether I had heard from the doctor, and sounding very depressed. At her request, she was given the name of a therapist who could work with her condition. At last word, she had followed up on the referral, was finally getting her first marriage annulled, and was to be married again.

As in Groups No. 1 and 2, in Group No. 3 there were frame variations of a similar nature, such as the bringing in of a male therapist to train and the abandonment by the therapist who terminated her services with the referral agency.

Conclusion

As the therapist became more experienced and aware of the many variables affecting the course of the symptoms as they emerged, the patients did not become so victimized by their illnesses. The resistance to growth through individuation; the reaction to variations in therapeutic framework; the changes in group composition, such as the termination of a member, often experienced by other members as a symbolic loss; and the therapist's need to rescue the patient from uncomfortable feelings were all factors that influenced the emergence and course of the symptoms. It seems that when patients were deeply entrenched in family systems, it was important that the therapist refrain from attempting to rescue them. The pressure on the therapist from patients developing symptoms to become the good mothering figure is difficult to resist. It is frequently at this time that the therapist, upset about what is occurring, varies the frame. The therapeutic process as a stress factor, in itself, needs to be further considered.

Since the patients in Groups No. 1 and 3 were depressed, it is interesting to note that there was an absence of paranoia in the separation process. Everything that happened to them was passively accepted. Their resistance to the expression of aggression was strong. They compensated for their feelings of loss by an effort to replace the lost object, no matter how toxic, rather than mourn and find a more appropriate substitute. The inability to tolerate or adjust to the loss by using appropriate channels for the expression of anger seemed to accommodate the cancer, so that it became a replacement for the lost toxic object. This gave the patients realistic and meaningful pain to relate to, talk about, and get attention for. The psychic pain resulting from the sadomasochistic relationship was now replaced by physical pain.

In addition to heredity, physiological predisposition, and environmental factors such as pollution, food additives, and the like that are related to cancer, one also needs to consider the identification with the lost object. It is known that stress does affect total body functioning, including hormonal secretions, so that if illness occurs during a state of low resistance and depression, then the body may be more prone to yield to the irregular growth of cells. However, this also may be related to the need to identify with the lost object who often had died of cancer. The realistic loss of the object through cancer is replaced by the patient's cancer, which becomes a psychological way to replace the lost object or to remain attached to the object, no matter how toxic (Menaker, 1979). In other words, patients become willing victims of the cancer cells just as they had been willing victims of their parents.

In these instances, then, the development of cancer during the treatment process may have been an indication of a treatment destructive resistance. If the goal of analysis is separation and individuation for the purpose of potentiating oneself, then the anxiety related to this process generates psychic stress which, if intolerable to the ego, is converted into physical stress or pain. If the patients are deeply embedded in a lifestyle of passive receptivity and strongly committed to the past, there will be a strong resistance to enlisting the aid of the therapist, at whom they are enraged, to help them confront the illness.

The many variations in the frame as indicated by the coming and going of a trainee, the raising of fees, and the termination of affiliations with clinics and referral agencies are all factors experienced by patients as losses. There seems to be little doubt that these frame variations add tensions and pressures to the patients' lives. As seen in the cases discussed, some patients react by somatizing. For them, communicating about their illnesses may be a way to express indirectly their repressed anger. They may actually say, "See, I am sick. Look at what is happening to me," though the more underlying communication may be, "Look at what you did to me." Such communication tends to arouse countertransference feelings of guilt in the analyst, who may see him or herself as responsible. In other words, countertransferential feelings occur as the analyst experiences the very feelings that the patient experiences toward the lost object.

Appelbaum gives many reasons for the resistance to health. He said:

> The person fantasies that his illness is an attack on those who he thinks have failed to care adequately for him, or it is triumphant proof that his resistance has been justified all along (1977, p. 520).

He goes on to discuss the concept of how the illness unconsciously may be a means by which the patient may remain weak and deficient. As in the suicide, the patient's means of reuniting with the lost object may be death. This concept may explain why patients so often are eager to go along with a recommendation for surgery before getting another opinion. For a variety of reasons, there is often great pressure placed on patients to undergo surgery, so that it is usually difficult to persuade them early to seek another opinion, wait, start the necessary dietary and care program, and evaluate whether the body will rally itself to repel the invading object. Patients may seem eager and anxious to go along with the recommendation for surgery or to be "cut into," which may represent an unconscious attempt to cut out the toxic introject, or, as Appelbaum states, "to ward off an ever greater fantasied punishment."

While the patient is undergoing stress, the therapist is also being affected. As has been shown, the therapist's countertransference and counterresistance may precipitate a change of frame which, rather than elicit repressed rage, may support the patient in some way to remain in the victimized position. The type of group the patient is in is also crucial to the course of treatment. In the situation described with Jim, the patients seemed to support and perpetuate his resistance, possibly as a vicarious manifestation of their own resistance to separation. Other groups whose members are more evolved toward separation may take a more militant stance, as did Group No. 2 concerning Celia's illness, which provides a greater opportunity to express anger directly.

It is hoped that this hypothesis that the development of cancer or tumorous growths during the course of treatment may be a form of treatment destructive resistance will open new vistas for medical and social research regarding the relationship of cancer to emotional and psychic stress as has already been established in relation to smoking, environmental pollution, and diet (Abelson, 1979, p. 11). If the development of cancer during the course of treatment may be related to resistance, then indeed continued study of resistances is indicated, including the role played by the therapist.

References

ABELSON, P. "Cancer—Opportunism and Opportunity." *Science,* Vol. 206, Oct. 5, 1979, 11.

AMMON, GUNTER. *Psychoanalysis and Psychosomatics.* New York: Springer, 1979.

APPELBAUM, S. "Refusal to Take One's Own Medicine" *Bulletin of the Menninger Clinic* Vol. 41, No. 6, November 1977, 511–521.

APPELBAUM, S. *Out in Inner Space.* Garden City, New York: Anchor Press/Doubleday. 1979.

FURGERI, L. "The Celebration of Death in Group Process." *Clinical Social Work Journal,* Vol. 6, Nov. 2, 1978, 90–98.

GIOVACCHINI, P. "Ego Equilibrium and Cancer of the Breast." *Psychoanalysis of Character Disorders.* Peter Giovacchini, ed. New York: Jason Aronson, 1975.

HOLDEN, C. "Albert-Szent-Gyoryi, Electrons, and Cancer." *Science,* Vol. 203, Feb. 1979, 522–524.

LANGS, R. *The Bipersonal Field.* New York: Jason Aronson, 1976.

LANGS, R. *The Therapeutic Environment.* New York: Jason Aronson, 1979.

MENAKER, E. "Masochism—A Defense Reaction of the Ego." *Masochism and the Emergent Ego.* Selected papers of Esther Menaker, edited by Leila Lerner. New York: Human Sciences Press, 1979, 52–67.

MITCHELL, J. S. *Study in Radiotherapeutics*. Cambridge: Harvard University Press, 1960.

ORMONT, L. "Acting In and the Therapeutic Contract in Group Psychoanalysis." *International Journal of Group Psychotherapy*, Vol. 29, 1969, 420–432.

REICH, W. *The Cancer Biopathy*. New York: Farrar, Straus and Giroux, 1973.

SELYE, H. *The Stress of Life*. rev. ed. New York: McGraw-Hill, 1976.

SKLAR, L., and ANISMAN, H. "Stress and Coping Factors Influence Tumor Growth." *Science*, Vol. 205, Aug. 3, 1979, 513–515.

SPOTNITZ, H. *Psychotherapy of Preoedipal Conditions*. New York: Jason Aronson, 1976.

THOMAS, C. B., and DUSZYNSKI, D. R. "Closeness to Parents and the Family Constellation in a Prospective Study of Five Disease States: Suicide, Mental Illness, Malignant Tumor, Hypertension and Coronary Heart Disease." *The Johns Hopkins Medical Journal*, Vol. 134, 1974, 251–250.

13 In the Leper Colony
Group Therapy for Cancer Patients

Steven G. McCloy and
Anita S. Lansner

This chapter is based on a two-year experiment in the use of a therapy group for patients with cancer and their families. The group is discussed in terms of its origins and development and how it affected the hospital and the larger community. Some concepts of the life and lifestyles of cancer patients and the impact of cancer on its host and on the host's loved ones are highlighted.

The first three sections describe the formation of the group. We have made this a detailed description with the intent of offering some guidance to those who might wish to organize similar groups. In the fourth section we present case material which illustrates psychosocial aspects of cancer for the patient, the family, and for those in the helping professions.

We have learned through our experiences in this group that what we initially viewed as circumstances unique to our patients in this setting were really reflections of the more universal experience of having cancer in this culture at this time. From this realization emerged the concept of the "leper" both as the patient experiences him or herself and as the patient is treated by others. The use of group therapy enabled the patients to confront this reality, to understand it, and to change it. Likewise, the group brought change both to the institution and to the therapists.

Formation of the Cancer Club

Origins

The "Cancer Club" began in the oncology clinic at Long Island Jewish/Hillside Medical Center (LIJ), a 350-bed university-affiliated hospital in the suburban New York City area. The clinic met one morning per week in the Ambulatory Care Unit of the hospital. The authors were full-time staff members of the Ambulatory Care Unit; Steven McCloy as its medical coordinator, and Anita S. Lansner as a social worker assigned to several individual clinics within the unit.

The oncology clinic patients arrived each Monday morning at 8:30 to have blood samples taken. If the blood counts were within acceptable range, patients would receive chemotherapy* later in the morning. They often had to wait two or more hours until laboratory results were received and the oncology clinic staff had arrived.

Because of this long wait, the patients usually remained in a back corner of the clinic area. They became acquainted, and would chat with one another. They often brought food to share. Cancer patients and family members generally did not mix with patients attending other clinics (who sat in another area), nor did they speak much with the staff of the non-oncology clinics except to inquire as to whether their "bloods were back" or "how much longer?". The Ambulatory Unit staff likewise often did not venture back into the oncology corner.

Thus, this group of people who became the "Cancer Club" pre-existed as an informal group before the club's formal innauguration.

The Oncology Clinic Staff

The clinic's principal physicians were private doctors who volunteered their time as a service to the hospital. Several of them had done so for years. In addition, there were "fellows" in hematology/oncology, physicians completing intensive training to become specialists in the treatment of cancer. Medical students occasionally worked for limited periods in the clinic.

The oncology nurse was a full-time hospital employee who spent the majority of her week in the radiation therapy program, but was also responsible to the oncology clinic. Many patients attending the oncology clinic had received or were receiving radiation treatment and were already acquainted with her.

Shortly after the formation of the Cancer Club, a reorganization within the hospital brought all activities of cancer research and treatment under the authority of a physician who was a full-time staff member. While he did not work in the oncology clinic itself, he did assign some of his staff to work there as a coordinator and as receptionists who could facilitate the flow of patients.

The oncology clinic, then, was a busy place with a steady resource of patients and staff. The Senior Physician in the clinic was there only once a week and had no ongoing authority to change clinic operations. The Director of Cancer Programs had the authority to make changes but was not di-

* Chemotherapy consists of tumor-suppressing drugs given orally or by injection. These potent chemicals are toxic to all body cells and often cause hair loss, nausea, vomiting, diarrhea, skin rashes, and suppression of immunity leading to lowered resistance to infections.

rectly involved in the clinic. The oncology nurse was both present in the clinic and familiar with hospital operations; however, she was not a physician, and therefore, somewhat outside of the hospital power structure.

Formation

The Cancer Club was formed in September, 1975. One of us (SGM) had been given the administrative task of trying to speed up the receipt of blood counts in order to decrease the cancer patient's waiting times. A host of hierarchical and bureaucratic roadblocks prevented any speedup of laboratory reports. SGM then proposed the initiation of a therapy group as a substitute for the seemingly purposeless waiting. He had an interest in the management of the dying patient. These cancer patients seemed likely to benefit from some discussion of death and dying. He sought a co-leader from the Department of Social Work Services. It was decided that the social worker already assigned to the radiation therapy program (ASL) might broaden her responsibility to include this other clinic population. She was intrigued with the possibilities and had prior group experiences.

We met with both the Senior Oncology Physician and the oncology nurse. The Director of Cancer Programs had not yet been named. We discussed in general terms our goals for the group and sought their cooperation in helping us to set up the meetings. They gave us names of patients whom they thought might especially benefit from participation.

Recruitment into the group was done on a volunteer basis. All clinic patients were approached and told that a group would be meeting to discuss some of the problems of cancer and its treatment. Some accepted; others did not. Those who had declined were approached periodically by both the group leaders and members. Some persons joined later, while others chose to remain outside of the group. Many who previously had sat in the back corner of the Ambulatory Care Unit sharing their waiting times and food simply transferred into the conference room where the meetings were held. The group size was ten to twenty people.

At the first session (and periodically as new members joined) these ground rules were laid down:

- Anything said within the group stayed there as confidential and was not to be repeated outside;
- Information given to the therapists outside of the group meetings could and would be brought back to the group—no secrets;
- The physician's role here was as group leader and he would not answer any medical questions. These were to be referred to the other physicians in the clinic;
- The purpose of the group was to explore what it is like having a malignancy or living with someone with cancer;

- We might occasionally split the group and meet separately with patients and family members;
- There were no taboo subjects and anything could be discussed;
- Silence would be respected although not encouraged;
- The group leaders' expectations were vague because this was an experiment. We had no specific agenda.

With these few guidelines we began. As a formal therapy group it was highly unconventional and broke many of the "rules" which apply to group therapy. Membership changed, sometimes weekly. These changes were the result of dropouts, addition of new patients to the clinic, the deaths of patients, and broken appointments. Some people were not seen in the clinic on a weekly basis and could not get transportation to the clinic unless they had an appointment. The group also was mixed by age (range from twenty-three to seventy-eight), marital status, diagnosis (all types of cancer plus healthy family members), and economic status (from medically indigent to middle class). Some were newly diagnosed. One had had cancer for eighteen years.

Psychiatric Liaison

In the group's ninth month, a psychiatrist joined the full-time staff of the Ambulatory Care Unit. He was asked to serve as a consultant to the co-therapists. He agreed to attend one session of the group each month and to meet with the co-therapists to share his observations, discuss their implications, and make suggestions as to topics which might be pursued in future sessions.

Before implementing this liaison, the group's agreement was sought. Although there was some resistance, agreement was given. The group came to accept the consultant's presence, his insistence on not answering direct questions, and to respect his wishes not to engage in individual therapy within the group. He consistently turned individual's questions back to the group and was otherwise silent.

In the follow-up meeting with the co-therapist, three main topics recurred: the unconventional aspects of our structure, the issue of the effect of this work on us personally, and the emotional problems of individual members of the group. The latter is discussed below (Psychosocial Aspects of Cancer).

The Non-traditional Nature of the Group

As described above, the Cancer Club did not adhere to many of the tenets of conventional group psychotherapy.[1] This group was a subset of the general cancer patient population. Many of its members had already been an "affinity group" before the co-leaders "formed" the group. Food was served at each meeting. The length of time for group sessions was not fixed. Despite our best efforts to dissuade them, the clinic staff summoned members from group sessions to administer chemotherapy.

We answered these criticisms of our psychiatric consultant primarily by pointing out that we were doing the best we could under the circumstances. We believed that the group should be available to all who wanted to use it and that we could not control when people were able to participate and when they were not. We did not set the patients' appointments or determine whether or not family members always accompanied them. Additionally, we believed that this group was serving a wider purpose than just as a therapy group—it was experimental, it was social, its members had differing agendas. Perhaps some members sensed that they would never leave the group alive and were not seeking the same remission of emotional pain as might be expected from a traditional therapy group.

The serving of food was viewed by the psychiatrist as disruptive to process, and he was correct. It was also the continuation of a tradition which the patients themselves had begun, as well as some recognition that to share food is to share love of one another.

His attention to the fact of people being called out of the session for their chemotherapy treatment put some decision-making power in the hands of the group. There was a recognition that they valued what they were doing. Some decided to resist outside interruptions by polite refusal to go when called. This was a sacrifice on the part of the patients, because it meant they were the last to be seen. Often they left the hospital five and a half hours after they had arrived.

The Emotional Toll of Caring

Our consultant was especially skilled in supporting us while we explored what the group was doing to us. It was becoming increasingly difficult to maintain an emotional detachment from the patients. It was difficult to turn off our involvement at 10:30 AM. ASL continued to be the members' social worker for the remainder of the week, and SGM saw many of them as his patients for general medical problems. Some of the psychosocial problems were so compelling that they could not easily be laid aside at the end of the session.

Some of our difficulties were functions of the jobs we held. Others might be viewed as "countertransference," or as overdeveloped "rescue needs." We believe, though, that there is a larger framework of what cancer means to the health worker who must attend to it daily.[2-4]

What is the personal cost of being the "cancer nurse" or "cancer doctor"? Years of training are taken in order to make people feel better—to cure. How often does one cure? How does the health worker maintain his/her own energy stores against this continual drain? A common observation of oncologists is that many appear to adapt by either leaving the field entirely or by becoming cold, dispassionate scientists. They describe themselves as dispensing "poisons" (the common nickname for chemotherapeutic agents), and they may develop all manner of clever euphemisms to avoid using the word "cancer."[5] They may set the cancer patients back in a corner of the clinic. Symbolically, they may have to set the human being aside and confront only the disease the human being has.

We suspect that some of these issues may have lain behind the frequent interruptions by the clinic staff of our sessions. As the group became more cohesive, it became stronger and had a raised level of consciousness. Individuals started to question, to expect some empathy and communication along with the chemotherapy. Some began to insist that they not be called out of a group that was important to them.

This increase in self-worth was a desired change. Its impact on the oncology clinic was not always pleasing to the clinic staff. Unfortunately, not all of the clinic staff had the benefits of a psychiatric liaison service to help them deal with the feelings they were having about helping cancer patients.

We found that the intimacy of helping the cancer patient through his best and bleakest days demanded from us skills which had not been taught in our formal training. As people came closer to death, the tools given us by modern medicine might fail. Other, human tools had to be called forth. We found ourselves often greatly fatigued from this and needing one another's support and comfort even more. We were grateful for the guidance of Elizabeth Kuebler-Ross.[6] We were also all the more admiring of her strength in carrying out her initial work against the resistance she encountered.

"Making Waves": Institutional Change

It is not usual within a hospital setting for an assortment of patients to group together for a prolonged period of time. Inpatients are in the hospital for only a few days or weeks. Childbirth preparation classes may meet continuously, but the membership changes regularly as new parents leave and prospective parents enter. The Cancer Club persisted. In doing so, it brought change outside the perimeter of the meeting room.

In the Oncology Clinic

The group members—like many consumers of health care—often were ignorant of their bodies, their disease, and how to obtain better services for themselves. Before the group began, these people had not been able to confront a system which could not supply quick the reports of an automated laboratory test. Instead, they waited.

The Cancer Club became a self-education group. Members taught one another about cancer, the different types of chemotherapy, and how to manage the side effects of the treatment. This kind of firsthand information supplied was far more usable than the theoretical information supplied by the physicians and nurses. Some patients shared their anti-nausea medication. They taught others how to take it to diminish the wracking nausea which occurs a few hours following most chemotherapy and radiation treatments. They encouraged one another to ask probing questions of the clinic staff and to insist on satisfactory answers. They talked openly of how they resented the paternalism they found in many members of the health professions.

It is perhaps, then, not too surprising that there was less than ideal cooperation on the part of the clinic staff with the Cancer Club's smooth operation. What *was* surprising was the unity of purpose which allowed the members of the group to resist efforts to call them out early, to telephone them in the meeting room, and to inquire as to what they were discussing in "that group."

In the Hospital

As the various cancer programs in LIJ were brought under the aegis of a single individual, there developed an increasing interest in the psychosocial aspects of cancer. (Also, as director of the hematology laboratory, he was able to have laboratory results expedited.) He worked to organize a day-long symposium to explore the topic of "Living with Cancer." Members of the Cancer Club attended. They talked poignantly about the unmet needs of the patient and family.

This symposium was followed by a series of four evening meetings to explore the economic, marital, family, and psychological damage people experience after diagnosis and treatment. Each session was attended by seventy-five to one hundred persons in small groups led by members of the LIJ Social Service and Psychiatry staffs. A growing circle of hospital personnel became involved directly with cancer patients and their families.

At the end of these four seminars, several of the attendees had grouped, either by diagnosis or because of geographic nearness, to form themselves into networks of self-helpers. These people continued to meet in each other's homes.

Beyond the Hospital

Coincident with this, a prominent association of cancer researchers (of which the hospital's cancer program director was an influential member) held an exploratory meeting on how to initiate research in the area of the psychosocial aspects of cancer. SGM was asked to report on the work going on at LIJ. Psychiatrists and practicing oncologists could agree that an understanding of the psychosocial aspects of malignancy was needed. Efforts to develop a clearing house for information began at that meeting.

Transition

In early 1977, both co-therapists simultaneously learned that they would be ending their involvement with the group. One of us was changing jobs within the hospital while the other was leaving to work elsewhere.

The best indication of the success of the group experience was that it continued after we left. The liaison psychiatrist became one co-therapist while the hospital budgeted a new position of social worker for the cancer programs. This was a substantial commitment in the presence of tight hospital budgeting. It is a long way from the back corner of the clinic to having one's own social worker.

We left the group work as we had begun—with ambivalance. The balance, though, seemed to tip toward the side of relief. It had been very hard work. In our busy professional lives, we seldom have the opportunity and challenge of such intimate knowledge of patients. The faces and names of these patients do not fade with time.

Some Psychosocial Aspects of Cancer

From our notes of over 150 hours of group therapy, we have culled the following issues for presentation here. Some were chosen for their prevalence, some because they were surprising, and some because they were dramatic. Our hope is that others, too, will explore this area and add to our understanding of the psychological mileau of malignancy.

The Leper of the Twentieth Century

The cancer patient is the leper of the twentieth century. He or she has a sneaky, unclean, smelly disease. The patient experiences this uncleaness just as the leper of biblical times. To say "I have cancer" is to ring the leper's bell so that the healthy can step out of the way of the contagion. Patients report, "People stopped hugging . . . neighbors stayed away . . . children used to spend a lot of time at my house. I was their 'grandmother.' Then they told me their parents didn't want them to come over any more." Husbands were less interested in intercourse, less attentive to foreplay, careful to avoid touching the tumorous breast or its mate.

Why do the healthy respond in this way? Our inference is that even well-educated and medically sophisticated people retain some notion that cancer is contagious. "I brought my Black Forest cake to the party. For years it had been a hit recipe. No one touched it."

In our culture no other disease evokes the same horror and revulsion as does cancer. Until recently obituaries cited death from "a long illness" rather than cancer. The image is of decay, disfigurement, wasting, and odor. The body turned against itself, housing a malicious growth which parasitically steals all nourishment until both are killed. When a physician finds high blood pressure, he is making a diagnosis; when he finds a malignancy, he is delivering a death sentence.[5]

One must conclude that we respond to cancer primitively, instinctively. We fear the cancer patient. The patient reminds us that we, too, may harbor a malignancy. Deep down we fear that we may "catch" it from the patient.

The publicity about Mrs. Gerald Ford's and Mrs. Nelson Rockerfeller's breast cancers brought many thousands of women to medical attention. We can hope that, through education, people can change their behavior toward the cancer patient. Not to do so seriously threatens the patient's physical and emotional well being.

Living with Cancer

One of the therapists' original goals was to create a forum for the discussion of death. For the patients, however, death was far less an issue than was *life*. Productive living—not mere survival—was what they sought. Within the group, disability ranged from none to extreme. Yet, they found that jobs were denied them, that their illness depleted whatever savings they might have accumulated, that family and friends considered them to be ill, that their social circle shrank, and that recreational activities, transportation, and travel opportunities were curtailed. The stigma of "handicapped" was nearly as strong for them as for the blind or the paraplegic.

For the wage earner, the loss of a half-day in the hospital clinic or of a day from the side effects of chemotherapy meant financial hardship. Young students lost entire academic years because of necessary absences from class. Full-time workers found themselves to be part-time workers—or suddenly unemployed.

Life and coping were greater issues than mere death. The group spent much time in exploring this.

Keeping the Patient Sick

As counterpoint to the patient's quest for fulfillment in living was the surprising discovery of some families' efforts to keep the patient in the sick role. At several junctures we divided the club into patients and non-patients. We met in separate rooms with the ground rule that family members were free to share or not to share afterwards what they had said about each other. This one breach of our "no secrets" rule was necessary to free up some of the more reticent participants.

Zachary and Sophie were a couple in their sixties. Pleasant and garrulous Britishers, they were stalwart group members. Zach had inoperable lung cancer which had been well controlled with chemotherapy. He had given up his business as a cabinetmaker. They were active in a fraternal organization which sponsored bi-weekly dances. Zach's only disability was some wheezing and shortness of breath on exertion.

In the patient group, Zach talked about his resentment toward Sophie's forbidding him to dance. He loved to dance, to flirt with the other wives, and to carry out his role as chaplain and toastmaster of the organization. He told of how his son had hired "outsiders" to lay new linoleum on the kitchen floor and allowed him only to supervise. He knew that he could have done a more skilled job. He wasn't allowed to carry groceries up the stairs from the car.

Meanwhile, Sophie shared with the family group her fear of Zach's wheezing and breathlessness. The wheeze reminded her of the growth in his lungs. She was afraid when he sat in his chair to catch his breath that "he might die sitting there." Because of his fatigue and wheezing, she rationed the sexual intercourse which they both enjoyed. She colluded with their son to carry in the groceries, chauffeur them, and perform his father's household chores.

These same themes ran through many families' stories. All seemed to believe that after diagnosis, ones days are numbered. Beneath a fascade of optimism was the face of a clock, the hands rapidly spinning, as in a 1940's motion picture. Time passing. Any exceptional exertion, any daily work, any extra wheeze would accelerate the clock.

The co-therapists intervened to make explicit this unconscious notion that extra effort would shorten life. We noted a relief and an ability of couples, parents, and children to talk, to explore what they valued, and to change their behavior toward the sick role. Patients began to rediscover activities which enhanced their self-esteem, while family members were relieved of their roles as watchdogs.

Dying from Cancer

There were deaths among the group. Carol's death occurred, except for its final hours, before our eyes. Carol had been born a "loser" and lived the loser's life for her twenty-nine years. Abandoned by her father in infancy, raised by a schizophrenic mother, Carol dropped out of school early to marry an alcoholic career military man whose own deficits would keep him from rising above the rank of petty officer. Drunk, he battered her and their children. He was usually gone—either to sea or to the hospital for alcohol detoxification.

Ignorant and medically indigent, Carol came to the group shortly after an ovarian cancer had invaded her intestines. The only surgical intervention possible was a colostomy to allow the passage of stool. Not only was her cancer untreatable, but also her psychosocial disabilities proved to be beyond the capacity of the Cancer Club, the hospital's social services department, the county bureau of child welfare, and the Navy.

Carol clung to her life most tenaciously. She became the vulgar mental image of cancer: yellow, waxy skin, wasted and skeletal, with frightened dark eyes shining from the deep sockets of a barely padded skull. The club members' pain and horror at this spectre were evident. They tried to exclude her from the group's meeting and to ignore her when she spoke. The therapists suggested that they were doing to Carol what they so resented being done to themselves. Carol clung to the group most tenaciously and would not be silenced. In her limited way she began to talk about dying, about her fear for the fate of her children and her optimism at the new temperance of her husband. Carol was readmitted to the hospital (to die) and became the only patient who requested to come in a wheelchair from her hospital bed to the club. She stayed away from one meeting when her bowel control was gone and died the following weekend.

It was our custom to announce deaths at the next club meeting. Usually little was said in response to these announcements. That time, the group spent the entire session eulogizing this simple woman and what she had taught them. We explored the ambivalence of their love for her and admiration of her bravery, and their horror. To us, it seemed that they were Carol. They were eulogizing themselves, too. After that, talking about dying was no longer taboo.

Denial and Noncompliance[7,8]

The smoker[9], the woman who does not examine her own breasts[10] or obtain a "Pap" smear for cervical cancer, or the cancer patient who does not take the prescribed therapy are labeled "noncompliant." As used medically, noncompliance describes patients' behavior—either willful or otherwise—in not participating fully in their treatment regimens. It is a topic of growing importance in discussions of improving the public health or in treating disease. Achieving compliance is a high priority among oncologists.

Mike manifested denial and noncompliance which greatly threatened his survival and the quality of his and his family's lives. He was a twenty-three-year-old Jewish man who became ill while on his honeymoon with his attractive Italian-American bride. They abruptly returned from Acapulco, and he was admitted to LIJ. Surgery demonstrated an inoperable pancreatic cancer, a rare tumor in this age group, and not amenable to chemotherapy. His physicians told him he would live only about six months.

He joined the club as a very angry man. He had decided to quit work. He was going to spend his days hunting and fishing. He drove recklessly. He boasted that whenever he was pulled over he told the officer that he did not care about a ticket because he was dying of cancer. Nothing much mattered. His sister accompanied him to the hospital while Joanne, his wife, stayed home. Joanne had been disowned by her Italian Catholic parents, who had boycotted her wedding. Mike's mother barely accepted her gentile daughter-in-law. Mother handled the couple's finances and attended to the filling of the insurance forms. She insisted that his sister drive him to the hospital. Despite this, Mike often missed appointments and, his sister reported, skipped his medications on non-clinic days. He was determined, he said, to "whip this myself." He became involved with faith healing and charismatic Christian religious sects.

Work within the group was stymied by Mike's bravado. The group may have sensed the frailty of his defenses and unconsciously admired his seeming bravery and acting out. The therapists used marital and family therapy techniques outside of the group in order to help make the group experience useful to Mike and to help bring his in-group antics under some control so that he did not sabotage the others.

An intensive multi-family and intergenerational intervention was planned and carried out. The immediate goals were to open up the communications between the married couple, to move the mother out of the controlling epicenter of decision-making and financial supervision, and to allow the sister room to quit being a "wife" and to pursue her own interests and education. A longer-term goal was to recognize that Mike would die and that Joanne would need the sustenance of her family of origin, since she could not expect much from her late in-laws.

Mike outlived the physicians' dire prognosis by more than a year. We were able to achieve the treatment goals. Mike was able to share his pain with his wife instead of "sparing" her and to discover her real strength. Given some means of venting his outrage against the cosmic unfairness of his fate, Mike became effectively compliant. He began to use his energy creatively through photography instead of dissipating it in antisocial acting out.

Does Cancer Create Psychopathology?

The co-therapists hypothesis at the outset of this experiment was that cancer was a special clinical circumstance which would create its own peculiar psychopathology. All chronic illnesses are known to cause special stresses in patients' lives.[11-13] We were curious to know whether there were some unique dynamics in malignancy. The experiences cited above might seem to support this hypothesis. However, our conclusions have been that *cancer is far more catalytic than causative.* We repeatedly found that the psychopathology and psychosocial dysfunction we observed in our patients had been there long before they developed cancer.

Mike's case would seem to support the causative hypothesis. However, in the course of his individual and family therapy, we learned that his problems far predated his cancer. He had a long history of antisocial behavior, of inability to hold down steady jobs, of ambivalent relations with women, and of a high level of neuroticism in his family of origin.

We interpreted his long-time trouble with male authority figures to relate to anger at his controlling mother and at his father for being too distant and passive. In the group, he said that he had linked his disease with the physicians who had diagnosed it.[14] The messengers were the message. In fighting the disease, he was compelled to fight the doctors. Thus he avoided being passive while continuing his struggle against authority figures.

Mike's malignancy prevented him from maturing into a more effective adult. It did not, we think, make him behave as he did. By understanding the psychological origins of his noncompliance, Mike was able to change his behavior and help himself to his treatment.

Anna's case also demonstrated to us that what seemed like cancer-induced psychopathology was not. She was a retired grammar school teacher in her seventies when she developed breast cancer which metastacized to her brain. Widowed, she lived with her maiden sister. Their most frequent complaint was that Anna's illness prevented their socialization with family and friends. Anna was embarrassed by the baldness which had resulted from her chemotherapy. Each week she complained about how little her sister would allow her to do. In separate sessions, her sister complained about what a burden Anna was becoming, and how she longed for a day to herself.

The club responded with offers to include them in its helping network. Members would visit. One offered to take the sister shopping while another would stay with Anna. To each offer, the sisters responded with some compelling reason why they could not accept. Finally, Ed, an outspoken veteran of Alcoholics Anonymous, confronted their refusals of help with a threat to come to their house the following Sunday. They answered, "We won't open the door."

In subsequent sessions, there emerged the picture of a mutually saprophytic relationship which had predated the cancer by decades. Anna's marriage (which we had been led to believe was a happy one,) was very brief "and never consummated." The sisters had spent most of their lives together, tightly bound in a relationship that excluded others. The sister's "martyrdom" in caring for Anna had been preceded by equal suffering in nursing their dying mother during Anna's brief marriage.

Anna's cancer may have intensified some of the resentments in their relationship and magnified some of their feelings of lack of fulfillment in their lives. The cancer did not create the relationship.

The group sought to help the sister in her frightened anticipation of the coming emptiness of her life. Following Anna's death the sister was asked to continue with the group. She stayed away for many months, though she continued to see ASL. She underwent a protracted period of deep mourning and profound depression.[15] She did eventually return for one visit to the group to thank them for their help but refused any further involvement.

Conclusions

We have attempted here to report some observations in a two-year experience with cancer patients and their families. This has been necessarily subjective and anecdotal. This type of treatment modality is new for cancer patients, and our Cancer Club was not designed as a formal research project.

We have described the dynamics of this group in the setting of a large hospital in order to describe some of the forces which helped to create the group and occasionally threatened its functions. This is offered in some detail both as a rough blueprint for those who might wish to implement such a program and as a warning that even a small effort may bring about radical change with all its fallout.

In the last section we have presented some case material which illustrates interesting psychosocial aspects of malignancy. The cancer patient is subject to some unique cultural pressures both from within and without. The malignant diseases exact high prices in social and economic terms, both for the host and the host's loved ones. Cancer patients are lepers. Their disease is an obscenity within our culture. Some of these psychosocial factors may coalesce into potent denial mechanisms which contribute to the patient's noncompliance. Yet, it was not our experience to find that cancer created *de novo* much psychopathology.

We close with an inevitably inadequate salute to our friends in the Cancer Club. They taught as they suffered. In their living and dying they demonstrated the underlying bravery of people in crisis. They took, they gave, and they shared. Despite their disease they asked to be viewed and treated as what they are, human beings.

References

1. YALOM, I. D. "The Selection of Patients." In I. D. Yalom, *The Theory and Practice of Group Psychotherapy*. (Basic Books, New York, 1975), pp. 219-245.

2. BULGER, R. J. "Doctors and Dying." *Arch Int. Med.* 112:327-332 (1963).

3. LASAGNA, L. "The Doctor and the Dying Patient." *J. Chron Dis* 22:65-68 (1969).

4. CASBERG, M.D. "Toward Human Values in Medical Practice." *Med. Opin. Rev.* 3:22-25 (1967).

5. NOVAK, D. H.; R. PLUMER; R. L. SMITH; H. OCHITILL; G. R. MORROW; and J. M. BENNETT "Changes in Physicians' Attitudes Toward Telling the Cancer Patient." *JAMA 241:* 897-900 (1979).

6. KÜBLER-ROSS, E. *On Death and Dying,* (Macmillan, New York, 1969).

7. FINK, R. "Delay behavior in breast screening." In Cullen, J. W., B. H. Fox and R. N. Isom. *Cancer: The Behavioral Dimensions.* (Raven Press, New York, 1976). pp. 23-35.

8. WEISMAN, A. D. "Death from Fatal Illness: Cancer." In A. D. Weisman, *On Dying and Denying.* (Behavioral Publications, New York, 1972), pp. 95-121.

9. SCHEWCHUK, L. A. Problems of High Risk Populations and High Risk Nonresponders: Smoking Behavior. In Cullen et al., op. cit., pp. 93-100.

10. FINK, R. "Delay Behavior in Breast Cancer Screening." Ibid. pp. 23-24.

11. FEDER, S. "Psychological Considerations in the Care of Patients with Cancer." In C. Bahnson and D. Kissen (eds.), Psychological Aspects of Cancer, *Ann. NY Acad. Sci.* 125:1020-1027 (1966).

12. LIPOWSKI, A. J. "Psychosocial Aspects of Disease." *Ann. Int. Med.* 71: 1197-1206.

13. LASAGNA, L. "The Tyranny of Senescence." In L. Lasagna, *Life, Death and the Doctor,* (Knopf, New York, 1968), pp. 201-224.

14. HOLLAND, J. C. "Psychological Aspects of Cancer." In J. F. Holland and E. Frei III (eds.), *Cancer Medicine.* (Lea and Febiger, Philadelphia, 1973).

15. PARKER, C. M. "The First Year of Bereavement: A Longitudinal Study of the Reaction of London Widows to the Death of Their Husbands." *Psychiatry* 33: 444-467 (1970).

PART V
The Family

Family therapy has been particularly useful with cancer situations, because the disease is not selective in its effect to just the cancer patient. The possible loss or incapacitation of any family member affects all the members of the family: roles have to readjust; loyalties can shift. Decisions about treatment choices are usually not unilateral, but rather involve at least one close family member. The contraction of cancer by any of its members is a psychological trauma to the family unit as well as to the individual.

As with the individual and group treatments, family therapies and theories are varied. The field has its prehistory in the origins of psychoanalysis. The first report of psychotherapy with a family was Freud's case of "Little Hans," where the child was successfully treated through the agency of the father. This case stands out from the usual psychiatric practice of that century in that treatment of patients was more typically conducted in abstraction from their interpersonal and social contexts. Acknowledgment of the importance of utilizing social psychological phenomena, as well as intrapsychic material, led to the field of child psychiatry, where first the mother, and later the father, were included as valuable additions to the treatment plan. Since the beginning of the development of family treatment, the field has had input from such diverse areas of inquiry as anthropology, sociology, small group behavior research, linguistics, kinesis, general systems theory, and communication theory.

In one sense, family therapy can be seen as live-play therapy. Rather than the child moving around dolls or other representations of significant figures, the actual primary objects are there to play themselves. Whereas in both individual and group treatment, the patient forms relationships with symbolic figures (the therapist or other group members) to replicate primary relationships, here the primary relationships are themselves the object of study.

The chapters in this section present ideas of family functioning in relation to the cancer patient. Yehuda Nir and Bonnie Maslin discuss the problems specific to having a child with cancer. Michael Kerr presents the systems approach, as developed by Murray Bowen, and applies this broad theory to his work with cancer patients. The next chapter, by Wendy Schain, explores those sensitive issues relating to sexuality of cancer patients. The selection ends with a case history of a cancer patient. Kathleen Philbin focuses on the family's involvement with the patient, his disease, and the treatment of his disease.

14 Psychological Adjustment of Children with Cancer

Yehuda Nir and
Bonnie Maslin

Medical advances in pediatric hematology and oncology during the past few decades have significantly influenced the survival and cure rate of children with leukemias and other forms of cancer. Even though ultimately he might die from the disease, the new therapeutic interventions have greatly extended the time a child can expect to live once the diagnosis of a cancer has been made.

The survival or the extended life-span is a result of prolonged and aggressive treatment with chemotherapy, radiotherapy, and surgery, either separately or in combination. On a daily basis, this treatment may include painful venipunctures, that occasionally result in infiltrations, lumbar punctures, and bone marrow aspirations. Loss of appetite, nausea, painful mucosal ulcerations, weakness (necessitating prolonged bed rest), and total loss of hair as side effects of medication are the grave consequences of cancer that confront the child. Chemotherapy may produce severe neutropenia, which requires periods of isolation and, consequently, sensory deprivation. It is important to remember that all of the above (and this is an incomplete picture) are the consequences of the procedures and side effects of treatment and not the disease itself.

This new medical reality creates a series of overwhelming problems for the young patient, his family, the physician-in-charge, nurses, and house staff. These problems are both physical and psychologic. It has been recognized that the child who is cured from cancer, while physically well, may remain emotionally handicapped. Koocher et al.[1] have shown that children who survive cancer suffer from residual depression, anxiety, and poor self-esteem. One hundred and fifteen patients, who were symptom free, off all treatments and at least five years post-diagnosis, were evaluated on measures of intellectual functioning, social maturity, depression anxiety, death anxiety, and self-esteem. Sixty percent of the pediatric cancer survivors had mild to severe psychiatric symptoms as compared to only 15 percent in the general population.

Although initially distinct the physical and psychological components tend to interdigitate in the course of the child's illness and, as the condition progresses. Toward the end of the child's life, psychological and physical issues become almost indistinguishable from one another. If treatment is to succeed, the physician must take both aspects into consideration.

At any point on the continuum of the treatment process the physician is confronted with two central themes:

1. the life-threatening aspect of the disease, and
2. the impact of therapy and the effect on the child and his extended environment.

How does one deal with these issues? How does one maximize the effectiveness of treatment while at the same time minimizing the amount of stress on both patients and the physicians?

In view of the multiple factors impinging on the management and the emotional well-being of the critically ill child, unless one provides psychological input and understanding into all elements that come into contact with the sick child, the medical intervention will not be optimally successful.

The child must be regarded as a part of a larger system. Psychological support programs which utilize the system theory must provide, through improved communications and development of common understanding, assistance to all persons central to the management of the critically ill patient. Support during the acute phases of the illness, and prevention of the psychiatric sequela of cancer therapy should be dual goals of this approach.

The general system theory, developed by Von Bertalanaffy,[2] Miller,[3] and others, perceives man and his environment as interacting wholes with integrated sets of properties and relationships. Applying this concept to a hospital setting, means that everyone in contact with the patient has to be seen as an interdependent part of the larger therapeutic network. The patient, then, has to be dealt with as both a psychological and biological subsystem.

Increased understanding and insight achieved by each person in the system will simultaneously facilitate the relationship between all members. It will reflect in a better coordination of efforts and improved cooperation resulting in an increased effectiveness of treatment.

To accomplish the goals of successful integration of care for the child with cancer through improved communications, one has to identify the components of the system. The following subsystems have to be considered:

1. the sick child
2. the parents and siblings

3. nurses
4. house staff: fellows, residents, interns, and medical students
5. attending physicians
6. mental health professionals (social workers, psychiatrists, psychologists)
7. Auxillary personnel (rehabilitation, volunteers, clerical staff, clergy)

Interventions may take place both within and between subsystems. Given the extensive number of pathways to intervene only the most critical interventions will be explored.

Caring for the Individual Child; Assessment and Therapy

Initiation of psychologic intervention is of paramount importance from the time the diagnosis of malignancy has been made in order to integrate it as a component of the total management of the patient. Once the child is diagnosed as having cancer a psychosocial profile of the patient and his family has to be developed.

The information is obtained by the pediatric psychiatrist, social worker, or psychologist attached to the unit. The intervention consists usually of two interviews with the patient and one with the rest of the family: the parents, and possibly siblings. To avoid apprehension concerning the psychiatric interview, early in the course of the treatment, the child and the family are told by the physician in charge, that this evaluation is a routine procedure, part of the therapeutic protocol. The goal of those conducting the profile is to assess the child's development level, his intelligence, ego strength, and ego defenses. In addition, the profile describes the family constellation, the stability of the marriage, and the family's style of coping with crisis. Attitudes toward recent death, and the family's way of dealing with it are a specific aspect of the profile. Reactions to recent death refers not only to people but also to pets. We have learned that the young child's attitude toward death may be influenced by the loss of a pet. Jason, a 4-year-old boy developed a rhabdomyosarcoma in the nasopharynx several months after his dog died. The family had the dog for ten years, and the mother described it to the consulting psychiatrist as "my first child." When Jason, at some point in his treatment, was given an I.V. in his scalp (for lack of a good vein), he asked his mother how long it would stay there. Trying to reassure him that he wouldn't be exposed to painful I.V. infusions she answered "indefinitely". Jason looked alarmed and asked his mother for the first time whether he was going to die. When his dog died he had asked his mother "how long will the dog remain buried," her answer then was also "indefinitely."

The psychological profile also includes testing consisting of a WISC or WIPPSI, human figure drawings, and the Bender Gestalt to assess intellectual and cognitive functioning also organicity. The Massachusetts General Hospital in its project Omega II has extended this profile to include *an inventory of current concerns, general coping strategies, and the index of vulnerability.*[4] Testing provides a baseline finding which is critical in view of reported intellectual impairment in children with cancer and leukemia after cranial radiation and intrathecal methotrexate. An important aspect of the psychosocial assessment is the fact that the process allows contact with the child without his moving into a therapeutic relationship.

Once obtained, the psychosocial profile is discussed with physicians and nurses directly involved with the patient's care, to facilitate a better understanding of his needs, and his style of coping with stress, pain, and fear. The profile is continuously augmented and expanded as additional information is obtained in the course of the child's illness.

During the initial stage, the first weeks or sometimes months, after the diagnosis, the child and family are usually reluctant to become involved with a mental health professional. Denial is still very powerful and is augmented by hope for a good outcome. In addition, the physical aspects of the illness and the side effects of the initial treatment are of such magnitude and place such high demands on the coping mechanisms that he perceives any in-depth exploration of feelings as an additional threat, an additional assault rather than consolation. However, the mental health practitioner must establish the initial contact early, because later on, when the patient is in the midst of his battle for survival or feels that he is succumbing to the disease, he might no longer be available any more for a new relationship, incapable of cathecting a new object.

The patient and his family's style of coping with the illness and its life-threatening consequences is the central axis around which both medical and psychological intervention have to take place. It is a complex, though not necessarily time-consuming task, critical for the development of successful treatment strategies. Coping can be divided into adaptive and maladaptive. An example of the former would be Albert, a fourteen-year-old boy with Burkitt's lymphoma who when seen before surgery tried to convince the psychiatrist that his tumor was miniscule, "almost invisible," while in reality he was told by his surgeon just a few hours earlier that it was the size of an orange. This degree of denial helped him to lessen his preoperative anxiety and accept surgery with less resistance.

The maladaptive aspects of denial can be seen in Kevin, a sixteen-year-old with Acute Lymphocytic Leukemia. During his first hospitalization he never mentioned his disease and kept talking about his return to his high school basketball team as soon as he got back home. He also had a date with his girlfriend scheduled for the weekend. The staff went along with his unrealistic expectations (a common countertransference problem among physicians caring for the child with cancer), reflecting a desire to protect the young patient, at least temporarily, from the full impact of the disease. Despite recognizing that massive denial of reality is maladaptive and potentially harmful, the staff did not act on this knowledge. Kevin went home and totally collapsed, when trying to get out of bed. This led to an overwhelming depression and his request to be taken back to the hospital and left there permanently.

It is important to distinguish between the contribution these two expressions of denial make to the coping process. Albert's distortion of the size of the tumor helped him to master his overwhelming anxiety, but Kevin's denial of the reality of his physical condition make him totally unprepared for discharge from the hospital.

Attempts at coping takes various and often unpredictable forms. Humor is a rare but important modality. Jonathan, a twelve-year-old with osteosarcoma made the following statement during his initial hospitalization. "A typical soap opera scene; the dying son, the neurotic mother, and the helpless father." When a resident brought him a little gift saying "I have something nice for you," Jonathan retorted, "I'm sure it's death." It is important to recognize that while the above statements are somewhat droll and should be responded to with a smile, they reflect massive underlying anxiety and feelings that his parents can offer him no protection.

Patient participation in treatment planning and implementation is essential for effective coping. This modality seems to be extremely effective and should be encouraged. Making the patient and his parents active participants in the fight for survival makes it possible to master some feelings of passivity and helplessness evoked by the diagnosis of cancer. Participation is a broad concept and covers numerous areas; from keeping exact records of chemotherapy and daily blood tests through detailed knowledge of the condition, the drugs used, and the side effects.

Patient's ideas of active participation can be surprising, leaving staff at a loss as how to respond. Unusual requests commonly come from older adolescents. One eighteen-year-old male patient asked to participate in a tumor board meeting when his case is being discussed. He wanted to see the x-rays, the CAT scans, etc., feeling that the information he had been receiving from his various physicians was too fragmented. Another request came from a young nineteen-year-old male with Gardner's syndrome who asked that his operation be video-taped so he could have an opportunity to view it.

The child's knowledge of his condition is another important aspect of coping. Clinical and research findings indicate that the child is generally less anxious when he knows his diagnosis. Waechter (1972),[5] in a study of 64 children ages six to ten demonstrated, using the thematic appreception test (TAT) and anxiety scales, that the less opportunity that the child had to discuss his illness, the higher was his core on the general anxiety scale.

While knowledge of illness may reduce anxiety the issue of how and what to tell remains a major problem for people who deal with children with cancer.

Cassem[6] suggested the following steps in conveying the initial diagnosis, "the bad news." First:

1. Provide information in a brief fashion, in two or three sentences. Example: "Tests have confirmed that you have leukemia."
2. "We will start treatment tomorrow"—this implies that the physician is going to do something about it.
3. "As things proceed I will talk to you about them and tell you about our plans"—this in turn implies that the physician is going to stand by the patient.

The first three statements should be followed by step 4, silence; waiting for the patient to respond, to see his reactions. The physician's willingness to silently accept the patient indicates his availability for a meaningful dialogue in the present or in the future.

The children's attitude toward death is another central concern of all who take care of children with cancer. While there have been many studies about concepts of death in healthy children Waechter found the situation different with fatally ill children; they revealed a significantly more specific concern about death. Every ill child evaluated used death imagery at least once in a response to the protocol. Images of loneliness also frequently exceeded those in the control group. These studies seem to confirm clinical impressions which indicate that children with cancer know about death at a younger age than the general population. The critically ill child seems to perceive the gravity of his condition, conveyed to him in a nonverbal fashion by increasing use of more drastic therapeutic measures that do not bring relief, and which in fact often aggravate the already existing symptom. The very young child frequently expresses his feelings through the non-verbal rejection of his parents. Christina, a two and a half year old Chinese girl with hepatoma was noncommunicative during the last two weeks of her life. She was lying in her bed with her eyes closed, ignoring her parents. She would only respond when a physician came in. She would then open her eyes and protest against more treatment. Her attitude toward her parents seemed to convey both disappointment and resignation.

By contrast, it is primarily the adolescent patient who verbalizes his feelings about death. It may take various forms: John, a fourteen-year-old with promyelocytic leukemia, while suffering a relapse from which he did not recover, would talk only about his previous hospitalization and his previous bouts with death. "I was sure then" he said "that I am going to die. I had a dream that I went to heaven and St. Peter seeing me said, 'This kid has to go back. He is too young to be here.'" While there may be this recognition of the seriousness of the illness, it is important to respect this defensive style of coping and not to probe it. A sixteen-year-old with Hodgkin's disease dealt with her fear of dying through a masochistic rescue fantasy. She thought that through her illness she could improve her parents' marriage and therefore she was willing to suffer. An older adolescent with a terminal sarcoma talked about the fact that instead of going to college he should have gotten married and had children. "I would have at least enjoyed a part of the life cycle." This pain about dying without having achieved much is common among terminally ill young people.

This individual assessment with a particular emphasis on coping strategies provides the mental health practitioner with a sense of what therapeutic modality is best suited for the child. Possible choices include;

Individual psychotherapy

Group therapy (Groups should be age related and are often the treatment of choice for adolescents.)[7]

Family therapy

Play therapy (This can be particularly useful with young children as preparation for surgical and other stressful procedures.)[8]

Hypnosis, biofeedback (These are invaluable in providing children with strategies to deal with painful procedures and effects of chemotherapy.

While individual interventions are the primary emphasis for the ill child, group discussions are the most effective strategy for the others involved in the management and treatment of the child.

The Group for the Nurses

The nurse has a very special position in the oncology team. On the inpatient service, as a function of her assignment, the nurse has to become both physically and emotionally involved with the patient. Her contact with the sick child and his family is the most intense one, both in the nature of her interaction and the amount of time she spends with the patient. Group discussion with nurses tends to take two formats:

The case center group: The patient, usually the most problematic one on the ward, is presented to the group and discussion centers around the child's problems, the staff's reaction to his behavior, and to individual attitudes as they enhance or interfere with the management. Issues commonly discussed are the parents' perceived interference with the nurses' tasks.

The feeling of being left out of the medical decision-making process is another common topic. Case-centered meetings usually lead to a better understanding of the child and result in a formulation of a treatment strategy, allowing for a more uniform and concerted effort. Specific recommendations arrived at are available to staff not present at a particular meeting.

The second format for a group of oncology nurses is psychotherapeutically oriented. The theme is "What does it mean to work with a dying child and what emotional price does one pay?" Of central concern is the problem of overinvolvement, mourning, depression, and ways of separating one's work from private life. This format is especially pertinent in areas of intense patient-nurse contact like the ICU's, bone marrow transplant unit, etc.

The Group for Parents

Groups for parents should be ideally run conjointly by a pediatrician and a mental health expert. The themes vary from issues relating purely to medical management to problems of how to tell the child about his diagnosis. It is helpful to have a spectrum of parents with children in various stages of remission, as they will reflect the scope of attitudes from which every parent can gain insight into his own struggle.

Siblings are a frequent topic. They seem to be a highly vulnerable group. They suffer from neglect during the sick child's acute illness, experiencing feelings of guilt and conflict around sibling rivalry. Melissa, a thirteen-year-old with Hodgkin's Disease returned home after a long hospitalization. She received upon her return a $100 gift from her grandparents. Her eight-year-old brother thought it was unfair that he did not get anything. Melissa's comment was succinct: "You can have the money—but togther with my illness."[9]

Siblings may become extremely hypochondriacal and talk about their own death attempting to get additional attention from unavailable parents. Others use the illness as a weapon. A five-year-old girl talking to her three-year-old brother who had recovered from neuroblastoma said, "If you don't eat you will get cancer again."

The group offers the pediatrician important insight into the parent's style of coping, thus allowing him to become more effective in his interventions. To the parents, the physician seen in another framework is perceived as more human, easier to establish contact with. In a sense the group can become a forum for improved mutual understanding and improved doctor-patient relations, a critical therapeutic ingredient.

The Group for Attending Physicians

And finally, the central component for creating an effective department of pediatric oncology is a group for attending pediatricians. The format, is a cross between a clinical case conference and an insight-oriented group discussion.

The psychiatrist is the group leader. Individual patients are presented, usually the most critically ill. The focus of discussion frequently centers around the physician's personal relation to the patient, positive and negative, counter transference, methods of care, and issues of helplessness and omnipotence.

An important subject for this group is the need to determine the point when continuation of treatment becomes futile and what criteria should be used in order to arrive at this decision. Finding an acceptable compromise between research goals and the patients welfare is central to the decision making process. Although such discussions rarely reach definite conclusions, the process of exploration is highly constructive. It allows for sharing of thinking and insight into personal motives behind the decision-making process, leading to rationally rather than emotionally motivated interventions.

Anticipation of a patient's death, the admission that all resources have been exhausted, is another critical topic for such a group as is physician recognition of the importance for child and parents to prepare for death rather than to be confronted with it unexpectedly. An example is a three-year-old girl, daughter of a wealthy businessman, who was suffering from a hepatoma. After all the surgical and chemotherapeutic interventions had failed, the parents started to travel with her to various medical centers all over the U.S., to Lourdes in France, and finally ended up in a clinic in Jamaica, where the child received Laetrile. As all this was fruitless, the child eventually returned to the hospital. The father, who, because of his wealth and power could not accept a passive role, continued to be aggressive and demanding toward all staff, leveling accusations of having been misled and demanding more treatment. Anticipating an outburst of rage with possible violence following the death of the child, a meeting was called "a premortem" conference. As ambiguous statements in the past were misinterpreted, it was decided that the parents would be told unequivocally that there was no hope for the child. No heroic, last-minute interventions would take place irrespective of the child's condition. This approach formulated by the attending physicians group proved highly successful. The parents calmed down when faced with a uniform attitude of the staff, and a week later the child died peacefully. The ability of the group to come up with a uniform approach made the resolution of this crisis possible.

Conclusion

The treatment of the child who has cancer is unquestionably the most difficult and taxing area of modern medicine. The rapidly advancing technological discoveries allow for sophisticated and highly complex medical intervention to take place. Frequently, however, the child is emotionally unprepared or possibly incapable of coping with this onslaught of modern technologies. The physician, the nurse, and the child's parents are thrust into a position of having to mediate between the child's attempt to cope with his illness and the effects of powerful medical interventions. In addition, the critically ill child upset the natural order of events in which, under normal circumstances, parents die before their children. Helplessness in preventing the reversal of this order adds to the magnitude of the already complex situation.

Increased understanding and insight achieved by each entity will simultaneously facilitate the relationship between them; i.e., it will be reflected in a better coordination of efforts and improved cooperation and will result in increased effectiveness of treatment. Although the child is the patient, the whole therapeutic system requires treatment. The child can be helped best and with the highest degree of efficiency when psychologic intervention is directed toward the most immediately critical individuals within the system. Often, as has been illustrated, helping either the parents or the physician is the most effective course of action. Dealing with the vast ramifications of this most devastating illness requires that one provides a psychosocial support system that will match in its comprehensiveness and sophistication the other components of therapeutic intervention.

References

1. KOOCHER, G. P.; O'MALLEY, J. E.; GOGAN, J. L., FOSTER, D. J. "Psychological Adjustment Among Pediatric Cancer Survivors." *Journal of Child Psychology and Psychiatry,* 21:163-173, 1980.
2. VON BERTALANFFY, L. *General Systems Theory.* New York: George Braziller, 1968.
3. MILLER, J. G. "Living Systems: Basic Concepts." In *General Systems Theory and Psychiatry* (Gray, W.; Duhl, F. J.; Risso, N. D., eds). Boston: Little, Brown, 1969, pp. 51-134.
4. WEISMAN, A.V.: *Coping with Cancer.* New York: McGraw Hill, 1979.
5. LEVY, A.M.; NIR, Y. "Chronic Illness." In *Child Development in Normality and Psychopathology* (Bemporad, J. R., ed). New York: Brunner Mazel, 1980.
6. CASSEM, N. H. "Treating the Person Confronting Death." In *The Harvard Guide to Modern Psychiatry* (Nicholi, A. M., Jr., ed). Cambridge, Mass: Belknap Press of the Harvard University Press, 1978, p. 589.
7. COFER, D. H.; NIR, Y. "Theme-Focused Group Therapy on a Pediatric Ward. *Psychiat. Med.* 6:541-550, 1975.
8. *Emotional Care of Hospitalized Children* (Petrillo, M.; Sanger S., eds). Philadelphia: J. B. Lippincott Company, 1980.
9. SOURKES, B. "Siblings of the Pediatric Cancer Patient." In *Psychological Aspects of Childhood Cancer* (Kellerman, J., ed.). Illinois: Charles Thomas, 1980, pp. 47-69.

15 Cancer and the Family Emotional System

Michael E. Kerr

This chapter examines the influence of emotional factors on the development and course of cancer from the perspective of *family systems theory*. Family systems theory was developed in the 1950's and early 1960's by Murray Bowen, first through the study of families with a schizophrenic member and later through study of families with symptoms spanning the full range of emotional problems (Bowen, 1966; Kerr, 1980b).

Systems theory can be contrasted with individually based theories such as psychoanalysis in the following way: whereas individual theories consider schizophrenia a *disease* of the individual and seek its "cause" within the individual, systems theory conceptualizes schizophrenia as a *symptom of a disorder of the family emotional system*. While systems theory has also conceptualized physical diseases as symptoms of disturbances in the balance of the family emotional system, the majority of systems-based research has focused on the emotional dysfunctions. The author has focused his research on cancer, attempting to study more adequately the consistency of systems thinking with what can be observed about the development and course of physical illness.

In addition to describing family systems theory and its applicability to helping understand emotional process in cancer, the chapter also includes an effort to extend systems thinking into understanding some of the biological aspects of cancer. A systems model for conceptualizing the physiological mechanisms involved in illness is proposed. Another model is presented that places cancer on a continuum with other disease states, emphasizing the role of the exaggerated use of normal physiologic mechanisms in the development of all of these conditions. The goal in presenting these models is to aid thinking about disease, not as something foreign that is inflicted on us from the environment, but as symptomatic of a disturbance in the balance of our own bodily mechanisms.

During any discussion about the influence of emotional factors in cancer, it is prudent to remind ourselves that cancer is not confined just to man, but occurs in other animal species and in plants. The concepts developed about cancer in man should be consistent with what is observed in the rest of nature. One day cancer will likely be seen as a phenomenon of natural systems, occuring at all levels in nature, its existence reflecting a disturbance in the harmonious balance of a natural system.

A Systems Model for Disease

For many centuries medical diagnosis was restricted to a description of the patient's signs and symptoms. Little was known about the basic causes of disease. The discovery of Pasteur of the relationship of germs to disease dramatically changed medical diagnosis. It became possible to classify disease based on specific etiological agents, for example, the tubercle bacillus as the cause of tuberculosis. Much of cancer research today continues in this mode by trying to identify specific viruses, genetic defects, or carcinogenic substances that might "cause" certain cancers. Such research is invaluable in that, if specific agents or defects can be identified and treated, a particular cancer might be rendered harmless. Identification of the pneumococcal bacterium and specific antibiotics to treat it, for example, has greatly lessened the danger of that type of pneumonia.

As time has passed, it has become evident that invasion by a bacterium or virus does not *necessarily* lead to the development of a clinical disease. In fact, in the majority of instances people can live in perfect harmony with these invaders or even with the presence of genetic defects without the development of a clinical syndrome. With this in mind, saying that the tubercle bacillus causes tuberculosis or that smoking causes cancer is not entirely accurate. In recent years, an attempt has been made to deal with this issue by proposing a *theory of multiple causes* (Cassel, 1965). This theory states that several conditions or factors must be present for a disease to develop. The presence of bacteria by themselves would not be enough.

A systems model goes a step beyond the multiple-cause model, conceptualizing the balance of the relationships between the various "causes" or factors as the critical determinant in the development of clinical disease. *A systems model for understanding the mechanisms of disease is a model that attempts to define all of the factors that interact to produce a particular clinical syndrome, viewing each factor as impacting on the others such that the behavior or activity of any one factor cannot be understood out of the context of its relationship to the others. Clinical disease is not the result of the presence of any one or all of the factors, but develops based on a disturbance in the balance of the relationship system between them.* The important question, then, is what disturbs this harmonious balance of biological relationships and leads to clinical symptoms? This systems model does not preclude the possibility that a specific defect or agent may be found for a given disease, without the presence of which a particular clinical syndrome could not exist.

Acne Vulgaris

The author was, to a great extent, taught the systems model by one of his own diseases, *acne vulgaris*. Acne is a perifolliculitis, an inflammation surrounding the sebaceous follicles in the skin. Muir has defined the following mechanisms in the development of an acne lesion (Anderson, 1976). *Corynebacterium acnes* is a bacterium that finds an occluded sebaceous follicle suitable for growth. This bacterium produces a potent lipase, an enzyme that chemically reacts with sebum, the neutral fat substance normally produced by sebaceous glands, splitting the sebum into substances called free fatty acids. Unlike sebum, when these free fatty acids leak into the tissues surrounding the sebaceous glands, they are potentially quite irritating to the tissues. The presence of the free fatty acids can be associated with a significant inflammatory response, causing the area surrounding the sebaceous glands to become swollen and packed with white blood cells. *It is then this inflammatory reaction that produces the redness and swelling that gives the clinical picture of acne.* If you think about this for a minute, you begin to realize that it is the response of our own bodily armies, our own immunologic system, that can create the picture of chaos and destruction we call disease. Since these are our own immunologic armies, to what extent is their mobilization under our control? To what extent is the deployment of these armies in disease states an unnecessary, even counterproductive, overreaction to the situation?

There are many other interesting questions posed by the disease acne. For example, why do some people never get it? There are people with high sebum output and people with high concentrations of the corynebacterium on their skin who have never experienced an acne reaction. Consideration of the factors influencing why some people never get acne is well beyond the scope of this chapter. But there is another interesting question that is relevant here. The question is, why do people who have acne experience exacerbations and remissions of their disease? Several years ago I began trying to identify some of the factors that influenced these cycles of activity in my own case. The exploration proved fascinating and contributed significantly to the development of a systems model for disease.

The first factor I identified was the consumption of foods with high sugar content. I speculated, perhaps inaccurately, that the extra sugar energized the bacteria in some way, triggering more lipase production, free fatty acids, and eventually an inflammatory response. Efforts to reduce sugar intake did lead to some improvement in the acne. The second factor I identified was mechanical irritation of the skin, for example, by shirt collars and shaving. What was interesting, however, was the gradual realization that excessive sugar and mechanical irritation did not *always* trigger much of an acne response. At times these stimuli were tolerated or adapted to rather well.

The third factor identified proved to be the most difficult of all to really see. For some time my wife had been telling me that she thought that when I was under more stress, the acne was more in evidence. I had heard the same thing from other people about their experiences with acne. It is one thing to be told that stress can be associated with acne, but it is another thing to see a really clear association between stress and the activity of a disease process within oneself. For me, it took time and careful observation during repeated cycles of the disease to become convinced of a clear association between fluctuations in my level of *chronic anxiety* and fluctuations in the activity of the disease. But I did become convinced. When anxiety was low, significant sugar consumption and mechanical irritations could be tolerated with only mild skin reactions. When anxiety was high, severe exacerbations of acne could be avoided by carefully avoiding excess sugar and mechanical irritations. The combination of all three factors in high "dosage" produced the worst reactions. The interplay fascinated me.

Later on, I resorted to the use of low dosages of tetracyclene on a regular basis to control the acne. College students flock to clinics around exam time to load up with tetracyclene in order to get through exam pressures without a full flowering of their acne. It usually works for them and, in my case, it completely cleared up the acne. Since no one is entirely certain about the exact mechanisms involved in acne, no one is sure why tetracyclene can help control the disease. Originally, I had imagined it controlling the reproduction of the bacteria. Later I heard the idea that tetracyclene interfered with the production of free fatty acids, thereby reducing the inflammatory reaction. In any event, it worked. But since I am one who only reluctantly takes aspirin for headaches, I never liked the idea of using tetracyclene to control the acne. I did like the idea of no longer having to worry about eating foods with high sugar content.

The reliance on tetracyclene continued for about two years. During that period, I learned a good deal about my anxiety and gained in my ability to control it. Acne had been an important teacher about anxiety. Eventually it became possible to get along without the tetracyclene, even while consuming foods high in sugar content and continuing to experience various mechanical irritations of the skin. The fact that I had significant control over the activity of the disease process through the control of my anxiety was mind blowing. To what extent was this possible with other diseases? This is not to say that the only reason acne can disappear is through the reduction of anxiety. Certainly there are other biological variables that can influence it. But when acne continues to be active, unquestionably anxiety is an important variable influencing the clinical course. Nor is this to say that people who have acne have it because of their "psychological" problems. Anxiety is a universal phenomenon, and acne is but one of a myriad of ways anxiety can be manifested.

It would be tempting to say that in acne anxiety is reflected in an overzealous inflammatory reaction. But it seems more accurate to think in terms of a systems model and say that anxiety disturbs the balance between all the various biological factors involved in acne. What probably occurs is that, as the disease process picks up momentum, the activity of each factor, for example, the bacteria, the enzymes, the white blood cells, etc., is increasingly modified by the activity of every other factor through a series of feedback loops. The disturbance is in the total balance of the system rather than any one part being the culprit. In other words, the activity of the inflammatory cells may reflect what is going on with the bacteria, sebum, lipase, and free fatty acids but *also,* the activity of the bacteria, sebum, lipase, and free fatty acids may be a function of the overzealous inflammatory response. The important point is not to pick out any one factor and blame the process on it. All of the players being observed are capable of living in harmony. It is the anxiety that can disrupt that harmony and turn peaceful coexistence into polarized confrontations.

Perhaps a fitting conclusion for this section is a quote by Lewis Thomas (Thomas, 1974): "Our arsenals for fighting off bacteria are so powerful, and involve so many different defense mechanisms, that we are in more danger from ourselves than from the invaders."

Acute and Chronic Anxiety

Having introduced the concept of anxiety and discussed its role in at least one disease process, let us now attempt some definition of anxiety and explore some of the differences between acute and chronic anxiety.

Bowen has offered a definition of anxiety that I have found particularly useful (Bowen, 1980). Bowen defines anxiety as *the response of an organism to a threat, real or imagined.* He makes a distinction between *acute* and *chronic* anxiety, acute anxiety generally occurring in response to a real threat, and chronic anxiety being more related to imagined threats. People typically adapt well to stressful situations that have tangible causes and are known to be time limited. People tend to be more worn down, physically and mentally, by situations in which the causes for the stress are not so obvious and there is no anticipated time of relief. Examples of imagined threats that can be sources of chronic anxiety would be anticipating that the worst might happen, overreacting to the uncertainties of a situation, or being preoccupied with whether one is being accepted or rejected by significant others.

In attempting to conceptualize anxiety, it is well to keep in mind that anxiety exists in other animals besides man. Presumably there is an equivalent to what we call anxiety in man in all other forms of life. Let us take as an example of manifestations of anxiety in nonhuman animals, the deterioration of social stability and marked increase in aberrant behaviors in the mice of Calhouns overpopulated colony (Calhoun, 1962). In the experiment, Calhoun begins with a colony of mice at ideal population density. Under these conditions, the mice demonstrate all of Wilson's criteria for optimum social organization, namely, cohesiveness, cooperation, and altruistic behaviors (Wilson, 1975). But as the population of the colony is allowed to increase to very high levels within a confined physical space, the social organization deteriorates. Cohesiveness is lost as the animals fragment into subgroups, cooperation is replaced by selfish behavior, and increasingly the animals work at cross purposes. I believe that the regression in the colony can be thought of as a manifestation of increasing levels of chronic anxiety in the mice. Interestingly, the incidence of cancer in the colony increases as the social stability deteriorates.

This example from the nonhuman animal world is given to emphasize that chronic anxiety can be a deep process in man, deep in the sense of being related to man as a biological being and closely tied to his evolutionary heritage. Chronic anxiety is deep also in the sense that when we are seeing manifestations of anxiety on the social interactional level, there can also be similar disturbances at the cellular level.

Let us now step back from a microscopic look at a specific disease and the role of anxiety in that disease and attempt to look at the problems on a broader theoretical level with discussion of some of the basic concepts of family systems theory.

Family Systems Theory

Family systems theory is a theory that conceptualizes the family as a system of relationships. This family relationship system is viewed in multigenerational terms in that what the family is in the present is understood in the context of what it has been in the past. A family's patterns of behavior, beliefs, values, types of emotional reactions, and particular problems can be observed to be gradually altered in type and intensity down through the generations. Viewing the family across many generations, it can also be observed that the various lines or branches of a family gradually diverge in terms of their apparent overall stability. From one set of original parents, say eight generations back, certain lines of their descendants can be seen to evolve to a level of adaptation higher than the level of adaptation of the original ancestors. These more adaptive segments of family demonstrate an unusual degree of emotional and apparent physiological stability. Relationships in these highly adaptive segments tend to remain intact, and the incidence of serious emotional, physical, and social dysfunction is amazingly low. In contrast, other branches of the family from the same original ancestors gradually show an increasing impairment of adaptiveness as evidenced both by frequent disruption of relationships, with segments of closely related family becoming significantly isolated from each other, and by a high incidence of physical, emotional, and social dysfunction. The dysfunctions in these poorly adaptive segments of family often occur early in life and are frequently quite serious and permanent. It should be apparent from the discussion that the physical, emotional, and social dysfunctions are being defined here as representing some degree of *failure in adaptation* by the individual and by the family.

If any family is studied over enough generations, all the gradations between the above described extremes of high and low level adaptiveness can usually be found. If you again start with two original ancestors and trace their descendants through say ten generations, all the segments of family that have survived can usually be observed to fall at many points along a continuum ranging from families with a level of adaptiveness better than the original ancestors to families with their adaptiveness much more impaired than the original two parents. As you observe the process across the generations, highly adaptive segments will be seen to spawn their less adaptive branches and poorly adaptive segments will be seen to spawn their better adaptive branches. It is a shifting, fluid process that courses through the generations, spinning off the least adaptive, least flexible segments that may eventually die out.

This evolving multigenerational family-relationship system is conceptualized to be anchored in and driven by emotional forces. These emotional forces are considered to be deep in the sense that they are a product of man's evolution and that they also exist in other animals. It is appropriate, in other words, to speak of an emotionally driven relationship system in a troop of baboons. It is likely that the emotional system of a baboon troop has principles of operation that are strikingly similar to the principles that govern human emotional systems. This is not to imply that man is the same as the baboon. Clearly man's intellectual capacities are far more advanced than those of other primates, but it appears that all too often man's intellectual system is governed by his emotionality; his intellect acts in the service of emotionality rather than maintaining enough independence from the emotional system to offer an alternative to an emotionally determined direction.

What systems theory is proposing then is that man is far more emotional, far more like other forms of life than he would usually like to believe. The emotional forces comprise the binding meshwork of a family and can be referred to as the *family emotional system*. The emotional system is transmitted down the generations with a precision and predictability approaching that of classic Mendelian genetics. It is the particular way that these emotional forces evolve that governs the variations in the adaptiveness of the different branches of a family. Although the particular evolution of emotional forces may prove unfavorable for specific branches of the family, the creation of these more impaired family segments serves a *function* in the evolution of the larger multigenerational family system. It is a fact of man's emotionality that the group can preserve its strength at the expense of some of its parts. In terms of cancer, it is a different matter when cancer occurs in a weakened branch or twig of the family that is dying out and when it occurs in the main trunk. The emotional substrates on which these tumors are growing are significantly different, and that difference appears to have an effect on prognosis.

If we look more closely at the family emotional system, we see that, like other biological systems, it consists of counterbalancing forces. There are two principal counterbalancing life forces in a family system, one referred to as the *togetherness* force and the other as the *individuality* force. The togetherness force is reflected in a need for emotional closeness and agreement. The individuality force is reflected in the capacity to be an individual in one's own right, to function autonomously. These forces are part of the make-up of each family member and are reflected in the balance of individuality and togetherness in family relationships. *It is a disturbance in the balance of these forces in a relationship system that is the critical emotional process influencing the emergence of clinical symptoms.* Said in another way, we all have a need for a sense of connectedness to others and a need to have some control over our own destiny, to be ourselves. The harmony of these things within us is intricately tied to the harmony in our important relationships. When those relationships are significantly disturbed, we become more vulnerable to disturbances within ourselves.

Families differ in the relative mix of individuality and togetherness that constitutes a state of balance for them. Some families are characterized by the strong influence of the togetherness force. Such families are referred to as highly *fused* families. Functioning in these families is strongly determined by people's need for each other and individuality is sacrificed to preserve apparent harmony and agreement. There are all gradations between highly fused and less fused families, the latter being characterized by a more optimum mix of the individuality and togetherness forces. In less fused families, people have the capacity to be themselves and at the same time maintain comfortable emotional connections with each other. The functioning of the individuals in a less fused system is not as *emotionally* interdependent as in a highly fused system, and consequently the functioning of one person is less dependent on and less likely to impair the functioning of another person. *These less fused systems are the more adaptive to stress.* Highly fused systems are so emotionally interdependent that, under significant stress, panic can prevail over cooperation, and all or some part of the family organism may collapse into dysfunction. *The relative mix of individuality and togetherness in a family system is the product of multi-generational emotional process.* As has been stated, families fall at many points on a continuum between the extremes of high and low levels of adaptiveness. There is no such thing as a family that is not fused; it is, rather, a matter of degrees of fusion.

These variations in the relative mix of individuality and togetherness forces that occur in different branches of a family over generations are primarily the product of two facts. The first fact is that parents become fused with their children and, classically, this fusion is more intense with one child than it is with the others. This fusion is manifested in the emotional overinvolvement people have in each other's lives, an overinvolvement that can range from overpositive to overnegative in character. The child with whom the parents are most fused reciprocates their overinvolvement with him, and it becomes a mutually reinforcing process. This most fused child grows up with togetherness needs that are more intense than those of his siblings and usually even more intense than those of his parents. The siblings who grow up with a less intense emotional overinvolvement with the parents develop a mix of individuality and togetherness that is similar to the parents' or perhaps with an even greater capacity for individuality than the parents. Most of the details of this process have been left out because of lack of space, but the important point to be made is that while the individuality and togetherness life forces are rooted in man's instinctual being, their basic mix within an individual and within a family unit can be modified based on the characteristics of relationships down through the generations.

The second fact that influences the alteration in the individuality-togetherness balance across the generations is that people select partners for marriage whose togetherness needs and capacity for individuality are equal to their own. Since parents are producing children with somewhat different capacities for individuality and somewhat different needs for emotional fusion, the marriages of those children will be somewhat different in their basic individuality-togetherness balance. The most fused child will have a marriage that is balanced slightly more toward togetherness than the other siblings. The least fused child will have a marriage balanced slightly more toward individuality than the other siblings. When these children have their children and the process is played out in yet another generation, then lines of increasing and decreasing fusion plus all gradations in between will gradually emerge. At one extreme, the most fused child produces his most fused child who produces his most fused child, etc. The togetherness needs of that particular line become greater and greater, and its adaptiveness gradually more impaired. At the other extreme, the least fused child produces his least fused child, etc. In this line, the adaptiveness gradually improves.

To summarize what has been said thus far, the lines or branches of family that are evolving toward more impaired adaptiveness are the lines that are becoming progressively more emotionally fused. In these segments of family, the togetherness force is significantly overriding individuality. As the togetherness force increasingly overrides individuality, the system becomes more vulnerable to the development of acute and/or chronic symptoms. The relationship between the individuality-togetherness balance and symptom development is a complex one, which will be examined here in some detail.

In thinking about the individuality-togetherness balance in a family system, it is important to keep in mind those factors that have influenced it across the generations as well as those factors that influence it of more recent origin. In both instances, changes in the level of chronic anxiety are the critical variable to be considered. Changes in chronic anxiety that occur gradually through the generations are much more fixed, much more built into the nature of things than are changes in chronic anxiety that are based on recent life events. Increases in the level of chronic anxiety, based on multigenerational process as well as that triggered by a variety of real or anticipated life events, is the primary disturbing influence on the balance of family emotional forces. Once the relationship balance begins to be significantly disturbed, *it is people's reactions to the fact of that disturbance that usually becomes the principal generator of anxiety*. Anxiety then feeds on anxiety in a vicious cycle.

Anxiety disturbs the balance of a family emotional system by increasing the activity of the togetherness force. Whether a family system is strongly balanced towards togetherness or only moderately so, increasing chronic anxiety disturbs that balance. The system reacts to this potential disturbance in its equilibrium by activating mechanisms designed to bind or wall off the anxiety into certain areas of the system, thereby preserving equilibrium of the system as a whole. When the intensity of this process reaches a certain level, the use of anxiety binding mechanisms becomes so exaggerated that the mechanisms contribute to the particular type of symptoms a system develops.

There are four anxiety binding mechanisms in a family system, namely, *emotional distance, emotional conflict, compromised spouse,* and *overinvolvement with children*. These mechanisms will be discussed in detail in a later section, but, basically, they influence the pattern or flow of emotional forces in a family. In any family, people come to function in certain characteristic ways in relationship to each other. The less fused a family, the less rigid or fixed are these functional patterns. These emotionally determined patterns of functioning and positions functioning people have in families are related to the way anxiety and emotional reactivity is managed. It is a mindless process, having less to do with man as a thinking being than with man as an emotional being. *It is the way people function in relationship to each other, the mechanisms they use to deal with anxiety, that determines where the system's anxiety comes to "rest" or surfaces.* When family anxiety is relatively low, these patterns of functioning usually do not create problems. Their presence reflects the fusion in the system, but the patterns are functional. But when anxiety increases, the patterns become exaggerated and then play a part in determining which family member develops a problem: physical, emotional, or social.

Family equilibrium in a highly adaptive system, a system in which the individuality-togetherness balance approaches an optimum level, is characterized by the complete absence of acute and chronic clinical symptoms. As family systems become progressively more fused, however, it becomes more likely that family equilibrium will be associated with the presence of chronic symptoms. Regardless of the level of adaptiveness, family disequilibrium is associated with the appearance of new symptoms and/or the deterioration of previously existing chronic symptoms. A family system generates a certain amount of chronic anxiety on its own, regardless of external events. The more fused the system or the more it is balanced toward togetherness, the more chronic anxiety it generates. The relationship of increasing levels of fusion to increasing levels of chronic anxiety is something more easily observed than it is explained. Any attempt at explanation is doomed to being inadequate, but one way to think about it is as follows: the more fused the system, the more people are leaning on each other to draw strength and a sense of well being, but at the same time the more pressure people are feeling from each other to function in ways that will make the other feel better. This leaning and pressuring are an apparent source of chronic anxiety and relationship instability. The more fused the system and the more chronic anxiety it generates, the more the chronic pressure toward emotional disequilibrium. As a consequence, the more fused the system, the greater the necessity for chronic and exaggerated use of anxiety binding mechanisms.

To summarize, over the course of multiple generations in a family, certain lines or branches are characterized by an increasing degree of physical, emotional, and social instability. These branches are referred to as having an impaired level of adaptiveness. The togetherness life force is overriding in these highly fused systems, the level of system-generated chronic anxiety is high, and there is a chronic exaggerated use of anxiety binding mechanisms designed to preserve system equilibrium. Such systems have low reserve and cannot maintain equilibrium without the presence of chronic symptoms. They are particularly vulnerable to going into disequilibrium with the appearance of new symptoms and/or deterioration or the chronic symptoms based on the occurrence of real or anticipated life events that generate additional increments of anxiety. Less fused systems, based on multigenerational process, have more reserve and therefore more adaptiveness to life events that are potentially anxiety producing.

The specifics about anxiety binding mechanisms and other emotional variables influencing symptom development will be discussed in a later section. But first we will look at some of the biological aspects of cancer and make some attempt to extend systems thinking into those areas.

Biological Aspects

Is the clinical impression of a sustained increase in the level of chronic anxiety as the critical emotional variable influencing symptom development consistent with what is known about the biological aspects of physical illnesses like cancer? Is there any evidence, in other words, of ways in which anxiety could be translated into the development of a tumor? The evidence to be presented here about possible biological links between anxiety and tumor development is quite limited in scope, but does point some directions for further research. This evidence is based on knowledge about the histology of the human skin in both normal and diseased states coupled with personal experience with yet another skin disease, psoriasis.

Normal skin

Look for a moment at your own skin. What you see is the most superficial layer of the epidermis, the *stratum corneum*. It is these highly specialized cells of the stratum corneum that form the body's water-resistant and fairly tough outer shell. These cells of the stratum corneum are so specialized that they have lost the capacity to reproduce themselves and are thus referred to as terminally differentiated. They are the end product of one of the most fascinating phenomenon of nature, the process of cell differentiation.

The skin consists of three basic layers: the *epidermis, dermis,* and *subcutaneous tissue.* The subcutaneous tissue is the bedrock of the skin, containing a variety of important structures, the most important of which for this discussion are the blood vessels. Tiny arterioles course to the most superficial layers of the dermis where, just beneath the epidermis, they narrow down into capillary networks that permit the exchange of life-giving oxygen and nutrients for carbon dioxide and tissue metabolic waste products. The epidermis is the outermost layer of the skin. This layer consists of many layers of cells that are increasingly more specialized or differentiated as they move from the deeper layers of the epidermis to the stratum corneum. The deepest layer of the epidermis is the *basal cell* layer. These basal cells are referred to as undifferentiated in that they can reproduce and form into several kinds of specialized cells. Based on mechanisms or systems that are not well understood, these basal cells divide and provide new cells for the epidermis at a rate that exactly equals the rate at which cells are sloughed off from the stratum corneum. Where a basal cell divides, the daughter cell product of that division gradually moves toward the surface, evolving through predictable stages of increasing differentiation along the way. By the time it reaches the surface, this now completely differentiated cell has lost its ability to reproduce, but has developed the abilities to make special proteins and perform special functions that make it suitable for the stratum corneum. It is a beautifully ordered marvel of nature. *Under normal conditions, the epidermal system is in a perfectly balanced dynamic equilibrium, maintaining the skin at constant thickness.* The epidermis and dermis operate in synchrony, each responsive to changes in the other.

Psoriasis

A microscopic look at a psoriatic skin lesion tells a very informative story. Looking at the skin grossly, it is thickened and scaling; it looks "diseased." But looking microscopically, one immediately realizes that *what is occurring is nothing more than exaggerated activity of normal bodily mechanisms.* The skin normally responds to injury or irritations with a hypercellular or *hyperplastic* reaction. Following injury, the capillaries dilate and flood the dermis with protein-rich serum and inflammatory or white blood cells. The basal cells begin dividing at an increased rate, and the epidermis thickens. When the irritating or provoking force is removed, the process subsides. The first step in the development of a psoriatic skin lesion has also been identified as dilatation of the dermal capillaries (Garelly, 1968). White blood cells begin escaping from these dilated capillaries and migrate up into the epidermis. It is these white cells that are believed to be a stimulus for the increased basal cell division that then occurs. The epidermis gradually thickens and, apparently because cells are being produced so rapidly and reaching the surface so quickly, they are not quite as mature and cohesive as normal stratum corneum cells and scaling develops. Psoriasis is a hypermetabolic process that likely gathers a certain momentum of its own as it progresses. *In psoriasis and other hyperplastic responses, the cells remain basically normal in function, differentiating through the orderly stages and maintaining their normal alignment and relationship to each other.*

In contrast to a hyperplastic response to injury or irritation, the puzzle about psoriasis is *what energizes it,* what drives the activity? Why are the lesions more active at some times and not others? What is the trigger for the capillary dilatation and egress of inflammatory cells? Certainly some of the stimulus comes from the very activity of the process itself, in that a hypermetabolic process does apparently stimulate capillary dilatation to gain more oxygen and nutrients. But that could explain only a part of the picture and is of no help in understanding what sets the process in motion in the first place.

There are a number of triggers for a psoriatic lesion developing that have been observed; mechanical irritation of the skin, for example, and even excessive dryness appear to play some role. Personal experience with the disease over the last twenty years coupled with careful observation of it over the last three years have convinced me that, like acne, psoriatic activity is a perfect mirror for fluctuations in anxiety level. Relatively small increases in the level of sustained anxiety will be manifested in three or four days by the appearance of a scaling lesion. Why the anxiety would be manifested in psoriasis as opposed to something else is beyond the scope of what is being discussed here. But if it is going to be manifested this way, it is an absolutely perfect indicator of changes in anxiety.

Chronic anxiety, then, is seen as the primary energizing force in psoriasis, the lesions themselves being only tips of the energy iceberg. In looking at the lesions microscopically, it is as if the anxiety is being absorbed, played out, or bound in increased cellular activity. Once looked at in these terms, psoriasis becomes a kind of friend, a built-in biofeedback, a potential teacher about anxiety.

Benign tumors

Many, if not all, of the benign tumors appear to be but slight variations on the hyperplastic response theme. Benign tumors are also characterized by *some degree of inflammatory cell activity in the dermis, marked increase in the rate of cell division, normal cellular differentiation, and normal cellular alignment and relationships.* As the tumor progresses, however, and an increasing number of cells are produced, there is a limit to how much the epidermis will continue to thicken before it begins to push outward into folds, drawing the dermis up inside the folds and producing a stalk for the tumor mass. If this occurs in the colon, it will grossly be identified as a polyp. The polyp is clearly not a strange creature, but is a product of exaggerated activity of normal bodily processes.

Precancerous lesions

The precancerous lesions are far more like the hyperplastic responses and benign tumors than they are different. In fact, all of these conditions extending all the way to cancer can be thought of as existing on a continuum, with each condition being but a variation of the previous one. *In precancerous lesions there is definite inflammatory cell activity in the dermis and a hyperplastic, thickened epidermis. What is new is the appearance of abnormal looking cells that have failed to differentiate properly. There is also a beginning disturbance in the normal alignment between the cells.* These precancerous lesions are localized, with no evidence of the abnormal looking cells having broken through the basal cell layer down into the dermis.

Squamous cell cancers

The cancers demonstrate all of the previously described characteristics of skin lesions, all of the exaggerations of normal body processes, but with greater intensity and more disruption of the normal order of the tissues. *The inflammatory activity in the dermis is quite marked, and poorly differentiated cells, also referred to as anaplastic cells, have migrated out of the local area down deep into the dermis, setting up new colonies of rapidly reproducing cells.* The spreading of the cancer cannot occur without the body's cooperation in that the inflammatory activity around the cancer cell nests provides the blood vessel supply and connective tissue support the cancer needs to exist (Masson, 1970). Amazingly, in the less malignant tumors, there is evidence within these cancer cell nests of some cellular differentiation still occurring. Cancer cells have the capacity to produce daughter cells that can differentiate into relatively normal cells.

Conclusion

Most of the prevailing concepts about cancer present it as a cell that has become defective, usually by virtue of a genetic mutation, and run wild, triggering all kinds of responses in the body. There may well be some truth to this viewpoint, but it seems a one-sided view and not a systems view. The goal of presenting the above descriptions of various skin conditions is to encourage looking at cancer on a continuum with other conditions, seeing how many basically normal bodily mechanisms appear to be involved in its development. It is likely too simplistic a view, but it would appear that in cancer the body's normal mechanisms have become so overreactive and exaggerated that the tissue collapses into chaos, permitting the development of cells that now compete against the body instead of cooperating with it. To what extent anxiety can be the overenergizing and eventually disrupting force remains speculative, but at least the clinical impressions about the role of anxiety appear consistent with what is occurring on the biological level.

Systems Thinking and Cancer

In beginning this section on the specific application of systems concepts to cancer, it is well advised to remind ourselves that what is being discussed is but one facet of the complex process that can eventually erupt in a cancer. Obviously, the role of genetics, viruses, carcinogenic chemicals, radiation, and other factors must be considered in the development of any cancer. The previously described systems model for disease was, at least, some attempt to think about the possible interrelationship of all the variables. Having given this reminder about the complexity of cancer, let me proceed with some observations about the apparent relationship of cancer to the family emotional system.

As is theorized to be the case with the emotional illnesses, *cancer can also be considered symptomatic of a disorder of the family emotional system*. Family systems theory, in other words, has been found to be consistent with what has been observed about the emotional process in cancer families. In my research on over one hundred cancer patients and their families, in the majority of instances a period of increased, intense, and sustained anxiety lasting from several months to a year or more preceded the cancer diagnosis. Furthermore, it has been a clinical impression that what happens to the level of chronic anxiety following the cancer diagnosis is an important variable influencing outcome. The range in intensity of the level of anxiety in the various situations has been fairly wide, with many cancers appearing in highly intense emotional situations, while in other cases, the intensity has been more moderate. As should be evident based on the earlier discussion of a systems model for disease, saying anxiety has a role in the development of cancer is not to imply it is *causing* the cancers. The impression drawn from the research is that sustained intense anxiety gradually erodes the organism's biological adaptiveness, thereby making it more prone to *something* going wrong.

In attempting to understand a specific family's vulnerability to the anxiety driven imbalance in the family emotional system that can contribute to the development of a cancer, there are four key areas to be considered in the assessment of that family. These areas have been discussed in a general way in the previous section on theory, but will be discussed here in more detail. The four areas are the following: the basic adaptiveness of the individual and the family, also referred to as level of differentiation; the level of chronic anxiety in the family system generated by reactions to real or anticipated events; the nuclear family's degree of emotional cut-off from the extended family and other important relationship systems; and, finally, the mechanisms the family uses to absorb or bind anxiety.

Differentiation

The concept of differentiation is the most important emotional variable to be considered in understanding a person's vulnerability to the physical, emotional, and social dysfunctions and in understanding their ability to recover from those dysfunctions. Differentiation defines an important way in which people and families are different, it being possible to place all people at various points on a continuum between the extremes of high and low-level differentiation. Where people fall on this continuum is a product of multigenerational emotional process. Differentiation can be thought of as the way people manage the individuality-togetherness mix within themselves. People with the higher levels of differentiation approach a more optimum mix of individuality and togetherness, are less prone to intense relationship fusions, and are more adaptive to stress. People at the lower levels of differentiation are more prone to be caught up in relationship fusions and are more dominated by the togetherness life force. The differentiation level of a family can be thought of as a product of the levels of differentiation of the people who make up the family. Presenting the contrasting profiles of two people at the opposite extremes of the differentiation continuum might help clarify this important concept.

A reasonably well differentiated person is one with a set of well defined beliefs that are consistent with each other. That person can act based on those beliefs and the principles that emerge from them, even in face of considerable emotional pressure from others to do otherwise. These beliefs and principles are not rigid or dogmatically adhered to, and the person can *choose* to modify them based on new knowledge. Such a person respects the opinions of others and does not pressure others to change their viewpoints; differences, in other words, are well tolerated. A well differentiated person is keenly aware of the difference between his emotional, subjective responses and his intellectual, objective ones and is cognizant of the value and limits of each type of response. He consistently has the ability to choose between actions based on his thinking or on his feelings in a given circumstance. The togetherness needs of the well differentiated person are toned down to an optimum level. While he has an emotional need for others and is aware of that fact, that need is not so compelling that it dictates decisions and actions. Approval has some importance but, again, not compellingly so. In emotionally close relationships, the well-differentiated person can be himself and does not function in a way that impairs the other person's ability to do the same. His expectations of himself and of emotionally significant others are realistic and not based on needing the other to be something different than he is. He is not holding the other responsible for his happiness, nor is he vulnerable to such claims on the part of the other. Periods of intense closeness are enjoyed, and periods of protracted distance are tolerated equally well. The well differentiated person is comfortable with the emotional needs and problems of the other and does not respond to them by withdrawal or by getting judgemental and preachy. Having been raised fairly calmly and not being constantly preoccupied with being approved of, being rejected, or with what he "should" or "ought" to be, the well differentiated person lives with a low level of chronic anxiety. His emotional reserves are great and are not easily drained by emotionally intense situations.

In contrast to the well-differentiated person, a poorly differentiated person spends most of his life reacting emotionally to situations and has little awareness of an alternative to such reactions. He is so unsure about what he believes and so hungry for acceptance from others that he will unthinkingly adopt the popular opinions of the groups to which he belongs. Since emotionality so strongly influences what he thinks, he will adopt views that are intellectually incompatible and not even be aware of the discrepancies in his belief system. Having adopted these beliefs, their emotionally determined base is betrayed in rigid, dogmatic adherence to them or in a ready willingness to change them under emotional pressure from the group to do so. Another possibility is that the poorly differentiated person will reject the group's beliefs, becoming a rebel. The rebel's belief system is emotionally determined and is always the opposite of what the group espouses. The togetherness needs of the poorly differentiated person are so intense that they seriously impair his ability to be autonomous. The needs for emotional closeness and approval and fears of rejection are so compelling that important decisions are made based on those feelings. The poorly differentiated person may either fuse intensely into relationships, seeking a sense of security and personal completeness through the relationship or, in contrast, may avoid close relationships because of his vulnerability to feeling swallowed up by or trapped in such relationships. In an intense relationship, his expectations of both himself and of the other person are quite unrealistic. An example of the unreality is feeling his partner's happiness is his responsibility *or* that his own happiness is the responsibility of his partner. The relationship of two poorly differentiated people frequently becomes fraught with anxiety when either partner encounters a problem. In these instances, one person can begin feeling drained and dragged down by the other's problem. It can be a vicious cycle, with one partner's overreaction to the problem of the other serving to undermine the other person's ability to cope with the problem. The poorly differentiated person lives with a considerable amount of chronic anxiety, anxiety that gets bound up in a variety of clinical and subclinical symptoms such as overeating, overdrinking, obsessions, phobias and other neurotic traits, psychotic thought patterns, physical symptoms, and behavioral peculiarities.

These two pictures of well and poorly differentiated people represent the extremes of a continuum of differentiation. All of us fall somewhere between these extremes, demonstrating a mix of the elements that have been described and a variation in the intensity of them. Bowen considered the highest level of differentiation as something man might evolve to, but has not yet reached. This continuum or scale of differentiation is not related to diagnostic categories. People on the lower ends of the scale can go through life with few clinical problems provided circumstances are favorable. Lower-scale people have a harder time keeping relationships in balance and are more at the mercy of their emotional environment, but if they are fortunate, their life can remain in relative equilibrium. By the same token, people toward the more differentiated end of the scale can develop clinical problems if they are subjected to enough stress-generated anxiety. They are less vulnerable to their emotional environment than lower-scale people, but it is a relative difference. People anywhere on the scale could develop psychotic symptoms, cancer, or any other problem, but the poorly differentiated person is more likely to experience a severe case, have it occur relatively early in life, and to have a less satisfactory clinical course.

Chronic Anxiety

It is useful to think in terms of two components of chronic anxiety, that which is built into the individual and the family and that which is generated by real and/or anticipated events. The built-in component is related to the lack of differentiation in the system as was discussed in an earlier section. In addition, there is a wide variety of events that have the potential for disturbing the balance of a relationship system and generating anxiety. Examples of such events are marriage or even anticipated marriage, births of children and all that entails, retirement, and the increased togetherness, deaths, divorces, and a long list of other events that are fairly well known.

People and families toward the lower end of the scale of differentiation generate enough chronic anxiety on their own that some types of chronic symptoms are almost always in evidence. The family can even become so oriented around symptoms and their chronic treatment that the orientation can provide an interesting kind of structure and stability for the family. Lower-scale families are extremely vulnerable to any additional events that load any more anxiety on the system. Additional increments of chronic anxiety can trigger deterioration of previously stable chronic symptoms or perhaps trigger the appearance of yet another new problem.

A family with a somewhat higher level of differentiation than the one just described may be able to maintain balance in the emotional system without chronic symptoms. The limited reserve of such a family, however, becomes evident when a series of events such as the husband starting a rigorous night-school schedule in addition to his job, the birth of their first child, and a move into a new home with accompanying financial and time strains sets off an escalating cycle of anxiety that eventually culminates in a serious symptom. The appearance of the symptom can further escalate anxiety. It is important to keep in mind that it is not the events but people's reactions to the events and their reactions to each other's reactions that is the problem. These emotional chain reactions take on a life of their own. A better differentiated family may also experience some buildup of anxiety in reaction to such events, but such a family's reserves and ability to adapt prevents the process from going out of control. But if enough things happen over a short enough period of time, the balance of an even fairly well differentiated system can be disturbed to the point of symptoms. When the anxiety subsides, equilibrium is restored and the symptoms disappear.

Emotional Cutoff

This concept in systems theory describes the way one generation cuts off emotional contact with the previous generation in order to avoid potential relationship problems.

The theory underlying the concept of cutoff is based on the observation that the excessive emotionality and lack of differentiation of the parents, to varying degrees, permeates their relationship with their children. As described earlier, typically, the parents' relationship with one of their children is characterized by more emotional reactivity and anxiety than with the other children. This emotional overinvolvement between the parents and most involved child can manifest itself as an intense closeness and dependency or as intense conflict and a pseudo-independence on the part of the child. Although all of the children are caught up to some degree in the undifferentiation of the parents and are shaped by it, the most involved child, being most caught up in it, will grow up with a level of differentiation that is less than his siblings. The parents, based on their undifferentiated relationship with the child, are transmitting their undifferentiation to him. They transmit their undifferentiation to the other children too, only less so. The end result is often parents raising one child who is less differentiated than they are, children similar in differentiation and perhaps one or more children a little better differentiated than the parents, the latter being the one or ones most *left out* of the family emotional problem. The greater the undifferentiation of the parents, the greater the amount that is potentially transmitted to the children so that the *average* level of differentiation of children from reasonably well differentiated parents is going to be higher than the average level of children from poorly differentiated parents.

Based on this undifferentiation in the parent-child relationships, when children grow up and leave home, they leave with a certain degree of *unresolved emotional attachment* to their families. The child most involved in the parental undifferentiation will have the greatest degree of unresolved attachment to them. Since the lack of differentiation in the relationship can foster anxiety and problems, this most involved child has the greatest tendency to cut off emotionally from the parents. This cutoff may be accomplished by physically moving a great distance from the parents, by rarely seeing them, or by staying in the vicinity of the parents and cutting off, using internal mechanisms such as withdrawal and limited communication. A good example of this is the schizophrenic-level person who alternates between denying his attachment to the parents and staying away and then going into a functional collapse and coming home and accepting a dependency on the parents. The cutoff exists based on the emotionality in *both* the parents and the child and can be initiated and promoted by either one. The parents pull back from the child to protect themselves from the drain and anxiety of continued overinvolvement. In contrast, the child with the most differentiated relationship with the parents can remain in comfortable emotional contact with them. It follows that poorly differentiated families are much more likely to be loaded with emotional cutoffs than better differentiated families.

Based on clinical observation, it is clear that while emotional cutoff can reduce the potential for day-to-day problems with the extended family, the cutoff also eliminates the positive aspects of viable emotional contact with the extended family. The sense of being connected, "rooted," or supported is impaired by the cutoff. These relatively isolated family units can be observed to be more vulnerable to escalating cycles of anxiety. So, in addition to basic levels of differentiation and the events that can generate anxiety, the degree of emotional cutoff is important to consider in understanding the family's ability to adapt to illness. A poorly differentiated family subject to a series of unfavorable events may escape without serious symptoms based on its viable emotional contact with the extended family. Non-family relationship systems can substitute for family to a certain extent, but non-family systems are usually not as effective.

Anxiety-Binding Mechanisms

The level of differentiation, amount of chronic anxiety, and degree of emotional cutoff are all factors that influence the vulnerability of a family system to symptom development. The "selection" of the particular person in the family who develops the symptom depends on which mechanisms the nuclear family uses to absorb or bind its anxiety. These mechanisms, as mentioned earlier, have the primary function of preserving the equlibrium of the system as a whole.

A family system uses four distinct anxiety-binding mechanisms, with some families using predominantly one or two of the mechanisms and others shifting around among all four. The mechanisms are emotional distance, emotional conflict, the compromised spouse, and overinvolvement with children.

(1) *Emotional distance*. This mechanism is similar to what was described under emotional cutoff, only here it refers to spouses cutting off from each other. This distance may range from avoidance of talking about emotionally charged subjects to not speaking to each other or even looking at each other for extended periods. The distance reduces the anxiety of too much closeness, and in that sense the anxiety is "bound" by the distance. The anxiety, in other words, is not evident in looking at people, but is evi-

dent in the distance between them. Again, this distance can be accomplished by physical avoidance or by the use of internal distancing mechanisms; for example, isolating oneself through drinking. The lack of differentiation in all of us is great enough that emotional distance, to some degree, is a component of all emotionally significant relationships. This is not to imply that being "totally honest" is the way relationships should be conducted. There is obviously a place for privacy in a relationship that is unrelated to people reactively distancing from each other.

(2) *Emotional conflict*. This mechanism permits each spouse's anxiety to be externalized onto the marital relationship. When taken toward the extreme, the result is a husband and wife who are functioning well individually and who have no clinical symptoms, but who are experiencing severe marital discord. This mechanism allows the anxiety of each partner to be bound in their blaming of each other and preoccupation with each other's alleged deficiencies. It is a battle over who is going to give in to whom, with each doggedly holding their ground. Presumably, the sense that each has about being "right" frees them from considerable internal turmoil about themselves.

(3) *Compromised spouse*. This mechanism is one in which relationship harmony is preserved by virtue of one spouse giving in or compromising to appease the other. While emotional distance and emotional conflict may play a role, this mechanism appears to be the most important one involved in cancer and the other dysfunctions that occur in a spouse. While both spouses are constantly adapting to and giving in to each other to preserve harmony, the one who chronically gives in the most is the one most vulnerable to symptom development. These marriages, which place a premium on peace and agreement, frequently demonstrate a reciprocity in functioning in which one spouse becomes an overfunctioner and the other an underfunctioner. This pattern can be reasonably comfortable for both spouses when the stress on the marriage is not very great and the pattern does not operate to an extreme. But with increasing stress and anxiety, the patterns become exaggerated and one spouse can begin to feel compromised. This most compromised spouse is the one making the most internal adjustments within the self to preserve harmony in the relationship. The most compromised one can be the chronic overfunctioner who becomes overloaded with all he is feeling responsible for and trying to manage, or it can be the chronic underfunctioner who gradually loses his sense of control over his life. These positions will be described in more detail in a later section on the cancer position.

(4) *Overinvolvement with children*. This final mechanism for binding system anxiety is one in which the anxieties and lack of differentiation of the parents are focused on one or more of the children. This mechanism can leave the individual functioning of the parents unimpaired and preserve

harmony in the marriage, but at the expense of the children's functioning. One or more children become absorbers of the parental problems and often grow up with less differentiation than the parents. At periods of high family anxiety, it is these overinvolved children who are most vulnerable to physical, emotional, or social dysfunctions.

These four anxiety binding mechanisms that have just been described are not to be regarded as "good" or "bad." They are simply ways in which anxiety and emotional reactivity can be shunted around and encapsulated in a family system. Each family member participates in this shunting process, each seemingly being motivated by a wish to relieve his or her own anxiety. While these patterns of interacting can lead to one person winding up in an anxiety-ridden, severely compromised position, the steps that led to that position were a series of mini-compromises designed to relieve the anxiety of the moment. People do not "need" to be in these positions. It is, rather, a mindless process that is dictated by anxiety. The mechanisms serve a function in the system in that they help preserve system equilibrium, albeit at the expense of some of its parts. It is their exaggerated use that can change the functional patterns into dysfunctional ones. If the dysfunction becomes extreme, it can begin to pull the whole system down with it.

Adequate family assessment, then, depends on consideration of all four of these above mentioned areas, namely, differentiation, level of chronic anxiety, degree of emotional cutoff, and the anxiety binding mechanisms. The lower the level of differentiation of a nuclear family system and the greater degree of its cutoff from the extended system, the more chronic anxiety it generates. In this instance, the anxiety binding mechanisms will be so active that system equilibrium will exist only with the presence of chronic symptoms. In a moderately well differentiated system, the situation with the majority of families, the anxiety binding mechanisms, though chronically active, are toned down enough that under most circumstances they do not lead to symptom development. It is only when additional anxiety builds in the system, based on real or anticipated life events or other factors, that the balance of emotional forces is sufficiently disturbed for symptoms to develop. When the anxiety is lowered, the symptoms subside.

Let us now back up from looking at some of the specific factors involved in symptom development and look more broadly at the ways in which the balance of a relationship system can be disturbed.

System balance

Since symptoms reflect a disturbance in the balance of an emotional system, an appropriate question to ask when a symptom appears is, "In what way has the balance of this system been disturbed?" As has been mentioned several times, a build-up of chronic anxiety is the principal disturbing force to the balance of emotional systems, but systems usually have a way of adapting to, binding, or spreading anxiety so that, for the majority of families, serious symptoms are the exception and not the rule.

One way a family has to cope with anxiety is that when pressure builds in the system, the family relationship network becomes more active, permitting emotional run-off from the hot spots in the system. Symptoms can develop when there is not enough relationship network available to diffuse the anxiety, and the system pressure gets contained primarily within one person or one relationship. For example, if the balance of emotional forces in a marriage is significantly disturbed by the birth of a child, viable emotional contact with the extended system can cushion this disturbance, preventing major disruptions.

The birth of a child is one way in which the balance of a relationship can be disturbed. Another example of such a disturbance is what sometimes happens when two people who had a comfortable relationship while living together get married. The marriage can trigger an escalating cycle of anxiety that can eventually disrupt the relationship. Prior to marriage, one or both had enough sense of an "out" to provide the distance needed to keep the anxiety of too much togetherness under control. The marriage of these two poorly differentiated people becomes a kind of emotional cage, and suddenly one or both feel trapped and panicked. The anxiety generated by this kind of emotional dilemma could manifest itself in a variety of ways, for example, as a physical symptom or in intense relationship conflict. If a child is born into such a relationship, its presence could relieve the anxiety in the marriage as the wife satisfies her needs for emotional closeness through overinvolvement with the child, and the husband achieves a comfortable distance from what he perceives as his wife's excessive neediness and intensity.

Most of the time the situations are more complex than these simple examples just given. The following is an example of a more complicated disturbance in the balance of a relationship system that contributed to the development of a cancer. Mr. and Mrs. C had been married for nearly twenty years. Their marriage was reasonably harmonious, but much of this harmony was preserved by the considerable amount of emotional distance between them. Mr. C was heavily invested in his work, and Mrs. C had moderate overinvolvement with her teenage children. Mrs. C also retained very close ties to her father, her "emotional sounding-board," calling him in reference to many of the personal issues in her life. Mrs. C's mother and older brother were both living too, but the brother had fairly severe emotional problems, and Mrs. C's mother often functioned in dependent and helpless ways. Mrs. C felt extremely vulnerable to getting overinvolved in her mother's problems and so distanced from her. Mrs. C's father was an overfunctioner, taking charge of most problems that developed with his wife and son.

After a number of years of relative family stability, a series of events in Mrs. C's extended system led to a marked build-up of tensions. Mrs. C's father, trying to manage all of it, suddenly dropped dead of a heart attack. In the aftermath of her father's death, anxiety in her extended family further escalated. Mrs. C began to feel overwhelmed by the prospect of now being the only one to deal with her mother and brother. Several months later, Mrs. C's best friend died, the other person besides her father from whom Mrs. C gained considerable emotional support. Mrs. C's husband tried to be more a part of things after the deaths, but too much involvement between the two of them could leave Mrs. C feeling "taken over" by him. Mrs. C pulled back even more from her husband and finally gave in to overtures for an affair. She had known the man five years and knew he had been interested in her, but now she felt a need for such a relationship, a need not felt previously. But the anxiety and sense of pressure continued to escalate within her and in the rest of her nuclear and extended systems. One year after her father died, her breast cancer was diagnosed.

The important point to be made here is that the emotional elements triggering Mrs. C's cancer could not be attributed just to her reaction to her father's death. The key elements are more related to anxiety in the total system and the shift in the balance of emotional forces. This shift left her in a *position of functioning* in the family that she had not been in prior to her father's death, namely, a position of responsibility for the emotional well-being of her mother and brother. This position for Mrs. C was, at least at that point in time, clearly a source of anxiety equal to, if not greater than, the anxiety generated by the loss of her father.

Let us now leave the broad view of the family system and look at the specifics of the position of functioning in a family that can be conducive to the development of a serious dysfunction like cancer.

The Cancer Position

The concept of a cancer personality, although certainly having some validity, is based in individual theories of human functioning. The concept of a cancer position is based in a systems theory of human functioning. In a family system, the functioning of each person is influenced and regulated by the functioning of every other person. The idea that one person's behavior "causes" another's is dropped, based on the recognition of the reciprocity in functioning of all family members. It is clear from the observation of family systems, particularly during periods of high anxiety, that certain positions of functioning in the system are conducive to dysfunction in the people who occupy those positions. These cancer "inducing" positions will now be described in some detail.

As mentioned earlier, the person who is vulnerable to developing a cancer, in the majority of instances, has experienced an increased level of chronic anxiety for a period of months to a year or more prior to the diagnosis. This is anxiety that, seemingly lacking other outlets, creates a significant disturbance in the person's physiological equilibrium. The person going through this experience frequently describes it as a struggle against things that are not easily defined or easily changed. They often have a sense of not making progress with their problems and that there is no relief in sight. A possible parallel to this situation in laboratory animals is doing things to an animal that stress it, and at the same time not allowing the animal any way out, any control over the situation. The limited options placed on people by an emotional system, based on recent events as well as multigenerational factors, can be every bit as confining as the restraints placed on a stressed experimental animal.

In my insatiable need to categorize my observations, I have defined two kinds of positions conducive to a cancer. There is much overlap between the two categories, and I do not consider them unique to cancer. The first category is situations where the person has experienced a disturbance in their most emotionally significant relationship system or systems, leaving them anxious and emotionally disconnected or isolated. The most obvious examples of this one are following the death of a spouse or following a divorce. In a divorce, the one who struggled to prevent it and who felt most undermined by it usually appears to be the more vulnerable partner. Most of the time, no one event would appear to be sufficient to trigger a serious dysfunction. It frequently appears to be an accumulation of factors, some spanning generations, some adding up over a lifetime, and some of recent origin. The death of a spouse can be the final event. But regardless of the contributing factors, emotional isolation accompanied by higher than average levels of chronic anxiety are the important variables.

Emotional disconnectedness can occur without deaths, divorce, or actual physical separation, but can occur related to sustained build-ups of anxiety in close relationships. For example, sustained build-ups of anxiety in a previously harmonious marital relationship can lead to people repelling each other, leaving one feeling isolated and anxious. People can feel more lonely living together than if they were physically separated. Characteristically in these kind of situations, one is focusing or venting their anxiety on the other and the other feels at the mercy of it. The emotional atmosphere may be overtly harmonious, with one spouse constantly focused on the physical and emotional well-being of the other. In turn, the other spouse may become increasingly preoccupied with this within themselves and become isolated in the process. In contrast, the emotional atmosphere may be overtly conflictual, with one spouse's sureness that he is right prevailing over the other's attempt to explain and defend himself or herself. These struggles can be as intense as the battles for dominance in nonhuman animal hierarchies. It is the loser, the compromised one, the one who has given in who is vulnerable to withdrawal and dysfunction. Again, it is well to keep in mind that this is an anxiety driven process that both partners are at the mercy of and that goes well beyond what either wants or needs. If the anxiety cycle can be broken, both will be relieved.

The second category of cancer position, keeping in mind the overlap between these categories, is the person who experiences getting progressively overloaded, overwhelmed, and who is feeling locked in with no outlet. There is a feeling of being alone coupled with a strong sense of responsibility for a situation they are unable to influence very much. A striving, struggling aspect in their approach to things seems especially important in the escalation to a serious symptom like cancer. There is frequently an exaggerated sense of responsibility for the emotional well-being of others, a constant need to measure up, to make things "right," to please, be approved of and accepted. These qualities make the person more prone to accepting the system's anxiety and to feel they have to make some adjustment within themselves and in their life to appease others. Typically, they are asking far more of themselves than anyone could realistically expect of them. All of the other members of the family are caught up in this process, for example, by allowing their own emotional functioning to get too dependent on the one who is feeling such an inordinate sense of responsibility for their emotional well-being. One breast cancer patient said, "I feel like I have been responding to the needs of my flock and that there is no me anymore." Obviously, this statement says something about the way she functions, but it also says something about the way those around her have functioned. People can be amazingly oblivious to the load one person in a system is trying to carry.

As mentioned, these qualities and positions that have just been described are not unique to cancer. In fact, they are perfectly compatible with good health. It is a question of the intensity of this process coupled with the presence of essential biological variables that is important in converting a state of health into a state of disease. That intensity is related to all of the previously outlined emotional variables, namely, level of differentiation, level of chronic anxiety based on reactions to recent life events, degree of emotional cutoff, and the mechanisms for binding anxiety.

Cancer vs. other dysfunctions

Why does a person develop a cancer as opposed to some other type of problem? What are the factors that influence symptom selection? These are fascinating but difficult questions to answer. Ultimately what will be needed to answer such questions is a theory that can integrate a vast array of variables; variables that include the biochemical, immunologic, emotional, genetic, etc. But for now, there are a few observations about these questions that appear reasonably accurate. Let us first look at family emotional process in the various types of dysfunction and then at the influence of the way anxiety is managed as a factor in symptom selection.

The patterns of family emotional process that contribute to the development of physical illness, emotional illness, and social dysfunction appear to be *basically* the same with each type of problem. Anxiety builds in the system and results in a disturbance in the balance of the system's emotional forces. The previously described anxiety binding mechanisms are activated to deal with the disturbance, and if the process is intense enough and protracted, certain people get into positions conducive to some type of dysfunction. The position of emotional isolation, for example, coupled with high anxiety can underlie the development of psychotic reaction, serious alcoholism, clinical depression, homosexual acting out, a variety of physical illnesses, and even criminal behavior.

But while the basic patterns of family process appear to be identical in all the various dysfunctions, there are some differences that can be identified between the individuals and families with different types of problems. These differences reflect the different ways people manage and manifest their anxiety. How individuals bind or manage their anxiety is an important influence on the type of symptom that develops. To the extent that anxiety is bound in one type of symptom, it can protect the person from other types of symptoms. To examine this binding process in a little more detail, let us look at a clinical example. Suppose, over a period of a few months, a family has experienced a series of unfavorable events that have led to considerable build-up of anxiety in the system. Based on the family patterns, the wife functions as an absorber of the system's anxiety. She becomes increasingly anxious, feeling overwhelmed and overloaded. The emotional cutoff from her extended family is such that it does not provide an emotional outlet. At this point, the compromised position she is in could contribute to a variety of outcomes. She might have an affair. The affair could relieve her anxiety and also stabilize the family system. An alternative path would be for her to begin to drink and develop an increasing problem with alcoholism. If the family gets focused on her drinking as the "cause" of the problem, it can exaggerate her symptoms. Still another possible outcome of this compromised position would be the development of a physical illness. A more unusual outcome may be finding herself in a department store shoplifting an item she does not need.

Describing the various ways in which anxiety can be manifested in symptoms still does not shed any light on the selection of a particular symptom. The particular selection of a way to deal with anxiety often seems to be based on many factors that are not easily defined. It seems clear that certain families tend to focus their anxiety on and overreact to specific kinds of problems, for example, physical illness. At times the anxiety at a specific symptom appears to play a role in creating the symptom. At other times, this is not so clear, and it is like the chicken and egg debate. Regardless of which comes first, once a symptom and family anxiety about the symptom are present, they can mutually feed on and aggravate each other, creating a vicious cycle. Studying multigenerational emotional process can also, at times, offer some understanding of the type of problems that emerge. One family, for example, may manifest three or four generations of acting-out behavior, culminating in the most recent generation with serious criminal behavior. At times, the transmission of these problems appears clearly based on patterns of interaction between people. At other times, the transmission seems "genetic." An example of this would be families with a lot of the same type of heart disease. At other times, the border between "environmental" and "genetic" seems blurred.

In any event, this is a complex area and one of the most exciting areas for further research. The next section is on families with a high incidence of cancer or other physical diseases and offers some speculations about the interplay of "genetic" and emotional process.

Cancer and Multigenerational Process

There are a spectrum of families in which cancer occurs where thinking of cancer on a multigenerational level becomes inescapable. These are the families in which multiple cases of cancer have occurred over the course of three or four generations. Aldred Scott Warthin, a pathologist at the University of Michigan, published one of the earliest reports about such families back in 1913 (Warthin, 1913). Even after the nearly seventy years since Warthin's report, our knowledge about high incidence cancer families is still quite limited. However, in recent years there has been considerable effort devoted to defining the possible genetic mechanisms underlying the high incidence of cancer in these families (Lynch, 1976).

Warthin's early observations about cancer families remain fascinating and suggest some sort of relationship of the phenomena observed in such families to multigenerational emotional process. After establishing that families with a high incidence of cancer did, in fact, exist, Warthin made several interesting observations about them. In addition to cancer susceptibility, the families had a marked susceptibility to tuberculosis, a disease quite prevalent at that time. There was also evidence of a reduced fertility rate in the family. Particularly interesting was the fact that *in families showing the occurrence of carcinoma in several generations, there was a decided tendency for the neoplasm to develop at an earlier age in the members of the youngest generations. In those cases of early age of onset, the neoplasm often showed an increased malignancy.* Warthin includes many examples of three and four-generation segments of family that finally extinct, with the cancers coming earlier in each generation. The fact that certain lines of family can extinct is consistent with the intensification of emotional process across the generations. My own studies of several high-incidence cancer families revealed them to be segments of family that were significantly cut off from the larger extended system. The level of chronic anxiety in such families was quite high and strongly focused on physical health. It seemed to be a kind of snowballing effect in which, as the families experienced more and more cancer, escalating anxiety about what else might happen seemed to accelerate the process.

The patterns that can be observed in high-incidence cancer families can also be observed in families that have a high incidence of some other disease. A nearly forty-year-old report about families with a high incidence of diabetes contains one of the most fascinating ways of conceptualizing disease that I have found anywhere in the medical literature (Woodyatt and Spetz, 1942):

> This gives us the picture of diabetes appearing in a family (that has not exhibited it before so far as we knew) and running a definable clinical course but in the family as distinguished from the individual case. . . . The whole course can be run in two generations, but it is more commonly completed in three or four and rarely in more. That is to say, we rarely find families with a history of diabetes in more than four generations.
>
> In this picture, those patients that develop the disease in later life appear as cases of first or second generation. They are offshoots of a vine that has been affected for only a limited time—expressions of a young family of diabetes. On the other hand, juvenile diabetic patients appear as cases of following generations. In families that show rapid (progression), they can be representatives of second generations, but average rates are more often of a third or fourth generation. They are shoots from a vine that has been diseased for a long time—expressions of an old family diabetes. Hence, the differences in the average course of diabetes in older and younger subjects.

In recent years, diabetes is talked about as several distinct clinical entities, and the above quote is frequently dismissed based on the lack of scientific knowledge of that time. But this is a period in medical research in which, as advances in technology permit us to know more about the details of disease mechanisms, we are constantly breaking them down into subcategories. Perhaps in this fascination with differences, we are losing sight of the importance of the similarities between the various clinical entities and the broader common patterns.

The research of Warthin and Woodyatt and Spetz stimulated me to comb the medical literature in search of reports about families that had a high incidence of other diseases. It appears that every disease can cluster in a family. *When this occurs, the families demonstrate the same patterns that were described by Warthin for cancer and Woodyatt and Spetz for diabetes.* This observation led me to think in terms of some sort of background process common to all diseases, the diseases then being thought of as *symptoms* of this process. I believe that it is possible that these common patterns exist because we are dealing with some sort of *unidisease* (Kerr, 1980a). My speculation is that the unidisease concept is tied to the balance of physiological relationships.

Now let us leave this somewhat abstract theoretical view and take systems ideas back to the clinical world. It is hoped that the clinical case can help integrate some of the theoretical ideas presented thus far.

Clinical Example

Mrs. B was a thirty-three-year-old married mother of two children when she underwent a mastectomy in January 1977 for an infiltrating ductal carcinoma of the breast. Three axillary lymph nodes were positive for cancer.

Mrs. B dates her problems back eighteen months prior to surgery to the summer of 1975. At that time she experienced what she felt to be a fairly abrupt development of serious tensions in her marriage of then thirteen years. She described her husband as becoming extremely critical and rejecting of her. After a few months of this tension, Mr. B announced that he had been involved in an affair and that he did not know if he wanted to stay together or not. The next year was tumultous. Although he apparently stopped the affair, the marital tension escalated. Mr. B alternated between being depressed and withdrawn or markedly critical of his wife, all the while talking about the possibility of separation. Mrs. B was panicked by the thought of divorce and fought to have them stay together. She was feeling increasingly "lonesome and vulnerable," a feeling she had never had before in the marriage. "His aloofness and criticism left me feeling I had no shoulder to lean on." In the middle of 1976, Mrs. B had a "desperation" affair that was short lived. She felt so guilty that she told her husband about it and he reacted "wildly." New threats of separation sent her to a lawyer for consultation and then briefly to a psychiatrist.

Toward the end of 1976, Mrs. B discovered the breast lump. The mastectomy was in January 1977, and the couple separated in March. Mrs. B joined the author's cancer research project a few weeks after the separation. She had also just embarked on what was to be a year-long course of chemotherapy.

Mr. and Mrs. B both grew up in Roanoke, Virginia, and began dating when both were in high school. They married in 1962 when Mrs. B had just graduated from high school and Mr. B was a junior at a nearby college. The couple moved to Washington in 1966 at Mr. B's urging. He apparently wanted to get away from both of their extended families, whom they both felt intruded a lot on their lives. Mr. B had also gotten into an affair about two years after they were married and wanted to make a "clean break" from all of his emotional entanglements. Mrs. B was not particularly eager to leave Roanoke, but agreed to go along with her husband's wishes. After arriving in Washington, Mr. B found a new teaching position, and Mrs. B continued work as a secretary.

The B's first child, a son, was born in February 1968. Their second child, also a son, arrived in July 1969. Mrs. B had miscarriages in 1970 and 1972 and after that, by choice, there were no more pregnancies. The period from 1966 to 1973 was a reasonably comfortable one for them. Mrs. B did not work for about two years while the babies came, but eventually did return to work in September 1969. But 1974 was a turning point in terms of a marked increase in family anxiety. Early in 1974, the older son, then six years old, began having frequent epileptic seizures. It was eventually diagnosed as petit mal epilepsy, and it took nearly a year of experimenting with medications to bring it under good control. Mrs. B became heavily preoccupied with her son's health. The older son was the one with whom Mrs. B was most emotionally overinvolved, even before the epilepsy. He was an intense worrier and, like his father, tended to down-play his abilities and express many fears about being able to succeed. Mrs. B worried endlessly about ways to bolster his confidence, diverting much of the emotional energy she used to devote to her husband and his problems to her son. In the spring of 1975, the B's bought their first house, something they could not easily afford. Mr. B later told his wife that he had mixed feelings about the house, wondering if he could manage the responsibility. It was that summer of 1975 that Mr. B got involved in the affair and told his wife about it a few months later.

Throughout the marriage Mrs. B had been an overfunctioner and major decision maker in the family, but at the same time she felt dependent on and felt in need of a lot of support from her husband. That need was particularly accentuated during this high anxiety period.

> I had always been the one to take care of everything, the bills, social arrangements, even my husband's clothes. It seemed to me that his unsureness created a void I had to fill. I would lead the way and he followed, but then he would turn around and blame me for taking over, calling me stubborn and wanting my way. It seemed that it was easier for me to make decisions than it was for him, but I felt I couldn't do it without his acceptance and support. When he began withdrawing from me and criticizing, my anxiety soared. He said if he allowed it, I would get too dependent and he seemed to run from that like the plague. But I've always needed to talk things out, gaining a release from that. When he withdrew and pushed me away, I had nobody.

Mrs. B was the only child of parents whose families had been in the Roanoke area for at least three generations. Her parents separated and eventually divorced in 1967, a fact that Mrs. B related to her own marriage, leaving the parents more to themselves. She described her mother as a person with whom she had been tremendously emotionally involved, almost as her "side-kick." At the same time she found her mother as a person "hard-to-know" and difficult to talk to, particularly about problems, without being "preached" at. "My mother maintains an aloof, strong image of herself and always expected that of me," according to Mrs. B. Interestingly, Mrs. B's father, a preacher by profession, was generally easier for Mrs. B to talk to, but she had grown quite distant from him since moving to Washington and since her father remarried. Another interesting fact about Mrs. B's extended family was that her maternal grandmother and two maternal great aunts were diagnosed late in their lives as having breast cancer. Only one, a great aunt, had died of the cancer.

Mr. B was the younger of two brothers born also to a family that had been in the Roanoke area for several generations. Both of his parents and brother lived in Roanoke, but Mr. B began trying to get away from what he perceived as his family's "dominating influence" when he was a teenager and had had very little contact with his family in recent years.

Mrs. B began psychotherapy sessions as part of the author's cancer research project in March 1977. At that time she was two months post surgery, three weeks post marital separation, and one week into chemotherapy! Her reactions to all these events were interesting. She had a fatalistic attitude about the cancer, believing it was something beyond her control and not something she was going to struggle over. She had felt depressed, but reasonably calm, calmer in some ways than she had been since 1974. I was convinced when she said, "I just don't dwell on the cancer. It doesn't bother me that much. I am more concerned about my loneliness and my marriage. I wonder if I can be acceptable to someone else."

The next several months were very interesting for Mrs. B. She drew emotional support from the psychotherapy sessions, but more importantly she responded to a suggestion about communicating her fears and anxieties about her situation to her parents by doing just that. She even made several trips back to Roanoke to see her family. The contact with her father proved extremely helpful toward her regaining a feeling of well-being and a sense of not being alone. Efforts with her mother were more difficult, but she saw the sense in gradually trying to work on that relationship. Part of the effort was to recognize her mother's preaching as evidence of her mother's anxiety and for Mrs. B not to be so reactive to it. Mrs. B also recontacted some of her aunts and uncles, most of whom she had not seen since she left Roanoke in 1966. Within a few months her depression had lifted, and her contacts with her husband were becoming quite relaxed. He never wanted to come with her to the therapy sessions, but did respond very positively to the change in his wife. While living on his own, Mr. B had begun to assume a lot more responsibility for himself. Mrs. B continued psychotherapy for about five months, terminating when the couple got back together. She completed the course of chemotherapy uneventfully and has remained in good health, now four years post surgery.

Impression

The emotional system of this nuclear family unit appeared to be in reasonable balance until 1974, when the older son's illness developed. One could ask what emotional factors may have influenced the appearance of the boy's symptoms at that particular time, but nothing emerged to be very tangible on that subject. The build-up of anxiety around that illness coupled with the events that followed all served to further disturb the balance of the system in a chain-reaction fashion. These events, such as the husband's affair, reflected the anxiety as well as serving to generate more of it. It was an escalating cycle of anxiety for which no one can really be blamed.

Mrs. B was clearly the one most emotionally compromised by the situation. She was struggling to preserve a marital relationship that she felt slipping away from her and, at the same time, as her husband withdrew and functioned less effectively, she felt increasingly overloaded and emotionally isolated.

The emotional cutoff that each partner had from family of origin was another important factor in the whole process. Mrs. B had no other relationship to turn to as the marital problem increased.

It is interesting that the cancer diagnosis served as a catalyst for doing something about the situation. The marital separation brought a relief of the tensions to a certain extent and that, coupled with Mrs. B's efforts with her extended family, did much to reduce anxiety. The overall reduction of anxiety made possible a reopening of relaxed communication between the B's and their eventual getting back together. This emotional system had enough flexibility in it to recover, and that appeared to favor a good prognosis for Mrs. B's cancer.

Anxiety and the Progression of Cancer

It is well known that even the most experienced clinicians and pathologists have difficulty predicting the clinical course of many cancers. Tumors of the same cell type and stage at time of diagnosis may go on to behave in amazingly different ways. At times, the cancer may completely disappear. The patient who was supposed to be dead in six months is alive and well ten years later without a trace of cancer. Other patients have been known to have cancers that neither grow nor shrink over the span of many years. Still other patients, obviously, experience progression of the cancer causing their eventual death. The variables that influence these different outcomes are not very well understood. Are these variables properties of the cancer itself, properties of the host in which it is growing, or properties of both cancer and host? Answers to these questions are for the future, but, for now, we can form impressions about what may influence this process. As cancer research continues, there will be clarification, no doubt, of the specific biological variables that influence outcome. But what I will focus on here are the emotional variables that seem to influence a patient's survival from cancer.

Some people who develop cancer are more differentiated than others. Some situations in which a cancer occurs have more flexibility in them than others. For some patients and families, the appearance of a cancer comes as part of an intense but rather acute upheaval. The problem situation has developed fairly rapidly and there is much potential for solution to the emotional dilemmas that exist in it. For other patients, the cancer appears at the end of an extended emotional process and the situation is much more fixed, with very limited potential for resolution. The inflexibility of the situation is a product of the characteristics of the relationship system and not just the characteristics of the patient. An example of an inflexible situation would be a family that had been getting progressively more fragmented for three or four generations with the cutoffs and emotional isolation between people and segments of family becoming too intense to ever be bridged. It is, in a sense, too late. The person with the cancer and the family are in too many emotional binds to have any real options.

The term flexibility in reference to a family system means the potential of the system for diffusing and reducing anxiety and reestablishing emotional equilibrium. As might be implied from all that has been said about the apparent role of anxiety in the emergence of a cancer, reduction of anxiety in the patient following the diagnosis seems to favor a better prognosis. There are so many factors that can influence the reduction of anxiety that I have had to focus on just a narrow range of them. The area on which I have chosen to focus is concerned primarily with family relationships. I have not explored, for example, the role of religious experiences in the reduction of anxiety. I have ignored the possible role of significant shifts in the way the patient manages and manifests anxiety; for example, the patient who develops a chronic psychosis following a cancer diagnosis. To what extent does binding his anxiety in a psychosis protect or stabilize his physical system's equlibrium?

To assess the role of some individual emotional factors and family relationship factors on the outcome of a cancer, I compared the group of patients who died relatively quickly of their cancer with the group of patients who survived. The impressions outlined here are based on that comparison.

The reduction of anxiety following a cancer diagnosis occurred in several different categories of circumstances. The first category was when a change occurred in the situation in which the cancer patient was enmeshed.

An example of this was a patient who returned home to her family after a period of striving to be independent. She had done well on her own for a time, but after a series of unfavorable events, she began feeling increasingly isolated and anxious. After the Hodgkin's disease was diagnosed, she returned to her family and was able to accept comfortably a more dependent role and felt considerably relieved. She also got into a highly supportive psychotherapy relationship. This reestablishment of a relationship or set of relationships for a disconnected person seems, at least in some instances, to make a difference.

In contrast, as opposed to connecting with people, a patient who gets out of a situation that has been eroding his ability to function often does better. He may, for example, initiate a separation from his spouse or may move away from his family. He may also insist another person move out, such as a problem young adult. These efforts to get *physical* separation can permit an emotionally vulnerable person to gain better control over his overanxious responsiveness to others, thereby reducing his anxiety. He simply had been unable to accomplish this in the physical presence of the other, in the same house, or whatever. Another physical separation affecting prognosis may be the death of a spouse, for example, the case of a sixty-three-year-old woman who developed first an ulcer and then a bone cancer during the first year following her husband's retirement. Two months after her cancer diagnosis, the husband died of a sudden heart attack. Though deeply grieved by the death of her husband, the wife soon began functioning with an independence and sense of direction that she had not felt for many years. Her physical health improved dramatically in the year following his death. She coped far better with loneliness than she did with the anxiety of too much togetherness she experienced following her husband's retirement. These situational changes, obviously, were not things the therapist recommended to people. These are actions some patients take in response, apparently, to the stimulus of a cancer diagnosis.

A second category of patients who seemed able to reduce their anxiety following the diagnosis were those with the ability to not get too focused on the cancer, not get too preoccupied with it. This was different than denial of the cancer in that they seemed to "accept" it and its reality risks. They usually invested their energies elsewhere, such as into specific goals or tasks unrelated to their health. In short, they sort of took it in stride, coped well with the treatment, and got on with the business of life. Again, this is not something a therapist can tell people to do. This kind of adaptation seems built into some people and not others.

The third category of people were those who fell into the overwhelmed, overloaded category and who were able to regain some sense of control over their lives. Physical separations were often used to aid this process, but others could stay in the situation and manage to take less on themselves. Adjustments other family members made were obviously important in this change. Such people often had a deep confidence in their ability to regain their equilibrium and did not regard the cancer as life threatening. They just knew they would make it if they could do certain things about their lives.

At the other end of the spectrum was the group that died of their cancers. The anxiety and emotional reactivity in these situations was usually high enough that it makes it difficult to sort out emotional variables, but some patterns do emerge. The person who is floored by the cancer to the point of giving up seems to be more at risk. Also the person who struggles against his cancer, fighting it in a wheel-spinning way with no reduction of internal anxiety. They are panicked themselves and are often surrounded by panicked family members. Family anxiety can be so high that it is extremely difficult for the cancer patient to regain any kind of control. Another group that did poorly were those who seemed so disconnected that the situation did not permit reestablishment of an anxiety reducing relationship.

The role of undergoing the whole process of medical and surgical treatments cannot be underemphasized for its potential to both relieve and generate anxiety in the patient and his family. For many people it is a severely eroding psychological and physical assault that literally surrounds the patient.

What has been reported in this section is my best observations after hundreds and hundreds of hours of interviews with patients and their families. The observations are, at best, inadequate. The roles of cancer cell type, staging of the cancer at diagnosis, and other biological variables were all purposely set aside in an effort to sort through the emotional variables that appear to affect prognosis. It is a complex process and all of these variables must eventually be integrated to give a complete picture.

Therapy

Working with a large number of cancer patients and their families has had a major impact on my professional development. I would rate the importance of the experience second only to my efforts to understand and modify my functioning in my own family system. The experience with cancer families challenged me to think on a theoretical level not previously attained and it also significantly modified my overall approach to psychotherapy.

Perhaps it is important that I began my work with cancer patients not to do therapy, but to do research. My goal was simply to attempt to understand the emotional process in cancer families, and I worried little about changing or fixing anything. The patients and families who entered the study quickly responded as thoughtful, interesting people whom I regarded as a tremendously valuable resource. Although no one patient or family could provide the unrealistically hoped for "answers," all of them stimulated my thinking and helped me become more fascinated by the cancer puzzle. Gradually, I realized that with this research-oriented approach to the families, I was learning more about the emotional process in cancer families and they, in turn, were learning more about themselves than the families I was seeing in my private psychotherapy practice. The research interviews were more relaxed, contained more humor, even in face of serious problems, and were more interesting for all concerned. *Perhaps more importantly, the research interviews were more "therapeutic" than the sessions in which I was trying to be therapeutic.* The contrasting parallel experiences of research and private therapy helped me realize how much pressure I could put on myself in a regular session to "fix" the problem, pressure that inclined me to impose my preconceived notions on the family, believing that is what they needed. I eventually came to believe that being comfortable with one's ignorance coupled with a desire to gain knowledge about human problems were two of the most important ingredients for doing effective psychotherapy. I only wish I could maintain this orientation in sessions more than I do.

The emotional process surrounding cancer is generally quite intense. I have watched many therapists get unproductively entangled in it. Some enter the emotional arena of a family with a cancer acting as if they know what is best for the family, while others enter that arena feeling sorry for people and get hopelessly overinvolved. In either case, either the family or the therapist will eventually do something to terminate the therapy. I believe that cancer patients and their families respond well to a therapist who is not all tangled up within him or herself with how he or she is supposed to be *helping* the family; a therapist is most helpful who can listen fairly calmly to what is in people's thinking and not keep pushing the focus back on what people are feeling. The emotional charge in the majority of families with a cancer is great enough that if the therapist pushes to "get the feelings out," it will impair the family's ability to cope with their problems. This toned down approach does not mean denial is being encouraged or issues are being avoided; it simply means creating a relaxed, sometimes even humorous atmosphere in which these issues can come up naturally and with the emotion under adequate control. If the therapist can foster this, the family is deeply appreciative. Most failures in therapy with cancer patients and families are the product of the therapist not recognizing and adequately diffusing the emotional intensity of the sessions. At the beginning of my research, really for the purpose of keeping the families coming and also for attracting more referrals, I set a goal of having the patient and family be more relaxed at the end of a session than they were at the outset. When it came time to end the interviews, nobody wanted to stop. As the session evolved, the families became increasingly objective and volunteered more and more of their innermost thoughts and feelings. *The most constructive expression of and talk about feelings came from not getting particularly focused on the feelings.* People dealing with cancer can be more thoughtful about life than most of us. They are the experts on the problem, not the therapists. The bulk of what they need from others is comfortable relationships and a tolerance of their anxieties about a set of very difficult realities. The family smells pity in a minute and is allergic to it. Pity is a problem in the one who pities.

When evaluating the cancer patient and family at the beginning and during the course of therapy, there are three general areas that are important to keep in mind. The ongoing assessment of these areas guides the course of the therapy. The first area is the level of existing anxiety in the patient and his or her important relationship systems. The patient's family and the medical treatment staff are usually the most important systems. The second area is assessment of the patterns of emotional process in the immediate family, the nuclear family. The third area is the relationship of the patient and his or her nuclear family to the larger extended family system.

One of the main obstacles to a patient dealing reasonably well with their own anxiety is the anxiety of the important people involved with the patient. Helping the patient's spouse deal with their own reactiveness and patterns of functioning can often be the most critical element in the therapy being effective. One of the more interesting examples of this was the case of a sixty-three-year-old man with cancer of the rectum. The patient and his wife had raised four children, all of whom were now married and out of the home. He had been retired for about four years prior to the cancer diagnosis, a retirement that had seemingly generated much anxiety in the couple. They had been thrown together in a way that was new to them, and the four years had been loaded with tensions and problems. After the husband's surgery, which included a colostomy, things went from bad to worse. Much of the husband's extended family was dead, and he was long out of contact with the few remaining members. His wife had gradually become his relationship life-line, but in recent years she had been so emotionally reactive to him, he could no longer relate comfortably to her. The wife's extended family was small too, but she did have a sister who lived cross country. Most of the couple's children lived in the area, but when they got involved in the situation, they took sides with their mother and further polarized the situation.

The initial sessions with the couple began about two months after the surgery and were done seeing the couple together. The sessions were quite reactive and not very productive. The husband constantly fell into the position of trying to explain himself, defend himself to his wife, and she could not let go of the view that he was the one causing all the turmoil. The husband was having a hard time adjusting to the colostomy and dealing with an enormous sense of isolation. After a few sessions, both began to talk about needing some time away from each other, but neither could implement anything. Finally, they began talking about the wife going to spend a couple of weeks with her sister and asked my opinion about it. "Go!" was my response. She went. The first week his wife was gone was one of the most difficult of the husband's life. I saw him for a session at the end of that week. From the moment he hit the chair he started sobbing, deep sobbing, and said that was the way he had been all week. He had serious doubts about whether he was going to make it. He sensed that if he involved his kids at this point, it would only make matters worse, they being too upset themselves. We were at least thirty minutes into the session, and I had not said anything. What can you say in a situation like that? Finally, when the timing seemed right, I kidded him about something he had been talking about. He looked up at me, saw my smile, and burst out laughing. I started laughing, and we both laughed uproariously for fully three minutes. I am not even sure what either of us said during the rest of the session, but when he left he was composed and warmly took my hand. When his wife came back, I again arranged a session for the two of them together. She started the session by telling me her husband was a sick man, both emotionally and physically, and presented her evidence to support that view. I listened. After several minutes of this, the husband told her to stop talking, he had some things he wanted to say. She looked a bit startled by his remark, but started in again. "Shut up!" was his next remark, and she did. At that point he turned to me and said he wanted to thank me for what I had done for him last week. "You were able to let me be me and be comfortable with it. I knew you or nobody else had the answers, but I can't tell you how much your attitude helped. These have probably been the two most difficult weeks of my life, but I think I have begun to sort out what is my problem and what is my wife's problem. I know I can't change her, but I think I am now getting a hold on what to do about me." I am not sure that this man could have arrived at this point without the brief physical separation from his wife. He again thanked me and said he did not think they would need any further sessions. I heard from them about a year later and although things were not great, each was more involved with his or her own pursuits, and the situation was under control. His health was remarkably better.

An anxious doctor and treatment setting can also be a significant source of anxiety for the patient and his family. Some physicians, nurses, technicians, and others are absolutely superb at calmly dealing with people. Other professionals leave much to be desired. The primary doctor's role is probably the most critical as an influence on family anxiety. The physician's anxiety can dictate giving the patient more information than is useful, less information than useful, jumping around on medications, overtesting, not returning phone calls, and a host of other things. Anxious professionals frequently wind up feeling angry and frustrated with the patient or the patient's family, further increasing their sense of anxiety, isolation, and lack of support. Although unproven, I have no doubt that the physicians who can relate comfortably to their patients and families have fewer treatment complications and better responses to treatment. I think this is why so many of the so-called "unscientific" therapies can be effective. It is related to the atmosphere surrounding the patient and the patient's confidence and belief in what is being done. It is testimony to the anxiety reducing potential of comfortable relationships.

The importance of being aware of the patterns of emotional process in the patient's nuclear family has probably been adequately emphasized by the examples that have been given. To think toward a systems-based therapy is to constantly be thinking in terms of the relationship system, understanding the thoughts, feelings, and functioning of the patient in the context of his or her *position of functioning* in relationship to others in the family. The position any one person is in is a product of the way everyone in the family functions. That is not to say that these patterns are easily modified, but if the therapist can at least help the family conceptualize this relationship process, with each person focusing on improving their own functioning, some change is possible.

The use of the extended family in therapy has also been talked about in the examples. This is a technique for which there are no rules. Probably the most important thing to keep in mind is that emotional cutoff between the generations can be the product of marked emotional intensity, and when that is the case, the cutoffs are not easily bridged. The clinical example showed one of the positive uses of the extended system, the wife getting more involved with her father and aunts, but there are other instances where pushing people in that direction is contraindicated. The basic emotional reactivity is just too great for people to engage it, particularly during a period when they are trying to cope with a potentially life-threatening cancer. One example of this is a woman with breast cancer who said that if she involved her parents very much in the situation, she would wind up ministering to them and their problems. She felt that the cancer was all she could deal with and preferred to keep her involvement with friends and other lower-key relationships. The therapist agreed. Maybe later when things were calmer, she could move toward her parents. Judgments about these situations depend on the skill and experience of the therapist. For the therapist to begin to know what will be useful, he or she has to have resolved some of this with his or her own family (Bowen, 1978).

The role of this kind of therapy as an influence on the progress of a cancer is difficult to assess. Frequently my role has been one of providing some emotional support to the family and trying to help reduce the incidence of emotional problems surrounding the whole process. This is particularly true with families in which the anxiety level is quite high, the flexibility of the system is markedly impaired, and the spread of the cancer is fairly rapid. At the other extreme are situations with more flexibility, more manageable anxiety, and in which the patient will seemingly do well regardless of whether a therapist is involved or not. Then there is the gray area between these extremes in which psychotherapy has the potential for promoting a better outcome of the cancer. I think medicine will eventually attach more emphasis to the emotional aspects of cancer and consider it vital, in some instances, to a favorable treatment outcome. As these concepts are better integrated into medicine and begin to permeate thinking about disease, I believe the effectiveness of their application in therapy will be enhanced.

References

ANDERSON, J. R., ed. *Muir's Textbook of Pathology* (1976). Tenth Edition. Chicago: Year Book Medical Publishers.

BOWEN, M. (1966). "The Use of Family Theory in Clinical Practice." *Comprehensive Psychiatry* 7: 345–374.

BOWEN, M. (1978). "On the Differentiation of Self." In *Family Therapy in Clinical Practice* by M. Bowen, pp. 529–547. New York: Jason Aronson.

BOWEN, M. (1980). *Anxiety and Emotional Reactivity in Therapy.* Videotape made by the Georgetown Family Center, Washington, D.C.

CALHOUN, J. B. (1962). "Population Density and Social Pathology." *Scientific American* 206: 139–148.

CASSEL, J. M. (1965). "Potentialities and Limitations of Epidemiology." In *Health and the Community: Readings in the Philosophy and Sciences of Public Health,* ed. A. H. Katz and J. S. Felton, pp. 432–445. New York: Free Press.

GARELLY, E. (1968). "Psoriasis Lesions as Shown by Histopathology." In *Psoriasis,* ed. E. Sidi, Z. W. Zagula-Mally, and M. Hincky, pp. 124–139. Springfield, Ill.; Charles C. Thomas.

KERR, M. (1980a). "Emotional Factors in Physical Illness: A Multigenerational Perspective." *The Family* 7: 59–66.

KERR, M. (1980b). "Family Systems Theory and Therapy." In *Handbook of Family Therapy,* ed. A. S. Gurman and D. P. Kniskern. New York: Brunner/Mazel.

LYNCH, H. T.; A. J. KRUSH; R. J. THOMAS; and J. LYNCH (1976). "Cancer Family Syndrome." In *Cancer Genetics,* ed. H. T. Lynch, pp. 355–388. Springfield, Ill.: Charles C. Thomas.

MASSON, P. (1970). *Human Tumors.* Detroit: Wayne State University Press.

THOMAS, L. (1974). *The Lives of a Cell.* New York: Viking Press.

WARTHIN, A. S. (1913). "Heredity with Reference to Carcinoma." *Archives Int. Med.* 12: 546–555.

WILSON, E. O. (1975). *Sociobiology: The New Synthesis.* Cambridge: Belknap Press of Harvard University.

WOODYATT, R. T. and M. SPETZ (1942). "Anticipation in the Inheritance of Diabetes." *JAMA* 120: 602–605.

16 Self-Esteem, Sexuality, and Cancer Management

Wendy S. Schain

Accurate information about the sexual needs and/or dysfunctions in cancer patients has been a seriously neglected area in total patient care. While health professionals are actively pursuing interests in other quality-of-life concerns, little attention is paid to the sexual performance or satisfaction of patients with malignant diseases. Longevity is not just living; it involves loving, and rehabilitation experts must develop skills to diagnose and treat sexual disturbances related to the diagnosis of cancer and ensuing radical surgery or aggressive therapies. Holistic health care requires that caregivers understand: (1) what the degree of sexual dysfunction is in patients with cancer in different organ sites and at different life stages; (2) what the resulting disability associated with specific treatments is; and (3) what degree of distress or emotional morbidity reported by the patient regarding quality of life is related to his/her sexual dysfunction.

This chapter is an attempt to present information with the intention of sensitizing health professionals to the premise that sexual functioning is a critical concept in rehabilitation of cancer patients. Until recently most of the emphasis in cancer care was devoted to technological advances which could prolong survival and provide patients with as much pain relief as was possible. Little interest was directed at the conditions of that patient's psychological state or concern for what factors improved or deteriorated the quality of that patient's survival time. Few professionals asked what conditions or experiences were perceived as making life worth living, for any given patient, and/or what conditions or experiences were perceived as not worth the effort to continue the struggle—a living hell, so to speak.

With the advent of a new cadre of health professionals who are exploring humanistic issues in oncology, more and more emphasis is being focused on quality of life concerns in the treatment and rehabilitation of cancer patients. Research investigations are now being directed at asking questions intended to identify factors which will optimize survival time and

This chapter will also appear in *Coping with Medical Issues: Living and Dying with Cancer,* edited by Paul Ahmed. New York: Elsevier North Holland, Inc., 1981.

maximize the quality of a patient's interaction with his/her physical environment and significant others.

Critical issues in the quality-of-life concept focus on activities of daily living, behavior on one's job, family interaction, psychological symptomatology, and utilization of leisure time. Very little, if any, attention has been directed at sexual functioning and satisfaction in the cancer patient. There is a paucity of knowledge about the degree of impairment of sexual function and body image associated with the major modes of cancer therapy, including ablative surgery and aggressive courses of either chemotherapy or radiation. In addition, there is no substantive data on the role of the health care provider in dealing with this problem. Does the primary physician, oncological surgeon, or floor nurse initiate inquiry or counseling of this area with the patient? Who is responsible for patients suffering serious sexual disturbances in conjunction with cancer treatments?

Accurate information about the sexual dysfunction and needs of cancer patients could lead to more effective rehabilitation programs designed to improve the quality of survival and reduce the anguish so often associated with this disease. Quality of life, which is a key concept in cancer, should include identification of and attention to a patient's self-esteem, body-image changes, and sexuality. If survival statistics do not seem to be significantly different for several treatment procedures (such as radical breast surgery compared to lumpectomy and definitive radiation), then one must seriously consider issues related to self-esteem and quality survival as major determinants in decisions about choice of treatment; bearing in mind a desire to conserve body integrity and sexual prowess without compromising chances for a cancer cure.

A Working Model

With the limited tools and assessment techniques that we currently have available to diagnose the extent of morbidity associated with sexual dysfunction related to cancer treatment, I propose a conceptual framework which can be operationalized by most clinicians to act as (1) a general guideline for understanding sexual development, and (2) as a resource tool for diagnosing strengths and weakness in the individual's self-esteem system. This framework involves combining a knowledge of the developmental stages in human growth with an understanding of the dynamics of the components of the self-esteem system. The health professional must then be able to ascertain the patient's relative strengths and limitations regarding his or her self-esteem. Secondly, he or she must understand the implications of the developmental stage at which the patient's cancer was diagnosed and treated; and third, what role body image and sexuality play in that individual's sense of adequacy and well-being. In order to provide holistic health care, one must acknowledge the intimate interaction among self-esteem, developmental stage, sexual functioning, and the patient's interpretation and reaction to his or her malignant condition.

A Self-Esteem Model

Self-esteem is the sum total of all that a person feels about him or herself. It is a fluid, dynamic concept which is capable of changing from positive to negative and back again. One structural model of self-esteem which seems pragmatic is to compartmentalize the system into four major component parts each containing subfactors (Gates, 1978). These four major compartments include:

1. *The body self,* which has a functional (what can I do) and an aesthetic (how do I look) subfactor.
2. *The interpersonal self,* which is comprised of both social and acquaintance relations as well as intimate, sexual interactions.
3. *The achieving self,* which contains elements of work or competition efforts such as career or school behavior.
4. *The identification self,* which is comprised of those attitudes and behavior which are related to spiritual, ethical, or ethnic matters.

These four component parts work in conjunction with one another to form a configuration experienced as self-esteem. At different times and due to different circumstances, a person may experience a sense of depreciation, loss, or insult in any one of these four psychic compartments. For example, the severance of a long-term relationship may be viewed as a rejection (an insult to the interpersonal self), and the person sees herself as devalued and begins to compensate by borrowing "good feelings" or "stroking" from the body image component of her self-esteem. She works hard at developing a beautiful figure and getting recognized for physical attractiveness. On the other hand, a child who does not feel pretty about herself and fears she will not get rewarded for beauty, may begin to work very hard in school, become number one, and get her good feelings about herself from her achievement component of the self-esteem system. This schoolgirl manages to improve her scholastic standing in order to compensate for her loss of value in the body-image area.

The self-esteem system may be fluid or fixed, brittle or malleable, and amenable or resistive to professional intervention. It is essential, however, to ferret out what experiences feel good to a patient and enhance the self-image and what experiences hurt or insult that person's self-esteem. One particular method for making these determinations is a metaphorical paradigm which compares the *psychological self-esteem system to a commercial banking system.* This economic paradigm permits analogies in establishing assets, recording debits, and rearranging one's psychological currency so that the individual can operate at a profit. There are infinite arrangements and permutations in which an individual can put in (deposit) and take out (withdraw) from his or her self-esteem bank account. Sometimes, however, the individual (patient in this case) seems fixated: restricted to an equilibrium (self-esteem balance) which works only fairly well and which may be subject to an impending major withdrawal such as radical cancer surgery. Such a crisis as this might require a sudden traumatic realignment of emotional currency due to changes in actual functioning. In addition, the patient may experience a depreciation or dimunition of feelings of value and competence.

Mastectomy, colostomy, orchiectomy, and radical pelvic surgery are all experienced as a major insult to the body-image component of the self-esteem system, and the insult may spread out to other areas of the self, such as loss of approval, impaired work productivity, or loss of a lover. Major shifts in psychological reserves or defenses to compensate for such losses may require professional assessment either through standardized tests or through informal diagnosis of the patient's emotional reserves. For example, with a breast cancer patient, it would be important to ascertain how critical her perception of her breasts are to her self-image and sexual identity. How significant are they in terms of her sexual arousal and gratification? If she is a mother, did she breast feed? What kind of experience was that for her, and will the absence of her breast have impact on her concept of herself as not only sexual but also as a nurturing woman? In regard to esthetics, how much emotional investment has she attached to being able to exhibit her breast area or cleavage in cocktail clothes, bathing suits, or nightime attire? What is the likelihood of her generalizing her feeling of mutilation from her chest wall to the rest of her body or, more significantly, to experiencing a generalized sense of depreciation and devaluation because of this lost body part? Does she have psychological reserves and positive feelings from other areas of her self-esteem to carry her through her surgery and subsequent adjustment? What can her treating physicians do or say to enhance her self-esteem and avoid disturbing or insulting alternative resources. Such decisions are not easy to determine, particularly in light of the fact that most health professionals are not trained in communication skills or in understanding the relationship between developmental tasks, sexual functioning, and self-esteem. Sexuality is a significant source of self-esteem and one of the most enduring characteristics of the self-image. Clinical interviewing is necessary, therefore, to ascertain how a particular patient feels about his or her body image and how important his or her sexual functioning is to a feeling of value and sense of satisfaction with life.

Developmental Stages

It is almost impossible to understand the significance of sexuality in one's self-esteem without intertwining this concept into the broader framework of psychosexual stages of development. The centrality of one's sexuality is best understood in terms of its constancy and unalterability over the years. For all people, their size changes, shape changes, and age increases annually; physical appearance can be reconstructed, moods change, and friends shift, but gender assignment (except when there is reassignment) remains the same from conception until death. Therefore, it is vital to reacquaint one's self with the concept of developmental stages and the psychological, social, and sexual tasks which must be mastered in order to move from one stage to the next in the hierarchy of life's tasks. A number of significant works (Erikson, Woods) will recount the unfolding nature of both the libidinal urge as well as the ego or self-concept. During this emerging process, a number of conditions can be identified which may stimulate healthy adaptation or retard growth and foster pathology. At every stage on this developmental ladder there is a struggle to resolve certain issues which must be mastered in order to deal with the subsequent concerns. If handled adequately, the individual moves along this sequence of stage development unencumbered. If impeded, either by biology, psychology, or environment, the person may be fixated, regressed to an earlier stage, or flagrantly dysfunctional. For most individuals, the process is arduous and conflicted but progressive. For the cancer patient, however, the transitions may be delayed, traumatized, or even threatened of being permanently arrested. The major psychosocial and sexual tasks on the developmental heirarchy can be very briefly condensed as follows:

STAGE	BASIC PSYCHOSOCIAL TASK	SEXUAL TASKS
Infancy (0–2 yrs.)	Acquiring basic trust, learning to walk, talk.	Gender identity.
Childhood (2–12 yrs.)	Acquiring a sense of autonomy and worth vs. shame and doubt. Entering and adjusting to school.	Pleasure-pain associated with sexual organs and eliminative functions. Masturbation takes place with resulting shame or acceptance. Secondary sex characteristics become evident.
Adolescence (13–20 yrs.)	Acquiring sense of identity vs. role confusion.	Mastery over impulse control, acceptance of conflict between moral proscriptions and sexual urges, handling new physiological functions (menses for girls and ejaculate for boys).

(Continued)

STAGE	BASIC PSYCHOSOCIAL TASK	SEXUAL TASKS
Young adulthood (20–45 yrs.)	Acquiring a sense of intimacy vs. isolation. Vocational effectiveness, interpersonal security, "sexual adequacy."	Sexual adequacy and performance plus fertility concerns and questions related to parenting.
Middle adulthood (50–70 yrs.)	Acquiring a sense of self-esteem vs. despair. Adjusting to diminuation of one's energy and competence. "Empty nest syndrome" plus care of aging parents or their death. Adjusting to change in physique and evidence of aging.	For the female, menopause and resulting vasomotor changes, atrophy of breasts, clitoral size, and vaginal lubrication. For the male, delay on attaining an erection, a reduced compulsion to ejaculate, episodic impotence, possible prostatitis.
Old age	Adjusting to loss of friends, family, confrontation with old age and dying, painful joint conditions, reduced hearing and visual acuity. Adjustment to social stigmatization of being "old."	Reduced vitality, fear of incompetence or injury (coital coronary). Fear of being viewed as "dirty old person." Unavailability of a partner (widowhood). Limited physical capacity and reduced options.

Impact of Cancer—General Considerations

For individuals who suffer no major trauma or disease, alterations in body image which occur naturally on the developmental hierarchy are often difficult to deal with but permit transitions to continue without serious upset or distress. If, however, superimposed on these natural unfolding changes are added the burden of a diagnosis of cancer, radical surgery, insult to self-esteem, functional impairment, and the threat of the ravages of a cancer death, one can hardly begin to comprehend the magnitude of the implications of this disease and its potential disruption. Irrespective of the age or stage in the life cycle at which cancer occurs, there are general concerns such as: (1) fear of death, (2) morbidity associated with the treatments, (3) fear of recurrence, (4) fear of abandonment, and (5) loss of functional ability, social value, self-esteem, economic competence, and familiar role behaviors. Added to these global concerns are the specialized trauma precipitated according to the particular developmental period at which the cancer occurs and the life tasks which may be compromised by the type of cancer and the organ site involved.

Impact of Cancer—Individual Considerations

In addition to the universal and existential aspects of cancer for all patients, there are always idiosyncratic issues which arise and influence adjustment to the disease. Therefore, it is essential to explore the individualized response in order to understand what the patient is experiencing in conjunction with the diagnosis and treatment of his or her malignancy, and in relation to the impact cancer may have on the patient's sexuality. The important questions to determine are:

1. What is the meaning that the individual has attributed to the diagnosis of cancer and of the particular organ involved?
2. What effects do the severity of disease, extent of ablative surgery, or impact of aggressive treatment(s) have on the individual's functioning and self-esteem?
3. What were the individual's pre-treatment sexual attitudes and responsiveness, and how has this been affected by the disease and ensuing management?
4. What is the degree of visibility of the organ alteration, and what is the assumed stigma associated with that change?
5. What has been the individual's pre-treatment personality profile and major coping strategies (i.e., denier, tackler, monitor)?

There is also a need to understand the individual's relationship with a support system, his or her life stage at the time of diagnosis, the former adaptation to stress, and whether this disease is likely to have a "catastrophic" or consolidating effect on the patient's defenses and self-esteem system. When the cancer diagnosis and treatment(s) are directly related to a sex organ or a sex-related organ (i.e., mouth, arm), the experienced distress may be exacerbated because of the patient's embarrassment in expressing his or her needs and the accompanying discomfort that most professionals have in addressing sexual concerns directly.

The following discussion and series of case studies will be presented in order to demonstrate some of the critical issues involved in cancer of the sexual organs and the ways in which patients may attempt to deny, overcompensate, accept, or resist the implications of their disease and the body part which has been affected.

It has been suggested that three major parameters be kept in mind in delineating the specific problems which arise in relation to the interaction between a specific neoplasm and the unique way it impacts sexual functioning and self-esteem (Wise, 1978). These three factors include conditions which are: (1) organic or biologic, (2) psychologic, (3) iatrogenic. The intertwining of these variables will help to explain the individual's emotional reactions and behavioral response to his or her disease.

After consideration of the universal and individual concerns of cancer, one must go on to interpret the unique psychological reactions associated with the specific organ site involved and the interpretation given that experience by the patient; an interpretation shaped by the above three factors as well as the influence of the cultural climate in which he or she lives.

Breast Cancer

Mastectomy is the first consideration in this article since it affects such a large population: 89,000 women annually. To put it another way, one in thirteen women will eventually be affected by carcinoma of the breast and, until clinical trials demonstrate the ineffectiveness of such surgeries, most will undergo mastectomy, often referred to as "the operation women fear most."

Some day cultural anthropologists may describe our era as the "Mammocentric Age." Such a label has emerged out of society's serious preoccupation with the female breast as a symbol of pulchritude and desirability. The media's message is that firm, round, full, beautiful breasts are tantamount to happiness and well-being and that the absence of one or, worse, both breasts, is a condition to be feared, avoided, and denied. Many women in our culture feel that to be breastless is to be valueless. Therefore, is it any wonder that when a woman faces the prospect of amputation of that cherished organ she is besieged by feelings of fear, anger, depression, and diminished self-worth? The loss of a breast which is generally not visible to the outside world is still experienced intensely by the woman herself, and may be viewed as a threat to sexuality, femininity, and nurturance (Schain, 1978).

Adaptation or maladaptation following treatment will be based on a complex number of factors, but certain clues to morbidity are more reliable than others. For example, how does the woman perceive the importance of her breasts in her overall sense of well-being? Does she have an available support person? Who in her family has died from cancer and carcinoma of the breast in particular? What have been her previous coping mechanisms in response to crises? Is this woman likely to use regressive maneuvers to handle her insult, or is she capable of compensating for the loss by drawing upon other resources from her self-esteem system? In response to both pre- and post-operative assessment, one can begin to plan intervention strategies to assist the patient to work through her difficulties and, optimally, adjust to her condition.

One patient I had been asked to see had entered the hospital for elective breast augmentation. She had no conscious awareness of any possible malignancy and was both horrified and resistant to the news that a medial lesion discovered during her surgery was found to be cancerous. The plastic surgeon did not put in breast prostheses as was intended, but instead recommended mastectomy. The then forty-six-year-old, recently divorced mother of two girls was unconsolable. She initially refused acceptance of her diagnosis, became agitated and depressed, and could not assimilate the impact of this new information. The shift from an anticipated "high" of an embellished self-image (due to planned augmentation) to a crashing "low" of recommended amputation of an organ (viewed as inadequate) was experienced as confirmation of a defect and a terrible blow to her self-worth. After short-term but intensive reality therapy and education about breast reconstruction, this patient agreed to have the diseased breast removed *only* after extracting a promise of receiving reconstructive mammoplasty following her ablative procedure. Psychotherapy focused around anger about this loss, her impoverished self-image, her temporary period of self-imposed celibacy, and her unwillingness to show her perceived damaged (now visibly altered) body to a partner. During her post-surgery convalesence Mrs. A became interested in a man and allowed herself to engage in sexual intimacy but kept her brassiere and her false breast intact. She made it quite clear that she wished to camouflage her defect and could only perform if her partner permitted this cover-up. One week prior to Mrs. A's consultation for her reconstructive breast operation she noticed three lumps around her mastectomy wound. These nodules were biopsied and the diagnosis of local recurrence was confirmed. The patient was consciously unprepared for such an event, and the experience precipitated reinstatement of dread and some frenzied behavior to try to refute this diagnosis. Sexual concerns lost their intensity as priority issues centered around survival and choice of treatment tactics. Currently this woman is still shifting back and forth between denial of the severity of her disease, realistic health care responses, and compensatory reactions to combat her depression over her massive disappointments (lost breast, lost opportunity for reconstruction, lost marriage).

Information about how the woman experiences her breasts in relation to her general sense of worth may be a clue both to her reaction to mastectomy as well as an indication of her desire for and satisfaction with reconstructive surgery. One patient who had a modified radical mastectomy and who, four years later, requested replacement of her breast, was met with considerable medical resistance. First, as was prevalent several years ago, her surgeon labelled her vain and immature and admonished her for not being grateful that her life was prolonged and her disease "cured." Due to her sense of self-assertiveness, her retort was that she felt as entitled to a breast replacement as did his (the doctor's) wife who had recently had a rhinoplasty and a face lift. Mrs. S. consulted a reconstruction surgeon and was told that she was a good candidate for the procedure, but he recommended reduction mammoplasty for the contralateral breast since she had a size 38 DD cup. Mrs. S refused the reduction surgery and stated she wished to project her old image with very obvious and exposed cleavage that could "titillate" spectators. Reconstructive mammoplasty was performed and she was quite pleased with her post-surgery appearance which, when naked, revealed one pendulous unaltered breast and a round, small mound on the other side under which she wears an external prosthesis. This "Picasso effect," so apparent in the nude, was adequately camouflaged in most of her attire. While the plastic surgeon felt the results were not cosmetically pleasing to him, the patient was delighted with the outcome and what she felt was a "reinstatement" of her former body image which she could now again exhibit to the outside world.

When a mastectomy patient first confronts her loss, the absence of a breast and the rawness of the incisional area, she may be overwhelmed. She may view herself as a freak, a lopsided caricature who is not worthy of love and regard. She may feel out of balance, mutilated or defective in only a small compartmentalized aspect of self, or she may experience a more generalized diminished self-esteem. If she feels negative about herself, she may communicate this undesirable attitude to her partner in such a manner that he would not want to approach her. What often happens is a cyclical phenomenon—the woman feels unloveable and she withdraws; her partner reads this reaction as rejection—he avoids her because he is confused and hurt; she interprets this distance as revulsion, and there is no intimacy or communication about the disturbing feelings and fears each member of the pair is experiencing. Often professional intervention at this point can be helpful in altering the chain of events to ward off painful feelings and a sense of devaluation.

If the mastectomy patient feels unattractive, vulnerable, or defective, she may withdraw from sexual activity temporarily or indefinitely. She may wish for testimony to her femininity but be fearful of risking failure or disappointment. The acceptance of a change in body image without depreciation in self-worth or sexual prowess is a state which the woman must achieve herself, but she may need help to reach this goal, either professionally or by a sensitive partner. Confirmation of her desirability and her ability to be a gratifying partner is crucial in facilitating the woman's regaining a positive self-image, and the role a partner plays in helping a woman to be convinced of her adequacy and acceptability cannot be ignored.

At the other end of the response continuim, a post-mastectomy patient may engage in promiscuous "acting out" in an attempt to deny her feelings of diminished attractiveness or compromised mortality. One fairly young woman in her early 30's had been a traditional wife and monogamous partner for all of her ten years of marriage until after her breast surgery. Sometime after her mastectomy, while she was actively struggling with feelings of defectiveness, loss of femininity, and precipitous infertility, she found a lover. Her choice of a partner and the aftermath was indeed a compensatory expression of many of her unresolved fears and unexpressed concerns, as well as an inappropriate means to try and gain control over events about which she felt helpless.

Interestingly, the lover she chose was an oncological surgeon who had performed several mastectomies and had often told "other" husbands or partners that a woman is no different after this type of surgery. While the assignation was short-lived, it was later understood by Mrs. T as a frenetic

effort to avoid the terrible feelings of not being in control and making concerted efforts now to seduce (and control) the man who (in a displaced
form) had taken away her breast.

Shortly after this interlude, Mrs. T became pregnant. It was discovered
in psychothrapy that she announced her pregnancy exactly two years after
her surgery and the time limit the doctor had imposed on her for any future
pregnancies. Intensive discussion and exploration revealed again Mrs. T's
efforts to control events around her, deny the implications of her arrested
disease, and visibly confirm her wish to be an undamaged (pregnant)
woman. Dream material also revealed this patient's painful conflict over
her desire to carry the pregnancy to term. While she wanted to validate her
capabilities of fertility, she was terrified over the image of a single-breasted
pregnant woman in the labor room, and the final show-down which would
acknowledge to the world that she was indeed only "half a woman." The
patient decided to terminate this pregnancy, since her need was more to
demonstrate a biological competency rather than to nurture any more
children. In addition, she did recognize the possible danger of hormonal
changes which accompany a pregnancy after mastectomy that might trigger
dormant cancer cells.

Case materials can elucidate the various defensive maneuvers which can
interfere with or facilitate adjustment to mastectomy. Pre-operative
counseling as well as stage-related interventions during pre and post-
hospitalization can influence the reactions of patients following their treatment. In addition, it has been found that counseling these women does
make a difference in their post-surgical sexual adjustment, but that such
counseling should focus on the woman's acceptance of herself rather than
her male partner's acceptance of her.

While there is little substantive data about the decrease in orgasmic
response or frequency of sexual contact following mastectomy, recent
studies do suggest evidence of distress associated with sexual issues subsequent to radical breast surgery, and the fact that women's sexual self-
image, attitudes, and actual behaviors do change following this type of
surgery. More scientifically controlled investigations will identify, describe,
and clarify the most frequently experienced problems and foster ideas for
more effective interventions.

Radical Pelvic Surgery

The next category that requires discussion here is pelvic cancer. In considering pelvic surgery planned to control or remove cancer of the female
organs, it becomes necessary to determine where the patient is on a continuum from experiencing distress from mild vaginal irritation to the threat
associated with internal irradium implants to removal of the vagina and

resulting loss of ability for coitus concurrent with the need for excretory conduits because of involuntary control of eliminative functions. In addition, it is crucial to know how much of the internal reproductive organs and/or the external female genitalia has been removed.

Here, too, it is essential to interpret the woman's unique reactions to her loss, which will be a mixture of physiological, psychological, intellectual, and cultural forces. What does the woman know about her surgery? Does she understand what will be removed and what will be left? Does she understand the functions of the various organs involved? What value does she place on the removed organs, and how important has the function and/or psychological reaction to this organ been. For example, if the surgical procedure removed the uterus, one must ascertain what the patient's perception of her uterus is. Women have described various functions associated with their uterus which include reproduction, excretion, regulation of bodily processes, maintenance of youth, and the "rhythms" of life. Some even view their uterus as a repository of vitality and strength. Feeling fertile may be significantly correlated with feeling sexual and feminine, and the old adage that a "hysterectomy removes the baby buggy but retains the playpen" may not be a welcome state for all women.

Removal of the reproductive organs may elicit fears of (1) premature aging, (2) diminution of libido, (3) difficulty in lubricating, (4) feeling like a "sterile" shell, and (5) rejection by one's partner. Such fears may be confirmed or refuted by a partner's behavior or vergal response. Some men will feel that their wives' attractiveness is diminished because they share the same fears or because they have inadequate information to assuage such myths. Psychosocial intervention for these women and their partners must include both emotional support strategies as well as accurate information and education to diminish the threat to a patient's sense of womanliness as well as her physical comfort and actual survival (Donohue, Valentina, 1978).

Radical surgeries which involve excision of the ovaries or the ovaries plus parts of the vaginal passage and parts of the external genitalia create additional trauma to body integrity and sexual functioning. Removal of ovarian hormones may lead to thinning of the vaginal wall with reduced lubrication, which may cause intercourse to be painful. If there has been either pre-operative or post-surgery radiation, the woman may have fibrosis, narrowing of the vaginal passage and/or dyspareunia. Estrogen replacement therapy may prevent or reduce some of the discomfort associated with steroid disturbance, but the improvement in comfort following radiation damage is less easily achieved. Understanding the physiological aftermath of radical pelvic surgery, the attendant emotional consequences to the end of the menses (particularly if the woman was in her childbearing years), and the reaction to the threat of cancer are all essential to providing effective therapy for these patients. In addition, it is crucial to ascertain what degree of dysfunction is due to (1) functional impairment (absence or alteration of the vagina), (2) arousal mechanisms (sensitivity changed, or (3) desire (purely psychological interest in sexual or affectional behavior). Treatment tactics must be directed at the source of dysfunction and distinction is made among problems due to arousal, desire, or performance.

Reactions to radical surgery and the diagnosis of uterine or pelvic cancer vary considerably and are largely influenced by the woman's characteristic defenses. For example, one young woman who had a hysterectomy for cervical cancer before she had borne any natural children of her own compensated for her childless state by intellectualizing her loss and sublimating her energies to become an active member in both the Planned Parenthood association and in the battle in her state to get midwives licensed to deliver babies and reactivate the "home birthing" concept.

In many types of hysterectomy and in oophorectomy, the removal of tissue is not visible except for the external incision. If, however, the female cancer patient has ablative surgery which leaves an ugly abdominal excision, one or more stomas as in the case of pelvic exenteration, or if she has a major portion of her vulva excised, cumulative distress may be anticipated (Brown et al., 1972). In addition, there is evidence to suggest there is increased dysfunction associated with radiotherapy for cervical carcinoma which creates shortening of the vaginal barrel and stenosis; both conditions interfere markedly with sexual gratification (Abitol and Davenport, 1974).

If added to the concern of infertility and vasomotor changes, the pelvic cancer patient experiences a major disfigurement and attendant fears about being abnormal looking, she may not be able to express her distress or seek assistance for her dilemma. She may subvocally ask questions such as, who can look at my body with so many holes and scars? Who will want to touch a vagina with no pubic hair? Who will want to caress legs swollen from lymph-node dissection? How can I cover the ugliness and still be capable of giving and receiving sexual gratification?

Another issue in this area of concern which needs to be addressed by health professionals is the issue of masturbation in addition to the desire for resumption of intercourse following pelvic surgery. Many women know very little about their genitals and may have to be taught what the remaining organ or pieces of organ can do. Even if the clitoris is removed, it may be possible to reach a climax with a combination of manual stimulation elsewhere in conjunction with fantasy. While there is still debate about whether vaginal or clitoral orgasm is the highest form of sexual fulfillment, some radical pelvectomy patients report being able to fantasize to orgasm (although they describe these sensations as if they occur during sleep and dreaming). It may be necessary for nurses, doctors, and sex therapists to teach women manually and visually to explore their altered vagina to learn its contours and its orgastic potential as a prelude to reentry to sexual activities involving a partner. It will also be important to determine what physical and physiological alterations are permanent and what conditions may be compensated for by new behaviors and the possibility of reconstructive surgery. Reconstructive vaginoplasty is a fairly new area in cancer management (but has been used in gender reassignment surgery), and most women do not know it exists or whether they might be possible candidates for such an operation.

Another terribly underexplored area in the whole field of sexual functioning in cancer patients is a discussion of variations which may be required for homosexual patients who have had radical surgery. If cunnilingus is a major aspect of two women's sexual pleasuring and the vaginal area has been disfigured, dry, and perhaps odoriferous because of surrounding stomas, major alterations in sexual expression may be necessary. Professional intervention may be required to assist both the heterosexual and homosexual patient adjust to the changes in body image and function before resuming satisfying sexual behaviors. Sensitive clinical interviewing to determine prevalent practice, anticipated fears, and fantasies is essential before making recommendations which will be intended to be helpful, but may unwittingly turn out to elicit resistance (i.e., assuming the patient is heterosexual when she is not).

Ostomy Surgery

The third category of cancer patients with special concerns about sexual behavior are the ostomates. This is one of the most dreaded procedures of all cancer surgeries because of the stigma associated with the loss of bowel and/or bladder control. This surgery generally elicits a host of psychological reactions which stem from both the physical changes which take place as well as the societal taboos about excretory functions. In this type of surgery the anus is surgically repositioned to the front of the body and, for the most part, voluntary control of bowel activities is destroyed—a major alteration in self-image and body function.

The critical concerns and conflicts of the anal stage of development may consciously or unconsciously be unleased after this type of surgery. Issues may reappear such as those associated with cleanliness, control over one's impulses, a sense of autonomy and self-direction, ambivalence over active or passive behavior, and the reactivation of negative feelings of shame and self-doubt.

Emotional or physical regression (particularly social withdrawal) may be a consequence following ostomy surgery. In a study by Druss, et al. (1969), it was discovered that two-thirds of twenty-two men and fourteen women had an initially unpleasant reaction to their stoma. One patient said, "it's a terrible thing to find this change in your anatomy." Another denied any emotional response by stating she did not remember her first reactions after surgery. Another study by Orback and Tallent (1975) found some men reacted to their operation as if it represented castration or demasculinization. Some men reported reacting to the early post-surgical bleeding of the stoma as if it were a menstrual flow. They discussed feeling feminized and/or asexual. Women, on the other hand, viewed the change in their body as similar to a rape experience or to feelings of having been sexually violated. A few reported sexualizing the behavior of cleaning the stoma and experienced a feeling analogous to masturbation in handling the opening in their body. There was also evidence reported that compulsive colostomy management was a means of handling the anxiety elicited by the loss of control over one's excretory functions.

The meaning of this surgery is highly individualized and plays a significant role in loss or impairment of sexual competency. The cause of sexual .difficulty may be: (1) organic—resulting from nerve damage during the surgical procedure, (2) psychological—fears and anxieties associated with the presence of the stoma, the obviousness of the defect, or the fallibility of the apparatus used for the repository of waste material, or (3) iatrogenic—dysfunctions imposed by medical treatments (i.e., post-op radiation burns).

In several studies examining sexual functioning after colostomy or ileostomy, a large portion said surgery did not decrease their sexual activity. Some said it increased the frequency of contact but it is not clear what explicit questions were asked and what the nature of the sexual contact was. Other studies revealed a significant number of men who became impotent after surgery and a large number of women who terminated intercourse around the time of their colostomy (Woods, 1975). Again, however, it is not clear what the pre-surgical frequency and satisfaction of sex was for those patients and whether the colostomy permitted a legitimization for cessation of intercourse. The literature is sparse with regard to carefully planned and controlled studies to gather information about psychological and physical changes in sexual behavior following ostomy surgery. While the reported results suggest that sexual intimacy was present and pursued by a large number of patients post-operatively, there was evidence to suggest that there was a decrease in frequency of multiple orgasms and extramarital affairs. Some women verbalized concern that their condition was a definite deterrent to future sex contacts or remarriage. There is also not much detailed information on the patterns of sexual responses or responsiveness in the single ostomate; guidelines discussing their needs and specific compensatory mechanisms need to be described.

It has been said that for the most part after colostomy, men are primarily concerned with performance and women with issues of acceptance or rejection. Another male colostomy patient whom I saw in therapy, aged fifty-two, reflected a combination of resistance to sexual interaction due both to cultural conditioning as well as surgical destruction of potency. Mr.

O had been happily married to the same woman for thirty-one years and was moderately interested in sex before his surgery. As a result of his abdomino-perineal, he was impotent. His wife was extremely supportive and nurturing during his hospitalization and convalescence (changing bandages, adjusting his appliance), and he expressed unmitigated devotion and appreciation of her reaction. After his crisis state, when he gained complete autonomy over his self-care, he withdrew from his wife's involvement and threw himself compulsively into his work and imposed a condition of celibacy, creating a state of avoidance of emotional investment at home. His wife came to see me depressed, anxious, and in the middle of a guilt-ridden first extra-marital affair. The couple's therapy was initiated and it was discovered that indeed Mr. O was suffering from the "masculine mystique of the male machine," which translates into "if you can't get it up and in, don't bother"; to score is what really counts. This man's early socialization combined with his marital conditioning had reinforced the premise that "penis in the vagina" was the ultimate goal in lovemaking and that all other behaviors (kissing, hugging, touching affectionately) were merely "foreplay." While these other behaviors may be necessary for successful lovemaking, they were not considered sufficient. Two months of exploratory therapy plus directive suggestions of pleasuring behaviors (sensate focus, nude bathing) liberated this man's energy enough to shift his focus from intercourse as the final outcome in sex to loving and pleasuring as the major activity for their intimate encounters. Potency did not return but libido and desire increased significantly so that the couple was making love about two times a week with the wife reporting both orgasm and psychological "climax" and Mr. O feeling an enhanced sense of well-being and effectiveness (if not biological potency). Mrs. O discontinued her affair and exhibited diminished depression and increased amour for her husband. The combination of supportive therapy and behavioral recommendations for sexual tasks was effective in facilitating this couple's reestablishing a satisfying sexual interaction.

Prostatectomy and Orchiectomy

A fourth group which will be considered her is the population of cancer patients (males) who have surgery performed either on their external or internal sexual organs. Major surgery or an amputation procedure performed on any age male is often viewed as a castration threat. What then is the reaction of a man who is indeed undergoing some type of ablative surgery on his genitals? The literature is scant on emotional responses of either the male patient who received this type of surgery or the physician who performs such operations. Yet one knows experientially that there is a need for specialized assistance in this area in terms of adequately preparing these men for such an operation and the consequences that are likely to be brought about by this radical surgery.

There are several distinctions which must be made about the differences between these two procedures, although some underlying similarities do exist because of the way the patient may interpret this insult. For the most part, orchiectomy (removal of a gonad) is usually performed on younger men, since the median age range for cancer of the testis is between twenty-nine and thirty-five. No doubt this is the "prime of life" and to have a castration during the years of fertile home life and critical career endeavors could be traumatic. Many of these patients are still capable of impregnating a partner, but a retroperitoneal lymph node dissection often required in addition to the original orchiectomy may produce retrograde ejaculation. Prostatectomy, on the other hand is a surgery often associated with older men and removes an internal gland with little obvious evidence of alterations of one's masculinity. Most of these patients experience impotence after prostatectomy for cancer, especially if this procedure was preceded by removal of the testes. The prostatectomy patient generally will experience reduced erectile function, particularly if there was sacral neural plexus damage during the operation. In addition, even if the patient can ejaculate with a flaccid penis, there may be reduced volume of fluid. It is unclear whether either one of these conditions alone would account for the high percentage of primary impotence reported. However, it seems likely that pre-operative counseling might protect potency and prevent secondary anxiety which plays a significant role in erectile dysfunction associated with this type surgery.

It is important to explore certain myths and misconceptions associated with sexuality in older men in order to gain proper perspective about the psychological sequelae to a prostatectomy. The classical joke of the man in his 60's who says "it now takes all night to do what I used to do all night" is only partially true. What is suggested by research in this area is that sexual potency in older age is a result of physical conditions, environmental stimuli (the availability of a partner), and habit strength, as well as psychological states such as guilt, shame, or embarrassment. A study by Finkle (1972) revealed that sexual potency was zealously sought by most older male patients in his sample and best retained by married men with available and willing wives. Various investigators have reported variable responses to prostatectomy but little subsequent data on psychosexual adjustment is available for either of these two sexually assaulting procedures.

Two case studies may help to illustrate the often neglected trauma associated with the ramifications of surgery to a man's sexual organ. One patient came to see me in the midst of a classical depression and after three sessions shared that he had had an orchiectomy two years prior at age twenty-nine. Since his surgery he was impotent and had not been able to impregnate his wife. While his own sense of loss was marked and he felt inadequate and guilty about his deficiency (an unresolved conflict from childhood), he was seriously distressed by the change in his wife's parents reaction to him. While he had formerly shared a close, caring in-law relationship with them, he now perceived them as distant, cool, and rejecting and had heard stories from his wife that her father thought a divorce would be appropriate since her husband could not father a biological child. Mr. L was lethargic, preoccupied with suicide, and highly distractible at his job as an auto mechanic. Group therapy was the chosen treatment modality along with individual sessions. It was several months before this patient could establish a self-respecting identity which was not contingent on his potency or fertility. At this point, couples therapy was instituted and after many months of confronting the issue of infertility and narcissism for both the patient and his spouse, Mr. and Mrs. L reestablished their marital contract and made plans to adopt a child.

At the other end of the age continuum was a second-hand report I received from a patient of mine who was very distressed about her eighty-six-year-old grandfather who had just returned home from the hospital after a prostate operation. A few weeks later she called me at home and asked for the name of a gerontology psychiatrist and explained that grandpa had become quite bizarre after surgery and was threatening to kill his second wife who was twenty-two years his junior. Apparently, the insult experienced by surgery to his genitals unleased considerable anger and threat, which was translated into a paranoid preoccupation that his wife was "cheating on him" with the pharmacist. His desire to kill her possibly resulted from his wish to remove the visible evidence to him of his impotence (his sexual partner). Anti-psychotic agents were administered and eventually controlled the distorted thinking. Mrs. D no longer felt genuinely in danger of being murdered and remained at home with her husband. The intensity of such a reaction documents the range and magnitude of possible disturbance subsequent to radical surgery on a patient's genitals. One must also be aware of the potential threat of this type of surgery even to an octagenarian, and therefore one needs to be alert to any warning signals which could suggest resulting psychic distress or serious decompensation.

It is essential to remember that there may be a host of psychological repercussions following an ablative procedure that is not only perceived as castration but, as in the case of calprostate, is in reality intended for that purpose. In this area, as in the other cancer surgeries such as ostomy, mastectomy, and radical pelvic operations, more research is necessary to define the problems, outline the severity of concern, document the need for interventions, and establish guidelines for supportive strategies.

In addition, it would seem valuable to explore the patient-doctor communication regarding this procedure. The popular press is certainly critical of the "male perspective and economic incentive" associated with the magnitude of the operation performed when a woman has a breast removed. Accusations have been made that male surgeons are insensitive to the importance and ego investment a woman has in her breasts. What comments are applicable to the man who, for medical safety must remove another man's sex organ, or at least part of it? How does he inform his patient of this? Is he communicative about the possibility of reparative procedures such as penile implants? Will a young male patient, with a reasonable prognosis, wish to reestablish potency (by surgical implantation) and to whom can such a patient turn to explore the possible risk/benefits of such a procedure?

This last issue leads naturally to the last concern of this chapter: the problem of intervention. Who and when should a health professional intervene with a patient about to undergo radical surgery for cancer which has serious implications for both survival and self-esteem? Most of the surgeons know quite clearly the signs and statistics for longevity associated with these various cancer operations. They seem to know considerably less about the psychological morbidity which generally ensues and the low priority rating that they assign sexual functioning in total patient care. If one is ready and willing to acknowledge that sexual counseling is an integral aspect of cancer rehabilitation, then one needs to ask specific questions about the following:

1. How to identify the patient with a problem and clarify the concern.
2. Who should intervene and when?
3. How should the intervention be administered?
4. Who should train the interventionists?

Not every physician is a consultant in sexual health nor should he or she be, but one should be able to recognize and diagnose a sexual problem in a patient. It is essential to identify the patient's problem and this must be done by conducting a detailed and skillfull sexual history. If a gastroenterologist wants to know about a patient's bowel disorder, he asks very specific questions about the onset, duration, and character of the dysfunction. He does not inquire, "How is your defecation life?" The same should be true for professionals conducting a sex history. The banal phrase "How is your sex life?" must be replaced with specific questions related to the patient's presenting complaints. Follow the medical practice model. Investigate specifically what the problem may be, the possibility of multiple origins, and the ramifications for sexual pleasure (not just performance). Do not wait until the patient describes his or her difficulties but sensitively inquire about the frequency of sexual intercourse, the pleasure associated with it, the pain involved, the actual feelings of discomfort, embarrassment, or apprehension. Also bear in mind that some older individuals are particularly uncomfortable about discussing sexual behavior, even with their doctor. Age and culture also have implications for the individual's view of sexual satisfaction and his or her responsibility in obtaining pleasure.

Therapeutic intervention aims primarily at helping the patient prepare (pre-operatively, if possible) and adapt to major changes created by the diagnosis and treatment of his or her disease. When the focus is on sexual rehabilitation, the goal is to facilitate the patient's reestablishing a happy and satisfying sexual relationship and acquiring a self-respecting way to handle sexual needs. It is not a request to join the sexual revolution. One must also remember that some patients will actively choose to be non-sexual after their procedure. Asexuality is an option and deserves equivalent respect, as does the desire for sexual release and interaction. Both conditions require exploration and acceptance from the involved professionals, and this can be accomplished by a variety of treatment strategies that range from full-fledged formally oriented uncovering types of psychotherapy to the less formalized but very effective approach known as the P-LI-SS-IT model (Annon, 1974).

The P-LI-SS-IT is a brief learning theory model which is highly flexible and adaptable to patients' needs in a variety of settings and to clinician's range of expertise. Basically, this conceptualization is a stage-related model with each level requiring increasing degrees of knowledge, training, and skill on the part of the involved professional or helper (one can gear the approach to one's own particular level of competence). In brief, this model is self-regulating, hierarchical, and provides both a screening technique as well as a guideline for active intervention.

The issue of training for the health professional who wants to assist patients in this matter is a burgeoning concern which is predicated on the needs of the patient population which one sees and the resources and responsibilities the professional wishes to actualize. There are good references today for the helping professional to find training in sex therapy, if he or she is interested. There are also some self-taught techniques such as the P-LI-SS-IT model which can raise one's sense of awareness and also enhance one's skills of inquiry and counseling. Helpful procedures extend from just listening and giving the patient permission to ask questions or ventilate sexual fears to the more intense dynamic psychotherapies and the systematically designed desensitization techniques. It is not essential for any one health professional to do all these therapies; it is only critical to be appraised of their existence and their usefulness in order to provide referrals to a patient.

Cancer is a terrible disease which wreaks havoc with one's body, diminishes one's personal financial resources, interferes with family life, and often disrupts sexual function. While technology in this field is making strides in reducing mortality, extending survival, and enhancing the quality of longevity, patients' sexual needs, problems, and potential are still being neglected. It is time to pay more serious attention to the patient's body-image concerns, his or her sexual needs, and how these two factors interact to influence self-esteem and psychological adaptation. Quality survival involves loving; not just living. Therefore, professional intervention must turn its focus on acknowledging, diagnosing, and treating sexual problems of cancer patients if holistic health care is to be achieved.

References

ABITOL, M. M.; and DAVENPORT, J. H. "Sexual Dysfunction after Therapy for Cervical Carcinoma." *Am. J. Obstet. Gynecol.* May 15, 1974, 119 (2):181–189.

ABT, V.; McGURRIA, M. C.; and HEINTZ, L. "The Impact of Mastectomy on Sexual Self-Image, Attitudes and Behavior. *J. Sex Ed. Ther.* 4:43–47, 1978.

ANNON, J. S. *The Behavioral Treatment of Sexual Problems.* Honolulu: Kapiolani Health Services, 1974.

BROWN, R.; HADDOX, V.; POSADA, A.; and RUBIO, A. "Social and Psychological Adjustment Following Pelvic Exenteration." *Am. J. Obstet. Gynecol.* 114: 162–171, 1972.

DONOHUE, V. "Sexual Rehabilitation of Gynecologic Cancer Patients. *Med. Aspects Human Sex.* Feb., 1978, pp. 51–52.

DRUSS, R. G.; O'CONNOR, J. F.; and STERN, L. O. "Psychologic Response to Colectomy. *Arch. Gen. Psychiat.* 20:419–425, 1969.

ERIKSON, E. H. *Childhood and Society.* 2nd ed. New York: Harper and Row, 1972, pp. 44–48.

FINKLE, A. L. "Urologic Counseling in Male Sexual Impotence." *Geriatrics* 16: 37–43, 1972.

FRANK, D.; DORNBUSH, R. L.; WEBSTER, S. K., et al. "Mastectomy and Sexual Behavior: A Pilot Study." *Sex. Disab.* 1(1):16–27, 1978.

GATES, C. *A Manual for Cancer.* Boston: American Cancer Society, 1978.

LEIF, H. I. "Sexual Concerns of Mastectomy Patients." *Med. Aspects Human Sex.* Jan., 1978 pp. 57–58.

ORBACH, C. E.; and TALLENT, N. "Modification of Perceived Body and of Body Concepts." *Arch. Gen. Psychiat.* Feb. 1965, pp. 419–427.

SCHAIN, W. S. "Prophylaxis, Therapy and Rehabilitation of the Psychosocial Concerns of Breast Cancer Patients. *Breast, Diseases of the Breast* (2):24–27, 1978.

WISE, T. N. "Sexual Functioning in Neoplastic Disease." *Med. Aspects Human Sex.* March, 1978, pp. 16–31.

WITKIN, M. H. "Sex Therapy and Mastectomy." *J. Sex Marital Ther.* 1(14): 290–304, 1975.

WOODS, N. F. *Human Sexuality in Health and Illness.* St. Louis: C. V. Mosby, 1975, pp. 140–160.

17 The Mysterious Case of Ichabod Crane

M. Kathleen Philbin

Ichabod Crane is the unsophisticated non-hero of the *Legend of Sleepy Hollow*. Compared with his enemy he is under-horsed, physically inferior, and hardly clever in battle. Until his final race he does not even believe that his enemy is real. He does, however, have the nerve to keep going, whether this is born of naiveté or fear. It seems a miracle that he makes it across the covered bridge, although, in the end, there is no certainty about his fate or, indeed, about the reality of the Headless Horseman himself.

This chapter is an expanded case history of a certain commonplace man who developed a malignant tumor of the pancreatic islet cells during his late fifties. The case is of particular interest because it is the story of a man whose cancer surely should have killed him, but somehow, did not. An analysis of the forces interacting during the course of the illness includes several psychological and physical variables. The isolation of these particular variables from the whole fabric of existence is somewhat arbitrary and probably cannot be considered to be "variables" in the sense of scientific research.

The first of these components of his recovery is the medical regimen. While medical intervention might initially appear to be a simple asset to recovery, it also involved grave, and in some cases, pointless hazards. In the case of Mr. C., the effects of medical "care" were notably mixed. Another influence on his recovery was denial (coupled with repression), operating in many ways and at many levels of his life. The ways that this unconscious psychological defense operated, utilized and refined over a lifetime, are particularly interesting in terms of their contribution to his recovery. A third variable was a sure personal faith in his recovery which persisted in the face of his wife and children's disbelief and in the midst of a family that was profoundly breaking apart. The dynamics within the family, in fact, constitute what seemed to be a powerful set of forces, a variable in itself, whose function may have been both to promote recovery through authentic contact and to undermine it. A fifth variable, and one that was impressive to many observers throughout his illness, was his drive for physical activity. The reader will notice the ridiculous contrast between his physical condition and the activity he chose to engage in.

Physical Factors

Surgery

Below is the report of the local surgeon who has been the primary care physician throughout not only this illness, but the last fifteen years of Mr. C.'s life. The report is an excerpt of the official medical record and covers both the initial surgery to relieve the intestinal obstruction and the subsequent removal of most of the malignant tissue.

> November 12, 1975. Exploration was performed under general anesthesia and carcinoma of the splenic flexure of the colon with metastases to the lymph nodes and the surrounding structures was found. A transverse loop colostomy was performed in order to relieve the obstruction.

> December 4, 1975. He was taken back to the operating room and exploration was performed. After lysis of multiple intra-abdominal adhesions, a large mass was found in the left upper quadrant of the abdomen, extending from the colon and encircling the splenic flexure and invading the hilum of the spleen. The rest of the tumor was completely obscured by a large spleen. After removal of the spleen, one could see extension of the tumor to the tail and body of the pancreas, with a large mass, the size of a medium orange. At that time I felt this was a hopeless case. The tumor was in the pancreas and could not be removed. The transverse colon was removed and anastomosis was done between the two ends of the bowel.

It seems almost too obvious to state that the removal of this large quantity of malignant tissue was vital to Mr. C.'s recovery. It not only got the proportions of what the body had to deal with "down to size," but also eliminated a well-known site of dissemination of the malignant cells, namely the spleen. This assistance to the body's own defenses did not come cheap, however. The body, being compromised in its recuperative powers by the cancer process, was at a grave disadvantage in recovering from the "insult" of the surgery itself. The pneumonia, abscess, and debilitation that ensued were at least in part by-products of the surgery. In retrospect it seems eminently wise (and lucky for Mr. C.) that the surgeon did not attempt a "definitive" procedure. His patient was bleeding a lot, the tissues were inflamed and not holding the sutures. The case looked hopeless, and he decided to quit while he was ahead. On the day of surgery the doctor reported privately that he really should have removed the entire transverse colon, descending colon, some of the ascending colon and their surrounding lymph nodes. In a tone that apologized for not doing a thorough job, he said he didn't see the point in it.

Treatment for the side effects of surgery

Following the surgery there was medical intervention to counter the effects of the surgery. This was not intended as treatment of the cancer but as treatment for the surgery. This is not a distinction that is usually made, but discriminating between the treatment of the disease and the treatment for the treatment is useful for a number of reasons.

1. *Antibiotics to treat infection.* One of the unplanned (although not unusual) sequels to the surgery was pneumonia. No doubt there were several influences working together to foster the growth of bacteria in the lungs. He was anemic from the cancer prior to surgery; the lung tissues were poorly nourished and, therefore, susceptible. He had four hours of anesthesia during which the lungs were less mobile, less well aerated, and chemically insulted. Following the surgery he very seldom turned or moved about in bed although this should not have been left to his discretion. This nursing function was left undone probably due to guilt at causing pain in a person who was universally well liked by the staff. Any bacteria which found their way into his lungs also found a likely place to rest and undisturbed and breed ad lib.

What is most paradoxical about this first pneumonia and the recurring pneumonias and abscesses over the next nine months is that they may have worked to mobilize the body's defenses against cancer, even though they constituted a life threat in themselves. There seems to be growing evidence that the body's own immune system may be able to fight cancer if it can be stimulated appropriately.[1,2,3,4,5,6,7] In the case of Mr. C., the series of infections (both pneumonia and lung abscesses) began within a week of the second surgery and continued off and on for about six weeks. These were treated with antibiotics. Another month or six weeks then passed before chemotherapy was started. It is possible that his body may have been powerfully stimulated in its immune responses by the viruses and bacteria that repeatedly invaded his lungs over the nine-month period from December through August. It is also possible that the chemotherapy which was begun in March prevented the immune system from acting as effectively as possible. This is possible in theory, at least, and in reality he did begin to improve dramatically when the chemotherapy was stopped in August. Since chloromycetin (an antibiotic with many undesirable and, in fact, dangerous side effects) was the only one able to affect the bacteria at that point in August, it was used to treat the severe pneumonia present at the time the chemotherapy was stopped. Perhaps the chloromycetin also had an effect on the malignancy.

2. *Blood replacement.* To maintain the sequence in which the elements in the medical regime entered the picture, let us go back to the immediate postoperative period and introduce the possibility that some of the blood

received during and after the surgery may have contained immunities to cancer. Needless to say, this blood was given because Mr. C. had a low blood volume (due to bleeding during surgery) and/or a low hemoglobin (due to the destruction of blood cells as part of the malignant process.) The blood was not given for the purpose of introducing someone else's immunities to cancer, although this may have been a powerful, unplanned side benefit.

Mr. C. received eleven pints of blood between December 1975 and August 1976. Since it seemed apparent that he was "terminal" his doctor was less cautious than usual about giving the blood, a procedure which does carry with it the very ominous potential of hepatitis or fatal allergic reaction.

3. *Hospitalization/confinement in bed.* Enforced confinement in bed was a negative force in the medical-hospital regime. As most nursing students can recite, prolonged confinement in bed increases the risk of pneumonia and decubiti (bed sores). It also weakens muscle strength and leads to muscle atrophy. It promotes absorption of calcium from the bones, thereby increasing the danger of broken bones. It interferes with kidney function and leaves the intestines without the necessary stimulation for regular bowel movement. The unchanging environment and social isolation promote depression and mental disorientation.

The Medical Center to which Mr. C. was sent was far more restrictive of his activity than the previous local hospital had been. The surgeon in charge was completely in favor of bed confinement out of fear of suit for an accident. He thoroughly expected Mr. C. to die either in the hospital or in a nursing home within a few weeks. He did not see any advantage in encouraging ambulation and did not see pneumonia as any worse risk than the cancer. He fiercely argued against the family's plan for discharge to home.

Diet

Concomitant with this scenerio of accumulating positive and negative forces for healing was the complicated problem of nutrition of malnutrition moving toward starvation. Working from a base condition of a typical high meat, high sugar, highly "preserved" low-fiber American diet, Mr. C. entered a postoperative period of poor appetite, muscular weakness, and physical pain which made eating an enormous problem. During his period of hospitalization, both at the local hospital and at the medical center, he received a "regular" diet with no vitamin supplements. Judging from the food that entered his room each day, there was no way of discriminating between him and the twenty-year-old man who was being treated for low back pain. Consider the illogic of this diet in the face of startling loss of both fat and muscle tissues, persistent infection, ongoing malignancy, and large areas of surgical intrusion.

When Mr. C. was returned home, the family attempted to institute a regimen of vitamins and meals in hopes to facilitate the recovery process. They found Mr. C. an unwilling patient, however. He was disoriented and extremely frail at this point and had no interest in nutritional programs. His only demand was that his wife cook exactly what she had always cooked. After forcing himself for more than two months to swallow hospital food as if it were medicine, he was fierce about eating familiar, "real" food. Unusual foods, such as vegetable juices, were flatly refused. This was a psychological drive for feeling "normal" and for experiencing himself as being at home rather than an interest in nutrition.

One important addition to Mr. C.'s diet had a profound psychological effect. The family felt that a small glass of wine with the evening meal might perk up his appetite. Mr. C. liked the idea but the wine "burned" his mouth, a symptom typical of vitamin deficiencies. At length, a cheap rather sweet rosé was discovered which did not burn, and he drank a glass of that with the evening meal each night. Propped at the table too weak to sit alone, that glass of wine not only sparked his appetite but seemed to indicate that this was a real meal, with real people. He was surprised to see wine on the first night at home and he took it, as it was intended, to signify that he was outside the official, institutional bond.

In retrospect, I do not think his diet was a significant factor in overcoming the malignant process itself. The efforts the family made to provide him with a balance of calories, proteins, and vitamins in his normal diet helped to fight the hospital/disease induced malnutrition, and also helped to hold back the wasting effects of the cancer. There is a great deal to know about diet in the treatment of cancer, and the family and physician knew rather little of it. The fact that he recovered without the proper nutritional assault on the cancer is certainly no recommendation that someone else take that risk.

Chemotherapy

Fortunately the infections (stimulating immune responses), the transfusions, and a couple of months recovery at home all preceeded the chemotherapy. From the very beginning the surgeon had said he would give Mr. C. some chemical treatment, and from the very beginning several of the children and his wife insisted that they were against it. He was plainly telling them the case was hopeless, and they did not wish to witness the miserable side effects in their dying loved one. The surgeon replied that he could not let his patient (or himself?) think that he had given up hope, and promised to stop or change the treatment if the side effects became apparent.

When Mr. C. had been home for about two months, he was noticeably better. He could walk without support, recall the time of day without reference to a watch, and had the coordination and strength to spear a piece of lettuce on his fork. The surgeon was seeing him weekly and decided to start giving him chemotherapy.

The *Medical Letter on Drugs and Therapeutics,*[8] is a respectable and conservative newsletter designed to present current drug information and research to doctors in a brief form. The 1976 publication cautions against vigorous treatment with chemical agents in hopeless situations. "Many patients with primary . . . pancreatic cancer . . . may be best served by not being given drugs that cause serious toxic effects without prolonging or improving the quality of life." The same publication[9] indicates that there is a mere 1 percent chance of survival of this type of cancer after five years. It might seem, therefore, that the decision to use chemotherapy was questionable. The local surgeon decided to use five-fluorouracil (5-FU), the drug of choice for adjunctive or palliative treatment of pancreas cancer, on the outside chance that it would help psychologically as well as physically. He avoided side effects by giving less than half the amount normally used and also by spreading the injections out to a weekly schedule of six month's duration, rather than the usual concentrated course of six weeks. Mr. C. received between 100 and 500 mgms. by vein once a week while the usual dosage for someone of his weight would have been about 885 mgms. each week or less as his weight dropped from 130 lbs. On these small doses he never did feel nauseated or have obvious side effects. He did develop a cramp-like stomach pain during or after each meal, but that could also have been due to adhesions following the surgery.

The chemotherapy was stopped after six months when it seemed that Mr. C. would succumb from yet another pneumonia.

Conclusion

It is apparent that the threat to Mr. C.'s life came from two sources: the cancer and the treatment of the cancer. If a West Point athlete had two successive, major surgeries a month apart, and then was confined to bed and fed relatively little for a month and not allowed to sleep undisturbed, was given barbiturates at night and narcotics during the day, and was also institutionalized and prevented from private communication with his family, that formerly well cadet would be in bad shape indeed. The human mind and body are so resilient, however, that they regularly overcome these very hazards all over modern America in persons who are not well, but ill. On top of all of the above conditions, Mr. C. was weakened by the systemic effects of the malignancy, pneumonias, and lung abscesses. It was the combination, the cumulative or synergistic effect, of the cancer and the treatment that resulted in severe debilitation and illness.

He was suffering the effects of the cancer in many subtle ways before the surgery. It was evident in his color and sudden "aging" about him. He was not, however, deathly ill. He was hiking, working, socializing, and generally feeling all right, but not great, even though a significant malignant process was at work in his body.

The sudden intestinal obstruction which made him very sick indeed was not an effect of cancer, per se, but of a mechanical blockage of the large bowel. A healthy child would get as sick and would be in just as much short-term danger from an intestinal blockage due to a lump of half-chewed peanuts. The child would also require surgery to relieve the obstruction, although the tissues would bleed less and heal faster, being disease-free and young. The immediate threat to his life came from the effects of surgery, immobility, anesthesia, dehydration, anemia, pain, and the psychological trauma of institutionalization. Having a cancer going on inside him made it very hard, and nearly impossible, for his body to counteract these other treatment insults and thus preserve itself. Because Mr. C.'s cancer was so extensive, the all-inclusive diagnosis that he was a "terminal cancer patient" was easily believed and, in fact, served as an unwitting cover-up. Staff interventions were based on that diagnosis, namely, that there was not much they could do. If the label had been "terminal hospitalization patient" the appropriate corrective actions might have been more apparent.

Psychological Factors

Denial

One might think about Mr. C's hospitalization and illness experiences in relation to the proposals of Elizabeth Kübler-Ross, who proposes a sequence of psychological responses to the perception of terminal illness which usually begins with denial and moves through anger and depression to acceptance and peace.[10]

Mr. C.'s unconscious self has made use of denial as a mainstay defense mechanism throughout life. It was not surprising, therefore, that he initially denied the cancer and settled for an "obstruction" as a diagnosis. What was surprising, however, was the extensiveness and the depth of his failure to "know" so much of what was going on, and also his persistence in that unknowing through time.

Health-care professionals are taught that a person with cancer who is using denial, for example, is denying (unconsciously) the fact of the cancer. Analytic theory seems to say that an appropriate therapeutic intervention would be to help him work through this unconscious stance toward the illness. If one believes that denial is harmful in some way and that denial in the hospitalized cancer (or cardiac or orthopedic) patient is stimulated by the cognitive awareness of himself as a diseased person, altering the denial might be a logical therapeutic approach to reinstating a reality-oriented integrity. That is to say, one might treat the patient as if his psychological reaction was an undesirable response to his disease state because it prevents him from coming to grips with reality.

From another point of view one could hypothesize the whole, immediate life situation, rather than the diagnosis and its meaning for the future, as the stimulus of unconscious defense mechanisms. In the case of a hospitalized patient, this stimulus would include the hospital and the treatment, as well as the disease. One could also view the evoked defense as beneficial or, perhaps, necessary in the presence of a noxious stimulus.

From this alternative perspective, one could argue that when a person is in the hospital, he might need to begin denying what was happening to his human dignity as a healthy way of remaining integrated. From the first implications of eating in bed, to sharing living space with a stranger during a time of stress, to finding out that the flu is really cancer, it seems that denial might as easily block out all awarenesses as well as only one or two. Once denial is operating it behaves like the unsophisticated chemotherapy agent, which affects nearly every cell in one way or another. Making this kind of paradigm shift, one might then see the therapeutic task as changing the environment and leaving the patient's defenses against it undisturbed.

There are fascinating studies of what happens to people in intensive care units which support this alternative viewpoint. For example, postoperative psychoses as well as other noticeable personality changes of a less severe nature have been observed in patients who have had open-heart surgery. At one time it was thought that some type of oxygen deficit during surgery, some other chemical problem attributable to the surgery, or the heart-lung machine was responsible. New work, however, suggests that it is the intensive-care unit itself combined with the stress of surgery that is causing the changes. Documented effects of the intensive-care unit on patients are illusions, auditory and visual hallucinations, and paranoid delusions of a transient nature.[11] While being hospitalized on a medical unit does not comprise a threat of the same intensity as being hospitalized on an intensive-care unit, it too is a powerful psychological event that is finally coming under serious scrutiny in nursing research.

Kübler-Ross' psychological stages of denial, aggression, depression, and acceptance may be useful or non-useful responses to a life-threatening situation such as a fatal illness. Regardless of the usefulness of the response in relation to the diagnosis, it may not be emotionally possible for the person to stop denying the nature of the disease if turning off that denial also means turning off his unawareness of his current life circumstances in the institution. To put it another way, the person who admits to himself that he is dying of cancer may also have to admit to himself that he is an unfree person in a potentially unsafe situation, dependent upon strangers who regard him as a work object. Acknowledging his illness, he may also begin to see and acknowledge the incompetence of the staff, the callousness in the system, and the misery in the patients around him. Denial is not a particularly selective force. It is very hard to stop denying some things and maintain the unknowing about others. Perhaps it is better in some circumstances to stay dumb all around.

Mr. C., for one, maintained his unknowing across the board. He never felt that there were problems with his medical care or the hospital regime. Although he was told explicitly that he had "cancer," he did not attend to or perceive the word for about two months. Maybe that was just as it should have been. Through the most desperate period of his illness the only thing that kept him going was his belief that what he had was a terrible case of pneumonia, and he knew of many (including an infant son) who had survived that. One wonders where he could have kept eating, turning, getting up for inhalation treatments, etc., if he also *knew* that he had a futile, fatal disease. It is possible that his denial saved his life. The same denial has also caused serious interpersonal problems for him. One would not recommend it as a panacea.

During this time he not only denied the fact of cancer, he also failed to see meaning in what was happening to his body before his very eyes. In December, when he was so critically ill, losing weight at a frightening rate and requiring a transfer to the state medical center, he was asking for a chain saw for Christmas. In January when he was cachexic and barely able to feed himself, he began planning out a fruit orchard which he intended to plant that spring. The impact of changing from a durable backpacker to a person who fell over trying to put on slippers and then couldn't get up did not impress itself. The situation was cooled of its existential meaning and was dealt with as an engineering problem.

"I fell down twice while I was in the Medical Center. The first time, I had gotten out of bed to sit in the chair looking out of the window. I was putting on my robe and turning around at the same time, missed the chair, and went down. No harm done except that a nurse heard the commotion and came flying in. The next time I was sitting on the side of the bed feeling around with my toes for my slippers. One had gone partly under the bed and reaching for it I went off on the floor. No one heard this except my roommate. I figured I'd get up before anyone came in and grabbed the wheel of the bed to pull myself up. But the wheel turned. There was a brake lever. I pulled that to lock the wheel, but this time the wheel swiveled. Meanwhile my roomie was pushing his call button hard enough to dim the lights in the operating room and in came a nurse and a big Negro orderly. He scooped me up in his arms and popped me back in bed with the comment, "We're trying to put you back together, not break you apart!"

From the point of view of the outsider, denial was at work in every conscious fact of his life. From his point of view, however, life at that time was a series of mountainous problems which could not be denied or ignored. From his point of view, the realities of life were these:

1. Eat! (Even though I can't open the milk carton much less cut the chicken from the bone.) Eat more than I want because there is no snack between now and dinner. Eat even though the tray is going to sit here stinking for an hour after I'm done.
2. Keep track of the aide I saw trying to steal my watch.
3. Keep track of time by remembering the meals (now that my watch is at home). Try to figure out what happened yesterday when dinner came after breakfast, missing lunch entirely.
4. Keep track of the old man in the next bed who talks about suicide after his sons leave.
5. Keep your wife and kids from causing trouble with the doctor.
6. Remember to tell the aide not to fill the water jug so full and not to put it out of reach.
7. Figure out how many days of sick leave and how much insurance money are left.
8. Before turning over remember to think for a bit about which arm to move first so I don't get stuck like yesterday unable to move or get the call button.

Looking at the world from this personal perspective, Mr. C. was not denying much at all. Philosophical considerations of life and death, even these, take a back seat when simply turning from one side to the other requires at least five minutes of sustained mental and physical effort, causes pain everywhere, and demands a conscious memory for the correct placement and sequence of hands and knees. Denial from one point of view may be irrelevance from another.

In the case of Mr. C., his strong mental set of "not knowing" brought many problems with it, both for himself and for others in the family. For him there was a tense, almost fierce (if one can be fierce and debilitated at the same time) determination about him. There was, of course, a need for constant effort just to keep going. The fact, however, that the tension came partly from the denial is clear to me from the periods of relaxation and sleep that followed the infrequent breaks in the unknowing. The few moments when he openly asked for help or prayer or experienced relief of having made it past a certain milestone were moments of deep feeling. In these moments he was in touch with the truth of the situation as others knew it to be. His experience of closeless to death was awesome for those at hand.

His ability to not know, in other words, was pervasive but not universal. His dreams particularly revealed an unconscious awareness of the seriousness of the life threat and of the overwhelming proportions of trying to struggle against it. There was an evolution in his dreams toward a clearer definition of reality. The changes in his dreams coincided with an increasingly conscious awareness of his uncertain circumstances and, paradoxically, with an improvement in his physical condition. The following dream occurred so often that at one point he dreaded going to sleep for fear of having to go through it again. He dreamed that he had to do something and that he was struggling very hard to do it. He didn't know what it was he had to do in some dreams, while in others there was a specific task. Always, however, something would come in the way of doing what had to be done. The thing that came in the way was horrible but had no specific shape or identity. He had no image of the thing but was aware of the feeling of horror and dread that it stirred up. In another version of this dream he was trying to do a task that involved walking past a certain pole that looked harmless, but was really an anti-matter pole. In this dream the pole was absolutely horrible in feeling and there was no way to complete the utterly compelling task without walking past it. The dream was so frightening and frustrating that it often woke him up. (These dreams continued for several months during which time he was taking percodan. Percodan is an addictive pain medication, but he used it only at night believing that it was a sleeping pill.) He told the dreams as if they were a curiosity and saw no meaning in them himself. They are dreams in his own symbolic currency of work and effort, containing perhaps to those who read this, powerful symbols which describe the stance of his conscious life in relation to cancer. On an unconscious level he knew that he was going about his business in the very face of anti-matter.

Another dream that came later on during the summer is more explicit and full of detail. At this point he was getting around by himself and was recovered from the more urgent effects of the hospitalization, but he was certainly not getting better in the sense of progressing past minimal independence. He was receiving minimal chemotherapy without side effect or benefit. He seemed to be at a skeletal standstill. He dreamed that he and his young son-in-law (who, in fact, resembles Mr. C. in several ways) were trying to put a heavy box on a high shelf in the basement work room. Mr. C. was lifting the box alone. It became too heavy for him and began to fall down on top of him. When he turned to George to ask for help he saw that George had turned into a werewolf. The dream was terribly frightening.

This dream also involves the sense of going about one's business as usual, doing one's work. But there comes the recognition that not only is one's body inadequate to do the job, but (in the dream-form of George's body) is transformed into a monster and adversary. The life-threatening element is no longer an abstract, harmless-looking rod whose killing powers are perceived only from an intellectual knowledge of it. The life threatening element in the form of a werewolf was just as deadly, but it also reveals itself in the way it appears, in the way it changes from friend to foe. In the first dreams he had only to avoid a pole to stay safe, even though it engendered fear and frustration by standing in the way of completing necessary work. In the last dream he was caught between the heavy box crushing him and the werewolf eating him alive. The sense of being trapped and of disappearing alternatives is apparent in the progression of the dreams.

As the sequence of the dreams suggests on an unconscious level, Mr. C. consciously began to acknowledge the reality of his situation over a period of time. Six months after the surgery, when he was past the crisis point, he began to acknowledge in conversation that his life *might* be in danger, statistically, since his own father had died of cancer. He did not feel, however, that dying of cancer was a realistic possibility for him. Three years later he speaks with awe about the closeness of his brush with death. The denial, it seems, worked when it had to, by protecting him from giving up, and receded when there was mental space to cope with reality. As he became healthier, he could grapple with the possibilities of dying. It seems uncertain that therapeutic intervention to help him overcome the denial would have been of any service to him. He was aware, at brief, discrete intervals, of how near the edge he was. Bringing this awareness into conscious interpersonal communication, however, would seem to have weakened what grip he had left for hanging on.

Belief

The idea does not seem noble, but one can consider that faith or belief may lie somewhere on the continuum with denial. That is to say, faith may be just another psychological defense against reality. Wherever it lies in some engineering diagram of human sentiments, the position taken here is that faith is much more than the opposite of denial and, therefore, is treated here as a separate variable.

1. *Faith in God.* Although Mr. C. has been a Methodist all his life, he does not consider himself to be a particularly religious person. He sings in the church choir, which involves practicing one night a week, and has been increasingly comfortable over the years in going to mass with the other, Catholic, members of the family. Although he says now that he did not think much about religion when he was sick, there were several very powerful moments with him when faith and God were at the center. The night of his youngest daughter's wedding is an example. The wedding had been cancelled when he became critically ill, but was re-scheduled during his time in the Medical Center out of a desire to have the ceremony while he was still alive. On the night of the wedding, two other daughters and an old family friend (a golfing partner of Mr. C.'s and priest) drove to the Medical Center in their wedding clothes so that he could feel part of it. He was disoriented, in pain and exhausted when we arrived, and the wedding

seemed suddenly trivial. Mr. C. was not aware that it had even taken place. He was too tired to talk, especially after the exertion of sitting up and the four people sat in silence for some time. At length, one daughter asked if he would like them to pray with him, falling back on the requests of her husband's grandmother whom she had been with near the time of that lady's death. The Priest said a beautiful long and extemporaneous prayer and then led them in the Our Father. In the unfamiliar space that followed, one daughter (a Catholic) told him how important his example had been in the formation of her own religious life. Her sister affirmed that this had been the case for her too. Their father, now alert, said that he had gotten to like the Catholic Church over the years, and had thought at times of joining it, but he didn't want to leave the Methodist Church, particularly because of the music. "The hymns mean so much to me," he said, "particularly the marches. There is nothing like that music in the Catholic Church." He could not think of his favorite marches though. His attention failed. He had slept only briefly for days due to pain in his joints from laying always on one side. Sitting up now on the edge of the bed, laying his arms and head on a pillow on the overbed table, he fell asleep. The three visitors sat there for nearly an hour feeling that their greatest kindness was bracing the overbed table with their feet so that he could sleep. They had to wake him to help him lay down. He seemed afraid to have them leave and asked the priest for his blessing, acknowledging aloud that in all their years of friendship he had never received his blessing. The priest gave a simple blessing and then stayed alone with him for another half hour. The sisters, waiting alone in the lobby in their wedding clothes, realized with some fear that their father was making his own peace.

There were other moments of prayer and other expressions of faith, particularly at the milestones of recovery. One has the sense that the strength of his faith helped to sustain him at least in the sense of maintaining his will to keep plugging. He was not involved with trying to talk God into sparing him, but with a more certain sense that there was a future in which he would recover. He believed, and still does believe, that he would not die of that disease. Being discharged from the hospital was a kind of proof for him that he would make it. The first morning that he woke up in his own bed and saw the sunlight, he cried like a young child. He said he was afraid at times that he would never see the sun in his own backyard again, but, he added very deliberately, "I always had supreme faith, supreme faith that I would come home."

2. *Faith in the Physician.* Mr. C. also believes in and trusts the judgment of his doctor, the surgeon in the local town. This man is culturally different from Mr. C. and speaks with an accent. He is, however, respectful toward people, calm, and honest about his limitations. He has no clever patter, and his eyes well up when he says there is nothing more he can do.

So when he told his patient that, in spite of the family history of intestinal cancer, he might be one of the ones who would make it, Mr. C. believed him.

The work of Hans Selye and others shows that the body's defense systems are weakened by stress. Is it possible that these same systems can be activated by positive mental states opposite to psychological stress? One wonders whether faith can activate the immune systems against cancer just as well as tuberculosis vaccine has been shown to activate them.

Disbelief

The other side of belief, namely disbelief, was important to the preservation of his faith in his ability to recover. Of course disbelief should not be confused with denial even though, in this situation, they did coincide regarding Mr. C.'s outlook on cancer.

While Mr. C. did not believe in cancer as a fatal illness for him, he did (and still does) believe in heart attacks. If he had become equally as sick from a heart attack, his family believes he would have died of it.

Mr. C. has been an employee of a large American conglomerate corporation for more than twenty-five years. This company has pioneered some of the practices in employee health care which are now standard in this country. Beginning in 1955, when he was thirty-nine years old, Mr. C. was asked by his company to participate in a longitudinal study of diseases affecting executives. This invitation coincided with a promotion and a transfer to division headquarters in Chicago. He was among the young or potential "executives," that is to say "victims." An extensive physical exam was done each year for a period of ten years or so. Among other tests, an EKG was done during each two day exam.

Being part of the "heart attack" study, as the employees called it, made an impression on him and on the entire family. His own fears about ill health tended to be expressed in terms of a heart attack, rather than any other type of illness. Both his own father, and his father- and brother-in-law had died of cancer. These experiences, however, were not as personally impressive in terms of his own health as the repeated two day medical examinations for the "heart attack study." Furthermore, he had been keenly impressed by Eisenhower's heart attack. For him Eisenhower was a giant figure and the power of a heart attack to strike this man even as he held the highest office made it a sure embodiment of death. In terms of the illogic of the unconscious, one might escape the diseases of mortals like one's aging father but one could not escape a disease that could strike at the gods. To put it another way, cancer might have been able to "get" him physically, but it couldn't "get" him psychologically because he did not believe in it, unconsciously, as a reality for him. He believed in something else (and still does), namely, heart attacks. The sense of his resemblance to Icabod Crane lies partly in this disbelief in his pursuer.

The Family Unit

In terms of a larger support system, no one in the immediate family could make a claim for some kind of systematic family belief as a strengthener of his faith in recovery. On the contrary, family actions attested to the belief that he would die. The daughter's decision about when to get married, the son's decision about when to come home from Europe, and the timing of the visits of near and distant relatives were all grounded in the belief that he did not have long to live. Even the efforts to get him out of the hospital and to work out a nursing care plan at home were founded in the conviction that he should be allowed to die in peace and in as much comfort and health as possible. Neither family nor professional saw his continuing to live as anything but a fluke. The insurance on his antique car was dropped, and some funeral arrangements were discussed. There was no essential faith in recovery, but rather a sense of waiting longer and longer for the other shoe to drop.

The family was also unable to remain integrated as a unit. During the period of his illness, every member of the family went through serious personal crises in their marriages. While the problems between Mr. and Mrs. C. seemed fairly obviously to be illness-related re-runs of old conflicts, the crises in the children's marriages seemed to be unrelated to his situation. Most likely they were. One older daughter and the only son were each divorced during the year that he was recovering. Mr. and Mrs. C. were divorced the following year after thirty-four years of marriage. Serious conflicts also arose between the parents and one or more of the children and also between various siblings. Some of the divisions that solidified then have remained firm to this day. None of these divisions were new at that time, but the impending death of the father somehow gave them a solid and lasting form. The myth that families come together in a time of trouble did not come true for this family. Rather, the family broke apart into separate dyads of relatedness. Several of the siblings had begun intensive psychotherapy prior to his illness with the effect that old patterns were no longer satisfactory and the skills for working out new ones were reasonably well developed. Some of the dyads have remained distant while others of these relationships now have a directness and honesty that was not experienced within the family as a larger unit.

Authentic Contact

One variable in favor of his recovery was contributed by family members, however, and this was staying in touch with him as a real person via authentic interactions which occurred only occasionally, but which were intense. For a variety of reasons, authentic interactions between many family members and their very ill relatives seem to happen rather seldom. This is unfortunate since it renders the ill person interpersonally dead and may lead to a self-perception of one who is fading from genuine human existence. This probably occurs because the authenticity of the contact would most likely bear in some way on the present, real circumstances of the persons' lives. Since serious illness is very threatening, it is easy to see why both sides of the communication might skirt such emotionally valid but difficult interaction.

It is possible, therefore, that Mr. C.'s particular family members inadvertently supported his sense of himself as a current (not fading) human being through occasional intense experiences with him. His son, for example, became very angry with him during the medical center period and told him pointedly that people were tired of driving for two hours each way to visit him only to be turned off and told to go away after they got there. The son demanded that his father talk to the ones who came, and not just tell them to do things, and to let him alone. Apparently Mr. C. heard him as he did stop being so remote and withdrawn when his family visited.

Mr. C., on the other hand, was very angry with the eldest daughter for arguing with his doctor about releasing him from the hospital. The unexpected phone call from the doctor took place at his bedside, and it was not congenial, although it was businesslike in an abrupt sort of way. He did not know that she was even planning to talk to his doctor. (She deliberately did not tell him what she was going to do because she knew he would forbid it.) The issue of self determination was a long standing battle between husband and wife into which the children were now being drawn. There was a coldness in his anger that was very cutting. The daughter apologized, reminding herself that he had a right to die of hospitalization if that was his wish. She acknowledged that she would be angry if anyone interfered with her rights in that way. The reconciliation which followed was a "first" between them.

There were also isolated but intense expressions of love and tenderness particularly from Mrs. C. during those risky weeks in the medical center. Although there were long periods of hostile withdrawal between them during the course of the illness, there was a bloom of compassionate contact in January when he seemed about to die and again the following autumn when he began to recover.

The importance of these intimate contacts lay in the real quality or emotional vividness of the interaction. This does not necessarily imply that each party in the communication was interpreting the event in the same way. For example, the issue of self-determination that arose between father and daughter was about death in some sense, but this was only from her point of view. From his point of view the issue was maintaining his own authority during a serious illness. Perhaps much of what went on between him and others in the family involved this same two-track kind of communication; one person thinking about death and the other about getting well.

In a medical setting one witnesses many family members who are afraid to talk about anything other than baseball with a dying person for fear that it will throw that person into a fit of depression or grief. The reality of the situation, however, is that one can cry at seeing someone in pain whether they are in pain from a gall bladder operation or from an inoperable tumor. If the ill person does not intend to get into a "dying" frame of mind the visitor is fairly safe in saying whatever they like regarding their own feelings about his present circumstances. It is a great help to the family member to express his feelings, to be authentic and genuine, especially when there will not be many chances left for closeness. It seems that the ill person could not help but feel some alive response toward one who genuinely cared about what was happening to him. Whether or not a person sees the interaction in terms of death and a final parting, is ultimately up to the perception of the dying person anyway. There seems, however, to be a terrific resistance to intimate communication among families and among staff. People are afraid to say how they feel. A common rationale for keeping feelings from the ill person (or the spouse, in the case of an ill child) is that "I should be the strong one now. She needs to lean on me. I shouldn't be leaning on her." People are reluctant to believe that saying how they feel is a way of giving, whereas they are comfortable in believing that their feelings are a burden to others, and, therefore, should be withheld. On a less intellectual level, perhaps the vividness of their own reactions to a very ill loved one is just too frightening to experience.

The Drive for Physical Activity

Among the professional and lay friends and family members alike, there is a consistent belief that Mr. C. is alive today because of his unrelenting drive for physical activity. His desire and struggle for physical activity are related in some ways to the denial, since many of the things he worked so hard to do while he was sick would have made no sense if he had believed he was dying. He had a number of long range projects underway at home at the time of the first surgery and he automatically assumed that he would go back to work on them as soon as he got home. Actually, he continued the mental work, in terms of planning and decision-making while he was still in the medical center. His conversations were reminders of a story about an American war prisoner who stayed sane by planning every detail of his dream house during his brainwashing imprisonment. Although Mr. C. began at one point to become disoriented regarding the time of day and the day of the week, he could talk lucidly about the fruit orchard he intended to plant. While his conversations about long range physical-labor-intensive projects were ludicrous and maddening to the family members, and labeled by them as straight out denial, or brain metastases, these conversations could also be seen as a healthy means of remaining psychologically integrated.

Mr. C.'s professional work involves repairing and designing modifications for enormous heavy industry machinery. While he does some desk work each day, he also does a great deal of walking about the factory. (Other workers in his kind of position ride golf carts or bicycles from one point in the plant to another.) At home, he spends most of his waking hours in his workshop on intricate and demanding "projects." For example, he has an old car which he has been restoring himself for fifteen years, and is designing and building a four cylinder steam engine by hand. While he was still ill he began digging and laying a system of clay drains around the farm house, and building a guest house on top of the garage. There are a half-dozen smaller projects as well as the restoration of the bicentennial farmhouse, which requires every repair that there is. As one might guess physical activity for him is closely linked with the maintenance of a familiar body image. Since he knows himself so much through his work, the planning and doing of physical work during illness was a way of staying psychologically whole as well as of discharging frustrations, of experiencing his powers, and therefore of fighting the depression that he felt about being so sick, weak, and thin.

It remains to be learned whether physical activity in itself does anything to stimulate the body to fight cancer. If nothing else, it indirectly promoted physical health perhaps allowing the body to then fight the cancer in some unrelated way.

While he was in the Medical Center, he forced himself to turn and move about in bed even though he was painfully frail. Besides avoiding a stasis pneumonia, his ability to push himself kept him alive by keeping him fed. By the time he was discharged from the medical center it took him about thirty seconds of effort to spear a piece of lettuce on a fork, and that was after he got the fork up to the plate. He did not have the strength to open the milk carton by himself, and the coordination required to spoon soup was out of the question. (The soup was out of the question anyway because it came with a tight foil lid that took two hands and strong nails to open. The soup inside stayed hot, though.) He could have gotten someone to feed him, but since it took a long time for him to chew and he had to rest between bites, it would have meant less food in the long run. An aid would not be able to spend an hour with a "feeder." He would have been patiently rushed through a few bites of each thing and the tray taken as she left.

Besides keeping him fed, his ability to push himself helped him regain muscle strength. Once he got home he decided, within two or three weeks to start going down to the basement work room. The family was decidedly against it. Falling in the bedroom was one thing. But falling down the basement stairs was something else. Nevertheless he began the month-long attack on the stairs by going down three steps with his wife holding onto him, resting against the wall for a few minutes, going the next three steps and sitting on the landing for ten minutes, and so forth to the bottom. At that point he walked a few steps to the playroom couch and slept the rest of the afternoon. Going back up was much slower. At the end of about a month of building up to it he was able to go downstairs unassisted, poke around in the shop for ten minutes, sleep on the couch for an hour to recouperate. Then come back up with his wife steadying his balance from behind. Whatever being busy in the shop meant for him, it must have been impressive to warrant that kind of strain.

Although it would have been much easier physically on both him and his wife, he absolutely refused to have a hospital bed, wheelchair, or even an overbed table at home. The implications of these items that he was physically unable were just too obnoxious. He also wanted to establish a clear break with the hospital, regardless of the pain and effort involved in getting into and out of a flat bed. Perhaps a very strong need for physical activity involves a diminished sense of the awfulness of physical discomfort.

Once he was able to leave the house by himself, he began driving out to the farm. Once he got there, it took him six months of daily effort to complete what he could have done in two weekends the year before. It was painful to watch him. There was no joy in the exertion, only grimness. He had to set up a long beach chair out there to rest on since the drive of twenty minutes over dirt roads was exhausting in itself.

On the one hand he seemed to be a lunatic. He certainly looked like a lunatic, emaciated and in work clothes leaning on a shovel. The effort he expended was out of all reasonable proportion to the results he obtained. On the other hand, he did get stronger, the projects did get done (eventually) and he never turned into an invalid. His surgeon wrote at one point:

> One thing I can tell you about him; he is a very determined, cooperative man that has a good will power and wants to get well. He loves physical activity and even in those darker days he was looking forward to seeing his farm and doing some work. Maybe that might have something to do with his unusual recovery.

> Why he should get well after being signed out as a terminal carcinoma of the pancreas is a mystery to me. Medications that I used on him could be counted on one hand. I was sure that some tumor was left behind at the time of the operation. I suspect that his immunity took over, but I certainly cannot explain the dramatic result.

By the summer of '78, Mr. C. had been working full time for a year. He went on a victory hike in Yosemite and Kings Canyon crossing several high passes. He hiked for five days at altitudes over 6,000 feet carrying a 40 lb. pack. The pace was slow but comfortable with grandchildren along.

He remained healthy until the summer of 1980 when another obstruction developed just beyond the pylnas. Surgery and cell studies revealed a large metastasis of undifferentiated tumor contained primarily behind the bowel. Once again, after grim forecasts and an uneventful recovery, he is gaining weight, working full time and receiving the same minimal chemotherapy at weekly intervals. He is beginning to become interested in nutrition in the hopes of avoiding repeated surgery.

And this is the conclusion of the mysterious case of Ichabod Crane, a middle-aged engineer turning farmer who somehow made it through the covered bridge with his head and life intact. The unreal, illogical quality of his recovery lends the feeling at times that, like Ichabod, he made it because of terrific effort, luck, and a certain lack of belief in the power of the enemy. One hopes that writing about these events does not tempt fate or break the spell for him, but only serves to benefit others living now in Sleepy Hollow.

Notes

1. J. U. Gutterman, et al., *Seminars in Oncology,* 1:409, 1974.
2. R. C. Bast, Jr., et al., *New England Journal of Medicine,* 290; 1413, 1458, 197.
3. L. Delmonte, et al., *Clinical Bulletin,* 6:31, No L, 1976.
4. H. E. M. Kay in P. G. H. Gell, et al., eds., *Clinical Aspects of Immunology,* Oxford: Blackwell, 3rd Ed., 1975, p. 623.
5. G. M. Mavligit, et al., *Lancet,* 1:871, 1976.
6. J. T. Evans, *Lancet,* 1:1248, 1976.
7. The New York Times Magazine, April 2, 1978, William Stocton, "A New Clue in the Cancer Mystery."
8. *The Medical Letter on Drugs and Therapeutics Reference Handbook,* The Medical Letter, Inc., New Rochelle, 1976, p. 33.
9. Ibid., p. 35.
10. Elizabeth Kübler-Ross, *On Death and Dying,* Macmillan, New York, 1969.
11. Donald Kornfeld, Terita Maxwell, and Dawn Monrow, "Psychological Hazards of the Intensive Care Unit," *Nursing Clinics of North America,* 3:41-51, 1968.

Index